Morality, Halakha
and the Jewish Tradition

THE LIBRARY OF JEWISH LAW AND ETHICS
VOLUME IX
Edited by Norman Lamm

President and Jakob and Erna Michael professor of Jewish philosophy

Yeshiva University, New York City

Morality, Halakha and the Jewish Tradition

By
Shubert Spero

KTAV PUBLISHING HOUSE, INC.
YESHIVA UNIVERSITY PRESS
NEW YORK

Library of Congress Cataloging in Publication Data

Spero, Shubert.
    Morality, Halakha, and the Jewish tradition.

    (The Library of Jewish law and ethics ; v. 9)
    Includes bibliographical references and index.
    1. Ethics, Jewish.   2. Rabbinical literature—
History and criticism.   I. Title.   II. Series.
BJ1280.s63   1982   296.3'85   82-21912
ISBN 0-87068-727-1

MANUFACTURED IN THE UNITED STATES OF AMERICA

199835

To
Iris
With Love

Contents

Editor's Foreword

The place of morality within Judaism and the relationships between morality and law in the Jewish tradition are complex issues about which much has been written and more remains to be said. The problems are more than semantic, although linguistic analysis clearly can make a creative contribution to the clarification of the subject matter. The issues themselves are substantive, and require, for their proper elucidation, mastery of a variety of disciplines: halakhic literature, Jewish thought and philosophy, ethical theory as it has developed in the Western world, and contemporary analytic philosophy.

These diverse branches of wisdom have all been brought together felicitously and focused on the problem of Judaism and ethical theory by our author, Shubert Spero of Cleveland. As both a rabbinic scholar and a teacher of philosophy, his credentials are impeccable for the task at hand. The reader will learn, to his delight, that Rabbi Spero's qualifications are matched by his achievements.

As editor of this series, the Library of Jewish Law and Ethics, I cannot refrain from commenting on one happy precedent this volume sets. This marks the first time we have published both a father and son. We recently issued Moshe Halevi Spero's *Judaism and Psychology: Halakhic Perspectives,* and now we publish a book by his father. This is not only a source of special gratification to Rabbi Shubert Spero, but a symbol of encouragement to the whole enterprise of Jewish scholarship in the United States.

Norman Lamm
Editor

August 27, 1982

Introduction
Judaism and Ethical Theory

The aim of this book is to examine the moral teachings of Judaism so as to uncover their implicit structures in order to develop what might be called an ethical theory of Jewish morality. A few definitions of basic terms are perhaps in order.

By Judaism we mean the religious beliefs and practices of the Jewish people in their fully developed and traditional forms as found after the major halakhic codifications of the sixteenth century and before attempts at liberalization were made under the impact of the modern period. We shall therefore look not only to the Hebrew Bible as our source for Jewish morality but to rabbinic literature as well. No one has ever denied that Judaism contains a morality or a moral code. Indeed, many have made the stronger claim, which has received general acceptance, that morality is a major feature, if not the essence, of Judaism. But what is morality? This question shall concern us in some detail in the first chapter. In general usage, however, the term "morality" usually denotes a set of rules which prescribe the way people ought to behave and principles which reflect what is ultimately good or desirable for men. Judaism certainly contains much material of this sort. Many books have been written describing the moral teachings of Judaism, praising its nobility, tracing its profound influence, or demonstrating its contemporary relevance and urging its observance.

Our interest in this study remains the morality of Judaism, but only to develop therefrom its *ethical* theory. What is the difference between morality and ethics? Morality has a more overtly regulative character, sometimes called a *normative* orientation. It includes several different elements: rules prescribing or forbidding certain types of actions, certain character traits to be avoided or cultivated, certain patterns of ends and means. These in turn are inculcated into the consciousness and behavior of people in a variety of ways. A morality can be implicit or explicit, depending upon whether its practitioners have ever brought to consciousness the principles by which they make their moral decisions. A morality can further be systematic or nonsystematic, depending upon whether its adherents have succeeded in tracing the relationships between their moral principles and have eliminated inconsistencies and achieved a degree of coherence.

Ethics, however, is a reflective enterprise. An ethical theory is a theory *about* morals and *about* moral systems. An ethical theory attempts to analyze the basic concepts and methods of a morality, to describe the types of phenomena involved such as a special feeling of "obligation" or perhaps certain ideal character traits, and to explain the relationship of the morality under study to other aspects of life, such as God and human nature and other moralities.

Philosophers have distinguished between what they call "first-order statements" and "second-order statements." The former refer to statements about the world around us or about the "good life"; i.e., knowledge of what *is* and knowledge of what *ought to be*. The latter involve inquiries about the grounds on which first-order statements rest. Regarding any statement one might ask, "What is the statement about? What are the grounds of the statement? Are they valid grounds?" Thus one can say that science deals primarily with first-order statements, while philosophy deals primarily, though not exclusively, with second-order statements. In this context, however, it becomes easier to state the distinction between morality and ethics. In morality we have the making of first-order statements telling us what people ought to do in order to attain the "good life." Ethics, however, deals essentially with second-order statements which comprise a philosophical examination of statements about morality.

Not much has been done in the way of subjecting the morality of Judaism to the analytic light of ethical theory since the pioneering work of Moritz Lazarus at the turn of the century. The Bible itself has no word for "morality" or "ethics" and does not seem, at least overtly, to recognize the special domain of morality. In the Talmud we have various "hints" and many insightful aphorisms which have to be mined for their philosophical significance. With perhaps the single exception of Maimonides, no attempt was made by the medieval Jewish thinkers to deal with morality as such. Recent works on Jewish ethics have been either apologetic, historical, or first-order studies of specific moral principles. Second-order analyses on the order I have defined as ethical theory have appeared in only sketchy form and are far from offering a systematic analysis of the morality of Judaism.

The present work is, therefore, undertaken in an attempt to fill this lacuna and to bring to bear the tools of philosophic analysis upon the moral teachings of Judaism. It is hoped that even a small contribution toward the development of such an ethical theory can deepen our understanding of the special character of Jewish morality, of the role of morality within Judaism, and thus of Judaism itself.

What Is Morality?

Learning From Philosophical Analysis

Before a competent surgeon begins an operation, he carefully lays out his instruments, making sure they are in proper condition. He also familiarizes his staff with the procedures he is going to follow. Only then is the patient wheeled in.

In a somewhat similar manner, it might prove helpful, before we plunge into our study of the moral teachings of Judaism, to briefly take stock of the tools at our disposal and of the methods we are going to employ. Much of these come from the results of philosophy of ethical theory as done during the past eighty years or so. What has philosophical scrutiny learned about morality in general? Are there agreed-upon answers to questions which touch upon all moralities irrespective of type or secondary differentiating characteristics? For instance, what is the general area of experience to which the prescriptions of morality apply? How do we distinguish rules of morality from rules of a game like baseball or rules of etiquette? What is the special function that moral predicates are called upon to perform within the structure of our natural languages? The answers to these questions can provide us with conceptual tools and categories, issues and distinctions which can enormously facilitate our analysis of any particular morality.

Recent ethical analysis has noted certain basic differences between various moralities. For example, it has been noted that some systems of morality look to the *consequences* of an act as carrying the moral weight of the entire action. This is in marked contrast to other moral codes that locate the right- or wrong-making characteristics in some quality of the act itself. This distinction will be explored in some detail later. The point we wish to illustrate, however, is that a general knowledge of the possible options open to moral systems enables us to gain a better appreciation of the peculiar emphasis of the particular moral system under examination.

Over the last few decades, considerable attention has been given to what is called the logic of moral discourse. This involves the basic question of the linguistic nature of a sentence containing moral predicates like "good" or "wrong." What role do these sentences play in our language? Are they indicative sentences, emotional eruptions, or prescriptive utterances? Are moral judgments reducible to a set of nonmoral sentences? Can prescriptive sentences be derived from a set of nonprescriptive sentences? Clearly, any understanding of these fundamental questions should be helpful in studying any morality and in particular a highly developed moral code such as contained in Judaism.

We shall start by assuming that all of us have some vague, intuitive understanding of what the terms "morality," "moral principle," and "moral judgement" refer to. Admittedly, we may not, if challenged, be able, at first, to give expression to that understanding with precision or clarity. Yet, in our daily conversations we refer to these terms with evident comprehension. We read our newspapers, in which these terms are constantly used, and we register no difficulty. We seem to be able to communicate successfully in this area. Can we make explicit some generalizations about how we seem to use the language of morality? Let us attempt to arrive at some formulation of the nature of morality in general, the special phenomena it refers to, and what function it performs in our ordinary discourse.

Does Morality Have Its Own Vocabulary?

There are certain words which are usually associated with morality, such as "right," "good," "virtuous," "wrong," "evil," "selfish," "ought." Most of these predicates, however, can be used in a non-moral sense as well. A "good knife" means "one that cuts well," and "He is the right man for the job" may refer to a burglary. Thus the language of morality is not identifiable by the use of certain words but by the context and the use to which these words are being put.

It is evident that most of the moral predicates are what we call terms of appraisal, which we use to evaluate cetain actions or certain individuals. But here again the distinction is too broad and the class into which we would place the language of morality is too large to be helpful. Obviously, there are many appraisal terms in our language, such as "beautiful" and "ugly," "useful" and "false," which are not part of the language of morality. When we say, "That painting is beautiful" or "That theory is true," although we are saying different things, we are undoubtedly making a positive evaluation of both the painting and the theory. But neither of them are moral judgments. Is there any special significance to a positive *moral* judgment, such as "It is right to help the poor"? Are we doing anything more than merely expressing our approval?

Some writers have pointed to the emotive function of moral language. They claim that what distinguishes moral appraisal is its ability to express feelings as well as to produce feelings concerning the act in question.

Further analysis results in the insight that moral language is not only appraisal language designed to express emotion but is prescriptive language. That is to say, it is a language which is deliberately used to suggest courses of action to people. Sometimes our moral judgments are in the form of overt imperatives like "You ought to behave more kindly," while at other times the prescriptive aspect is only implied.

It should, however, be kept in mind that in most usages, evaluative words, including moral ones, will have a descriptive meaning as a secondary aspect.[1] Thus, if I refer to my breakfast omelette as "a good egg," the hearer has learned something about the egg because we have rather fixed standards for assessing the goodness of eggs which are well known. However, if I say, "That poem is good," it is less clear what information has been conveyed about the poem. This is because there is no accepted criterion of goodness in poems. The same observations hold for moral evaluations. In addition to the emotive, evaluative, and prescriptive meanings, which are primary, there can be a secondary descriptive meaning if, for the language-users involved, there are fixed and accepted moral standards.

Assuming the above to be the general function of moral language, to what type of phenomena do we apply moral judgments? An old distinction tends to associate morality with "practical reason." In contrast to the quest for theoretical knowledge, ethics is expected to tell us how to behave. But clearly there is a considerable amount of behavior in which we are involved in the course of the ordinary day which has nothing to do with morality, where moral issues do not arise, and where moral judgments are not called for.

Determining What Is A Moral Issue

Some observations may be made to enable us to narrow the possible location of the moral sphere.

1. Moral judgments apply only to human beings and their behavior. One does not morally condemn an animal or weigh the ethical qualities of a plant.
2. The actions of human beings not subject to choice would not be considered subject to moral judgment. A necessary condition for praising or condemning a person morally is his ability to have acted otherwise than he did. An individual compelled either physically or psychologically to perform an act is not a moral agent. In order to be a candidate for moral judgment, an act must somehow reflect the "self" or character of the person.
3. Both of the above conditions are still not sufficient to create a moral situation. It is necessary that we have a situation in which a moral rule or moral principle is relevant. I rise in the morning and decide not to brush my teeth. This behavior satisfies conditions (1) and (2), but not (3) and is therefore a nonmoral situation. However, add the factor that there is only a dab of paste left in the tube, and knowing my wife's addiction to the stuff, I decide to leave it for her, and you have a morally praiseworthy deed. For we perceive here the relevance of the moral principal of benevolence.

But we still have not answered the question of how to detect the *moral* principle or rule from among other rules. Perhaps the best answer we can give is as follows:

4. A moral rule is one which it is believed ought to govern the conduct of human beings as human beings; a rule which we expect every human being to follow simply because he is a human being.

This is in contrast to all the many other sorts of rules that people may feel themselves called upon to observe because they are members of a certain class or because they have a special role in life. You may be obligated to obey the one-way street sign because you are a car driver. If you are a dinner guest, you are bound by the rules of etiquette. If you are wearing the uniform of the New York Yankees, you are subject to the rules of baseball, not qua human being but qua baseball player. But to say this is to suggest that the uniquely moral aspect of any rule or principle or standard is its claim to universal applicability. For to say that a moral rule governs the conduct of human beings as human beings is to imply that it is a rule which all human beings, regardless of time and place, ought to observe when in similar circumstances.

Another system of social rules with which morality is often confused is the law, which also includes critical standards of behavior designed for purposes of guidance. How do morality and law differ, and what is the relationship between them? This question is particularly significant in the light of our interest in the moral teachings of Judaism. For the prescribed observances of Judaism have usually been conceived as a code of law with the moral rules somehow included therein. Indeed the word *Torah* itself has frequently, though misleadingly, been translated as "law." It might therefore be helpful to review briefly some of the main distinguishing characteristics of legal rules.[2]

Morality And Law

Let us begin by noting some of the obvious similarities between legal and moral rules.

1. Both are conceived as binding independently of the consent of the

individual and are supported by social pressure for conformity.
2. Both include rules that govern behavior in situations constantly recurring in life.
3. Compliance is regarded not as a matter of praise, but as a matter of course. That is to say that in both law and morality there is a standard level to which all are expected to conform. This is as far as moral duties are concerned. There is, however, in morality a dimension we might call moral ideals, which extol virtues, such as benevolence or patience, whose realization is a matter of degree and where unusual achievement *is* deserving of praise.

The differences between law and morality may be summarized as follows:

1. Moral rules are considered of greater importance than legal rules, and their observance is expected even at the cost of hardship and sacrifice. The charge that one is immoral is generally considered more horrendous than the charge that one has performed an illegal act.
2. Laws can be added to or changed by deliberate enactment. Indeed a legal system includes specific rules of change which prescribe how one can modify or repeal existing laws. Morals generally enjoy "a certain immunity from deliberate change."
3. Whether an act is a moral offense depends heavily on its voluntary character, more so than in the case of a legal violation. One must usually be able to show intentionality in a moral act before either praise or blame can be accorded.
4. Legal rules are enforced by threats of punishment. Moral rules are maintained more by appeals to respect for the values involved or by generating a sense of guilt when they are violated.
5. A legal system performs certain functions which are not found in moral systems. Law provides for certain acts or instruments which confer powers. For example, if a legal contract is drawn, it assigns rights and imposes obligations upon certain individuals which they did not have before. It is a *moral* rule which tells me that I ought not to take what belongs to my neighbor. But it is a *legal* rule which, by recognizing certain acts as acts of purchase, informs me what it is that belongs to my neighbor.[3]

The relationship between law and morality is an intricate one, and the fact that they overlap and intersect in all sorts of ways has contributed to the complexity. There is no doubt that in almost every society the law has been heavily influenced by the dominant views of morality. Generally, the principles of the conventional morality were seen as emanating from some higher source which transcended society itself.

1. It was generally assumed that the laws made by man to govern his society should conform to the accepted moral principles.
2. Sometimes important moral rules themselves would be incorporated into the legal system and given the force and authority of law.
3. The legal system as a whole might be seen as resting upon a moral value. To the question, "Why ought I to obey the law?" the answer could very well be in terms of morality: "Because you would be ungrateful to enjoy the benefits of this society and reject its obligations."
4. Basic to the entire legal enterprise is the concept of justice, which is a moral principle. All of the laws are sometimes seen as nothing more than an attempt to regulate the affairs of men in conformity with justice, fairness, and equity. But these are moral principles. So that in effect those who are involved in the law constantly use the concepts of justice to apply the law and to interpret the law. We often appeal to morality to judge the law itself. Indeed laws, as well as legal systems as a whole, are tested by conformity to the moral principles of justice.

What is clear from the above is that it is to be expected that law and morality will be intertwined. We now have at least some idea as to how to distinguish one from the other.

Morality and Universalization

The universal aspect of moral judgment is so deeply imbedded in the structure of morality that some have claimed it to be a part of the very logic of moral language. Consider an individual P who upon seeing Q do a certain act (R) makes the statement S: "That was a most immoral thing to do!" The statement (S) as it stands is a judgment about a particular action (R) performed by a particular individual. Yet the grammar or logic of moral language seems to be such that on the basis of that particular statement alone, we would be justified in inferring that P is committed to the moral principle of which that particular action was an instance. Thus, if P himself, in relevantly similar circumstances, does the same act and claims there is nothing wrong with it, we can accuse him of inconsistency. For, having asserted S, he necessarily commits himself to a universal form of S. If it is acknowledged that it is morally wrong for Q to do R, then it must be wrong for any person in similar circumstances to do R. The structure of moral language seems to have this built-in feature of universality because morality is seen to apply to man qua man.

The observation we made earlier, that the moral predicates are terms of appraisal, words by means of which we express our approval or disapproval of certain acts, is the source of one of the main approaches to morality. To say that "the table is round" or that "the chair is red" is to report something about the world of fact. What, however, are you doing when you say, "The act is morally wrong," or, "His character is noble"? Are the "wrongness" and the "nobility" part of the factual world in the same sense as the "roundness" and the "redness"? The difficulty in locating the "wrongness" and the "nobility" leads us to the often-made distinction between facts and values. Moral judgments seem to be about values. The world of fact comes to us unlabeled and ungraded. It is value-neutral. Facts are simply there, neither good nor bad, right nor wrong. Facts are perceived, given names, and catalogued, their existence and properties confirmed by the experience of others. The process of assigning importance or worth or value to certain things seems to be a different process altogether, something rather confusing and something of which both aesthetics and morality seem to be a part. But things in the world seem to have a value only *for* persons and for different reasons. I can approve of something because it is useful or it gives me pleasure, so that any value judgments, like matters of taste and entertainment, seem to be *subjective* in nature. That is to say, a statement like "The steak is good" does not predicate some quality, such as "goodness," of the steak, but is to be translated, "I, the speaker, find the steak enjoyable." Something has been predicated of the *subject,* the person who made the statement. Are we prepared to accept the same analysis of the values referred to by moral judgments? Do these statements as well, in spite of their predicative form, say nothing about the world of fact, about the objective world, but simply register our own or society's likes and dislikes?

Morality As Value: The Search For The Good

At this point another distinction is in order. The conviction that the foundation of morality is the search for *summum bonum,* the supreme good or ultimate value, goes back to Aristotle, who defined it as "an end of action which is desired for its own sake while everything else is desired for the sake of it."[4] The suggestion is that the moral action lies in the pursuit of the intrinsic good rather than in the merely instrumental good. Money, for example, is valued not for its own sake but for what one can buy with it. Many seek success in their profession for the fame it will bring them or the recognition of their peers. Morality, however, is to be associated with the intrinsic good, which is that value which is desired for its own sake only. Precisely what this intrinsic value might be is, of course, to be found in the history of ethics from Aristotle onward. Some, like Aristotle, felt it to be a sort of happiness with stress on intellectual contemplation. The utilitarians saw it as the maximization of pleasure for the greatest number of people. Others spoke of self-fulfillment.

Those ethical theories which associate the unique moral phenomenon with a perception of the intrinsic good and define the "right" in terms of the good, so that the right moral choice in any situation is that which leads to the good, are sometimes called teleological theorites. In these systems the goodness or badness, rightness or wrongness of an act is judged by its consequences.

What remains in question is the nature of this intrinsic good. Did this also start as a subjective feeling, which because of its social importance was moved to the apex of the value structure, and in order to endow it with authority was given a grammar which suggests obligation and universality? Many thinkers today would answer in the affirmative. There was, at least one influential philosopher in recent times who argued that the ultimate good is an objective, nonanalyzable, and non-natural quality which can be intuited by anyone who cares to consider the question. He said, "By far the most valuable things which we can know or imagine and are worth having purely for their own sakes, are certain states of consciousness which may be roughly described as the pleasures of human intercourse and the enjoyment of beautiful objects."[5] He argued that even where there were no human beings actually present, an ideal observer would have to acknowledge that a world which contained beautiful objects was somehow better than one which did not. It does seem difficult to make out a convincing case for the objectivity of intrinsic value, particularly when these evaluations seem to be conferred on the object by considerations of human interest and satisfaction and seem empty without them. What is the relationship of the human being to value? Does he create it or merely discover it?

An important difference should be noted among those moral theories which emphasize the *summum bonum* and the value factor. Theories such as utililtarianism and the writings of Hume, for example, are purely empirical in approach. Hume stated that "to have the sense of virtue is nothing but to feel a satisfaction of a certain kind. . . . The very feeling constitutes our praise."[6] Bentham claimed that pleasure and absence of pain constitute the only intrinsic good because as a matter of fact that is the only end that people value for its own sake. If, at a later stage, Mill felt it necessary to distinguish between higher- and lower-quality pleasure, he did so only on the stated basis that those who were acquainted with both would opt for the higher pleasure. All was rooted in the sensations and subjective reactions of people.

As early as Aristotle, however, some writers were not prepared simply to consult the *vox populi* or to leave the determination of value to simple sensory perception. We do not *feel* our way to the *summun bonum*; we *reason* our way. This point, of course, would have to be granted by all theories, at least to the extent that it takes reason to distinguish between instrumental goods and intrinsic goods. Aristotle, however, went further and, while acknowledging that human happiness was the *summum bonum,* denied that it was a mere matter of subjective feeling on the part of the individual. Feelings can mislead. Thus, a person could feel fine and conclude that he is in excellent health, yet a medical examination might show otherwise. Aristotle and others who followed him could not deny that if a person feels contented and happy, he really is contented and happy. However, "being satisfied or contented or happy must always involve being satisfied or contented or happy *in* something or *with* something or *by* something."[7] Few people would agree that an individual who has an activated electrode hooked to the pleasure center of his brain and thus is in a constant state of ecstasy has reached the *summum bonum*. Reason, therefore, must guide us to that set of pleasure-giving activities which are characteristically human. Aristotle, of course, believed that reason can detect a natural end or function for man which fully satisfies man's natural aspirations, tendencies, or potentialities. Self-conscious striving toward fulfillment of that natural end will provide man with a truly happy life.[8] More recently F. H. Bradley conceived an ethical theory in terms of an even more fully developed notion of self-realization. Several considerations seem to commend such a rational reconstruction of our concept of the supreme good. One is the fact that what is good for any living thing does seem to depend on the nature of that thing. Birds thrive in the air and drown in water; fish prosper in water and die in the air. You must know the species to determine its good. But what is the nature of man? Can we determine, as Aristotle and Bradley thought we could, man's natural end or function which would disclose the supreme human good?

Another argument which leads away from a purely empirical grounding of the good is the tendency of reason to set up criteria of what the supreme good should look like. Thus Aristotle stipulated that whatever is proposed as the supreme good must be "final and self-sufficient"; i.e., must be such that the addition to it of lesser goods does not make the person happier than before. The supreme good must also be such as to assure a certain permanence to this experience of happiness.[9] Armed with such criteria, one can then review the values offered by the empirical approach with a result that finds them wanting. Thus Bradley attacks the notion that pleasure can be the supreme good by pointing out that pleasure as an experience is "an infinite perishing series"; each pleasurable sensation comes and goes; and when it goes, we are no longer satisfied. Says Bradley, "We are told: 'get *all* pleasures and you will have got happiness' but . . . a series which has no beginning and no end can not be summed; there is no *all*. . . . what is the sum of pleasure and when are we at the end?"[10]

Undoubtedly questions of this sort lead to the distinction between what *appears* to be good and the *truly* good, between the desired and the desirable. We shall see later that much of this road has been traveled by religious ethics.

Morality As Duty: The Search For The Right

In contrast to those who identify the central phenomenon of morality with the intrinsic good, there is an equally venerable group which argues that morality is uniquely grounded in our consciousness of a sense of duty and obligation, so that the primary moral predicate is the word "right." For these philosophers, the crucial fact is said to be obedience to rules rather than the satisfaction of desires. The goal of life is to be judged not in terms of the kind of satisfactions the individual has realized but in the extent to which his conduct has displayed a fulfillment of the demands and obligations to which he as a human being is subject. The chief good of life is thus a matter of doing what is *right*. If we examine our moral experience, we are told, we will discover some special *ought*-quality which seems to attach itself to sitations like promise-keeping or helping someone in need or refraining from an act of injustice. Since the experience of "rising to do one's duty" often sets one against one's own natural inclination and self-interest, it is easier to perceive moral experience as an "objective" reality than as a "subjective" desire. The moral ought seems to come from some principle or standard which in some sense seems to be "outside" the orbit of self-interest. Once we accept "duty" and "the right" as basic and "good" as derivative, the value of moral virtue considered as one who always performs his obligations does seem to be incommensurable with the values of the other, nonmoral goods.

However, here, too, as in the case of "good," one must be careful to distinguish the moral use of "ought" and "right" from the nonmoral. The comment to a friend during a meal, "You are not doing the right thing," is probably referring to his weight-watcher's diet rather than to any moral principle. Similarly, the judgment "You ought to go to the convention" or "You ought to stop smoking" must be understood in terms of an unexpressed hypothetical: "if you wish to secure that teaching appointment" or "if you wish to safeguard your health."

This has sometimes been called the prudential in contrast to the moral use of "ought." These prescriptive statements simply point out a certain means-ends relationship and depend for their force upon the acceptance of the particular end involved. Thus, if I am not interested in my health, it does not follow at all that I ought to stop smoking.

It was for these reasons that Kant spoke of the truly moral act as being seen as a *categorical imperative*; i.e., where the principle behind the act is accepted on its own merits and not as a rule for gaining some desired end. When one apprehends an obligation or duty as binding simply because one is a rational human being and is prepared to perform the duty for duty's sake, then one has entered the moral sphere.

Moralities which focus on the concept of "right" as being central to the moral enterprise are prone to be backward-looking rather than forward-looking. Rather than concentrate on what lies ahead, on the consequences of the act, these theories look more to the past, to the set of relationships in which the act is embedded. On this view the moral duty to keep a promise is grounded in the fact that I gave my word, on the nature of the act itself, rather than in any projection of what a policy of keeping rather than not keeping promises would bring about. Theories of this type, in contrast to the teleological theories described above, are sometimes called deontological moralities.[11]

Duties are usually expressed in the form of rules or laws or commands. Rules and laws are characterized by their generality, which once again brings to our attention that feature of moral judgment which we earlier called its universality. Kant made this component a central part of his theory, utilizing it as the criterion of the moral act. As he put it: "Act only according to that maxim by which you can at the same time will that it should become a universal law."[12] Any action, the principle behind which fulfills the requirement of universality, is sanctioned as a moral law. Kant saw this as a requirement of reason which would obligate all rational beings. Through the form of universality, a person restricts his inclination to do as he pleases and makes his actions conform to a universal law. As I am about to break my promise, I must ask myself: "Could I in all consistency will that all others in my circumstances should act likewise?" Clearly I could not, since if everyone broke his promise, no one would accept a promise, in which case I could no longer benefit from my nasty practice. But to consider a practice right for myself but wrong for all others, without there being a significant difference in the circumstances, does seem to involve one in some sort of inconsistency. This would appear to be the rather tenuous connection between acting on a universal principle and the process of reason.[13]

The Source Of The Ultimate Moral Principle

However, there still remains the question of the *source* of the ought, the *ground* of the obligatoriness, the *force* of the imperative. If one speaks of law, one may ask, "Who is the legislator?" If one speaks of command, "Who is commanding and by what authority?" Kant believed the answer was to be found in man's nature as a rational being. Others taught that the moral duty can be immediately apprehended as a self-evident intuition where the sense of obligatoriness is a part of the apprehension itself.

It is interesting to note that in both the teleological and the deontological camps, whether the "good" or the "right" is seen as primary, we ultimately arrive at a position which states that the uniquely moral quality is an immediate and irreducible datum of our experience. One of the important considerations which pushes in the direction of such a development has to do with the logic of moral language. An insight first found in Hume points out that no "ought" statement can be derived from a series of premises which contain only "is" statements. "Is" statements are factual, informative assertions which describe states of affairs in the natural world. "Ought" statements are sentences of our moral language which are normative, telling us what we ought or ought not to do. Thus consider the following deduction:

(1) Premise: Cigarette smoking leads to early death.
(2) Conclusion: People ought not to smoke.

As it stands, the conclusion does not follow logically from the premise. The reason why (2) is usually considered as properly entailed by (1) is that there is an additional tacit though unexpressed premise which it is assumed most people would generally agree to; namely, (1a) Rational beings ought to do nothing that would shorten their lives. Once this is made explicit, the deduction looks as follows:

Premise (1): Rational beings ought to strive to preserve their lives.
Premise (2): Cigarette smoking leads to early death.
Conclusion: Rational beings ought not to smoke.

The deduction as now stated is valid, but this is because there is now an "ought" statement in the premises. This simple insight has profound implications for ethical theory and holds even where the "is" statements are of a metaphysical nature. Consider the following deduction:

Premise (1): God exists.
Premise (2): God has commanded us to respect our parents.
Conclusion: We ought to respect our parents.

Now, even if (1) and (2) be accepted as true, (3) does not follow from those premises. This might come as a surprise to those who always assumed that religious belief offers a strong basis for moral observance. If that is the connection between religious beliefs and the moral conclusion, then the deduction might read as follows:

Premise (1): God exists.
Premise (2): God is omnipotent and punishes sinners.
Premise (3): God has commanded us to respect our parents.
Premise (4): Rational beings ought to avoid unnecessary pain.
Conclusion (5): Rational beings ought to respect their parents.

In this form, the deduction is valid, but the conclusion is no longer a moral rule but one based on prudential motives. These considerations help pinpoint an importatant problem that will require our attention in our analysis of the morality of Judaism. We shall have to explain the relationship between the will of God and moral principle and the grounds of the moral ought. What brought Hume to his understanding of the impossibility of drawing a moral conclusion from purely descriptive statements was not only logical considerations but also the roles he assigned to reason and emotions in man's decision-making process.[14] He believed that both reason and emotion, or sentiment, play an essential role in moral judgment, but that the roles are quite different. Reason is completely confined to matters of fact. The knowledge that reason yields cannot lead us to approve or disapprove of any particular end or value. This, according to Hume, is a matter of attraction or repulsion, and as such is a matter of sentiment and depends upon our emotional makeup. Reason, therefore, cannot help us in our choice of ends as distinct from means. On this view, our cognition of the world of fact provided by reason, no matter how extensive, can offer no clue as to ultimate moral choices. The ought cannot be grounded in the *is* alone.

From this view that moral propositions are not deducible from nonmoral ones, other thinkers went on to proclaim that moral properties are not definable in terms of nonmoral ones. Thus G.E. Moore developed a wholesale refutation of any ethical theory which defines the good in terms of any natural quality. He accused such naturalistic theories of committing the "naturalistic fallacy." Since Moore believed that goodness is simple in nature and unanalyzable in terms of anything else, it followed that goodness could not be explained by any account of the contents of the universe. Others have attempted to expose the naturalistic fallacy by resorting to what is sometimes called the technique of the "open question." This is based on the assumption that in a correct definition (A means B), to assert that X is A is to preclude any doubt that X is B. Thus, for example, if the correct definition of "atheist" is "a person who denies the existence of God," it would be senseless for someone to say, "I know what Leonid Brezhnev is an atheist, but does he deny the existence of God?" If the definition is correct, it is no longer an open question. Yet if we consider any of the naturalistic theories in ethics, such as the one which states that "Good *means* productive of the greatest happiness," it still seems perfectly sensible to ask, "I know this action will produce the greatest happiness, but is it good?" In terms of our ordinary discourse and our understanding of these words, the question seems perfectly sensible. The fact, therefore, that this remains an open question implies, according to Moore, that the definition of good in terms of "greatest happiness," or, by extrapolation, in terms of *any* natural quality, is an arbitrary one in defiance of the plain meaning of our language.

It would appear from our brief survey that all of the main types of moral theories face significant philosophic challenges. Naturalistic theories like utilitarianism must reply to the Hume-Moore challenge and explain the source of the "ought." Intuitionist theories that assert that both intrinsic value and the "ought" are aspects of reality itself will be hard put to explain the diversity of moral opinion. After all, if values or obligations can be immediately apprehended by the mind, one would expect more general agreement in moral matters. Metaphysical theories are touched by both the challenges mentioned above plus some special problems of their own. The general attitude of relativism and skepticism which exists today in regard to matters of ethics rests upon these two foundation-stones: (1) the seemingly obvious relativity of all known moral norms and standards of value (as a matter of fact); (2) the obvious neutrality to ethics of all actual facts and occurences within the real world (as a matter of principle).[15]

Types Of Moral Theories And The Logic Employed

For the purposes of this study, it will be helpful to see moral theories as divided into the following three major groupings:

1. There are naturalistic theories which attempt to explain the moral life on the basis of natural facts and nothing else. In one formulation of this type, moral rules are simply generalizations of what men have found commonly to be satisfying to their basic desires. Another version might attempt to explain the "ought" in terms of the principles of Freudian psychology.
2. What might be called "autonomous" theories are those that reject the idea that moral experience is grounded in anything outside of itself. They insist that morality belongs to the fundamental nature of reality or to the fundamental nature of the self. They believe morality to be an expression of the ultimately rational and the ultimately real.
3. Religious theories of morality are those in which the meaning and authority of the ethical experience are related to something beyond nature and rooted somehow in God. What remains to be explained is the exact nature of the relationship. Does religious theory of

necessity exclude the first two approaches? As we examine the moral teachings of Judaism, it will be our task to determine whether indeed the morality of Judaism is a religious theory in the sense that it differs completely from types (1) and (2) above.

Beyond these special problems of a logical nature, there is a broad area in most moral systems which has been called their vertical lineage, whereby moral conclusions are derived from some general premises and the progression is governed by the canons of traditional logic. Thus, for example, a morality may have as its supreme principle, "Act always for the general happiness," and from that principle, in conjunction with certain factual assertions, deduce particular moral rules. The logical progression would look like this:

P_1 One must always act for the general happiness.
P_2 Monogamy leads to general happiness.
Conclusion: Monogamy is a system which ought to be supported.

The major philosophic difficulty in justifying moral systems is generally associated with the major premise or the supreme moral principle. As we have seen, we run into trouble if we attempt to derive them from factual statements or claim that they are irreducible data of our experience or intuitions of some kind. The factual or descriptive assertions that are involved in moral judgments or systems as a whole require justification in the same manner as all scientific statements. Very often disagreement in moral questions can be traced to their factual components, in which case the dispute can be resolved. Where the disagreement centers about the moral principle and is rooted in a disagreement in attitude, the only reasons that could be advanced for or against are not rational but rather support the argument psychologically and seek to persuade rather than to prove. However, assuming the premises in the above deduction to be true, the conclusion follows by ordinary deductive logic and does not require any special ethical reasoning or moral faculty. Similarly, in moral disagreements an appeal to consistency is always in place, as in the following exchange:

a. It is always wrong to break a promise.

b. You speak without thinking. There are many cases of that sort which you regard without the least disapproval.[16]

It may therefore be concluded that reasoning in matters of morality does not generally require any special logic but utilizes principles of deductive inference, as when particular cases are subsumed under general rules and in practical issues of moral choice. Inductive inference is employed to determine the most likely consequence of an action.[17]

The Effect Of General Beliefs On One's Moral Views

A final consideration of a general nature before we bring this chapter to a close: An examination of diverse moral theories reveals that embedded within their inner structures are assumptions about the world and about human nature which are themselves not moral principles but which are operative within the moral theory. A recent writer has referred to these elements of any moral theory as its existential perspective ("existential" meaning a way of viewing existence), or stage-setting. He defines the existential perspective of an ethical theory as "its view of the world and its properties, man's nature and condition in so far as these enter into its understanding of moral processes and moral judgment."[18] In attempting to understand any ethical theory, it is suggested that we seek to determine in what ways, if any, the following elements are present and operative in its functioning:

A. a particular view of the world and its constituents
    a particular theory or model of its processes and mechanisms
B. a particular view of the nature of man and his dominant aims
    a particular reference to unavoidables in life and action (birth, maturation, reproduction, aging, death)
    a particular theory of man's faculties—intellectual, emotional, practical—and their relations and an image of the self
C. a particular image of community—its nature, bonds, extent
D. a particular consequent view of the degree of knowability of the world, human life, community, and their processes
    a particular view of determinateness and indeterminateness in their patterning

a particular expectation of dominant dangers (e.g., illness, human aggression, etc.)

a particular assessment of control-possibilities, including (where it exists) any estimate of morality itself as a control-instrument

As an illustration of the wide range of influence which elements of this stage-setting can have upon an ethical theory, let us for a moment consider the utilitarianism of Bentham and Mill. As a naturalistic theory, its stage-setting is very much our temporal world of men, with individual human beings being seen as the unit of moral agency. Causality is taken for granted in the operation of man and nature. It is further optimistically assumed that men can reason and calculate and successfully plan and generalize and apply the lessons of their experience. It is expected that once men fully realize that certain lines of conduct mean increased pleasure, they can be counted on to follow them. The tie-in of these existential perspectives with the structure of utilitarian ethics is quite plain. The understanding of man's basic striving—i.e., pleasure—is directly incorporated into the definitions of ethical terms. The assumed rational abilities of men and the steadiness and dependability of the environment make it possible to ascribe an inductive methodology to ethics. That is to say, experience will teach us what is productive of the greatest pleasure, and our intelligence will not only enable us to trace out the expected consequence of various policies but will motivate us to choose the "good" so perceived.

In our effort to develop an ethical theory for Judaism, it shall likewise be our task to identify its existential perspectives and indicate the ways in which they relate to the inner structure of the morality of Judaism.

The Place of Morality in Judaism

The Pentateuch—i.e., the Five Books of Moses, or the *chumash* of the Hebrew Bible—is the scriptural source and legislative core of Judaism. For the believing Jew, its writings embody the revealed will of God and describe the covenantal relationship between God and the Jewish people. Later biblical books, traditionally divided into the Prophets (*neve'im*) and the Writings (*ketuvim*), continue the history of the Jewish people through the postexilic period and preserve the teachings of the later Hebrew prophets. The prophetic writings contain no new legislation and are primarily exhortatory in nature, calling upon the people to observe the Mosaic legislation.[1] Nevertheless, as we shall see, the prophetic writings have a vital contribution to make to our understanding of the special nature of Jewish morality. The division called Writings includes books that belong to what scholars call Wisdom literature: Proverbs, Job, Ecclesiastes, and portions of the Psalms. We shall learn something very important about morality from these portions of the Torah as well.

In attempting to understand the place of morality in Judaism, it is essential that we begin our survey with the Pentateuch, for it is here that the basic material and behavioral content are to be found.

Moral Teachings In The Pentateuch Take Different Forms

As we examine the Pentateuch, we find that the moral elements appear in several different forms: (1) as values or character traits implicit in the narrative portions of Genesis and Exodus; (2) as particular rules or commandments included in the various codes in Exodus, Leviticus, and Deuteronomy; (3) as broad principles of great generality sometimes included in the codes; (4) as attributes ascribed to God. Let us consider these individually.

In the early narrative portions of Genesis and Exodus, moral deeds and events involving moral issues are found in abundance. There are, for example, the approval of offerings brought as an expression of gratitude to God; the punishment of Cain for murdering his brother; the "violence" of the generation that brought on the Deluge, suggesting moral sin; the early prohibition against murder[2]; the hospitality of Abraham and his pleading for the people of Sodom; the search for moral character in a wife for Isaac; the praise of Abraham for his moral traits; the implied condemnation of the brothers for their cruel treatment of Joseph; Joseph's self-restraint in the house of Potiphar; the repeated intercessions of Moses on the side of the exploited and victimized, and many more.

Many of these biblical stories, in addition, contain information about God and human nature which constitutes what we called in the previous chapter "existential perspectives."[3] These underlying assumptions, while themselves not moral in nature, greatly affect the moral teachings associated with them. For example, the Torah's depiction of man's capacity for evil is closely related to the kind of moral duties imposed upon him.

Why Moral Rules Are Not Listed Separately

In the various codes and legal compilations in the Pentateuch, the moral rules, while many and varied, are not labeled as such, nor are they grouped together in one section.[4] Thus we find:

> He that sacrificeth unto the gods, save unto the Lord only, shall be utterly destroyed. And a stranger shalt thou not wrong, neither shalt thou oppress him, for ye were strangers in the land of Egypt. Ye shall not afflict any widow or fatherless child. (Exod. 22:19–21)

> If thou at all take thy neighbor's garment to pledge, thou shalt restore it

unto him by that the sun goeth down. For that is his only covering, it is his garment for his skin; wherein shall he sleep? And it shall come to pass, when he crieth unto Me, that I will hear; for I am gracious. Thou shalt not revile God, nor curse a ruler of thy people. Thou shalt not delay to offer of the fullness of thy harvest and of the outflow of thy purses. The first-born of thy sons shalt thou give unto Me. (Exod. 22:25–28)

Ye shall fear every man his mother and his father, and ye shall keep My sabbaths: I am the Lord your God. Turn ye not unto the idols nor make of yourselves molten gods: I am the Lord your God. (Lev. 19:3–4)

Thou shalt not take vengeance, nor bear any grudge against the children of thy people, but thou shalt love thy neighbor as thyself; I am the Lord. Ye shall keep My statutes, thou shalt not let thy cattle gender with a diverse kind; thou shalt not sow thy field with two kinds of seed . . . (Lev. 19:18–19)

Turn ye not unto the ghosts, nor unto familiar spirits; seek them not out, to be defiled by them; I am the Lord your God. Thou shalt rise up before the hoary head, and honor the face of the old man, and thou shalt fear thy God: I am the Lord. (Lev. 19:31–32)

When thou buildest a new house, then thou shalt make a parapet for thy roof, that thou bring not blood upon thy house, if any man fall from thence. Thou shalt not sow thy vineyard with two kinds of seed; lest the fullness of the seed which thou has sown be forfeited together with the increase of the vineyard. (Deut. 22:8–9)

This has given rise to the erroneous notion that the Pentateuch was not aware of the distinction between moral rules, governing relations between human beings, and other rules.[5] We shall show, to the contrary, not only that the Pentateuch was very much aware of the difference, but that a very special significance was attached to moral rules and moral ideals.

We find in the Pentateuch that several different terms are used to refer to classes of rules or laws. These are *mitzvot* (commandments), *torot* (rules), *chukkim* (statutes), *'edut* (testimonials), and *mishpatim* (judgments). The first two terms, on the basis of etymology and usage, are quite general and imply nothing as to the type of commandment or rule that might be subsumed under their heading. In the context of the Pentateuch, they focus on the *source* of the rules rather than their content; i.e., these are the *mitzvot* or *torot* of God. The word *'edut* seems to be rather specific and refers to rituals of a commemorative or symbolic nature which "testify" to certain events or concepts. The word *chok* or *chukkim* is often used in combination with *mishpatim*. The roots of the latter term (from which we derive the noun *shofet*,—"judge," the verb *lishpot*,—"to judge," and the noun *mishpat*,—"judgment") indicate that we are dealing with a process of litigation involving claims and counterclaims between parties. This view is supported by several passages where the word *mishpatim* appearing alone introduces what are primarily civil laws arising out of and to be applied to interhuman relations.[6]

Thus, while *mishpat* is a complex term that even in biblical literature developed many interesting extended uses, its primary use in the Pentateuch may be said to refer to moral rules, the proper or just relationships between people as far as these can be brought under a rule.[7] It is not difficult to imagine how the language in its development proceeded from a consideration of *mishpatim* as particular decisions rendered by particular judges to the abstract concept of *mishpat* as justice, or that quality which *ought* to inform all proper judgments.[8] While the utility and practical benefits of *mishpatim*, properly rendered, are obvious to all, there are other rules, such as *chukkim*, which are legislated by authorities both temporal and divine for purposes sometimes known and sometimes unknown. The etymology of the word *chok*, suggesting the process by which the laws were "inscribed" or written, points to their origin in authority rather than to their demonstrable consequences. It is thus both in contrast and as complementary to *mishpatim*, that the Pentateuch so often urges Israel to hearken to the *chukkim* as well as the *mishpatim*, the *mishpatim* as well as the *chukkim*.[9] For, as we shall show it is the central theme of biblical religion that God has concluded a historic covenant with Israel which commits her to a national existence, and whose goals are for Israel to become a "kingdom of priests and a holy nation." As such, Israel must observe both *chukkim*, which express her special relationship to God, as well as *mishpatim*, which govern the relationships of the people of Israel to each other. This is required because the biblical God, unlike other deities, is vitally concerned with both the moral and the ritual areas. The God who is holy demands that His people be holy; the God who is merciful and kind demands that His people be merciful and kind. Thus, in order to overcome the natural tendency to bifurcate the world of obligation into the social and religious, duties to man and duties to God, the Bible deliberately interspersed the two types of rules, *chukkim* and *mishpatim,* so that all can be seen as emanating from the same authority, as equally binding and therefore to be observed with equal diligence. When a code is composed with the intention that it is to be used by a professional group in the study and execution of the law, a purely logical and systematic organization is to be expected. The biblical material, however, is directed to the people as a whole: "And these are the judgments you shall set before them." It was essential, therefore, that each unit section of the Pentateuch reflect the full range of the covenantal way of life: the ritual as interpenetrated by the moral in an organic and inextricable sort of way.[10]

The Torah Was Aware Of Morality As Such

Another indication that the Pentateuch was aware of the special nature of a certain class of moral rules is to be found in the fact that a promise of blessing is held out for the observance of some of these commandments. For example, in connection with lending money without interest, we find the promise, "that the Lord thy God may bless thee in all that thou puttest thy hand into." In "sending forth the dam," ". . . that it may be well with thee and thou mayest prolong thy days." In restoring a poor man's pledge, ". . . and it shall be righteousness unto thee before the Lord thy God." In setting free the Hebrew slave with gifts, ". . . and the Lord thy God will bless thee in all that thou doest." In lending money to the poor prior to the Sabbatical year, ". . . thou shalt surely give him and thy heart shall not be grieved when thou givest unto him, because for this the Lord thy God will bless thee in all thy works."[11]

It has been noted by Nachmanides that the promise of God's blessing after individual laws is to be found only in connection with those commandments that reflect "love and righteousness" (*chesed u-tzedakah*) but not for observing commandments such as "Thou shalt not steal" or "Thou shalt not deceive," which are required by the attribute of justice.[12] The Pentateuch's usage, which consistently restricts such a locution to commandments reflecting a positive love for one's neighbor, would appear to constitute evidence of an awareness of their special character.

The most striking evidence, however, for the proposition that the Bible was aware of the special nature of moral rules and accorded them a special significance is to be found in the composition of the Decalogue, which we must now carefully examine. Our approach will be more literary than historical, for we must try to understand the Decalogue within the context of the Pentateuch. What was the place within the Mosaic legislation and revelation as a whole of these ten statements inscribed on two tablets of stone? How was the Decalogue regarded by those who accepted the Pentateuch as a unitary work and as constituting Scripture?

The Decalogue As Evidence Of The Centrality Of Morality

It cannot be the case that the significance of the Decalogue lies simply in its being the revelation or even the very first revelation of God's will. The theophany at Sinai, which resulted in the Decalogue, is immediately followed by a series of detailed laws and commandments that seem to constitute the main legislation of the Torah.[13] For what reason, then, were these ten commandments (if there be ten)[14] or ten statements given separately as a unit before the others, given publicly to the people without intermediaries, and recorded in a different manner than the others? The Bible itself provides the answer. On several occasions the Decalogue is referred to as "the words of the covenant" or "the tablets of the covenant."[15] That is to say, the Decalogue represented the conceptual expression of the covenant-relationship that was now being entered into between God and a group of people who were now committing themselves to become a covenanted community called Israel. Once Israel has come into existence, the legislation follows through the mediation of the prophet. But the act that establishes the covenant is the giving by God and the accepting by Israel of the two tangible and permanent tablets of stone inscribed with the words which promulgate the unified common life which must now characterize

Israel.[16] It is in this sense that the Ten Commandments are "the words of the covenant," and the tablets, "the tablets of the covenant," and the ark where they were stored, "the ark of the covenant," a sense which does not apply to the other commandments. Thus considered, recitation of the Decalogue can be seen as a "speech act" which reenacts the covenant at Sinai and constitutes a reaffirmation of its terms and conditions by the individual. This explains why the Decalogue was often associated with the *Shema* and with the *tefilin* as a Jewish affirmation of faith.[17] However, what is of crucial relevance to our question of the place of morality in Judaism is the peculiar composition of the Decalogue. In order to facilitate our study, let us review the contents of the Decalogue.

THE TEN COMMANDMENTS

I I am the Lord thy God who brought thee out of the land of Egypt, out of the house of bondage.

II Thou shalt have no other gods before me. Thou shalt not make unto thee a graven image; nor the form of any thing that is in heaven above, or that is in the earth beneath or that is in the water under the earth; thou shalt not bow down thyself to them nor serve them; for I the Lord thy God am a jealous God visiting the iniquity of the fathers upon the children upon the third and the fourth generation unto them that hate Me; And showing loving-kindness unto the thousandth generation, of them that love Me and keep My commandments.

III Thou shalt not take the name of the Lord thy God in vain; for the Lord will not hold him guiltless that taketh His name in vain.

IV Remember the Sabbath day to keep it holy. Six days shalt thou labor, and do all thy work. But the seventh day is the Sabbath unto the Lord thy God; in it thou shalt not do any work, neither thou, thy son, nor thy daughter, thy man-servant, nor thy maid-servant, nor thy cattle, nor thy stranger that is within thy gates; For in six days the Lord made the heavens and the earth, the sea and all that is in them, and rested on the seventh day; therefore the Lord blessed the Sabbath day and hallowed it.

V Honor thy father and thy mother; in order that thy days may be prolonged upon the land which the Lord thy God giveth thee.

VI Thou shalt not murder.

VII Thou shalt not commit adultery.

VIII Thou shalt not steal.

IX Thou shalt not bear false witness against thy neighbor.

X Thou shalt not covet thy neighbor's house. Thou shalt not covet thy neighbor's wife, nor his man-servant nor his maid-servant, nor his ox, nor his ass, nor anything that is thy neighbor's.

The traditional manner of presenting the Decalogue, with five commandments on one tablet and five on the other, has no real warrant from the Pentateuch itself. Indeed, the rabbis in the Talmud discussed the matter and suggested several different possibilities. [18] As we examine the Decalogue, we are immediately struck by the fact that the last five commandments deal with relationships between human beings and are clearly moral in nature. Of the first five commandments, the fifth, which has to do with filial respect, is likewise a moral rule; the first three are concerned with our relationship to God, while the fourth, concerning the Sabbath, is a ritual command with clear social implications. Here, no attempt was made, as in the later codes, to intersperse the ritual and the moral commandments. Instead, the order is logical and sequential. The Decalogue quite literally begins with "the Lord thy God" and ends with "thy neighbor." We are first introduced to God who redeemed us from Egypt, who forbids the worship of other deities and demands respect for His name and His Sabbath day. But if these are but expressions of the love and fear of God, then the remaining utterances are but ways to realize our love of man.

What is remarkable, then, about the contents of the Decalogue is that more than half of the rules are moral in nature and refer to human relations. If the Decalogue constitutes "the words of the covenant" and expresses what it is that the Lord requires of Israel, then we have here the Torah's own view of the essence of Judaism, the founding principles of the covenanted community.[19] Where are all the sacrifices? Why no mention of the Passover or of circumcision? The testimony of the Decalogue seems overwhelming: Moral rules regulating relations between human beings are primary. Morality is the essence of Judaism. According to David Tzevi Hoffmann, the later prophetic writings show a keen awareness of the startling nature of the theophany at Sinai in that it did not call for, nor was it accompanied by, votive sacrifices.[20] Hoffmann points out that Moses, who had been told to expect a "service" at the mountain as the culmination and climax of the Exodus, was looking forward to a festival that would include elaborate and unusual sacrifices.[21] This is evident from his reply to Pharaoh: "Thou must also give unto our hand sacrifices and burnt offerings that we shall sacrifice unto the Lord, for we know not with what we must serve the Lord until we come thither."[22] But much to their surprise, the God of Israel did not include in the Sinai covenant any request for sacrifices. This important disclosure as to what is really the essence of the divine demand is alluded to in the well-known declaration of Jeremiah: "For I spoke not unto your fathers, nor commanded them in the day that I brought them out of the land of Egypt, concerning burnt-offerings or sacrifices; but this thing I commanded them, saying, 'Hearken unto my voice, and I will be your God, and ye shall be My people.'"[23] Since there is nothing authoritative about the five-five arrangement of the Ten Commandments, we might consider an alternative arrangement which would look as follows:

I introduction

II	III	IV	} theological
V	VI	VII	
VIII	IX	X	} moral

On this view, all of the Ten Commandments were repeated on each tablet. This, in effect, provided two copies of the Decalogue. Since a covenant is struck between two parties, the two tablets could be viewed as symbolizing that a copy of the agreement had been given to each party.[24]

Various theories have been advanced to explain the particular sequence of the Ten Commandments.[25] The above arrangement, however, seems most plausible, as the first utterance contains no imperative and should rightfully be considered introductory in nature. This leaves three commandments which are clearly "religious" and speak of Israel's relationship to God. The remaining six constitute rules of morality. The arrangement is both logical and architectonic. There are additional considerations which incline us to the view that implicit in the composition of the Decalogue is an awareness of morality as constituting a special area of religious obligation. A reading of the Decalogue reveals significant stylistic differences between the first five commandments and the last five. The name of God appears in each of the first five comandments but not at all in the last five. Instead, the term "thy neighbor" appears four times in that last group. In addition, each of the first five commandments contains an explanatory clause introduced by the word *ki*, "for," or *lema'an*, "in order that," which either gives the reason for the commandment (4) or describes the consequences of obedience (5) or disobedience (2 and 3) in terms of punishment or reward. No reasons are given for any of the last five commandments, nor are sanctions threatened for disobedience or rewards promised for compliance. These striking differences are rendered intelligible once we see them in relation to the character of the last five utterances as moral rules. Evidently, these rules, and the principle of the inviolability of the human being upon which they are based, were considered so self-evident and their social utility so obvious that they need only be stated.[26] Their inclusion on the tablets of the covenant was to proclaim that the God of Israel, who was now entering into a covenant with this people, demanded as a prime condition of such a covenantal relationship individual and group compliance with these principles of morality. Viewed as such, we can understand why the moral commandments are predominantly negative in form, inasmuch as they embody the essentials of *social* morality. As we shall attempt to demonstrate later on, what was unusual and perhaps unique about the morality of the Decalogue was not the essential content of the moral rules but rather the source of its authority, which endowed the entire system with special qualities.[27] The point is that the entire Decalogue—all of its commandments, the *chukkim* as well as the *mishpatim*—is subsumed under the identical heading: "I am the Lord your God. . . . Thou shalt . . ."

Moral Principles And Moral Rules

Scattered in the Pentateuch are certain prescriptions which appear to be moral *principles* rather than moral *rules*.[28] Although these prescriptions are not designated as principles, either by location or by superscription, it seems plausible to assume that these passages must always have enjoyed a special status for two reasons: (1) as they stand, they are so general and abstract that by themselves they do not prescribe any specific observance; yet (2) they seem to subsume any number of particular rules as instances of the principles they embody. Thus, for example, if you accept the principle of "Love thy neighbor as thyself," it follows that you will not murder your neighbor or steal from him, since these are things you would not want done to yourself.[29]

These moral principles include the following: "But thou shalt love thy neighbor as thyself"; "And thou shalt do that which is right and good in the sight of the Lord"; "Righteousness, righteousness [*tzedek*] shalt thou pursue."

What initial meaning can we assign to those fundamental moral concepts that occur again and again throughout the Bible: *tzedek* or *tzedakah*, translated as "righteousness," and *mishpat*, translated as "justice"?

As we examine the occurrences of the term *mishpat* in the Pentateuch, we find that it sometimes means "the entire process of administering the law" or "the specific verdict delivered in a certain case" or even simply, "the way a thing was customarily done."[30] However, it was also used in the abstract sense of "justice," as when Abraham exclaims before God, "Shall not the judge of all the earth do *mishpat*?" While it is obviously impossible to explicate with any precision the meaning of the biblical concept of justice, it would appear generally to denote fairness, balance, giving each person his due. *Mishpat* in this sense refers to the quality of actions and implies a state of equilibrium and harmony. *Tzedek,* on the other hand, seems to refer to benevolence, kindness, and generosity, and could be taken to describe the quality of a person.[31] Thus, the noun from *tzedek* is *tzaddik,* "a righteous person."

From certain passages in the Book of Deuteronomy, it seems clear that moral principles like *tzedek* were regarded as "second-order" standards by which "first-order" rules and statutes were judged. Evidently, the Torah realized that there was nothing unique or terribly impressive in the mere fact of a people being given "statutes and judgments," no matter how elaborate or particular they may have been. The highly developed Hittite and West Semitic codes must have been known to the ancient Hebrews. What the Book of Deuteronomy did find noteworthy was the special moral quality of Israel's God-given "statutes and judgments."

> Behold, I have taught you statutes and judgments even as the Lord, my God commanded me, that ye shall do so in the midst of the land whither ye go in to possess it. Therefore observe and do them; for this is your wisdom and your understanding in the sight of the peoples, that, when they hear all these statutes, shall say, "Surely a wise and understanding nation is that great nation." For what great nation is there that hath God so close to them as is the Lord our God whenever we call upon Him. And what great nation is there that has statutes and judgments that are *righteous* [*tzadikim*] as all this law which I place before you this day?[32]

This remarkable passage assumes that each nation will have its own set of statutes and judgments but makes the bold claim that Israel's code will be acknowledged superior when judged by the moral standards of righteousness. This is also seen in the passage, "And ye shall judge the people with *righteous* judgment."[33]

God's Moral Attributes

The role of morality in Judaism as reflected in the Pentateuch may be surmised not only from the importance given to it in the instructions to Israel but also in the moral nature of the qualities attributed to God.

In the course of renewing the covenant after the sin of the Golden Calf, Moses asks to be shown and is revealed the "ways" of God. There follows the statement of what the rabbis refer to as the "thirteen attributes [*middot*] of mercy":

> The Lord, The Lord, God merciful and gracious, long-suffering and abundant in goodness and truth; keeping mercy unto the thousandth generation, forgiving iniquity and transgression and sin and that will by no means clear the guilty, visiting the iniquity of the fathers upon the children and upon the children's children unto the third and unto the fourth generation.[34]

According to Cassuto, our text, in its opening words, provides an explanation of the name of the Lord—the Tetragrammaton—which is repeated twice as if to say: "The Lord, *who is* the Lord," which is tautological but perhaps the only thing we *can* say about God (compare "I am that I am" of Exodus 3:14), who can nevertheless be described as "God, merciful and gracious . . ."[35] The impressive theophonic manner in which this is revealed to Moses, as well as the frequent references to the attributes by the later prophets, testifies to the importance attached to this information.[36] However, it can be shown that many of these "ways of God" were already known and referred to by earlier personages in the Bible from Cain through the Patriarchs. The question that arises, therefore, is, wherein lies the special significance of this revelation if God's moral ways were known even before? Some commentators revert here to mystery and hint at the esoteric. Others find its importance in its being a formula given to Moses as how to supplicate God effectively by evoking the attributes of mercy in prayer. It might be suggested, however, that the importance of the description of God in our text lies in its grammatical form. That is to say, God is not merely said to perform *acts* of mercy but is referred to as *merciful*. He is *rachum*. Implicit in this grammatical difference lies a distinction already recognized by Aristotle, and built upon by Maimonides, between the performance of individual acts of, let us say, justice and the development in the individual, by such repeated acts of justice, of a just disposition.[37] While the ontological nature of dispositions remains unclear, the practical advantages of referring to such theoretical entities *is* clear.

If, for example, all that is known of a certain person is that he has performed one or two acts of justice, I am not justified in predicting anything about his future behavior. However, when a person is described as a "just man," this warrants an expectation of consistently just behavior on his part. As Aristotle put it: "Like activities produce like dispositions."[38] Dispositions were seen as resident character-structures of the personality which would continue to condition the individual to act in accordance with the virtue involved. In our ordinary language we would say that the moral virtue of justice had become a part of that person's character, or a character trait. It is interesting to note that while the Pentateuch describes individuals as performing all sorts of actions, moral and immoral, wise and foolish, they are rarely ascribed specific attributes or character traits. The rare exceptions are Noah, who is once referred to as a "righteous and whole-hearted man," and Moses, who is described as "very meek, above all the men that were on the face of the earth."[39] In the light of this reticence, the description of God as "merciful and gracious, long-suffering and abundant in goodness and truth" must have been perceived as a revelation which in some sense ascribed these moral qualities to God as part of His essence or character. God has been known to perform acts of kindness in the past, but now we are being given to understand that kindness is an abiding quality of God Himself.

Of course, the Jewish theologians of the Middle Ages, who worked hard to refine the concepts of God's essential unity and simplicity, were horrified by such a suggestion and denied its implications. Sa'adiah already declared that in spite of the grammar, "all attributes of this class go back, as far as their ultimate meaning is concerned, to God's actions."[40] Maimonides is even more explicit in denying the implications of the text:

> Our sages called these ["merciful and gracious"] *middot* [characteristics] and speak of the thirteen *middot* of God. They also used the term in reference to man: "There are four different *middot* among those who give charity." They do not mean to say that God really possesses *middot* but that He performs actions similar to such of our actions as originate in certain psychological dispositions; not that God really has such dispositions.[41]

The theological problem notwithstanding, the ethical implications must be drawn. The fact remains that in this pivotal biblical text, the God of Israel, in response to Moses' pleas, "Show me now thy ways" and "show me . . . thy glory,"[42] is described as possessing certain qualities which are moral in nature. God is revealed as a moral God but not merely because He demands moral living from His creatures. Rather, it seems to be the other way around. God demands of His creatures, first and foremost, obedience to moral rules because morality is of the very essence of His own being.

> Now, this concept of God, this Hebrew protest initially was only negative: no image. But the concept demanded also some positive, although metaphysical meaning: "Show me thy Glory" or "what is His name?" And the concept responded to the need—"I will cause all my *goodness* to pass before thee" and "Lord, Lord, God, merciful and gracious" with positive attributes almost all denoting mercy. God then is gracious . . . which is the heart and soul of all the laws and of the entire national chronicle.[43]

It is but a short step from these considerations to the concept of *imitatio dei,* which is first fully articulated by the Rabbis. Judaism asks of man to walk in God's way, to act as He does, in short to imitate Him.

The strong implication of the thirteen *middot* of God's close identification with morality leaves little doubt concerning the high priority of morality in Judaism. This link between morality and God finds strong echoes in the Book of Psalms:

> The Lord is righteous, He loves righteousness. (Ps. 11:7)

> Righteousness and justice are the foundations of His throne. (Ps. 97:2)

> The king's strength loveth justice, Thou didst establish equity; Thou hast made justice and righteousness in Jacob. (Ps. 99:4)

God's identification with morality is absolute: God is goodness.

It is in this that Judaism differed from what had gone on before. "The source of justice and morality in the pagan conception was *wisdom*—human or divine. . . . In the Israelite conception justice and morality belong to the realm of prophecy not wisdom. . . . The prophet brings the divine imperative from a God over whom no evil impulses hold sway, whose will is essentially moral and good."[44]

Morality In The Prophets

The books of the later prophets, covering a period of about three hundred years from Amos and Hosea to Malachi, contain essentially what scholars have referred to as literary or classical prophecy. While many of these prophecies were originally spoken to the people in personal confrontations, they were recorded by the prophets themselves or by their disciples and preserved by the nation.

The classical prophets are rooted in the Torah of Moses; in its concepts of God, history, and the covenant relationship of Israel. They saw themselves as links in a chain of divine messengers extending back to Moses. That the prophets were familiar with the Torah book itself is evident from certain correspondences between Jeremiah and the Book of Deuteronomy and between Ezekiel and the Book of Leviticus.[45] Their special task as spokesmen commissioned by God was to denounce the people for their transgressions and call them to repentance, to prophesy the fall of the Northern and Southern Kingdoms, and then to console the exiles and encourage the remnant to return. The relationship between the later prophets and the Torah may be summed up in the following way: "The Torah legislates and commands; the prophets exhort and censure; both call for faith and trust in God."[46]

The historical background for the appearance of an Amos and Hosea was the rise of new and threatening world empires on the political scene and the emergence of sharp social cleavages which intensified social problems in both Israel in the north and Judea in the south.

What emerges quite clearly from the writings of the literary prophets is the primacy of morality, the concept that what God demands of Israel more than anything else is righteousness and justice. In the Book of Deuteronomy we read:

And now, Israel, what doth the Lord thy God require of thee but to fear the Lord thy God, to walk in all His ways, and to love Him and to serve the Lord thy God with all thy heart and with all thy soul.[47]

By contrast we find in the Book of Micah:

It has been told thee, O man, what is good, and what the Lord doth require of thee; Only to do justly and to love mercy and to walk humbly with thy God. (6:8)

Or in Jeremiah:

But let him that glorieth, glory in this, that he understandeth and knoweth Me. That I am the Lord who exercises mercy, justice, and righteousness in the earth; for in these things I delight, saith the Lord. (9:23)

Or in Ezekiel:

But if a man be just and do that which is lawful and right and hath not eaten upon the mountains, neither has he lifted up his eyes to the idols of the house of Israel, neither hath defiled his neighbor's wife, neither hath come near to a woman in her impurity. And hath not wronged any but hath restored his pledge for a debt, hath taken naught by robbery, hath given his bread to the hungry, and hath covered the naked with a garment. He that hath not given forth upon interest, neither hath taken any increase, that hath withdrawn his hand from iniquity, hath executed true justice between man and man, hath walked in My statutes and hath kept Mine ordinances, to deal truly; he is just, he shall truly live, saith the Lord God. (18:5–9)

There is no doubt that in the Deuteronomy passage, the moral imperatives are contained in the general command to "serve god with all of one's heart and soul" and in particular in the injunction "to walk in His ways." The point, however, is that here the morality is not explicitly singled out, whereas in Micah and in the other prophets the stress is very clearly on morality.

In many of the utterances of the literary prophets which affirm the importance of morality, the positive emphasis upon man's relationship to his fellow man is accompanied by a negative view of the sacrifices and other ritual observances. This is usually expressed in the form of a preference. Thus Hosea:

> For I desire mercy and not sacrifice, the knowledge of God rather than burnt-offerings. (6:6)

And Amos:

> I hate, I despise your feasts, and I will take no delight in your solemn assemblies. . . . But let justice well up as waters and righteousness as a mighty stream. (5:21, 24)

And Isaiah:

> Saith the Lord;
> I am full of the burnt-offerings of rams
> And the fat of fed beasts. . . .
> Yea, when you make many prayers,
> I will not hear;
> Your hands are full of blood,
> Wash you, make you clean,
> Put away the evil of your doings. . . .
> Learn to do well
> Seek justice, relieve the oppressed,
> Judge the fatherless, plead for the widow. (1:11–17)

It is generally acknowledged that the prophets did not come to repudiate the Temple and its sacrifices or to deny the value of feasts and assemblies or to replace Temple worship with moral living. Precisely because the sacrificial cult was so highly regarded as the way to the divine, the prophet used it to shock the people into a realization that the truly supreme act was morality and not sacrifice. The prophet is denigrating only the worth of a cult that is not morally informed. Indeed, only sacrifices performed by immoral individuals and burnt-offerings brought by unrepentant evildoers are "despised" and a burden to God. Nevertheless, these statements choosing morality *rather than sacrifices* do seem to imply that the ritual commands are of instrumental value only, whereas morality possesses intrinsic and absolute value.[48] If sacrifices were of intrinsic value, it would not make sense to reject them simply because they were brought by individuals who were not fulfilling their obligations to their fellow men, even as we would not reject moral behavior on the part of agents who did not worship God. Belief in the intrinsic value of morality is consistent with the teachings in Exodus, already alluded to, that moral values are somehow of the essence of God Himself.

Another teaching of the literary prophets which reflects their sense of the primacy of morality is their warning that morality is the decisive factor in determining the national destiny of Israel. While in the Pentateuch we read that the political fortunes of Israel are dependent upon her obedience to the commands of God, no special reference is made to the moral transgressions.[49] The only sins that are singled out are idolatry and neglect of the Sabbatical year. Amos, however, thunders:

> Thus saith the Lord: For three transgressions of Israel, yea for four, I will not reverse it.
> Because they sell the righteous for silver and the needy for a pair of shoes;
> That pant after the dust of the earth on the head of the poor.
> And turn aside the way of the humble. . . .
> And flight shall fail the swift,
> And the strong shall not exert his strength,
> Neither shall the mighty deliver himself. (2:6, 14)

Of special interest is the fact that the moral transgressions referred to in these contexts are not grave ones like murder but the "everyday" variety, such as oppression, exploitation, and the perversion of justice.[50]

But if moral sins are weighty enough to cause Israel's downfall and exile, then moral virtues are worthy enough to bring about the redemption: "Zion shall be redeemed with justice, and they that return of her, with righteousness" (Isa. 1:27).

The Book Of Proverbs And Personal Morality

The third grouping of scriptural materials, known as the (*ketuvim*) or Hagiographa, includes, in addition to the five Scrolls and several historical works, the books of Job, Psalms,[51] and Proverbs. This last work contains collections of *mashalim,* or "wise sayings," attributed to King Solomon and other sages. They are all short, pithy aphorisms or epigrams that were used to teach the good and wise way of life, particularly to the young.

What is the relationship of the moral maxims of the Book of Proverbs to the moral teachings of the Pentateuch and the prophets? In its basic orientation the morality of Proverbs coincides with the morality of the prophets: God is the source of morality. The key word in this book is *chokhmah,* or "wisdom," which is understood as the skill or ability to make wise choices and to live in accordance with the moral norms of the covenant community. However, the "beginning of wisdom is the fear of the Lord," who is the source and guarantor of moral understanding.[52] All the moral rules of the Decalogue are to be found in the Book of Proverbs.[53] Many of its admonitions are attributed directly to God.

> There are six things which the Lord hateth . . . (6:16–19)

> Lest I be poor and steal and profane the name of my God. (30:9)

> A false balance is an abomination to the Lord;
> But a perfect weight is His delight. (11:1)

> Everyone that is proud in heart is an abomination to the Lord. (16:5)

We even find an echo of the primacy of morality that we observed in the prophets:

> To do righteousness and justice is more acceptable to the Lord than sacrifice. (21:3)

> By mercy and truth iniquity is expiated. (16:6)

> The sacrifice of the wicked is an abomination to the Lord. (15:8)

There is, however, a special flavor to the moral teachings of Proverbs, as seen in its unmistakable appeal to prudence and to the principle of utility. Morality is urged not only because it is pleasing to God but because (perhaps as a very consequence of this) it fits into the practical order of things so that it is the way through which a person will find satisfaction in life. Thus, we are urged to avoid certain practices because of the unfortunate consequences which are sure to follow: slander will lead to retaliation (30:10) and adultery to inevitable punishment (6:26–30). In short, morality is the most worthwhile policy because it leads to well-being.

Historical research has determined that among the ancient cultures of the Middle East, particularly in Egypt and Mesopotamia, there existed as early as the second or third millennium B.C.E. a wisdom literature consisting of instructions by parents and teachers in those skills or moral standards that had proved advantageous in actual experience. It seems clear from the form and style of the Proverbs of Solomon, which are universal, individual, and humanistic, that they are related to this international wisdom movement. Indeed, the existence of such a transcultural wisdom is implied in the statement that the wisdom of Solomon "surpassed the wisdom of all the people of the east and all the wisdom of Egypt."[54] Except for its emphasis on God, there is little in the content of Proverbs that cannot be paralleled in the wisdom of Israel's neighbors.[55] Thus, in the *Instruction of Ptah-hotep,* his son is urged "to be modest, reliable, honest and to follow justice and truth." In the *Instruction for King Merika-re,* his son is told to "do justice, not to oppress the widow." And in the *Instruction of Amen-em-ope,* we find the following precepts: "Do not encroach upon the boundaries of a widow, do not bear witness with false words; do not laugh at a blind man."[56]

The inclusion of the Book of Proverbs in the body of Holy Writ may be seen as an attempt to support the apodictic moral commands of the Pentateuch with the evidence of sapiential wisdom. The same moral imperatives are presented, but now under the aspect of the confirmation of long and varied experience. These moral rules have been tested in the crucible of life and have been found to work. Many of these character traits have been cultivated by people, with certain observable consequences that are most instructive. Acquiring this knowledge can advance man on the "road of life."[57] What takes place in the Book of Proverbs is the equation of the morally good with the rational. To do the good and avoid the evil is the intelligent thing to do, as demonstrated repeatedly by experience. Thus, the wise man is identified with the righteous man, and the wicked person with the fool.[58] Just as the books of Job and Ecclesiastes represent a confrontation of certain values and principles of the Torah with areas of human experience which seem to contradict them, so Proverbs presents those aspects of empirical reality that seem supportive of traditional morality.

In terms of the overall development of morality in Judaism, the material in Proverbs constitutes an advance in at least two respects. By identifying that faculty in man which deliberates in moral judgments as "wisdom"—i.e., a skill or ability—it follows that it, like all skills, can be learned and can be improved upon by training, diligence, and discipline. This is stated quite explicitly: "If thou seek her [wisdom] as silver, and search for her as for hid treasure, then shalt thou understand the fear of the Lord, and find the knowledge of God" (2:14), and again, "Those that seek Me earnestly shall find me" (8:17).

What this suggests is that moral training may involve much more than merely informing one's student of the moral rules. Later generations will go on to identify the efforts called for in Proverbs with specially devised methods and procedures for moral training.

Since the moral perspective of Proverbs is from the side of human experience, we find an emphasis upon character traits, both good and bad, which are identified with certain clearly drawn personality "types." This is in contrast to the Pentateuch, where morality is presented primarily in the form of rules referring to particular acts and sometimes to general principles but rarely to dispositional traits resident in persons.

Thus, in Proverbs we have an entire gallery of positive moral types, such as *tzaddik,* the *chakham,* and the *yashar,* and an even greater variety of unsavory types, such as the *rasha,* the *avil,* the *kheseil,* the *letz,* and the *peti.* This suggests that moral virtue or vice is to be achieved not by concentrating on individual moral acts but rather by learning to recognize and to emulate certain good personality types, such as a *tzaddik* or a *yashar,* who is associated with an entire cluster or family of good behavior patterns.

A "scorner" (*letz*) is one who does not hear rebuke (13:1), loves not to be reproved (15:12), instigates strife, and should therefore be cast out (20:11).

The "fool" (*kheseil*) considers doing wickedness a sport (10:23), despises his mother (15:20), is always saying things that get him into trouble (18:6), despises wisdom (23:9), and is unreliable (26:6). Never sink to his level of discourse, but deflate his pomposity (26:4–5).

The "thoughtless one" (*peti*) believes everything (14:15), ignores danger (22:3), attracts folly (14:8), and loves thoughtlessness (1:22), which will ultimately destroy him (1:32).

One can perceive here the beginning of an attempt to understand the underlying characterological structures that would give rise to an entire complex of desirable or undesirable behavior patterns. There is also implicit a horizontal linkage that would relate, for example, different vices as typical of the same character weakness. While we have no evidence that moral theory actually went this far in this early period, these considerations are suggested by the terminology of the Book of Proverbs.

In general, the orientation of the Book of Proverbs can best be described as that of "personal morality." A moral code designed from the point of view of society would insist upon strict justice and have little patience with lawbreakers. In Proverbs, however, we are urged to be "slow to anger," and to have compassion upon a thief "if he steal to satisfy his soul when he is hungry."[59]

Morality In Rabbinic Literature

After the Bible, the second primary source of Judaism is the teachings of the rabbis, which have come down to us in the Mishna, the Talmud, and other midrashic works. Believing themselves to be in possession of an authentic oral tradition as to the meaning of Scripture, the rabbis proceeded to analyze, interpret, and amplify the biblical teachings.[60] Accepting the Torah as divine revelation and as the embodiment of the divine will, the rabbis looked upon all its parts, the ritual as well as the moral, as of equal validity and authority. Hence their process of interpretation and amplification was directed to the ritual as well as the moral, to the philosophical and historical as well as to the legal. While the dynamics of the exegetical process of the Talmud carried the ritual and legal material to its ultimate expression in the form of fixed and definitive rulings called the Halakhah, the ideas and concepts of Judaism, called the Aggadah, which did not lend themselves to behavioral rules, were left in a rather fluid form and were generally not resolved in a dogmatic fashion.

The elements of morality that we noted in the Pentateuch were likewise subjected to the talmudic process and, depending upon the form they took in the Pentateuch, found their way into both the Halakhah and the Aggadah. Thus, for example, a specific rule obliging a householder to build a parapet around his roof, obviously intended to prevent injury to himself and others, was clarified, interpreted, and given a legal structure which resulted in both expansion as well as limitation. The command is found in Deuteronomy: "When thou buildest a new house, then thou shalt make a parapet for thy roof, that thou bring not blood upon thy house, if any man fall from thence" (22:8). In clarifying this rule, which is expressive of the moral responsibility one has for the safety of one's fellow, the Halakhah specified the height of the parapet and limited its application to dwelling places of a certain minimum height, to the exclusion of barns and storage structures. At the same time, perceiving the principle behind the rule, as expressed in the words "that thou bring not blood upon thy house," the Halakhah broadened the admonition to include open cisterns, tunnels, and any other hazards, on one's property. Further extensions of this principle to encompass precautions for the health and safety of people brought under its rubric all of the rabbinic warnings against unsafe drinking water, contaminated utensils, and half-eaten fruits and vegetables.[61] In our day it would certainly include responsibility for safety devices in shops and factories, inferior products, harmful chemicals in foods, and the long-range ecological damage of discharging waste products, fumes, and noise.

Another example of a moral rule handled halakhically is the hallowed: "Honor thy father and thy mother" and "Ye shall fear every man his mother and father."[62] In the analysis given to these commands by the rabbis, vague admonitions were spelled out in concrete terms so that these moral concerns could be realized in the ordinary and varied situations of life. Thus, "honor" is construed as the obligation, should it be necessary, to feed, clothe, shelter, and escort one's parents, from the parents resources when possible, but if not, from one's own resources. "Fear" is interpreted as reverence, to be expressed in not sitting in one's parent's chair and in not interrupting their conversation—being respectful in speech and gesture, no matter how great the provocation. Parental authority is limited to the framework of the Torah. That is to say, parents need not be obeyed when their commands are contrary to the rules of the Torah. The rabbis also ruled that one did not have to follow his parent's advice in the selection of a mate. They also discussed the priorities that should obtain in honoring father, mother, and teacher. The principle was expanded to include one's older brother and the obligation to honor parents even after their death.[63]

Moral teachings which could not be reduced to behavioral rules were treated by the rabbis in the parts of their literature that we called Aggadah. In the Mishnah, the first written codification of rabbinic law—redacted by Rabbi Judah ha-Nassi about the year 200 C.E.—a total of sixty five aggadic teachings of central theological and moral significance were judiciously included, usually at the end of a chapter, tractate, or order.[64] In addition, a special treatise on morals entitled *Avot* (Fathers) was included in the Mishnah.[65] In this work, the moral and theological teachings of the rabbis, often expressed in marvelously concise aphorisms, are presented in chronological order. The form of the teachings is varied. Sometimes specific actions are recommended or condemned, such as, "Say little and do much" or "Greet all men with a cheerful mien" or "Do not console your fellow while his dead is before him." Sometimes certain personalities, historic or generic, are held up as models of behavior to be emulated:

Moses was himself righteous and led others to righteousness.

Be as the disciples of Aaron. . . Be as the disciples of Abraham. . . .

Be as the servant who serves his master. . . .

There are seven marks of the wise man . . .[66]

The rabbis, in their treatment of morality, gave new and important emphasis to what can be called personal morality! Realizing that a broad range of morally undesirable acts can be the result of a single bad character trait, the rabbis shifted their instruction to the prevention or elimination of bad character traits (*middot*) and the inculcation of good ones. Thus, pride or arrogance (*ga'avah*) is condemned and meekness extolled; anger and lust and envy are condemned, while a "good eye" (generosity) and a "good heart" (self-control?) are praised.[67]

In a passage which was seen as containing the outline for an entire program of training in piety, one rabbi offered a series of stages in the religious development of the individual which included several moral traits, such as saintliness and humility.[68] Most important, however, is the conclusion in the Talmud that of the virtues enumerated, *chasidut*, "kindliness," is the greatest of all, which differs with another view that "humility" is the greatest of all. The fact, however, that both of these candidates for the supreme religious value are moral in nature and are selected above a virtue such as *kedushah*, or "holiness," would seem to support the claim that morality was recognized as the supreme value in Judaism.

In truth, these one-word names for extremely complex moral and religious values are necessarily vague and tend to overlap. A study of the sources seems to indicate that *kedushah* is the supreme attribute of God revealed to man. This has been variously defined as referring to the unlimited sovereignty of God, His infinite, all-encompassing nature, the "numinous" quality of religious experience, God's being "wholly other," or God as the ultimate good. But what does it mean when man is given the commandment, "Holy shall ye be, for holy am I, the Lord your God"? Following this command in the Pentateuch is the sublime code of Leviticus 19, which contains most of the important moral teachings. To be sure, ritual commands are also included, which prompts Lazarus to speak of "ritual holiness" as well as "ethical holiness."[69] However, a comprehensive study of the concept seems to warrant the following conclusion:

> The application of holiness to the life of man sheds light on its meaning in reference to God. The commandment "Holy shall ye be, for holy am I, the Lord your God," can hardly mean that man is exhorted to be "wholly other" like the "Wholly Other" Who dwells in His holy habitation. It contains rather the call to a total withdrawal from everything that is impure, ignoble, and unworthy, and the appeal to strive for the attain-

ment of a likeness of God in terms of whole-hearted dedication to goodness, compassion, love, and purity. God is holy because he possesses in
full all the attributes of goodness.[70]

The concept of *kedushah,* therefore, would appear to be the most
general and all-embracing term by which Judaism designates the highest religious quality that can be attained either in space, in time, or in
man himself and that brings one closer to God, or into communion
with Him. But, since in Judaism, the essential core of religion is
morality, it follows that holiness for man is "basically an ethical
value,"[71] the "perfection of morality" and the "ethical ideal of
Judaism."[72]

The concept of holiness is also found in connection with the dietary
laws and the rules governing sexual behavior.[73] These too, however,
must be seen as ultimately contributing to the development of the personal morality of the individual, i.e., his inner character traits and
moral dispositions. For clearly, we are dealing here with the two
strongest urges or appetites in man, which are biologically grounded
and thus have "natural" and useful channels of expression. Yet there is
something in man that can convert these passions and sources of great
creative energy into an "evil urge." It is the "imaging of the designs of
his heart"[74]—which Buber understands as "play with possibility, play
as self-temptation . . . images of the possible from which ever and
again, violence springs"[75]—that is called evil and can transform a
neutral passion into lust and gluttony. While Judaism accepts the pleasures of food and sex as legitimate and as a positive good, it seeks, by
the imposition of guidelines—by laying down rules for the "how,"
"when," and "with whom" of these activities—to encourage the individual to exercise a degree of control. Armed with deep insight into the
psychology of desire and the dynamics of hedonism, Judaism strove to
have man avoid the extremes of repression and obsession and instead
cultivate an approach that would preserve for the individual the simple
and satisfying joys of food and sex. One of the effects of the many rules
regulating eating and drinking in Judaism has been thus described:

> As often as one is about to satisfy the impulse of eating and drinking, the
> Torah brings one, from early youth, to that pause which converts impulse

to will. The pause may be exceedingly brief but the very withholding of the immediate fulfillment of the demands of the impulse, the very questioning and the very performance of actions other than through the medium of impulse, but after the examination and deliberation, are indeed what separate fundamentally and basically the man whose impulse has the better of him from him who can master it.[76]

Judaism, however, recognizes that man is neither an ascetic animal (which leads to neurosis) nor a pleasure-seeking animal (which leads to obsessional indulgence), but a human being, created in the image of God, whose every biological activity is interpenetrated by the human psyche, which demands meaning and significance.[77] Only self-transcendence can save these activities from ultimately becoming stultifying and empty.

Our task is not to renounce life but to bring it close to Him.

What we strive for are not single moments of self-denial but sober constant affirmation of other selves, the ability to feel the needs and problems of our fellowmen.

There is no joy for the self within the self. Joy is found in serving rather than in taking.

We are all endowed with talents, aptitudes, facilities, yet talent without dedication, aptitude without vocation, facility without spiritual dignity, end in frustration.[78]

In Judaism, the desires for food and sex are scaled down so that they can take their proper place as "team-players" within the structure of a unified human being. This makes it possible for them to be expressed in ways which are right and just when other human beings are involved. But, in addition, these impulses are harnessed, by means of the ritual law, to serve wider social and religious values and thus become effective vehicles for the bringing of holiness into all areas of life.

Were The Rabbis Aware Of Morality As Such?

That the rabbis were aware of the special moral content of *Avot* and of the moral foundations of that entire section of the Talmud dealing with *Damages* is clear from the following suggestion: "He who wishes to be saintly [*chasid*], let him fulfill the words of *Avot* . . . let him fulfill the words of *Damages*."[79]

Instead of simply urging their disciples to "depart from evil and do good," the rabbis continued in the "wisdom" tradition of the Book of Proverbs and sought, on the basis of experience, to suggest the conditions, in terms of the actual life-styles or psychological mind-sets, which will keep man far removed from the forbidden acts or volatile desires.

> Consider three things and you will not fall into the power of sin.
>
> Excellent is the study of Torah together with worldly occupation for the toil in both puts sin out of mind.
>
> Go out and see which is the good path that a person should choose.

On the other hand, there are considerations which predispose man to immorality:

> Midday wine . . . sitting in the meeting houses of the ignorant put a man out of the world.
>
> Jesting and levity lead man on to lewdness.[80]

We noted earlier that some of the moral teachings of the Bible are found in the form of principles—i.e., as rules of great generality and abstraction, such as, "And thou shalt love thy neighbor as thyself." Were the rabbis aware of the special nature of these formulations? Did they distinguish between rules and principles? From the following passage it would appear that they did:

> R. Akiva said of the command "Thou shalt love thy neighbor as thyself" that it is a great principle [*kelal gadol*] of the Torah. Ben Azzai said there is a principle that is even greater: "This is the book of the generations of Adam . . . in the likeness of God made He him" [Gen. 4:1].[81]

While scholars may differ as to the precise nature of the issue between Rabbi Akiva and Ben Azzai, there can be no doubt that the

word *kelal,* often used by the rabbis in their halakhic discussions, had
the meaning of a general principle or universal that subsumed many
particulars. It is not important at this stage to determine whether or
not the rabbis saw in this principle the "ultimate criterion of
morals."[82] Suffice it to note that as *kelal gadol,* they saw this principle as
capable of generating an unlimited number of particular imperatives
in all sorts of concrete situations. This same perception of the very
general nature of the command to love one's fellow as oneself led Hillel several generations earlier to assert that the passage "That which
thou despiseth, do not do to your neighbor" is the entire Torah.[83]

Some far-reaching teachings that the rabbis saw as grounded in the
"Love thy neighbor" principle included the one that a man must not
marry a woman without seeing her first, lest he learn to hate her and
violate the love precept.[84] In a completely different context, but
also appealing to the principle of "Love thy neighbor as thyself," the
rabbis insisted that every measure be taken to ease the pain and ensure
the dignity of those to be executed by the courts.[85]

In general, it has been noted that for the rabbis, the commandments of the Torah were objects of theoretical reflection, and that
"particularly in regard to ethical questions, a high degree of abstraction was reached."[86] A truly remarkable example is the teaching of
Rabbi Simlai:

> Six hundred and thirteen commandments were given to Moses on Sinai.
> David came and reduced them to eleven, as we read: "Lord, who shall
> sojourn in Thy tabernacle? . . . He that walketh uprightly and worketh
> righteousness" [Ps. 15:1–2]. Then came Isaiah and reduced them to six,
> as we read: "He that walketh righteously and speaketh uprightly" [Isa.
> 33:15]. Then came Micah and reduced them to three: "And what does the
> Lord require of thee, only to do justly and to love mercy and to walk
> humbly with thy God" [Mic. 6:8]. Then came Habakkuk and reduced
> them to one: "But the righteous shall live by his faith" [Hab. 2:4].[87]

Clearly, Rabbi Simlai is not suggesting that succeeding generations
reduced the 613 commandments to eleven and then to one in the sense
that the eleven or the one are now to replace the 613![88] This teaching
is, rather, part of the search on the part of the rabbis for ever more
inclusive principles of Judaism and Jewish morality—principles of

greater generality and abstraction under which all of the rules of the Torah could be subsumed and new ones, perhaps, generated.

Other principles, such as "And thou shalt do what is right and good" (Deut. 6:18), and "That thou mayest walk in the path of good men and keep the paths of the righteous" (Prov. 2:20), were construed by the rabbis as imposing a moral obligation upon the individual to benefit his neighbor beyond the strict requirement of the Halakhah.[89] The precise nature of this area, which the rabbis called *lifnim mi-shurat ha-din,* and which others have identified as "equity" and "morality" or the "way of the *chasid,*" remains to be analyzed.[90] The point, however, is that the special nature of these principles, as contrasted to the particular *mitzvot,* was recognized.

We would have to agree that the rabbis did not have a special term for "morality." That is to say, they did not have a word or phrase by which they designated with precision all aspects of morality and only morality. Thus, the term *derekh eretz* was used by the rabbis to refer to morality but also on occasion to many things besides morality.[91] The phrase *bain adam le-chavero,* "between man and his fellow man," while including the moral sphere, obviously does not cover a man's relation to animals, which is very much a part of the morality of Judaism. While it may be true that the specific phrase *bain adam le-chavero,* when used as a designation for a special class of *mitzvot,* is only found in occurrences "limited to a specific context and a particular idea"—namely, sins committed between man and man[92]—there are other rabbinic expressions and formulations from which it can safely be concluded that the area of intersubjective relations was seen as a special one and was associated with qualities that we identify with morality.

Thus, we find the following teachings in the *Mekhilta* and the *Sifre* respectively:

Rabbi Shimon said: Why did judgments [*mishpatim*] precede all the other *mitzvot* of the Torah? Because when judgments are pending between man and his fellow man, there is rivalry between them. When the judgment is decided, peace is made between them.[93]

What message did the Torah bring to Israel? Take upon yourselves the yoke of the Kingdom of Heaven, vie one with the other in the fear of God, and practice loving deeds toward one another.[94]

The Talmud also distinguishes between a *tzadik* who is "good" and one who is not good, defining the former as one who is good to heaven and good to humanity, and the latter as one who is "good to heaven and bad to humanity."[95] Similarly, the *Sifre* speaks of being "good in the eyes of heaven" and "straightforward in the eyes of man."[96]

All of these passages imply that the rabbis recognized a special class of *mitzvot* that applied *bain adam le-chavero,* to relations between man and his fellow man, resulting in conditions that we recognize as morally right and good.[97]

Scholars have noted that two different approaches, each virtually the opposite of the other, seem to have been employed by the *midrash halakhah,* the rabbinic method of exegesis, in interpreting the biblical laws.[98] Sometimes what seems to be operating is a policy of contraction, limiting the law in question to the exact conditions specifically mentioned in the text and considering the slightest deviation from these conditions as sufficient to render the law inapplicable. On other occasions, the exegesis seems to be following a policy of expansion, extrapolating the law to similar situations and thereby broadening the area of its applicability beyond the specific terms of the biblical formulation.

The observation has been made that the expansion approach seems to be used overwhelmingly in regard to laws grounded in the principle of kindness, justice, and peace, which we have suggested can be considered the essence of the Torah. Therefore, if one can assume that one has insight into the guiding principle behind the law, one can proceed to widen the scope of the law with confidence that one is still within the area intended. This roughly coincides with the group of laws dealing with matters *bain adam le-chavero,* "between man and his fellow man." Some examples of the method of expansion culled from this area follow.

Concerning a "hired servant" who is "poor and needy" we are told, "in the same day thou shalt give him his hire." Yet in spite of the explicit reference to his being "poor and needy," the rabbis interpreted this to apply to any hired servant, be he rich or poor.[99]

On the passage "Thou shalt not take the widow's raiment to pledge," the interpretation was, "whether she is rich or poor."[100]

The prohibition "Thou shalt not muzzle the ox when he treadeth out the corn" was understood to apply even when the ox was muzzled from before.[101]

The injunction "No man shall take the mill or the upper millstone to pledge" was interpreted to apply to any object necessary to produce food.[102]

The method of contraction, however, was utilized, it would seem, in regard to the ritual laws called *chukkim* or *gezerot ha-katuv,* whose rationale was not clear, or to laws that carried with them certain stated punishments. In regard to the former, the approach of the rabbis was to confine the law to the precise conditions mentioned in the text. Not understanding the underlying principles, the rabbis had little choice. Thus, the passage "You shall offer no strange incense thereon" whose intent is quite clear, was understood to mean that the individual person could not contribute any incense.[103] However, concerning the oil of anointment, the Torah said, "Upon the flesh of men it shall not be poured." The rabbis restricted this to "flesh of men," excluding animals, vessels, and the dead from the prohibition.[104] In regard to the redemption of the first-born, "All the first-born of thy sons [*banekha*] thou shalt redeem" was strictly interpreted as meaning sons but not daughters, although sometimes the word *banim* was understood to mean "children."[105] Similarly, the biblical prohibition of combining meat and milk was interpreted as applying only *derekh bishul,* "if arrived at through cooking," in accordance with the wording of the passage: "Thou shalt not seethe a kid in its mother's milk."[106]

In dealing with punishment, which is, in a sense, an area *bain adam le-chavero,* the rabbis were guided by the principle "and the congregation shall deliver" to lean toward leniency and mercy in their interpretations.[107]

If it is true that two different approaches, contraction and expansion, can be discerned as operating in connection with these different groupings of *mitzvot,* then we have here another strand of evidence that the rabbis had a profound awareness of the difference between laws which hold *bain adam le-chavero* and those *bain adam la-makom.*

It is interesting to note that Maimonides, who expresses reservations about the logical rigor of distinguishing between the commandments on the basis of "between man and man" and "between man and God," nevertheless employs the distinction to explain a variety of halakhic and aggadic issues.[108] Thus, there is the *Mishnah* in *Pe'ah* which reads:

> These are the things of which a man enjoys the fruits in this world while the stock [principal] remains for him in the world-to-come; honoring father and mother, deeds of loving-kindness, timely attendance at the house of study morning and evening, hospitality to wayfarers, visiting the sick, dowering the bride, attending the dead to the grave, devotion in prayer, and making peace between man and his fellow; but the study of the Torah is above all.[109]

Maimonides, in his commentary on this *Mishnah,* explains that the *mitzvot* can be divided among those that regulate relations between man and his fellow man and those that relate to man in his relationship to God. The reward for observing any of the *mitzvot* is to be understood in terms of bringing the person closer to the spiritual perfection of the world-to-come. This *mishnah,* however, draws our attention to the fact that the *mitzvot* that deal with man and his fellow man confer the additional reward of "fruits in this world"; i.e., the social benefits of reciprocated harmony and benevolence in human affairs.

In dealing with the laws of *Blessings,* Maimonides states that the rabbis ordained that the performance of any *mitzvah* relating to God is to be preceded by the recitation of a blessing containing the formula ". . . who has sanctified us with His commandments."[110] Evidently, Maimonides was attempting to explain the curious fact that the *mitzvah* of giving *tzedakah* (charity) was not assigned a blessing. The proffered "explanation" would lie in the fact that since "between-man-and-man" rules are "rational"—i.e., their social benefits commend their observance—this, in some way, compromises our ability to pronounce a blessing which proclaims the act as pure *mitzvah* and the action as response to the will of God. Once again Maimonides found a group of rabbinic teachings which he thought could be best elucidated by application of the *bain adam le-chavero–bain adam la-makom* distinction.

In the sixth chapter of his justly famous introduction to *Avot,* Maimonides presents what appears to be a disagreement between the philosophers and the teachings of the rabbis. The philosophers assert that a person who is moral and correct in his actions but exercises this control only after constant struggle to overcome and repress wayward desires and passions is not as highly regarded as one whose heart no longer lusts after the forbidden and whose very desires correspond to the will of God. Yet a number of rabbinic texts extol the virtues of the individual who must exert great effort to do what is proper above one to whom obedience comes naturally and without much effort. Maimonides quotes the dictum of Rabbi Simeon ben Gamaliel: "Let not a man say, 'I find it impossible to eat milk and meat together,' or 'I find it impossible to wear clothing of sha'atnez,' but rather, 'I find it possible but what am I to do—my Father in heaven has forbidden me.'"[111]

The resolution suggested by Maimonides employs the distinction between *mitzvot* between man and man and those between man and God, only this time he does not use these terms, preferring to speak of the *rational mitzvot* as opposed to the *traditional mitzvot*. His point is that in regard to those moral prohibitions which are universally held to be evil, such as murder, theft, requiting good with evil, etc., anyone who is attracted to these acts or who harbors a desire for them is definitely lacking in moral fiber and is inferior to one who naturally recoils from them. However, in regard to those ritual commands which, as Maimonides said, would not be evil at all were it not for the Torah, there is no reason why a person may not be attracted to them and say, "I would love to have milk with my meat, but alas, God has forbidden it." If he disciplines his desire to obedience to God, he stands higher than one who is naturally repelled by that food combination.

This analysis goes further than the others. For not only does Maimonides use here the moral-ritual distinction as a heuristic device, but he implies a most important substantive difference between the two types of *mitzvot*. The distinction that Maimonides makes can be rendered intelligible only on the view that the moral *mitzvot* are of intrinsic value; intrinsic good and intrinsic evil—whereas the ritual commands are only of instrumental value.[112]

The Primacy Of Morality Affirmed

We have established that the rabbis were amply aware of the special nature of man's relations to his fellow man as differentiated from his relations to God, and that these relations are the subject of a substantial number of *mitzvot* and are the matrix out of which grow the moral

qualities we call justice and righteousness, mercy and kindness, peace
and love. We can now proceed with the next question: Do the rabbinic
teachings reflect the same sense of the primacy of morality that we
found in the Pentateuch and in the prophets? An examination of rabbinic literature leads us to reply in the affirmative. Consider the following teachings, which we present in an ascending order in terms of their
implications of the primacy of morality. Beginning with statements
which indicate merely that morality is a necessary condition of man
fulfilling his religious obligation, we conclude with statements which
imply that morality is the most important component and indeed the
essence of the entire Torah.

1. In the Torah, in the Prophets, and in the Writings, we find that a man
must perform his duty to his fellows exactly as he does to the Omnipotent.

2. "Say ye of the righteous that he is good" [Isa. 3:10]. Is there then a
righteous man who is good and one who is not good? He who is good
toward God and toward his fellow man is a righteous person who is good.
He who is good toward God but evil toward his fellow man is a righteous
man who is not good.

3. He in whom the spirit of his fellow creatures takes delight, in him the
spirit of the Omnipotent takes delight, and he in whom the spirit of his
fellow creatures takes not delight, in him the spirit of the Omnipresent
takes not delight.

4. He who acts honestly and is popular with his fellow creatures, it is
imputed to him as though he had fulfilled the entire Torah.

5. When a person is brought before the heavenly tribunal after death, the
first question put to him is, "Have you been honest in your transactions?"

6. Hillel said, "What is hateful to yourself, do not do to your fellow man.
This is the entire Torah, the rest is commentary. Go and study."

7. Jerusalem was destroyed because honest men ceased therein.

8. The Torah begins with deeds of kindness and ends with deeds of kindness.

9. It is written [II Chron. 15:3]: "Now for long seasons Israel was with-

out the true God, and without a teaching priest, and without law." What does the expression, "without the true God" mean? Said Rav Huna: "He who occupies himself with the Torah but does not observe loving-kindness is similar to one who denies God."

10. Better is one hour of repentance and good deeds in this world than the whole life of the world-to-come.[113]

Morality In Later Jewish Thought

It is almost paradoxical that morality, which was so central to Judaism in all of its primary sources, did not receive the same attention and development in later Jewish thought as did other aspects of Judaism.

In all probability there were talmudic discussions of tractates *Avot, Derekh Eretz,* and *Kallah,* just as there were of the other components of the Mishnah. Such discussions, had they survived, would certainly have amplified and clarified these moral teachings but unfortunately they were not preserved. In the aggadic portions of the Talmud and in the midrashic literature, moral teachings were subject to the same limitations as Aggadah generally in that they did not receive the systematic attention of the codifiers and the *posekim* (halakhic decisors). Only those moral rules which were specific biblical commands with behavioral implications entered into the halakhic process and were further developed.

The more comprehensive philosophers of the Middle Ages like Sa'adiah and Maimonides included discussions of morality in their presentations. In the eleventh century there appeared the first so-called *musar*[114] or "ethical" work, the *Chovot ha-Levavot,* or "Duties of the Heart," by Bachya ben Joseph Ibn Paquda. In his introduction, the author criticizes the one-sided emphasis on the "duties of the limbs"—the external physical acts, or practical observances, of Judaism—with little attention by scholars to those duties of the Torah which are emotional and attitudinal—inner experiences such as beliefs, intentionality, purity of motive, love and fear of God, repentance and humility.

This work was followed centuries later by the *Sha'arei Teshuvah,* "Gates of Repentance," by Rabbi Jonah ben Abraham Leon Gerondi, who drew attention to the way in which personal perfection and proximity to God are dependent upon attitudes and speech. In a later period there appeared a work that became a classic of this genre, the *Mesillat Yesharim,* or "Ways of the Righteous," by Moses Chayim Luzzatto, who outlined the main steps which can lead to inner piety and holiness.

It is important to note that none of these works treats of morality as a separate subject, and none of them discusses the duties between man and his fellow man as such. Personal character traits, such as humility and *chasidut* and purity, are perceived as stages in self-development leading to reverence for God. Traits such as the aforementioned, which have clear implications for morality, are treated together with purely religious attitudes, such as faith and trust in God.

In the early sixteenth century, a body of "ethical" writings appears in connection with the *Chasidei Ashkenaz.* These included the *Sefer Chasidim* by R. Judah he-Chasid of Regensburg and the *Sefer ha-Rokhe'ach* by Eleazer of Worms. The Kabbalist school contributed its "ethical" works as exemplified by the *Tomer Devorah* of Moses Cordovero and the *Reshit Chokhmah,* by his disciple, Elijah de Vidas.

Chasidic literature in the late eighteenth century and throughout the nineteenth was to a large extent "ethical" in the above sense. Among its works are the *Sefer ha-Middot* by R. Nachman of Bratslav and the *Tanya* by R. Shneur Zalman of Lyady.

The more recent Musar movement associated with the work of Rabbi Joseph Zundel of Salant, Rabbi Israel of Salant, and Rabbi Isaac Blaser, which arose in the nineteenth and twentieth centuries in rabbinic and yeshiva circles, did place a direct and conscious emphasis upon the moral sphere, upon relations between man and his fellow man. This was done in response to a perceived distortion in the prevailing norms of Jewish observance and notions of Jewish piety. Whereas the Jewish masses of the time had developed a high degree of sensitivity to the ritual *mitzvot,* such as *kashrut,* festivals, and prayer, and external customs, such as dress, there had not developed a corresponding sensitivity in areas involving speaking slander, respecting the rights and fortunes of others, and the eschewing of arrogance, vulgarity, and ostentation.[115]

The Musar movement was essentially practical—i.e., didactic and pedagogical—in its orientation. Its purpose was to develop in the individual a sharper consciousness of the personal, pietistic, and moral dimensions in Judaism. Toward this end many of its leading thinkers applied their knowledge of psychology and human motivation in order to develop effective educational methods by which to develop character.

For many, this considerable literature does not sufficiently redress the imbalance in Jewish scholarship, which has persisted for too long, in which proper attention has not been focused on that which is, after all, the essence of Judaism—its moral teachings.

Morality Within The Jewish World-View

Judaism, along with other major philosophic and religious systems, constitutes, in part, a comprehensive theory or world-view which attempts to offer an intelligible account of God and the universe, man and history, in a unified manner. A conception of morality is usually a component of such a world-view. In attempting, therefore, to understand the place of morality within Judaism, it becomes necessary to examine not only the manner in which moral teachings are treated in the scriptural texts but also the logical role of morality within the context of the Jewish view of man in the universe.

Early in this chapter we alluded to the fact that in the opening narratives of the Book of Genesis, which speak of the creation of the world and of man, we find certain existential perspectives within which morality is accorded a pivotal role. Thus, we are told that in the latter part of the sixth day, after bringing into existence a world which He pronounces "good," God proceeds in a direct way to create man "in His image" and gives him "dominion . . . over all the earth." In subtle but unmistakable ways, the texts suggest that, while the other creatures attain full actualization of being with the gift of existence, man has much to do before he may be said to achieve fulfillment. After the creation of man, the Pentateuch does not make the usual comment, "and the Lord saw that it was good." This implies that man at his inception was not yet "good" but must work toward such a condition.[116] Similarly, while it is announced that man will be created in God's "image and likeness," the act of creation is described in terms of

God's "image" only. The rabbis drew the implication that it is up to man himself to become "like unto God" by his subsequent actions.[117]

While no clear indication is given in the text as to the precise meaning of "image of God," tradition has variously identified it with such uniquely human capacities as freedom of the will, reason, self-consciousness, moral deliberation, invention and use of language (conceptual symbols), and cultural creativity.

Initially the only task given to man beyond the "natural" ones of to be "fruitful and multiply . . . and subdue the earth" is to obey the command of God.[118] While the first sin of primal man brings into the world death, birth pangs, toil, and fatigue, it does not introduce any change in man's nature and in his propensity to sin. Judaism rejected any interpretation of this biblical account that might have inclined the Jewish view toward the Pauline doctrine of "original sin."[119] According to this latter view, not only did Adam's sin bring death into the world but it caused a deterioration in the nature of all future generations which inclined them all to sin, so that even the Torah itself is not capable of changing or redeeming them. In the Jewish view, however, while the human environment may have changed, the human capacity and the human task remain essentially the same. God has given to man life and the commandments. The first gift results in man's awareness that he is God's handiwork, fashioned in His image with the capacity to walk in His ways and be "like unto Him." The second informs man that he is called upon to live and work for God. Man is not merely a creature but a creature with moral responsibility, an ethical personality who can and ought to "choose life and the good."[120]

By choosing the moral life, which is the "way of God," man by his own actions fulfills himself and completes the work of creation. The Christian diagnosis of man, with its understanding of the Fall as somehow involving the whole creation in evil, had to look toward an external metaphysical event as embodied in the incarnation and atonement to somehow set things right for man.[121] Judaism, however, believing man's nature to be unaffected by any "Fall" and still grounded in the "image of God," looked to a moral development within man initiated by man and leading him on the divine path of justice and righteousness, love, and mercy. This, within the context of Torah, was thoroughly capable of fulfilling man's divine potential.

In this connection it should be noted that the Jewish thinkers of the Middle Ages did not give adequate recognition to the moral component in Judaism. This is particularly apparent in their inability to relate morality to the perfection of the soul and the attainment of immortality in the world-to-come. Maimonides, for example, taught that immortality of the soul (*olam ha-ba*) depends upon the actualization through knowledge of man's intellectual power. While the knowledge of God that man must attain does include an understanding of the ethical activity of God, moral perfection does not really touch man's essential core. Disappointingly, most of the other medieval thinkers, like Maimonides, regarded morality as a necessary condition of human perfection, but appreciated it primarily for its social utility. As Guttmann concludes, "He [Maimonides] was unable to distinguish between the meaning of moral communion with God, as taught but not dogmatically formulated by Judaism, and the idea of the communion of the knowing spirit with God, as held by Aristotelianism."[122] Maimonides' opponents were quick to point out that it is reasonable to assume that whatever serves as the key to human salvation ought to have the following characteristics: "It should be readily available, easy to acquire, universal in its application, and not quickly lost."[123] Clearly, an intellectual love of God based on abstract metaphysical concepts is too lofty and difficult a requirement upon which to hinge higher salvation.

Hasdai Crescas broke out of the rational bias of his predecessors and shifted the essence of the God-idea away from thought to goodness. He denied that knowledge is man's highest good. Communion with God and eternal happiness come about for man through love of God, which is attained through observance of the divine commandments.[124] Earlier, Juda Halevi had already taught that the chief purposes of the Torah is to achieve for man eternal happiness by developing a love for God as expressed through worship and obedience to the *mitzvot*. These approaches sounded more plausible in that they looked to a "religious" or "spiritual" factor to produce a "religious" or "spiritual" consequence. It seems to make sense that "love of God" should lead to communion with God, the ultimate consequence of which is for the soul to partake of the eternity of God. It also put the highest good within reach of every man. The thinker in that period who came closest to an appreciation of the moral component in this context was Joseph Albo, albeit still not for the right reasons! He saw the Torah as divided into three parts: ideas, statutes (ritual commands), and judgments (moral commands), each with their positive and negative formulations. Indicative of the crippling presuppositions under which they operated is the following most curious question:

> Now it is clear that perfection may be acquired through the theoretical part of the Torah. . . . Similarly, perfection may be acquired through the part containing the statutes, i.e., the rules concerning those things which are pleasing to God and those which are displeasing. . . . The thing that requires explanation, however, is how can perfection of the soul be acquired through the third part, which embraces judgements? It is hard to conceive how any of its parts, positive or negative, can give perfection to the soul. *Commandments like "Thou shalt not steal" and "Thou shalt not oppress thy neighbor"* . . . *are no doubt right rules for the preservation of social life, but by what merit does the soul of a mortal man acquire perfection by means of them?*[125]

Albo answers his own question by pointing out that when moral rules are performed with the right intention as commandments of God, the act takes on a religious character and does more than simply improve the state of society. It is now an expression of the love of God, and therefore gives perfection to the soul of the agent. He cites an interesting passage in support of his thesis that moral deeds can bring about ultimate human perfection. We find in Isaiah: "And the work of righteousness shall be peace; and the effect of righteousness, quietness and confidence forever."[126] Says Albo, "peace" refers to the immediate social benefits, while "quietness and confidence" refer to the long-range consequences of moral behavior in terms of conferring immortality upon the soul, which is "forever."

However, what all of these writers should have realized, and what was explicitly taught by Rabbi Judah Loew of Prague about one hundred years later, was that the religious and spiritual aspects of morality do not lie merely in its being a command of God, which one performs out of love for God, but rather that there is a more fundamental and substantive connection.[127] All that we know of God is His moral nature, so that when we act morally we are "walking the ways of

God," "imitating Him," and fulfilling our "divine image." This is the most direct way by which man can "cleave unto God" and have fellowship with Him. Acts of injustice and cruelty remove a man from God, while kindness, love, and concern draw him closer. More than that, "love of God" is not to be construed as some simple, primitive emotion. The sublime religious feelings of "love" and "fear" of God are themselves based upon moral sentiments, such as gratitude, justice, and responsibility. Samson Raphael Hirsch is said to have taught that "justice is the sum total of life and is the sole concept which the Torah seeks to interpret. The Torah teaches us justice towards men, justice towards plants and animals and the earth, justice toward our own body and soul and justice towards God who created you for love so that you may become a blessing for the world."[128]

There is a profound sense in which love of man is related to love of God. In the words of Buber: "Every particular *Thou* is a glimpse through to the eternal *Thou*; by means of every particular *Thou,* the primary word addresses the eternal *Thou.*"[129]

Therefore, to the evidence of Scripture and rabbinic teachings, we must now add the role of morality within the structure of Jewish theology. It would appear that in the Jewish view, morality is the bridge by which man reaches out to God. It is the relationship which unites man and man through values which are divine. Morality is the fabric out of which man weaves for himself an ethical self and society achieves its redemptive goal.

3

The Grounds of Morality

In our examination of the place of morality in Judaism and the particular form it takes in the Bible and Talmud, we have already encoun-
tered considerable evidence in support of the supposition that morality
in Judaism is theonomous in character. Thus, we have noted that God is
the source of the moral commands in the Torah as He is of the ritual
commands.[1] Furthermore, God reveals Himself to Moses as moral in
nature, as describable in terms of moral attributes. Finally, it was suggested that doing justice and righteousness is not only the path of God
but the path *to* God. Moral virtue constitutes "knowledge of God,"
which in the Bible implies interrelationship and *devekut.*

However, it is of the utmost importance that the relationship
between God and morality be submitted to careful analysis so that we
may arrive at a correct understanding of the grounds of morality in
Judaism.

There are two distinct, although related, questions which are
involved in any understanding of the grounds of a particular morality.
The first is the question of moral cognition, or how we arrive at a
knowledge of the requirements of morality. The second touches upon
the nature of the obligatoriness of morality. Why ought I be moral?
What are the ends of being moral?

Knowing What Is Morally Right

In answer to the first question, it would appear that the Bible comes
down hard on the side of revealed morality. We know what is good

64

presumably because "It has been told to thee, O man,"[2] by God in His revelations to Israel in the Decalogue and elsewhere in the Torah. Are we to infer from this that in the absence of such special revelations man would have remained ignorant of his moral obligations? Two considerations, one empirical and one textual, argue against such a conclusion. As we saw earlier in connection with our discussion of the Book of Proverbs, there is considerable historical evidence that as early as the third millennium B.C.E. the cultures of Egypt and Mesopotamia incorporated a positive perception of such moral principles as justice and benevolence. How did ancient man come upon such moral knowledge? Of course, this could be explained in terms of the tradition of the "seven *mitzvot* of the children of Noah," a rabbinic doctrine, based on the Bible, which states that as a result of an earlier pre-Sinaitic revelation, seven basic commandments, including the prohibitions against murder and idolatry and the obligation to establish the administration of justice in society, were somehow given to man.[3] This would explain the source of the moral insights possessed and developed by the Patriarchs and in the name of which Abraham appeals to God to "deal justly." Whether the seven Noahide *mitzvot* were "given" to primal man in the form of a prophetic revelation or whether, as one Jewish thinker has suggested, the principles behind them were implanted in the minds of all men as some sort of intuitive or a priori truth is not clear.[4] In either case, the point is that the existence of a knowledge of moral principles among men prior to the Sinaitic revelation may be said to have been assumed by Judaism.

We noted in the previous chapter that one of the terms by which the rabbis referred to morality was *derekh eretz* ("way of the world"). This term has different uses and sometimes may refer to nonmoral areas, such as the useful and the prudential.[5] In all of its uses, however, it carries the general connotation of matters which are common to all mankind. This can be understood in many different senses: that they are generally observed; that they are derivable from the accumulated experience of men; that they serve ends which are universally approved. The rabbis made it clear that *derekh eretz* is included in Torah and thus that we can often learn *derekh eretz from* the Torah ("The Torah teaches us *derekh eretz*").[6] But at the same time they pointed out that *derekh eretz* is prior to Torah, not only logically but chronologically: "*Derekh eretz* preceded Torah by twenty-six generations."[7] The material in *Avot* and in tractate *Derekh Eretz* seems to indicate that even after the Torah was given, we can continue to derive insights of *derekh eretz* from experience. But if, as we have seen, *derekh eretz* includes morality, the rabbis were clearly acknowledging the existence of morality in pre-Torah times.[8]

Is man naturally equipped, either through his reason or through some special "moral sense," to acquire moral knowledge on his own? There is no clear position on this to be found in the primary Jewish sources, although the question has important implications for our study.

Some point to the fact that in the Bible, Cain is held accountable for the murder of his brother, although prior to the incident there is no explicit statement that murder is wrong.[9] Moreover, the acceptance by God of Abel's offering and the rejection of Cain's seem to assume some understanding on the part of rational human beings as to the proper gifts to be offered one's benefactor.[10] Rabbinic texts which are usually taken to suggest a "natural morality" are not really unequivocal in their implications. There is the well-known *Sifra*: "'My judgements [*mishpatim*]' [Lev. 18:4]; that is, precepts such as laws of robbery, chastity, idolatry, blasphemy, and bloodshed, which if they had not been written down in Holy Scripture, justice [*din*; i.e., practical reason] would have demanded that they be put in writing."[11] As Urbach correctly points out, in the light of the examples, which include blasphemy and idolatry, all we can take this to mean is that these "judgments," in contrast to the *chukkim,* can be rationally justified in the light of the obviously beneficial consequences.[12]

Another oft-quoted text is the talmudic teaching, "If the Torah had not been given, we would have learned modesty from the cat, aversion to robbery from the ant, chastity from the dove."[13] The significance of this teaching is limited by its context, which is to explain a passage in Job which seems to indicate that some wisdom can be learned from animals.[14] Moreover, at best, these creatures can only be said to provide in their behavior patterns examples of similarities to certain well-known and admired human traits. In the actual absence of any moral sensitivity, would anyone really be able to generate a moral "ought" merely from the behavior of the ant or the dove?

An important bit of evidence indicating that the rabbis believed in some kind of innate moral knowledge is to be found in their use of the concept of *sevarah,* by which they meant "self-evident reason" or "common sense." Often they would accept this as a direct source of a particular *halakhah* without any further recourse to a text. Frequently the *sevarah* was quasi-moral in nature.[15]

Jewish thinkers during the Middle Ages like Sa'adiah and Maimonides, who had fallen heir to the presuppositions of a powerful rationalism and divided the commandments into rational and traditional categories, saw in the above-mentioned biblical and rabbinic texts support of the view that "reason is capable of reaching through its own powers the content of divine truth,"[16] or at least the moral content of revelation. This, of course, led to the problem of the need for revelation if all truth necessary for man is accessible to unaided reason. By the middle of the fifteenth century, however, Joseph Albo had no difficulty in demonstrating the way in which divine law based on prophetic revelation was superior to natural and conventional law based on human experience and was therefore essential if man was to reach human perfection. While Albo acknowledged that we find a general agreement among men that certain principles, such as justice and gratitude, are good, and others, such as injustice and violence, are evil, these principles are very general and do not provide adequate guidances in particular situations.[17] This had already been suggested by Sa'adiah: "Man is fundamentally in need of the prophets not only on account of the traditional law which had to be announced but also on account of the rational laws . . . for the prophets must show us *how* to perform them. . . . Reason disapproves of theft but gives no definition of the way in which some objects of value become a man's property."[18] It is clear that when these thinkers speak of "reason" as a source of certain kinds of knowledge, they did not have in mind rational necessity but rather the evidence of common experience or those things which command general approval.[19]

On the basis of the material presented so far, we can safely conclude that in the Jewish view:

1. From the very beginning, men were considered moral agents and held responsible for their behavior, as reflected in the events in the Book of Genesis.

2. Although the Torah, God's revelation to Israel, includes a set of moral rules and principles, men generally were aware of the basic demands of morality even earlier.

The Case For Moral Intuitionism

In response to the question as to how man became aware of moral value and moral obligation, I support a view similar to the intuitionist or moral-sense outlook. To accept this view is to accept a moral apperception not only in primal man but in all men. It is not suggested that this portion of our ethical theory is explicitly found in the primary Jewish sources or is uncontestably implied by some text, but only that it is compatible with what is known from the sources and explains in the most economical and thorough way several features of the traditional account.[20]

1. If a *prophetic revelation* to primal man was the source of mankind's moral awareness, it would be vulnerable to the vagaries of transmission of a tradition. Entire segments of humanity might be exempt from moral responsibility on the grounds that they were not privy to the tradition. The accountability which the Bible extends to all men makes no allowances for such excuses. Even today it would restrict moral responsibility to those parts of the planet which have been exposed to the Judeo-Christian tradition.

2. Rabbi Akiva said, "Beloved is man, for he was created in the image [of God]; an even greater sign of love, *it was made known to him* that he was created in the image of God."[21] Clearly, Rabbi Akiva refers to generic man. But how was it made known to man that he was so created? Here again it is difficult to claim that this knowledge came to mankind through Jewish scripture. But if all men are endowed with an ability to apprehend moral values in some way, then from the fact of his own moral consciousness man might come to realize that he is created in the image of God. Indeed, to say that man is created in the image of God is to suggest that man has some fundamental insight, however vague it may be, of God's nature. But if God is good, then it is to be expected that man will have some understanding of what is right and good.[22]

3. Albo states, "Since the first man was created alone, there must be something in man's essential nature by which he can distinguish between good acts conducive to the perfection of his soul and those which are not good."[23] The sequence of biblical events suggests that the entire concept of a covenanted people, of which the Sinaitic revelation was the base, comes about after man's failure. But if, according to the original intent, man was to function without revelation, then clearly, as Albo suggests, he must have been naturally equipped to acquire moral knowledge, which is indispensable for human fulfillment.

4. A passage such as "This Torah . . . is not far from thee nor is it on the other side of the sea . . . but rather it is in thy mouth and in thy heart to do" has suggested to some the notion of a natural moral faculty in man—a flicker of conscience within him that facilitates the fulfillment of his service to God.[24]

Why Be Moral?

We shall shortly return to a further analysis of the nature of man's moral intuition. Let us now consider the second question involved in an understanding of the grounds of morality. What is the nature of the obligatoriness of morality? Why should a person be moral? We indicated earlier that God is the source of the moral commands in the Bible. How shall we understand this? Does it mean that a certain rule is to be deemed moral because God has ordained it, or does it mean the reverse, that God ordains certain rules because they embody moral principles? The latter would appear to be the case inasmuch as the Torah identifies the "ways" of God by appealing to well-known and apparently approved moral traits. When the "Glory of God" is revealed to Moses, only moral attributes are listed, such as "mercy, long-suffering, and kindness."[25] This would suggest that morality is prior to our knowledge of God not only in an epistemological sense but in an axiological sense as well. But insofar as man can know the essence of God's being, if what he gets to know is a moral essence, then morality would appear to be, in some sense, divine. Morality, therefore becomes obligatory for man, not because of the arbitrary fiat of divine legislation but because morality, whose value and obligatoriness man has always dimly perceived, is now identified with God, who is absolute value, the prototype of all morality.[26] In a sense, God has no choice but to ordain moral rules. The moral God cannot command rules that are not moral. "You shall be holy, for I the Lord your God am holy."[27] Similarly, because He is moral, you shall be moral. It is because of this logic that Abraham with complete confidence is able to confront God with the demand for justice: "Shall not the judge of all the earth do justly?"[28] The ultimate purpose of man is to be moral but morality is divine. Hence, the ultimate purpose of man is to become like God, to seek fellowship with Him. One can start at the other end and come to the same conclusion. Man ought to seek self-fulfillment, but he is created in the image of God. Let him, therefore, seek to be like God. But God is merciful and righteous. Let man, therefore, strive to be merciful and righteous. It is in this unique concept of God as possessing a moral nature that there lies the key to our understanding of the grounds of the morality of Judaism.

> The value and power that are inherent in Hebrew monotheism are not due to a numerical unity but to what that unity stands for. The significance of Hebrew monotheism does not lie in the fact that one God is greater than the many gods or that He by Himself is what they all taken together are, but in the fact that He is different from them. He is the Holy One, the cause and guarantee of the one thing, the good, the righteous, and to Him men can draw near only through the one thing: only by doing justice, loving mercy and walking humbly with God.[29]

When Moses asks of God, "Behold, when I come unto the children of Israel and . . . they shall say to me: What is His name? What shall I say unto them?" The reply is given, "I am that I am."[30] This enigmatic reply has generally been interpreted to mean that God is to be understood as the ultimate ground of all being: the eternal Omnipresent. The rabbis, interpreted it to mean, "I will be with them in this trouble as I will be with them in their bondage by other kingdoms."[31] In other words, the rabbis conflated here the ontic and the axiological components of our understanding of God. At the same time that God is the source of all being, He is the source of value. God is not only absolute Being, the eternally present, but absolute value, the eternally compassionate.

Kant And Moral Autonomy

A most persistent stumbling-block in the way of an objective appreciation of this view has been the historical infatuation of Jewish theologians with the philosophy of Immanuel Kant. From Lazarus and Guttmann to Fackenheim, they have felt impelled to somehow reconcile the moral view of Judaism with the views of the sage of Koenigsberg.[32] Jewish morality had to be shown to be autonomous rather than heteronomous; self-legislated rather than imposed by outside authorities; chosen out of a sense of duty for the moral law as such rather than for any other consideration.

Sustained analysis of Kant's moral teachings has sorted out for us those essential elements which are in accord with common moral experience and therefore valid from the irrelevant portions which are not implied by the essential elements and which actually seem contrary to common moral sense.

Kant's first formulation of the categorical imperative, "Act only on that maxim through which you can at the same time will that it should become a universal law," is certainly acceptable as a negative test for principles of moral behavior. We would have to agree that any contemplated policy which could not be universalized could not be a moral policy. Let us see why. One reason why a policy may not be universalized is that I place myself in a favored position and allow myself privileges I do not wish to accord to others. This can be construed as inconsistent and in a sense irrational or as opposed to the principle of equity. Another reason for not being able to universalize a certain policy could be that it would lead to a calamity.[33] But this assumes a recognition of the principle of utility; i.e., the existence of certain universally accepted desirable ends. The formal character of the categorical imperative is thus exposed as being only "skin deep." [34] "The categorical imperative itself can be formal prescinding from and not concerning itself with any particular ends for a quite unmysterious reason. It is a test of maxims and it need mention no ends since the maxims themselves will." Kant's hope that he has revealed the ground of moral obligation to be something "pure" and "unconditioned" and uncontaminated by ends, interests, or utility is not realized in fact.

For all that Kant hoped to make morals absolutely a priori, it is "the nature of man" and "the circumstances of the world in which he is placed" that finally determine rightness and wrongness. What is right can be universalized, what is wrong cannot; but this is as far as one can speak a priori. What can be universalized and what cannot, depends on the contingencies of the economy of the human situation; how man is made and to some degree how and where he finds himself.[35]

Obviously there will be many instances in which duty will clash with self-interest and inclination. At such times the test of universalizability must be applied objectively and the results heeded. But while duty may be opposed to inclination, it does not have to be. "Duty is essentially indifferent to inclination, as indifferent to its opposition as to its concurrence."[36] There is no good reason to agree with Kant that if a person's moral duty happens to coincide with his self-interest or his duty to God, then his performance of his duty with due regard for his interest is devoid of all moral content.

In confronting the moral demands of Judaism, a Jew may learn to appropriate these values for himself and observe them because he is convinced they are right and moral. He therefore no longer needs the additional motivation supplied by the fact that God commands these observances. But if in practicing justice and righteousness, the individual is aware that he is emulating divinity, who is moral, or even more if he is actually attracted to morality out of a strong love for God, then God need not be, and indeed cannot be, eliminated from the moral experience; cannot be, because to understand morality correctly is to understand that it is grounded in God; need not be, because in performing a moral act, to be motivated by love of God as well as by a sense of moral duty does not impair the moral content of the act. Actually the terms "autonomy" and "heteronomy" as basic concepts are rather obsolete and not very useful in discussions of morality, certainly not the morality of Judaism.[37]

Some writers have maintained that there is a fundamental conflict between the concept of worship, which requires total subservience to God, and the role of moral agent, which in the Kantian tradition involves autonomous decision-making. However, once we spell out the implications of the Jewish view of God's moral nature, it would appear that the religious believer "has good reason for supposing that

God would not, indeed, could not command anything which a well-informed autonomous moral agent should be unable to accept.[38] It might, however, be objected that this suggests that the moral agent sits in continual judgment on God's commands, evaluating them by his own moral standards. Is this in keeping with the religious attitudes of obedience and humility required in the presence of the supreme power which is God? P. L. Quinn has suggested that we must distinguish "between unqualified obedience to a command which is of divine origin" after the divine origin is accepted and "unqualified acceptance of the claim that a command is of divine origin."[39] The former condition is undoubtedly required by the concept of worship and represents the preferred religious attitude. The latter, however, is not only not required but is downright foolish even from a religious perspective. The rational person must indeed weigh very carefully any claim to divine origin and authority. From the false prophets of biblical times to the contemporary founders of cults, this particular challenge is very much with us and requires a very deliberate response. Surely, one of the criteria by which we judge whether a certain command is of divine origin is to evaluate its moral character. Indeed, as we indicated earlier, the Torah itself urges us "to see that the Lord is good" and that "He is righteous and straightforward," which obviously requires moral judgment.[40]

Thus, the close relationship between God and morality in Judaism collapses the supposed conflict between the requirements of the worshipful attitude and the concept of moral autonomy. For each time we consider an action that God requires us to do and conclude that the action is morally right, we are making a moral judgment as a responsible moral agent.

Lishmah And The Power Of Personal Appropriation

While the framework of Jewish morality remains theonomous, Jewish thought went to great lengths, first, to stress the importance and desirability of the element of freedom, voluntary acceptance, and appropriation, and second, to affirm the element of intrinsicality—desiring the good for its own sake and not out of expectation of material rewards.

But it is doubtful that when the rabbis spoke of *lishmah,* "for its own sake," they had in mind Kant's notion of "duty for duty's sake." The intrinsic value of the good and the right was inextricably bound up with love of man and love of God. Having in mind the "ends" of the law in this way does not adulterate the moral worth of the action as would, for example, expectation of material reward. The well-known teachings of Antigonus of Sokho, "Be not like servants who serve the master for the sake of receiving a reward, but be like servants who serve the master without the expectation of receiving a reward; and let the fear of heaven be upon you," was seen by one of the foremost medieval commentators as allowing for the urge to spiritual self-fulfillment and personal salvation as legitimate motivation in the service of God.[41]

Again and again the rabbis extolled the importance of actions and observances which Israel as a whole, or particular individuals, took upon themselves over and beyond what was required by the normative Halakhah.[42] In a truly startling expression of the power of personal appropriation, the Midrash states: "Rabbi Yochanan said, 'Whosoever performs one precept truly is accounted as though he had enacted it and promulgated it from Mount Sinai.' . . . Rabbi Yochanan said further, 'Whosoever keeps the Torah truly is accounted by Scripture as though he had made himself.'"[43]

Even as man by developing his own personality becomes a partner with God in the work of creation, so too does man by freely apprehending his obligation in the *mitzvot* renew its promulgation. This appreciation of self-directed activity seems to conflict with the rabbinic dictum: "Greater is he who is commanded and fulfills the precepts than he who is not commanded yet fulfills them."[44] However, as Professor Urbach has correctly pointed out, this comparative judgment intends by the phrase "not commanded" to refer to one, such as a blind person or a non-Jew, who is exempted by the Halakhah from the observance of the precepts. It is not intended as a comment upon those who are "commanded" but freely appropriate the obligation to the point where the presence of God is experienced not as imposed commander but as *value* that draws the worshipper in love.[45] The view of the rabbis on the latter situation is perhaps best expressed by the teaching of Rabbi Simeon ben Lakish:

The stranger who converts is more beloved than Israel when they stood on Mount Sinai. Why is that? For, had they not perceived the lightning, the thunder, the trembling mountain, and the *shofar,* they would not have accepted the Torah. Whereas, this one who has not experienced any of these comes and seeks to live in harmony with God and accept the Kingdom of Heaven! Is there anything more beloved than this?[46]

Morality As Grounded In The Nature Of Man

What, then, are the grounds of morality? We have already referred to the morality of Judaism as being theonomous, or grounded in God. But since God created man in His image, morality may be said with equal validity to be grounded in the nature of man as well. What does Judaism teach us about the nature of man? Biblical and rabbinic literature make it clear that man is not like the other creatures, completely a part of nature, but like God stands apart from and, in some sense, transcends nature. This we learn not only from the specific instructions given to man in the Pentateuch to have "dominion over" the other orders of creation, but from an important stylistic innovation.[47]

All of the other portions of the universe, including living creatures, are brought into existence without any prefatory remarks as to what God has in mind or is intending to do. Only in the case of man is the description of the creative act preceded by the announcement: "And the Lord said, 'Let us make man in our image, after our likeness.'"[48] Furthermore, in bringing into existence all of the other living things, God, as it were, addresses portions of nature already in existence and commands, "Let the earth bring forth . . . Let the waters swarm . . ." Only in the case of man does God exercise His original creative power in a direct, unmediated fashion: "Then the Lord God formed man of the dust . . ."[49] In regard to the creation of man, we are told: "And God created man in His own image, in the image of God created He him." "Then the Lord God formed man of the dust of the ground and breathed into his nostrils the breath of life; and man became a living soul."[50]

It is not clear whether "image of God" is identical with the inspiration of a divine soul. Rabbinic usage seems to indicate that the concept of "image of God" carries the additional implication of a special dignity which attaches itself to the body of the person as well as to his soul.[51] The rabbis saw this mode of creation as expressive of a "special love" on the part of God which fashions man as a dual creature belonging to both the "lower" and "upper" orders.[52] There is something distinctive in man, which has its source in God, and which might be associated with the capacity to think and speak conceptually, to choose freely, and to be self-reflective, that makes man a responsible moral agent.

Thus, the passages which describe man as "giving names to all the beasts of the field" seem to suggest a degree of intelligence which involves empirical observation, conceptual power, and linguistic skills.[53] Furthermore, man is commanded, held responsible, and punished for disobedience, all implying the freedom that gives rise to moral agency. "I call heaven and earth to witness against you this day that I have set before thee, life and death, the blessing and the curse; therefore choose life, that thou mayest live, thou and thy seed."[54]

Finally, whatever the exact nature of the "knowledge of good and evil" acquired by man, it is evidently a sort of moral cognition that invites divine comparison: "Behold, the man is become as one of us to know good and evil."[55] This, of course, may not mean "one who is able to determine what is good and what is evil" but simply "one who knows that there is good and evil in the world."

But, should man in his "awful freedom" choose wrongly, the very gift that makes for divine-likeness can cause man to sink lower than the beast. Human selfhood devoted to the wrong ends can become demonic. Both the Bible and the rabbis never wavered from their keen awareness of the double potential inherent in man.

> When I behold thy heavens and the work of Thy fingers, the moon and the stars which thou hast established, what is man that Thou are mindful of him? And the son of man, that Thou thinkest of him? Yet Thou hast made him but little lower than the angels, and hast crowned him with glory and honor. Thou hast made him to have dominion over the works of Thy hands. Thou hast put all things under his feet.[56]

The concept of man as created in the image of a God who is infinite and eternal, pure subjectivity, and the source of value, confers upon each individual person selfhood and subjectivity, dignity, and intrinsic value. In other words, man is always to be regarded as an end in himself.

A most important rabbinic source for an understanding of the morality of Judaism is the following:

Rabbi Akiva said of the command "Thou shalt love thy neighbor as thyself" that it was a fundmental principle of the Torah [kelal gadal ba-Torah]. Ben Azzai said there is a principle that is even more fundamental [kelal yoter gadol], "This is the book of the generations of man . . . in the likeness of God made He him."[57]

The views of the two rabbis are not mutually exclusive. What Rabbi Akiva affirms is not opposed by Ben Azzai, and vice versa. The issue between them may rather be, Which is the most general of all the moral principles of Judaism? Rabbi Akiva offers the most general moral prescription in the Torah. Ben Azzai, however, goes beyond prescriptions and offers an account of the origin of man, which on another level may be seen as the grounds of the morality of Judaism.

The Mishnah teaches:

Man was first created a single individual to teach the lesson that whoever destroys one life, Scripture ascribes it to him as though he had destroyed a whole world, and whoever saves one life, as though he had saved a whole world. And to declare the greatness of the Supreme King of Kings, the Holy One, blessed be He, because a man strikes many coins from one die and they are all alike. But God strikes every person from the die of the first man, but not one resembles another.[58]

Man is not species-dependent. His value does not rest on his being one of a group. Man is first created as a single individual to teach us that with the appearance of a single human being, the entire creation reaches its fulfillment. In the beautiful turn of Kariv's insight:

It is not merely that man is in the world but that the entire world is in man—in his perceptions and in his personalized experience of it all. By means of the single person who carries the world within himself, the world outside becomes world. Therefore whosoever destroys one human life, it is accounted as if he had destroyed the entire world.[59]

But the value and dignity of each individual person is further reinforced by an astonishing fact. Although each person is "fashioned in the same die" as primal man and as such acquires his absolute value as stand-in for the entire world, this value is not diminished by the fact that there are now many people in the world. For no human being is an exact duplicate of any other. The element of uniqueness, which is a part of selfhood and of subjectivity, and which is true of God and was true of primal man, applies in this sense to every man. Thus, the Mishnah concludes: ". . . therefore is every man obliged to say, 'For my sake was the world created.'"

Every human being, by virtue of his divine image and his uniqueness, which preclude his saying, "Let others do it," assumes the responsibilities and the opportunities of the first man alone in a newly created world.

This idea of the value implicit in man can now be reformulated in more general terms to make explicit its implications for morality. One of Kant's formulations of the categorical imperative was in terms of man: "Act in such a way that you always treat humanity, whether in your own person or in the person of any other, never simply as a means but always at the same time as an end." What this implies operationally is that we must not "use" other people or exploit them for our own purposes in ways which do not respect their desires and plans for themselves. This is suggestive of Buber's "I–thou, I–It" distinction. In relating to other people, I must always remember that over against me is another center of consciousness, another self as autonomous as I am, who sets for himself ends even as I do. In this respect, persons are unique. Everything other than a person can only have a value *for* a person. This applies not only to objects, which have only instrumental value, but also to products of the human spirit, such as an epic poem, which also have intrinsic value. Even such things will have value only because they are experienced or felt to be of value by human beings and are chosen by them from competing alternatives.

Thus, of everything it will be true to say: "If X is valuable and X is not a person, then X will have value for some individual other than itself. The values, however, do not need to be valued as ends by someone else. In just this sense, persons and only persons are *ends* in themselves."[60]

For Kant, the fact of the existence of a rational nature, of a human being's having an autonomous self, is what constitutes value and the possibility of value in the world. This is what makes any other human being worthy not only of our forbearance in the sense of recognizing his rights, but of our active help and support in advancing his welfare. For Judaism, man is what he is, a unique self-conscious being capable of setting for himself ends of his own choosing, even to the extent of defying God because of the work of God. But once formed, man must be respected for what he is. This is seen in the fact that God thought enough of man to create him and so valued him that He provided him with means to obtain self-fulfillment.

The process that leads from rational man to moral man may, therefore, be viewed as follows: God created man free in respect to nature. Man as a rational being has self-determined ends. He is already, in this sense, transcendent. He is then called upon to achieve a second transcendence. As self-conscious subjectivity man may imagine himself as the supreme value, as be-all and end-all. But, in truth, he is not the only person in the world. He must learn to transcend himself and always consider the other person as an end. Through this double transcendence man becomes moral. In the words of Hutchins: "A single man might be the world. Two men establish for each other a limit and each for the other establishes a positive self-hood."[61] This is perhaps the "great principle" that Rabbi Akiva saw reflected in the biblical command, "And thou shalt love thy neighbor as thyself." If man is the source of value, then morality begins with our awareness of our obligation to treat humanity, whether in ourselves or in the persons of others, as ends.[62]

The Source Of Moral Obligation

Our analysis thus far has located the source of value in the Jewish view of morality. Can this, however, serve as the source of the *obligation* that is generally felt to be present in moral consciousness? Many feel that a sense of obligation is necessary to provide a justification for certain positive aspects of morality, such as benevolence. Kant, who speaks so explicitly of duty, law, and imperatives, attempted to ground all of this in the concept of a rational being. However, it is difficult to see that there are any ends with regard to which it could be inferred from the concept of a rational being that he would find them desirable or any principles that he would recognize as right. In terms of Kant's first formulation of the categorical imperative, it can be argued that for an individual to act on a maxim which he could not will to become a universal law would involve him in a sort of logical inconsistency: If something is right for me and we are the same in relevant respects, why should it not be right for you as well?[63] Therefore, we might acknowledge that a rational being would reject any cause of action based on a principle that would violate the categorical imperative. However, we cannot infer from this that a rational being would accept any principle whose acceptance would not involve him in logical inconsistency. More than that, it can be shown that universalization itself—i.e., the correspondence of a policy with the categorical imperative—only implies that a contradiction has been avoided. It does not of itself call for positive implementation. Indeed, not all universalizable policies are ipso facto based on maxims of moral action. They may be nonmoral or even trivial.[64]

Value itself does not seem to create obligation except in the negative sense that perhaps I ought not to destroy value, or if man created in the image of God is an entity of irreducible value, he ought not to be exploited as a means only. But then, what is the source of moral *obligation* in Judaism?

It is generally believed that the element of "obligation" in Judaism is provided by the theology; i.e., by the fact that morality is commanded by God. We have already indicated in the first chapter, however, that there is a logical difficulty in attempting to infer "ought" conclusions from any set of exclusively "is" premises, even where these latter include statements such as "God exists" and "God commanded me to be moral." One still has to answer the question: Why ought I to obey God?[65]

Why did the Bible think Israel ought to obey God? It does not appear that the Bible thought this proposition to be self-evident. Two different approaches seem to be present in the Pentateuch, one explicit and one implicit. Often Israel is called upon to remain faithful to the covenant and to observe the commandments, moral and ritual, in gratitude for all that God has done for His people.

Do you thus requite the Lord,
O foolish people and unwise?
Is not He thy father that hath gotten thee?
Hath He not made thee and established thee? . . .
But he [Israel] forsook God who made him,
And contemned the Rock of his salvation. . . .
Of the Rock that begot thee thou was unmindful,
And didst forget God that bore thee.[66]

Between these accusations of ingratitude, the Bible describes all of the many kindnesses and benefits that God has bestowed upon Israel, from their liberation from Egypt through all of the tribulations in the wilderness, that should have evoked thankfulness and loyalty. But arguments of this kind assume that somehow the moral obligation to show gratitude is acknowledged even by those who are prepared to repudiate the covenant and what it calls for.

The frequent appeals to Israel to obey the covenant contain a covert argument suggested by the term "covenant," i.e., an agreement formally entered into by two or more parties. This is taken most seriously by the Bible as obligating, first, God, who has promised to bring this people into the promised land and preserve them, and, second, the people collectively and individually, who freely committed themselves to the terms of the covenant. When the people proclaimed the "we will do and we will obey," the covenant became binding upon the community of Israel, "not only upon those that standeth here with us this day but also with him that is not here with us this day"—namely, all future generations to be born into the community of Israel.[67] But this argument as well rests upon a presupposition that one ought to keep a promise, honor an agreement, stand behind one's word. Thus, while the Torah contains a moral code revealed by God to Israel, it is urged upon Israel because of moral principles of gratitude and promise-keeping, with the implication that these are somehow binding prior to the Sinaitic covenant.[68] This is consistent with the point made earlier that rabbinic tradition, in its concept of the seven *mitzvot* of the sons of Noah, assumed a basic morality known to all men. However, it is nowhere stated that the original Noahide *mitzvot* were formally accepted or a covenant entered into, so that primal man might have raised the question: "Why ought I to obey the commands of my creator?"[69] One could, of course, respond in terms of reward and punishment, but that would involve considerations of prudence rather than morality. The only answer that suggests itself is the factor of gratitude: man ought to obey his creator out of gratitude for the gift of existence.[70] But how do we know that a person ought to show gratitude to his benefactor? If we accept the proposition that a moral "ought" cannot be logically derived from "is" premises, then we are compelled to say that somehow these basic moral principles, such as gratitude and promise-keeping, are self-evident in the sense that any rational human being who understands the meaning of these words will immediately perceive an intrinsic relation of fittingness between the emotions we call gratitude and the person we call benefactor.

This relation of fittingness is what we refer to as *right* in the moral sense and thus must be said to incorporate the concept of "ought." For it would appear to be a self-contradiction to say: "I know this is right, but I don't think I ought to do it." But if to perceive the *right* is to perceive the *ought*, which is the moral obligation to do the right, then to acknowledge the self-evidence of certain right relationships is to acknowledge the self-evidence of certain moral obligations. Returning now to the observation that the ultimate appeal of the Bible seems to be to gratitude and promise-keeping, we are led to the conclusion that in Judaism the self-evidence of these moral obligations is assumed. Logically speaking, it is not the case that I do what is right because this is obedience to God but rather I obey God because it is right to do so. The teaching "*derekh eretz* precedes the Torah" may be interpreted not only in a chronological sense but in a logical sense. This is strongly implied by the following Rabbinic teaching:

> Why were the Ten Commandments not given at the beginning of the Torah? This may be compared to a person who came to a land and said to the inhabitants, "I will rule over you." The inhabitants replied, "What have you done for us that you should rule over us?" Upon which the stranger built for them a wall, brought in water, led them in battle, and then said again, "I will rule over you." They replied, "Yes, yes." So, too, the Almighty liberated Israel from Egypt, split for them the sea, caused manna to fall, and brought forth water. *Then* He said to them, "I will rule over you." They answered, "Yes, yes."[71]

The suggestion here is that acceptance of the commandments is based upon gratitude for services rendered.[72]

If we examine the matter further, we can perhaps discover a metaphysical basis for this sense of moral obligation. The rabbis taught: "It is against your will that you are born, it is against your will that you live, and it is against your will that you will have to give account."[73] When man stops to consider that he did not bring himself into being, and that he cannot bring himself to believe that he was blindly thrown into being, he begins to sense that his very being is a response to a "let there be." Thus, human existence is experienced as a transcendence, as a life imposed upon and as an imposition of freedom. In the words of Heschel: "Commandment and expectation lie dormant in the recesses of being and come to light in the consciousness of being human. What Adam hears first is a command."[74] This may be understood as a consequence of the biblical doctrine of creation. If my entire being is in response to a command, then I exist because I ought to exist. There is a sense, then, in which the "ought" precedes the "is" or is at least built into the very essence of human existence. "Being created implies being born in value, being endowed with meaning, received value. Living involves acceptance of meaning, obedience and commitment."[75]

"It is against your will that you are born . . . that you live . . . that you give account." The way man experiences this "ought" is in the form of a generalized awareness of being called upon to answer; that something is expected of me, something is demanded of me! Once we sense the demand, we become aware of our being a center of value; and once we realize we ought to respond to the demand, we have discovered the source of obligation. To refer again to Heschel:

Indebtedness is given with our very being. It is not derived from conceptions; it lives in us as an awareness before it is conceptualized or clarified in content. It means having a task, being called. It experiences living as receiving, not only as taking. Its content is gratitude for a gift received. . . . Man cannot think of himself as human without being conscious of his indebtedness. Thus it is not a mere feeling but rather a constitutive feature of being human. "How shall I ever repay to the Lord all his bounties to me!"[76]

A more explicit rabbinic source for a metaphysical basis for the sense of moral obligation is to be found in a teaching by Rabbi Simlai:

> What does the fetus resemble in its mother's womb? A writing tablet lying folded: its hands rest on its two temples, its two elbows on its two legs . . . a lamp burns at its head , and it looks and sees from one end of the world to the other . . . and it is taught the whole of the Torah . . . but as soon as it comes into the world an angel arrives and slaps it on its mouth and causes it to forget the whole of the Torah . . . and it does not go forth until it is made to take an oath. . . . "Be righteous and be not wicked; and even if the whole world says unto you, 'You are righteous,' be wicked in your own eyes . . . for the Holy One, blessed be He, is pure, and the soul that He placed within you is pure. If you guard it in purity, well and good; but if not, I shall take it away from you."[77]

Although the soul is pure as it comes from God, it cannot be depended upon to be a force for the good only, since once it becomes a "self," it acquires the power of free choice and may be attracted to evil. It is therefore compelled to take an oath to be righteous. This reinforces the self's good inclination, since it must now, as it were, keep its "word"; it has already made a commitment. Just as Israel's loyalty to God as a people is based on the fact of a commitment given, so in the case of the individual do the rabbis seem to ground the "ought" in the concept of an oath. "This *aggadah* also seems to lay the groundwork for a sense of self-doubt ("be wicked in your own eyes") and an existential anxiety of falling into nonbeing ("if not I will take it away from you").

The fact that man was created—brought into existence against his will and in response to a command by a moral being—sets up a general awareness of being called upon, of being waited for. But the disclosure that man was created in the image of God with a component that transcends nature has an additional phenomenological consequence. Man will ultimately find that he experiences a vague yearning for something he cannot quite define, a hunger which nothing mundane can assuage. The rabbis expressed this thought in a commentary on the passage: "All the labor of man is for his mouth. And yet the appetite [Heb. *nefesh*] is not filled."[78] Now the straightforward meaning of this passage is simply the well-known phenomenon that man's needs and desires are such that no sooner is one satisfied than another arises. This idea appears elsewhere as well.[79] Rabbi Levi, however, read the word *nefesh* as "soul" rather than "appetite" and saw in this passage a metaphysical truth rather than a psychological one. He perceived here the hint that the soul, because of its transcendent origins, introduces into man's conscious life a hunger for things which nothing in the physical world can satisfy. "This may be compared to a townsman who married a princess. Although he provides her with the finest delicacies in the world, it is not enough. Why is that? Because she is a princess. So, too, all that man does for his soul is inadequate because it comes to him from above."[80]The implication is that what the princess is yearning for is something more than food and material comforts. Since she was brought up in a palace surrounded by graciousness and royalty, the princess misses the values associated with a different sort of existence altogether. So, too, the soul of man, coming from a spiritual realm, will not be satisfied with material pursuits alone. Man may be distracted for a time by "the labors for his mouth," but the "still small voice" within him will continue to call for something spiritual.

This consequence of bearing God's image is negative in character. There is, however, a positive element which gives direction and content to the awareness of being called upon or commanded. In an earlier context we made reference to the Jewish teaching that man is urged to "imitate" God, or to model his behavior after that which is reported about divinity. Let us examine this doctrine in detail.

Imitatio Dei

Martin Buber in a memorable essay has already pointed out how early Greek notions of "following after God" were based on the demythologized creation of an image of Zeus, while the later concept of the "imitation of Christ," involving his poverty, suffering, and death, was based on the remembering of a human life and, as such, constituted a mediation in man's effort to imitate the divine.[81] It was only in Judaism that we confront the full paradox: How shall man be able to imitate God, the invisible, incomprehensible, unformed, not-to-be-formed? Indeed, there is even a certain arrogance and foolhardiness in the suggestion as noted by the Rabbis:"'After the Lord your God shall ye walk." How shall man be able to walk in the footsteps of the divine presence? Is it not written: "The Lord thy God is a devouring fire'?"[82]

Throughout the Book of Deuteronomy, Israel is called upon "to walk in all His ways."[83] But this expression was already used in Genesis, before the Sinaitic revelation, in reference to Abraham: "For I have known him [Abraham] in order that he may command his children and his household after him, that they may keep the *way of the Lord* to do righteousness and justice."[83a] This would indicate that these values are not merely the ways which God has commanded man to walk in but that they are actually God's ways—i.e., the ways in which God Himself walks. These "ways" are later revealed to Moses, when he asks to be shown God's "glory," as *middot,* attributes of moral qualities: "merciful, gracious, long-suffering, abundant in loving-kindness."

The rabbinic teaching of *imitatio dei* is found in several statements:

> What means the text, "Ye shall walk after the Lord your God"? Is it then possible for a man to walk after the Shekhinah? . . . but the meaning is to follow the attributes of the Holy One, blessed be He; as He clothed the naked, so do you clothe the naked; as He visited the sick, so do you visit the sick; as he comforted mourners, so do you comfort those who mourn; as He buried the dead, so do you bury the dead.[84]

> "To walk in all His ways," that is, the characteristics of the Holy One, blessed be He; as it is said: "The Lord, the Lord, a God full of compassion and gracious, slow to anger, and plenteous in mercy and truth." . . . As the All-Present is called compassionate and gracious, so be you also compassionate and gracious; . . . as the Holy One is called righteous, be you also righteous; as He is called loving, be you also loving.[85]

> "This is my God and I will adorn Him [*ve'anvehu*]." Is it then possible to adorn God? Yes, by resembling Him [reading *ve'anvehu* as *ani vehu*], I will make myself like unto Him. As He is compassionate and gracious, be also compassionate and gracious.[86]

It should be pointed out, however, that the essential sources of this teaching are not the commands to "walk in God's ways" but rather the existential premises in the Bible concerning the nature of man that have already been treated: Man is created in the image of God. If we examine the relevant biblical passages, we find there the occurrence of two terms: "image" (*tzelem*) and "likeness" (*demut*). The passage reads: "Let us make man in our image, after our likeness."[87] The rabbis saw the term "image" as referring to a fixed universal component which confers irreducible value upon man, while the term "likeness" refers to his destiny rather than to his origin, to a state to be achieved rather than to something already possessed. The rabbinic interpretation is to the effect that while God creates man in His "image," the "likeness," which is the process of *becoming like,* lies in the hand of man. Man can achieve this by walking in the ways of God, by clothing the naked and visiting the sick, by being merciful and kind.[88]

Once man becomes aware of his nature and his potential, he already has the matrix out of which to fashion a response to the existential anxiety that something is expected of him. If to be human means to have been constituted with the potential to become like God, then this is what I ought to do. By seeking to fulfill and realize my "image," I requite my indebtedness.

Man's troubles from the very beginning has been that he could not quite figure out precisely who he was. In the words of the poet:

> Placed on this isthmus of a middle state
> A Being darkly wise and rudely great; . . .
> He hangs between; in doubt to act, or rest;
> In doubt to deem himself a God, or Beast.[89]

If man could determine his nature, he might, by using Aristotle's method of reasoning, arrive at a notion of what is good. Aristotle believed that if we examine nature or our ordinary human experience, we find that things have their natural capabilities and potentialities and are oriented toward certain goals or ends in their growth and development. Few of us would care to quarrel with the statement that an oak is the natural end of an acorn. There is something about an acorn that leads us to connect it in some way with a future oak tree. Of course, the acorn may become diseased or be eaten and not attain its characteristic end. We could not call these occurrences "unnatural." But certainly from the point of view of the acorn itself, there is a sense in which it is proper to say that the above occurrences are "bad" for it.

For Aristotle, therefore, "goods" and "values" are to be found in natural orientation of things, in their natural ends or goals. But if plants and animals all have their natural states of maturity toward which their very being is ordered, could not man be presumed to have some characteristic end toward which his life is oriented and which may be called the human good? If such an end could be found, a theory of value and of morals could possibly be built upon it. The difference, of course, is that if conditions are favorable, acorns will naturally grow into oak trees and animals will develop to maturity. Human beings, however, do not seem to have a natural end or intrinsic orientation. They have no innate sense of what they should do with their lives. A human being must somehow attain a conscious recognition of what the human end is and then must strive to attain it by act and design.

We would have to agree with contemporary thought and allow that no amount of empirical inspection of man and his history discloses any "natural orientation" or "end" for man as a whole. Aristotle attempted to find man's "good" in that faculty which was distinctive to man, his rational faculty. We may not wish to go so far as to argue that the contemplative life of pure rational activity is the highest end for man. We can, however, endorse the idea that as a rational creature, man has the obligation to seek a life in which his knowledge and intelligence are employed not as mere means for the achievement of irrational ends, but as tools in trying to determine the ends themselves.

In the Jewish view, however, once it is revealed to man that he is created in the image of God, whose attributes are moral, he can be expected to move in the direction of self-realization by fulfilling his divine potential in a life of service to man and God. The teaching of Rabbi Akiva mentioned earlier now takes on an even greater significance: "Beloved is man, for he was created in the image [of God]. An even greater sign of love is that it was made known to him that he was created in the image of God."[90] If man has been given the knowledge that he was created in the image of God, then it indeed is a sign of great love, for it inspires man to live morally, to redress injustice, to help the needy. In the words of Buber: "The fact that it has been revealed to us that we are made in His image gives us the incentive to unfold the image and in so doing to imitate God."[91]

What is the relationship between one's conception of the nature of man and one's moral code? The Humean contention that one cannot logically deduce an "ought" from an "is" statement would lead us to deny that there can be any beliefs about human existence B and any moral judgments M such that to affirm B and reject M, or vice versa, would result in a formal contradiction. However, there does seem to be a less formal, albeit logical, connection of some sort.

Man does seem to be central to the entire enterprise of morality. What is morally right is always something I must do as man and something which is binding on all men, as men, similarly positioned. Analysis of the moral consciousness shows that the sense of moral obligations usually pertains to the person rather than to the act. For what morality tells me is not merely that something must be done but that *I* must do it. If morality, therefore, is the science of what men ought to do as men, then surely the question of "What is man" must be relevant to morality! At the very least it should enable us to give reasons for our particular moral judgments and to give a "background of intelligibility" to our moral system.[92] Another writer has suggested that the existential premises contributed by religion are not part of the reasoning processes that go on *within* the realm of moral discourse. They may, however, be related to that realm on another level. Let us paraphrase an example offered by Toulmin:[93]

Q.—Why ought one to do what is right anyway?

A.—That is a question which cannot arise, for it is to query the very definition of "right" and "ought."

Q.—But why ought one to?

A.—Because it is God's will.

Q.—And why ought one to do His will?

A.—Because this is the way we can realize ourselves as human beings created in the image of God and become more Godlike.

The point is that after "the resources of ethical reasoning are exhausted," religious explanations may still be appropriate in that they "help us to embrace" moral duties and "feel like accepting them."

Conclusion

Let us draw together what has been said in terms of a general response to the question of the grounds of morality. Having freed ourselves from the straitjacket of the sharp autonomous-heteronomous dichotomy, we can state that the Jewish understanding of morality includes many elements associated with moral autonomy.

1. Certain general moral principles were recognized by man prior to the Sinaitic revelation.
2. These moral principles are universal, a priori, and self-evident and are often appealed to as grounds for serving God.
3. Even after Sinai morality possesses intrinsic value and ought to be practiced for its own sake.

Yet, having said all this we can and must at the same time affirm the proposition that morality for Judaism is "nothing less than a three-term relationship involving man, his human neighbor, and God himself."[94]

The rabbinic source for this concept is found in the cryptic comment on the passage: "If anyone sins and commits a trespass against the Lord, and deals falsely with his neighbor in a matter of deposit or of pledge or of robbery, or has oppressed his neighbor . . ."[95]

> Rabbi Akiva says: "What do we learn from the phrase 'and commit a trespass against the Lord'? Those who borrow and lend and trade do so only with contracts and witnesses, so that when one falsifies he falsifies the contract and the witness. But one who entrusts an object to his friend does not wish anyone to know except the Third One who is between them. When one, therefore, falsifies, he falsifies against the Third One."[96]

Rabbi Akiva observes the fact that although the Torah seems to be dealing here with transgressions against one's fellow man, it is called a "trespass against the Lord." Rabbi Akiva seems to be suggesting that in all interhuman relationships, there is the invisible presence of a Third One (*shelishi she-beineihem*)—God Himself, who symbolizes the trust, the obligation, the moral dimension.

However, we need not see the role of God in the morality relationship as one "term" among several or as an intruding element which compromises the "purity" of man's moral relationship with his neighbor. The presence of God in the moral relationship operates on a different level than man the agent or his neighbor at whom the action is directed. God, as it were, is within or perhaps beyond the intersubjective relationship.

When I accept my moral duty, I do so with the awareness that I have an obligation. But who am *I*? I am man created in the image of God. When I respect my neighbor as a center of consciousness, creativity, and rationality, I do so because I recognize in him intrinsic value to be treated as an end in himself. But when I track things back to their source and realize that God is the ultimate ground of all value, I recognize in my neighbor a self likewise created in the image of God. And when I realize that my particular relationship to my fellow human being urges upon me a certain action that I recognize as morally right, I decide to do the right because it is right but at the very same time joyously embrace it as the "way of God" and all that it entails.

In the words of a medieval Jewish thinker and a more recent non-Jewish thinker:

> Now since God is the absolute Good in whom there is no evil at all . . . the love of God is the love of the Good because it is good.[97]

> "Many religious persons would probably say that the motive of obedience or the love of God was the highest. But those who take this view would generally say that obedience and love are due to God as a Moral Being possessing the attributes of Infinite Wisdom and Goodness and not otherwise: and if so, these religious motives would seem to be substantially identical with regard for duty and love of virtue, though modified and complicated by the addition of emotions belonging to relations between persons.[98]"

To conclude with a familiar metaphor: "Rules of life are the twigs; moral virtues are the branches; the moral personality is the trunk; and the root is the divine likeness which God set in the mind of man.[99]

4

Morality and the Will of God

In previous chapters we have repeatedly alluded to the close relationship between God and morality in Judaism. However, the two terms are obviously not interchangeable. In fact, their relationship is an asymmetrical one: God is moral, but morality does not exhaust the concept of God. "Morality" is an abstract term referring to systems of rules or principles and ideals that are supposed to govern the relations between human beings. The word "God" refers to the living reality who is omnipotent, omniscient, and omnipresent and is the ground of all being. In the Torah, God manifests Himself not only as a revealer of laws moral and ritual, but as a powerful will or agent to whom certain acts are ascribed, who directs individuals and groups to do particular things, such as to travel to a certain country, and who announces events that are to come about in the distant future, makes promises, threatens punishment, and presides over a world He has brought into being.

What we shall consider in this chapter are problems arising out of the fact that the will of God, as manifested in word and deed, ranges over an area that is broader than the moral sphere and, at first glance, does not seem reducible to morality and on occasion seems to contradict morality. Theoretically, if God is moral as we have described Him, then everything God is or says or does ought to be in consonance with morality. But is this always the case? Let us consider several classic problems whose root issue is the question of the relationship of God's will to His morality.

Akedat Yitzchak: A Teleological Suspension Of The Ethical?

One of the best-known and most beloved stories in the Torah is the story of the sacrifice of Isaac. In what is explicitly announced as a test of Abraham, God commands the Patriarch: "Take now thy son, thine only son, whom thou lovest, even Isaac . . . and offer him there for a burnt-offering."[1] Abraham, according to the Torah, with perfect faith and in complete obedience, proceeds to carry out the word of God. But at the last moment, when the knife is already in his hand, Abraham is stopped by the angel of God, who discloses that it is all a *nisayon*—a trial or test. The rabbis regarded Abraham's faithful response as the climax of his career, decisively qualifying him to be the progenitor of the people of God and laying up for his seed a store of "merit" upon which all future generations can draw and to which they can appeal. This portion of the Akedah—the Binding of Isaac—was therefore incorporated into the daily morning service and made a major theme of the Rosh Hashanah liturgy.[2]

The theological problem that this story poses is the apparent conflict between the command of God and the dictates of universal morality. For a man to take the life of his innocent son would in most contexts be considered murder. How could a moral God have asked this of Abraham, and how could a moral person like Abraham, for all his faith, decide to do something so immoral and, in the words of Maimonides, "so repugnant to nature"? Kant, to whom the imperatives of universal morality were absolute, condemns Abraham and argues that the Patriarch should have doubted the authenticity of the call. The Danish theologian Sören Kierkegaard sees in the *Akedah* evidence that faith can sometimes make demands that go beyond morality; he calls this doctrine "the teleological suspension of the ethical." How are we to understand God's command to Abraham to sacrifice his son Isaac? Is the will of God in conflict with morality?[3]

Kierkegaard's treatment of the *Akedah* is profound and searching. As a brilliant and deeply religious thinker, he approaches the biblical story with the utmost seriousness. In one respect, his analysis is quite correct, independently touching upon a theme recognized earlier by the rabbis. God, in commanding Abraham to sacrifice Isaac, was in effect contradicting Himself. Abraham had been solemnly promised by

God, "For in Isaac will thy seed be called." Abraham's entire hope for a future, for the realization of all the promises made to him from the beginning, was predicated on the son that God had mercifully blessed him with in his old age. But if God now commands Abraham to bring Isaac as a "burnt-offering," what will become of the hope and the promise?[4]

This was certainly part of the agony of the experience. And as Kierkegaard points out, Abraham, the man of faith, believed fully and perfectly in both propositions: Isaac would be brought as an offering, and in Isaac would his seed be called! And if the two propositions are paradoxical, so be it! Such is the power of faith! But while we can agree with Kierkegaard that to Abraham the command of God must have appeared irrational, we cannot agree that it appeared immoral. Only a few chapters earlier in the Pentateuch, when told of God's intentions to destroy the Cities of the Plain because of their evil, Abraham courageously and tirelessly pleads on their behalf, refusing to accept the judgment of God because it appears to be unjust. Would Abraham then have hesitated to plead for his son Isaac if he sensed something immoral in the command? Surely the fact that it was his own son in this instance would not have inhibited Abraham from interceding on his behalf. Abraham's forthright actions on behalf of the people of Sodom renders untenable the approach which argues that before the Sinaitic revelation, the full extent of God's moral nature was not grasped. Clearly, Abraham was very much aware of God's moral commitment and was prepared to challenge God Himself on moral grounds.

Unfortunately, Kant's moral rigorism blinded him to the contextual nature of moral judgments. Thus, for example, he would never have been able to appreciate or agree with the rabbinic teaching that one may tell a lie for the sake of domestic peace. There is, however, today a broad consensus that agrees that an act is defined by its context. Not every taking of a life is murder and therefore immoral. Killing in self-defense, for example, is not blameworthy. Abraham himself engaged in war in order to rescue his nephew, Lot. Therefore, when God, the creator of us all, asks for the "return" of Isaac in the form of an offering, Abraham did not see this as morally questionable, for all of the personal anguish involved. Certainly it was incomprehensible and appeared irrational in the light of God's earlier promise. For Abraham, then, the *Akedah* was the supreme act of sacrifice. He was being asked to give up the son he loved. He did not see this as a command to *destroy* his son, but to restore him to God, which is the ultimate destiny of us all. He was also being asked to surrender his entire understanding of God's historic plan for him and his descendants. For Isaac, the central demand of the *Akedah* was an act of martyrdom. And indeed for future generations, the Binding of Isaac remained the archetypal symbol of the supreme sacrifice to God of life itself: the voluntary martyrdom of individuals, families, and communities for the sake of *kiddush ha-shem*—sanctification of the divine name.

There is, however, a moral dimension to the *Akedah* in a somewhat different sense. Abraham can choose martyrdom for himself. Does he have the right to do so for his child? Does a father have a right to determine the life of his child when he is convinced that it is the right thing to do, even though he realizes it might lead to suffering and to death? But, of course, parents have always assumed this responsibility, not only as a privilege but as an obligation. Parents must decide and act for children until they reach maturity. In moments of crisis, heads of families are often called upon to be the deciding voice in embarking upon moves that are fraught with peril. These decisions are made in the interests of all, according to the best knowledge and values of the leader. Such judgments may sometimes involve a deliberate decision to incur short-term privations for the sake of long-range benefits.

Jews have always realized that the offspring they bring into the world are exposed, by the very fact of their being Jews, to special dangers and possibilities of suffering. From the first blood and pain of circumcision to the ultimate act of killing one's children before killing oneself, as recorded of the martyrs of Masada and the martyrs of Mayence, Jews have understood the generational commitment to be part of the Covenant of Abraham. Jews freely choose this destiny as "people of God," accepting the blessings and the burdens. They can do no less for their children.

Of course, by the fact that God stops the hand of Abraham and bids him, "Do not do anything to him [Isaac]," the Torah makes the powerful point that, in truth, God does not require that one literally offer one's son as a "burnt-offering." This is a point that had to be made in pagan times, clearly and unequivocally. Yet, as Shalom Spiegel points out in his classic essay, rabbinic tradition could not free itself of the idea that somehow in some way Isaac *had* been sacrificed![5] This is because throughout Jewish history, from Hannah and her seven sons to the martyrs of York, again and again, Abraham *and* Isaac, hand in hand, found themselves in circumstances where they felt themeslves duty-bound to mount the smoking altar.

If there are basic moral issues involved in the *Akedah,* they merge into the general problem of theodicy—the question of why the omnipotent, moral God is involved with a world and a process in which there is pain and suffering and evil—so much of it seemingly undeserved!

Acting Out Of Duty Or Out Of Inclination

It was pointed out in the previous chapter that since moral deeds are intrinsically good, it is appropriate that they be performed for their own sake. Bearing in mind that God is at once the Good One and the embodiment of the Good, we can appreciate the teaching of Antigonus, "Be as the servants who serve the Master without the expectation of receiving reward."[6] Such rabbinic teachings may be said to be implicit in the biblical command, "And you shall love the Lord your God with all your heart and with all your soul and with all your might."[7] To truly love with all one's heart would not leave room for any other motivation. In terms of the usual distinctions made in ethical theory between a deontological ethic and a teleological ethic, one would expect to categorize Judaism as a deontological system where the emphasis is upon duty for duty's sake, simply determining what is right in every situation and then doing it.[8] However, as we examine the Torah, we find many expressions wherein actions and policies are urged in terms which appear to be plainly teleological and almost utilitarian in spirit. Certain special conditions of an explicitly pleasurable and happy nature are held out as rewards. "In order that it shall be good for you, and you shall lengthen your days." "Because of this God will bless you." "That a man may do them and live by them."[9] Also, certain states which are plainly negative and unpleasant are threatened as punishment to the individual for violating the commandments, as, for example, ". . . that soul shall be cut off."[10]

Clearly, then, the morality of Judaism is much too complex to be classified simply as a deontological system. Let us attempt to disentangle its various strands.

In terms of the overall purpose of the Torah and the commandments, both the Bible and the rabbis felt it important repeatedly to make the point that all ultimately points to man. The significance of this emphasis is man *and not God,* thus rejecting any magical-mythical quality to the precepts. In the words of Rav, "The precepts were given only for the purpose of trying [refining] people thereby. For what difference does it make to the Holy One whether one slaughters at the neck or at the nape? This proves that the purpose is to try mankind."[11] This process of "refining" or "trying" was interpreted in various ways: as augmenting man's "merit" or spiritual reward or affording him a variety of opportunities to fulfill the divine image within himself. That the overall purpose of the precepts resides in some benefit to man or Israel as a whole rather than to God or the upkeep of some celestial order may be the thrust of the many biblical promises such as the following:

> And thou shalt keep His statutes and His commandments which I command thee this day, that it may go well [*yitav*] *with thee* and with thy children.

> Ye shall walk in all the way which the Lord your God hath commanded thee, that ye may live and that it may be well [*yitav*] with you.

> And the Lord commanded us to do all these statutes, to fear the Lord our God for our good [*le-tov*] always, that He might preserve us alive.[12]

In all these passages the Hebrew root of the expressions that we translated "be well" and "our good" is the same, *tov* ("good"); i.e., general welfare or well-being. Rather than a promise of some specific reward, this should be interpreted as another reiteration to Israel that the goal of the Torah as a whole is to benefit man rather than God.

On a much more specific level, however, the Pentateuch seems to urge the observance of the commandments, both ritual and moral, by promising material rewards of all sorts for compliance and severe punishment for disobedience. These are found in graphic detail in covenant reaffirmations and throughout the farewell address of Moses in Deuteronomy. Also there is an entire penal code contained in the Pentateuch assigning various punishments for individual violations of the commandments, ranging from monetary fines and flogging to various forms of capital punishment and the "cutting off of the soul."[13] In the Decalogue itself we have the sublime "Honor thy father and thy mother," motivated by the inducement, "that thy days may be prolonged and that it may go well with thee."[14] How shall we reconcile this emphasis upon rewards and punishments, particularly material rewards and punishments, which introduces extraneous pressures for compliance, with the notion of the intrinsicality of moral values and its implication that the right ought to be done because it is right and morally preferable and for no other reason?

Role Of Rewards And Punishments

The appeal of the Torah to material rewards and punishments can be understood only if we remind ourselves of a fundamental characteristic of Torah legislation. Although the Torah is aware of a universal moral law that was known from ancient times and assumed that men were familiar with various cultic practices, such as sacrificing and temple worship, it did not hesitate to incorporate and adopt many of these rules and practices into its codes. It did this without any qualms about its claims to originality. For what is "new" and special about the Torah was the prophetic and national character that it gave to morality. Moral principles, once considered the dictates of "wisdom" derived from experience, were now seen as the imperative of a moral God. The universal moral law was now given anew to Israel as part of a covenant, as a national-religious obligation. As Kaufmann points out, biblical morality is societal and national. "Nation and society are responsible for its maintenance; their welfare is conditioned upon its observance."[15] While the Jew was always forbidden to murder because of a universal rule given human beings created in the image of God, he now renewed the obligation as a Jew whose national covenant with God included the command: "Thou shalt not murder."

One of the important implications of perceiving the Torah as a moral-cultic code "fixed in a national framework" is the fact that the Torah addresses primarily the group, the people as a whole. In the words of Kaufmann, "The covenant calls into being a new moral entity: the people of Israel. The Laws of the Torah are given to the whole nation at once; all as one are obliged to carry them out . . . the community becomes corporately responsible."[16]

As a code imposed upon an entire society, the moral and cultic rules take on a *legal* character, and in order that compliance be achieved, an enforcement policy supported by sanctions is included. Hence, if the Torah embodies the law of the covenanted society, then the judicial system which it establishes can be expected to authorize penalties for the obvious purpose of deterrence: "In order that they may hear and be afraid and not sin."[17] The rewards and punishments contained in the Torah are therefore pedagogical means of inducing compliance, a method familiar to every society, and should not be confused with the ultimate value of the rules themselves.

This view of the Torah as addressed primarily to the nation as a whole may provide the key to the problem of why material rewards are stressed to the near-exclusion of spiritual rewards, such as immortality of the soul and the sheer ecstasy of fellowship with God. Spiritual rewards of this nature are directed primarily to the individual. They attach themselves essentially to the self and to the ego. It makes little sense to speak of a nation collectively enjoying the hereafter or of an entire community, as such, meriting immortality in some spiritual sense.

Now it is clear that the promises referring to the nation as a whole cannot be spiritual, for even if the nation as a whole is righteous and deserving of life in the world-to-come, we cannot say that the wicked man in it deserves future life for the sake of the "fifty righteous men." It would be unjust to bestow future life on an absolutely wicked man and treat alike the righteous and the wicked. It is clear therefore, that the promises which refer to the nation as a whole must necessarily be material. That is, if the majority of the country or of the nation are righteous, the country or the nation will escape exile or famine or pestilence and universal punishment in general because good or evil decrees pronounced upon nations depend upon the character of the majority of the population.[18]

Furthermore, the entire concept of Jewish peoplehood as an entity covenanted *in toto* to God was designed to operate in the arena of mundane history, exhibiting its special qualities to the nations of the world, where the ultimate goal is the Messianic vision of universal redemption: peace, brotherhood, and recognition of God. Rewards and punishments are therefore presented in terms of empirical conditions which affect the nation as a whole on the social and historical level in the sight of all. Just as the individual is provided with psychological inducements for compliance by means of sanctions enforced by the courts and various social pressures, so is the nation provided with pedagogical inducements in terms of providentially ordered sets of conditions: political tranquility, peaceful borders, and economic well-being versus defeat in war, economic disaster, and exile.

Acting Out Of A Sense Of Purpose

Another aspect of *mitzvah* observance which must be considered separately is what can be called the "meaning" conponent. The rabbis, following the example of the Pentateuch itself, would often assign reasons for some of the individual precepts. Thus, they might point out the significance of the fact that sacrifices were restricted to the Tent of Meeting or why the knot in the phylacteries faces front or why the Torah is more severe in its punishment of the thief than the robber.[19] Let us consider a case where the Torah itself assigns a very explicit reason for a particular commandment. In regard to the building of booths on the Festival of Sukkot (Tabernacles), the Pentateuch states: "Ye shall dwell in booths seven days . . . that your generation may know that I made the children of Israel to dwell in booths when I brought them out of the land of Egypt."[20] Once a person believes himself to know the significance of the observance, it is possible for that knowledge to become the overriding factor in his actions, with a possibly negative outcome. He may, for example, reason thus: "Since I am thoroughly aware of the meaning of the observance, which is its ultimate purpose, surely it cannot be that important that the booth I construct conform to all the minutiae of the Halakhah." Already Philo reported a tendency to dispose with the actual observance altogether once its symbolic significance was grasped.

The dominant attitude of the Rabbis was that the reasons are not a condition of the fulfillment of the *mitzvot*. Although the Halakhah required that a person observe the commandments with the *kavanah,* or intention, of fulfilling his religious duty, it was not required, in most cases, that his *kavanah* encompass the reason or conceptual significance of the commandments. Thus, when we speak of the proper motivation that an individual should have in performing the *mitzvot,* the focus still remains on the *lishmah,* on simply directing the action to the service of God.[21]

There is a point, however, where the reason and the reward and the value of the commandment seem to converge. The rabbis believed that the ultimate reward of the *mitzvot* as a whole was their efficacy in bringing a person into the "world-to-come" (*olam ha-ba*).

In the words of Rabbi Jacob: "This world is the antechamber of the world-to-come. Prepare yourself in the antechamber that you mayest be admitted into the banquet hall."[22] In the works of Maimonides and others, the concept of the world-to-come was interpreted as the capacity of the soul or self of the individual to attain immortality in some sphere of spiritual reality after physical death. Maimonides viewed this as a developmental concept; i.e., man at birth possesses only a potential for immortality, which is conceived as the ultimate self-fulfillment or human salvation. The cumulative effect of properly motivated observance of the commandments is to develop the spiritual quality of the self to the point where it acquires self-subsistence in the hereafter. Now, what if a man honors his parents or loves his neighbor with a clear and deliberate intention that he is doing this in order to acquire *olam ha-ba,* in order to achieve immortality of the soul? Is this proper motivation? True, this is, in a sense, a "reward" for observing the commandments, and we are told by Antigonus not to serve God for the reward. But *olam ha-ba* is not an extrinsic reward but the consequence and purpose of the *mitzvah* itself, the ultimate end of all the commandments! The reward and the reason converge. Can this serve as the content of the motivation? Better yet, *ought this* not to be the preferred motivation?

According to Maimonides, true *lishmah* requires that we transcend even the desire to gain *olam ha-ba.* He describes the intrinsic value of Torah in primarily cognitive terms: "The end of truth is to know that it is the truth. . . . Torah is truth and the purpose of knowing it is to do it. . . . Believe in the truth for the sake of truth itself." This is how Maimonides expresses himself in his code:

> Whosoever serves God out of love occupies himself with the study of the Law and the fulfillment of the commandments and walks in the path of wisdom impelled by no external motive whatsoever, moved neither by fear of calamity nor by the desire to obtain material benefit: such a man does what is truly right because it is truly right, and ultimately happiness comes to him as a result of his conduct. This standard is indeed a very high one; not every sage attained to it. . . . It is the standard which God through Moses bids us to achieve, as it is said: "And thou shalt love the Lord thy God with all thy heart."[23]

Maimonides refers us to the rabbinic statement: "Lest you say, 'I shall study the Torah that I may be called Rabbi, that I may sit in council, that I may enjoy length of days *in the world to come,*' the Torah enjoins us 'to love'; study without thought of gain and the honor will come in the end."[24]

In his commentary on the Mishnah, Isaac Abarbanel rejects the interpretation of Maimonides and insists that Antigonus is speaking of material rewards. Only such considerations render the service of God imperfect.[24a] However, Abarbanel sees nothing wrong in being motivated by a desire to achieve the spiritual rewards of the *mitzvot,* such as *olam ha-ba,* as promised by God. In an alternate interpretation, Abarbanel concedes that the individual acting out a desire for any sort of reward is surpassed by one who approaches the commandments out of a sense of love for God, out of a sense of gratitude for benefits received. I ought not think of any reward in performing the precept because, in a sense, I have already received my "reward" in advance. The decisive teaching of the rabbis in this matter seems to be reflected in the unqualified assertion of Rabbi Eliezer: "Happy is the man that feareth the Lord; that delighteth greatly in His *mitzvot,* but not in the reward of the *mitzvot.*"[25] This is supported by the rabbis' consistent use of the locution *lishmah* in referring to the proper motivation in performing the commandments. *Lishmah* literally means "for its own sake"; i.e., for the sake of the action itself. The narrow focus here, at least in the first instance, is neither upon the cognitive meaning of the *mitzvah* nor even upon God, to whom the *mitzvah* is directed but rather

upon the act itself. This also seems to be the thrust of the teaching in
Avot: "The reward of the *mitzvah* is the *mitzvah*."[26] Regardless of
whether we take this to mean the *mitzvah* that has just been performed
or the next one that one might now be prompted to perform, the
emphasis is again upon the act itself, to the exclusion of other considerations.

What we have attempted to sort out from the welter of considerations which surround the performance of a precept, moral or ritual, is
the following:

1. *Rewards and Punishments.* These are psychological and pedagogical devices to induce people to obey the *mitzvot*. On the individual level
these may range from the sanctions of corporal punishment meted out
by the courts to the natural consequences of morality, which are the
social benefits of benevolence, the experiental joy of serving God or
one's fellow man, and ultimately spiritual bliss in the hereafter. On the
national level these include the providentially ordered "Blessings and
Curses" held out in the Bible for obedience or disobedience. Since all
of these constitute egotistical considerations, they are excluded by the
requirement of *lishmah*.

2. *Meaning Components (Reasons).* Here we have reference to the
kinds of considerations offered as the rational purpose or significance
of either the entire network of precepts, single precepts, or even portions of precepts. These answer the question of why the *mitzvot* were
commanded or what role they play in the divine plan or what their
underlying philosophy is. The most general kind of "meaning component" is the sort of response that sees *mitzvah* observance as constituting the fulfillment of the individual person as the "image of God" with
consequences that lead to *olam ha-ba*, here conceived as a cognitive
experience. Although these considerations are more abstract and
"spiritualized," they are still extraneous to the act itself and cannot be
regarded as constituting the proper motivation.

Once the concept of *lishmah* directs us to the act itself, we are compelled to distinguish between precepts of morality and the ritual precepts. Since the ritual commands are only of instrumental value, we
cannot remain fixed on the action itself and must relate the action to
God. We must somehow sense in the act service of the living God, to
whom we must reach out in love. Acts of morality, however, possess
intrinsic value and are themselves divine qualities. Hence, by perform-

ing the acts *lishmah*, for their own sake, we are already involved in a moral relationship not only with our neighbor but also with God.

The rabbis were quite realistic and realized that this kind of "pure" or disinterested motivation is difficult to achieve. However, since they placed great store in the efficacy of the commandments and their power to influence the doer, they counseled: "Let a man do the *mitzvot* even if it be from extraneous motives [*she-lo-lishmah*], for doing the *mitzvot* from whatever motive will ultimately lead him to to do them for their own sake [*lishmah*]."[27]

The Summum Bonum Of Judaism

In discussing rewards, it might be relevant to examine the vision of the final good, or *summum bonum,* as found in Judaism. The prophets are quite explicit in downgrading the ordinary values, such as wealth, wisdom, and power, in favor of the "knowledge of God," which they seem to have equated with moral values.

> Thus saith the Lord: Let not the wise man glory in his wisdom. Neither let the mighty man glory in his might. Let not the rich man glory in his riches; but let them that glorieth, glory in this, that he understandeth and knoweth Me, that I am the Lord who exercises mercy, justice, and righteousness in the earth, for in these things I delight, saith the Lord.[28]

Throughout the Torah, prophet, psalmist, and sage agree that true blessing and the ultimate good is to be found in fellowship with God attained through the study of Torah, performance of the precepts, and the pursuit of justice and righteousness.[29] The rabbis reinforced these teachings and enthroned the study of Torah as the highest value. However, they did not reject the pleasures, the ordinary enjoyments, the beauty and joy of life. These, too, constitute blessings and goods. Thus, the Bible describes how the Patriarchs, Abraham, Isaac, and Jacob, attained high levels of material wealth, and this constituted part of their "blessing." These are certainly not the highest good, certainly not the good which alone can bring man deep and abiding satisfaction, but they are not to be disparaged. These values are important adjuncts to man's life as a whole. They are subsidiary goods which make life sweet, lower rungs on the ladder of values. In this light we can understand the dictum of Rabbi Simeon ben Yohai: "Beauty, strength, riches, venerable age, and progeny are ornaments to the righteous and ornaments to the world."[30] This basic approach of the rabbis seems to have been grounded in their understanding that varieties of pleasurable experiences, the exercise of power, and the broadened outlook that comes with knowledge are all ways and opportunities for man to grow, develop his talents, expand his horizons. All of one's experiences can be directed to God in accordance with the celebrated dictum of the rabbis: "Let all of your actions be for the sake of heaven."[31] But even if they are not, they contribute to the development of a complete, richly complex self which, when it finally turns to God, is worthy of Him and is not a shrunken, underdeveloped, one-dimensional person. Thus the Talmud teaches: "There are three things that broaden the mind of a person: a beautiful dwelling, a beautiful wife, and beautiful furniture."[32]

Rabbi Kook is reported to have commented on the oft-repeated promise in the Torah to bring Israel to a land that "runs with milk and honey" that it portrays the ideal national life that the people should aspire to establish and attain. The vision is not one of bare necessities or of mere subsistence, but one in which there is "honey" to make life sweet and pleasant. This, he explained, is because Israel is destined to be a spiritually and culturally creative people who will require broad margins of comfort in order to recharge and stimulate their energies.[33] But if this interpretation is correct, then we have here a tacit assurance that Israel will in the long run be able to handle luxury and avoid its pitfalls.

Judaism was amply aware of the dangers of wealth and satiation and most sensitive to the powerful attractions of acquisitiveness. Yet it was not impressed with poverty either and believed that deprivation is an unnatural, demeaning, and debilitating condition for man. The prayer of the sage in Proverbs expresses this well: "Give me neither poverty nor riches; feed me with mine allotted bread; lest I be full and deny and say, 'who is the Lord?' or lest I be poor and profane the name of my God."[34] Moderation is, of course, the preferred approach; but if God blesses one with wealth, it ought not to be feared or rejected. Do not let it turn your head. Understand from whence it comes to you, and use it all in the service of God.

Rather than directly reject the generally desired values of wealth, power, and wisdom as did Jeremiah, the rabbis would sometimes attempt to retain the name but change the content, a sort of trans-valuation of values: "Who is rich? He who is happy with his lot. Who is wise? He who learns from every man. Who is strong? He who conquers his evil spirit."[35]

In their solution to the problem of why the Nazirite had to bring a sin offering, one trend among the rabbis explained the Nazirite's wrongdoing as being his original desire to take upon himself self-denying abstinence.

> Rabbi Eliezer ha-Kappar says, "What do we learn from the verse, 'And it shall atone for him for having sinned on account of the soul.' On account of which 'soul' has he sinned? His own, by afflicting himself with absti-nence from wine. This teaches a lesson: since he who merely denies him-self the consumption of wine is already a sinner, the sinner who afflicts himself with abstinence of all other kinds, how much more would he be considered a sinner."[36]

In general, it can be said that the rabbis frowned upon asceticism, for the reasons mentioned above. The greater one's appreciation of the world, the greater one's appreciation of its Maker. "On the Day of Judgment, man will be held accountable for everything he beheld and did not partake of."[37] It must, however, be acknowledged that tenden-cies toward asceticism in Judaism drew upon sources deep in the reli-gious consciousness. There are many for whom deprivation and self-denial for the sake of God generates holiness and a sense of piety. From the very beginning, as evinced by the Nazirite practice and the Rechabites, through the Essenes in the period of the Second Temple, and on to the medieval Chasidei Ashkenaz and beyond, the ascetic strain in Judaism waxed and waned but always remained alive.

We conclude that Judaism embraced life in all of its complexity but set up a hierarchy of values. Recognition was given to all of man's needs and interests, so long as the behavior they called forth was in accordance with moral norms. Judaism rejected no basic human drives. It demanded only that all be organized and oriented toward the apex of the pyramid—love of man and love of God.

Why Does God Permit Evil In The World?

One of the oldest and sharpest challenges to the belief in God's moral nature is the fact of evil in the world. The problem takes many forms. There is, first, the metaphysical question of the origin of evil and sin, given a creator who is all-good. Secondly, there is the question of the pain and suffering in the world today and its reconciliation with the concept of God's mercy and justice. The accepted term for this subject is "theodicy," from the Greek words for "God" and "justice"; i.e., the justification of God's justice and righteousness in the face of evil.

In terms of religious thought, theodicy is a type of theological problem which arises out of a conflict between theoretical beliefs and the jagged edge of human experience. In Judaism, theodicy represents the first fruits of religious reflection."[38] Both in his individual life and his national history, the Jew had occasion to experience misfortunes which he found difficult to understand on the basis of deserts or retribution. If God controlled events and therefore sanctioned what was happening, where was justice and mercy? In the Torah we find the concepts of responsibility and retribution, both individual and collective, entrenched from the very beginning. From Abraham and Noah through the kings of Israel and Judea, individuals or groups who sin or disobey God are punished in ways which are appropriate to their transgressions, while those who are good and righteous are saved and blessed. This principle is also implicit in the codes, which speak of individual sin, guilt-offerings, and expiation. The working-out of the moral order, even from the beginning, was not seen as a single, immediate cause-and-effect sequence. Included in the Torah are sets of "auxiliary assumptions" to facilitate the explanation of God's ways: affliction may be a test of men's loyalties; God is often patient with the world, giving people an opportunity to repent or waiting until some unspecified measure of sin has been filled.[39]

While the books of Psalms and Proverbs are completely enthralled by God's justice and righteousness and claim to see its manifestations all around us in the empirical world, prophets such as Jeremiah and Habakkuk are upset by the reality of a world which seems to run counter to the moral order and inquire of God, "Wherefore doth the way of the wicked prosper?" or "Thou that art of eyes too pure to behold evil, and that canst not look on mischief, wherefore lookest Thou, when they deal treacherously, and holdest Thy peace, when the wicked swalloweth up the man that is more righteous than he. . . ?"[40]

The problem of theodicy receives its fullest biblical treatment in the Book of Job. Here, as elsewhere in the Bible, the form in which the problem is presented is not such as to seek an explanation for suffering or evil in general, but rather to focus on the suffering of the righteous. Judaism never strayed away from the belief in the moral quality and purposive nature of God's will. However, men are compelled to question the justice of God, and indeed the entire moral order, once we contemplate the fate of a Job. The challenge of Job's experience consists precisely in this. The *tzaddik* in Job believes in God. The thinker in Job accepts God's existence but demands that we separate God from ideas of morality and justice. For it appears clear that God's rule is not moral. The Book of Job rejects this separation. Once God appears to Job and causes him to experience the "grace of revelation," God's concern for the world is clear. Job is now able to accept the principle that God's ways are hidden from man. Out of an "immediate certitude of divine majesty," Job regains his faith in the meaningfulness of God's acts. The Bible's last word on the problem of theodicy is that, all experience to the contrary, the concept of God necessarily includes the moral idea.[41] "For all His ways are justice . . . just and right is He."[42]

In rabbinic literature these biblical approaches are continued and deepened. The principle of desert and retribution, or that God governs the people of the world in accordance with the rule of reward and punishment, is affirmed and reaffirmed with one major modification. The arena for the carrying out of these rewards and punishments is explicitly broadened to include *olam ha-ba,* the world-to-come, the life after death.[43]

The Torah, as the book of the national covenant, was not primarily concerned with the question of the ultimate destiny of the individual. And although the question of the suffering of the individual is raised in the Book of Job, a general solution is not offered. Kaufmann considers it an "astonishing and remarkable feature of Biblical religion" that although the Torah believed that the soul or spirit of the dead lives on apart from the body, "Biblical faith draws no religious inference from this notion." That is to say, the Torah does not explicitly employ the notion of an afterlife as a solution to the problem of the suffering of the individual. The rabbis, however, who were extremely exercised by the problem of theodicy in terms of the everyday life of the individual, did not hesitate to develop fully the theological implications of the hereafter, or *olam ha-ba*. Rabbi Tarfon said, ". . . and know that the giving of the reward of the righteous will be in the time to come." And "One hour of spiritual delight in *olam ha-ba* is better than an entire life in this world." There is a suggestion here that perhaps the experience of the world-to-come, which is all spiritual and involves enjoying "the rays of the Divine Presence," can actually roll back or redeem, in some retroactive way, the pain and suffering experienced by the righteous in this world.

A concept such as this is related to God's unity and love as well as to His justice. Just as *achdut ha-shem* necessitates an ultimate Messianic redemption on the historical level, which constitutes the fulfillment of His will so that all may see that "God is one and His name is one," so, too, does God's love require the possibility of a final chapter to every individual life: a final accounting in which no person need go unperfected and no suffering remains unredeemed. "Every Israelite has [the possibility of] a share in the world-to-come."

How the rewards and punishments are distributed between the "here" and the "hereafter" was a matter on which the rabbis held differing views. These ranged from those who maintained that no reward at all was to be expected in this world to those who felt that while the "capital" was stored up for the individual in the world-to-come, the "fruits" are enjoyed in this world.[44] Others maintained that only the wicked could expect to be "paid off" in this world, while the righteous will be chastised for their few transgressions here, leaving the world-to-come to be for them an experience of uninterrupted blessing.[45]

However, the jagged edge of experience again and again challenged the rabbis and their theories. There are two commandments for whose observance the Torah explicitly promises long life: honoring one's parents and "sending forth the dam." Now consider this case: "If his father said to him, 'Go up to the loft and fetch me some pigeons,' and he ascended to the loft and let the dam go and took the young [in accordance with the precept], and on his way down he fell and died. Where is his 'happy life' and where is his 'length of days'?"[46]

On the national level, the Hadrianic persecution constituted a particularly grave and jarring crisis for rabbinic thinking on the subject of theodicy. It was not only that the widespread suffering affected both wicked and righteous alike, but the fact that the resolve to observe the *mitzvot* was itself the cause of death and suffering![47] The rabbis developed their own arsenal of "auxiliary assumptions" to try to explain the suffering of the righteous and the well-being of the wicked. One approach, alluded to above, distinguishes between one's out-of-character deeds, which are requited in this world, and deeds in line with one's characteristic personality, for which one is rewarded or punished in the hereafter. This is usually mentioned in connection with the rabbinic concept that the criteria of judgment may differ between the righteous and the wicked. Because of the greater awareness and deeper sensitivity of the *tzadik,* more is expected from him. He is hereafter judged more rigorously than others, even for deviating "a hair's breadth."[48]

Another concept of major importance is the rabbinic notion of "scourges of love"; i.e., suffering which may come upon a person not as punishment but as a sign of God's love; as an opportunity to grow and to "purify" one's relationship to God, in accordance with the passage: "For whom the Lord loveth He correcteth, even as a father the son in whom he delighteth."[49]

Ultimately, however, the rabbis were convinced that in spite of all the explanations, which included the ability of the world-to-come to redress all moral imbalances, the problem of theodicy constituted a mystery which in terms of any particular case defied rational explanation. Thus, we find the statement of Rabbi Yannai: "It is not in our power to explain the well-being of the wicked or the suffering of the righteous."[50] As a recent work on the problem of theodicy put it:

> The problem does not consist in the occurrence of pain and suffering as such; for all can see that a world in which these exist in at least a moderate degree may well be a better environment for the development of moral personalities, than would be a sphere that was sterilized of all challenges. The problem consists rather in the fact that instead of serving a constructive purpose, pain and misery seem to be distributed in random and

meaningless ways with the result that suffering is often undeserved and often falls upon men in amounts exceeding anything that could be rationally intended.[51]

We are also told in the Talmud:

> When Moses ascended to heaven to receive the Torah, he was shown Rabbi Akiva ben Joseph sitting and deriving heaps of *halakhot* from each jot of the Torah. Moses said, "Master of the Universe, you have shown me his Torah, now show me his reward." Moses then saw the Romans peeling the skin of Rabbi Akiva with combs of iron! And Moses cried: "Master of the Universe, is this the reward of Torah!" He was answered: "Be silent. This is my will." ("So has it come up in thought before me.")[52]

Even in the face of mystery, the rabbis held fast to their faith in the moral nature of God. ". . . the world is judged by goodness, yet all is according to the amount of man's work."[53] Aside from the theology, the Jew was seen as having a religious obligation to justify the Divine Judgment. "The Rock, His work is perfect"—when Moses came down from Mount Sinai, all Israel came to him. They said: "Moses, our teacher, tell us, what is the nature of the attribute of justice on high?" He replied: "I do not only say when the righteous are cleared and the guilty are condemned but even when the reverse takes place: He is a God of faithfulness and without inequity."[54]

The problem of theodicy is usually formulated as a dilemma: If God is perfectly good, He must want to abolish all evil; if He is all-powerful, He must be able to abolish all evil; but evil exists: Therefore, either God is not perfectly good or He is not all-powerful. Some theologians have been tempted to seek a solution by proposing equivocal meanings for the moral predicates. That is to say, "What is good in the eyes of God is not necessarily what is good in the eyes of man." This would enable us to affirm that although we see much injustice and suffering all around us, by God's standards this is all just and good. But this is not an option that is open to Jewish thinkers.[55] For as we have seen, God's attributes serve as a model and inspiration for human beings in their relationships to each other. If what is good in the eyes of God is not good in the eyes of man, then the entire point of a moral

God and the concept of *imitatio dei* collapses. When Abraham charged God, "Will the judge of all the earth not do justice?" God should have simply answered: "My understanding of justice is different from your understanding of justice!" What, of course, can be argued is that only God has the larger perspective, the cosmic view, and alternatively that only God has the penetrating view which looks into the heart of man. It may very well be, therefore, that if we could possess the information or the perspective that God has, many things which *appear* unjust and evil might indeed not be so. However, the standards of good and evil, right and wrong, remain identical for God and man.

Much of the evil in the world is moral evil brought about by man, who is given freedom of choice by a good God. Sometimes unintentionally and sometimes deliberately and viciously, some of man's most painful agonies are brought about by other men. But this cannot be used as an argument against God's goodness. For the freedom that God has given man is in itself the greatest good, the necessary condition for man to become a responsible person capable of entering into a personal relationship with his Maker and capable of freely and responsibly reacting to the commandments and developing the divine likeness within himself. The fact that man can then use his freedom and powerful intellect to turn against God and his fellow man is a risk that had to be taken and a tragic cost that had to be borne. Furthermore, God cannot be expected to intercede by miraculous means to save the righteous and the innocent, because then, the experiences which make for moral qualities and help to develop a sense of responsibility would no longer exist, and with them, moral virtue and responsible persons.

> It would mean that no wrong could ever have bad effects, and that no piece of carelessness or ill judgment in dealing with the world could ever lead to harmful consequences. If a thief were to steal a million pounds from a bank, instead of anyone being made poorer thereby, another million pounds would appear from nowhere to replenish the robbed safe; and this, moreover, without causing any inflationary consequences. If one man tried to murder another, his bullet would melt innocuously into thin air, or the blade of his knife turn to paper. Fraud, deceit, conspiracy and treason would somehow always leave the fabric of society undamaged. Anyone driving at breakneck speed along a narrow road and hitting a pedestrian would leave his victim miraculously unharmed; or if one

slipped and fell through a fifth-floor window, gravity would be partially suspended and he would float gently to the ground. There would be nothing wrong with stealing, because no one could ever lose anything by it; there would be no such crime as murder, because no one could ever be killed; and in short none of the terms connoting modes of injury—such as cruelty, treachery, deceit, neglect, assault, injustice, unfaithfulness—would retain its meaning. If to act wrongly means, basically, to harm someone, there would no longer be any such thing as morally wrong action. And for the same reason, there would no longer be any such thing as morally right action. Not only would there be no way in which anyone could injure anyone else, but there would also be no way in which anyone could benefit anyone else, since there would be no possibility of any lack or danger. It would be a world without need for the virtues of self-sacrifice, care for others, devotion to the public good, courage, perserverance, skill, or honesty. It would indeed be a world in which such qualities, having no function to perform, would never come into existence. Unselfishness would never be evoked in a situation in which no one was ever in real need or danger. Honesty, good faith, commitment to the right would never be evoked in circumstances in which no one could ever suffer any harm, so that there were no bad consequences of dishonesty, bad faith, or moral vacillation. Courage would never be evoked in an environment devoid of all dangers; determination and persistence would never be evoked in the absence of any challenges and obstacles. Truthfulness would never be evoked in a world in which to tell a lie never had any ill effects. And so on. Perhaps most important of all, the capacity to love would never be developed, except in a very limited sense of the word, in a world in which there is no such thing as suffering.[56]

Once it is acknowledged that in the dilemma posed by theodicy, Judaism must always affirm God's goodness and justice, then it would appear that Judaism would tend to agree with Leibniz that this is the best of all possible worlds.[57] Since God is good, it would be inconsistent with His own nature to have chosen any other world than the best. But here we must ask: "best possible" for what purpose? Clearly, the world that would best serve the purpose that God is seeking to fulfill by its means. That is, the world as a "vale of soul-making"; as an environment wherein men can develop as responsible persons, as moral agents exercising freedom in a world whose natural laws are stable enough so that man can learn and predict and be responsible. But if

God is all-good, why did He not create a world with less suffering and with less pain? The answer would appear to be that yes, God, too, would have wanted such a world. But again given His purpose, which requires man's freedom, even God could do no better! It would appear that this view saves God's goodness by compromising His omnipotence, for we are saying that God does not have the power to make a better world. Thus, while God's *gevurah* is absolute and has dominion over all nature and history, He does nothing when hearing the insults and blasphemies of a Titus who spitefully desecrates the Holy of Holies.[58] And when the God of Mercy sees the suffering of His people and does nothing, the rabbis describe Him as "weeping." This can best be conceived as the concept of a "self-limiting" God, who must restrain His power, as it were, in the interests of His overall plan for the world, suffering His creatures to experience momentary evil.[59]

Some are still shocked by the assertion that certain things are impossible even for God. Yet it can be shown that such an acknowledgment does not constitute a limitation or an imperfection. For even as God is bound by the laws of logic[60]—He cannot make a square circle—so, too, the process of soul-making, with its possibility for personal fellowship with God, necessarily involves freedom for man with a large degree of noninterference by God, which inevitably spells suffering and pain. Thus, the Torah in Genesis seems to suggest not only that man's disobedience results in direct punishment to himself but that it brings about a deterioration in man's entire environment, making for general hardship as a "given" condition for all men. In this connection, let us examine the expression, "And it repented the Lord that He had made man on the earth and it grieved Him at His heart."[61] Surely even a rudimentary notion of God's omniscience would find such surprise, regret, and grief on the part of God rather anomalous, to say the least! But perhaps this should be seen as the Torah's way of saying that in spite of God's omnipotence and omniscience, there was no other way for God to have proceeded to give man freedom except as He did. If it should then be asked why God is so surprised when man chooses badly, the answer is that God's goodness nevertheless cannot make peace with the idea! God "regrets" and God "grieves" because the reality of man's corruption and suffering, while in a sense inevitable and expected, cannot go unnoticed by God. The Torah assumes all the risks of anthropomorphism in order to teach that God's goodness and mercy, however you understand them, are in disharmony with the evil on earth.

While the Torah describes God as pronouncing an unequivocal "good" over all of His creation, the rabbis in a number of homilies raised certain questions about the wisdom of creation and the goodness of some of its aspects. In connection with the creation of man, for example, the Midrash describes God as consulting with various groups of celestial beings as to the advisability of His act.

> When the Holy One, blessed be He, sought to create man, He created a company of ministering angels and said to them: "Is it your wish that we should create man in our image?" Said they before Him: "Sovereign of the universe, What will his deeds be?" He replied:
> "Of such and such a nature shall his deeds be." Said they before Him: "Sovereign of the universe, 'What is man that Thou are mindful of him, and the son of man that Thou dost care for him?' [Psalms 8:5(4)]." He thereupon put forth His little finger among them and burned them. The same happened with the second company. The third company said before Him: "Sovereign of the universe, when the former angels spoke to Thee, what did they achieve? The whole world is Thine; whatever Thou dost will to do in Thy world, do!" When it came to the men of the generation of the Flood and the men of the generation of the Tower of Babel, who acted wickedly, they [the angels] said before Him: "Sovereign of the universe, did not the former angels speak rightly before Thee?" He replied: "Even to old age I am He, and even to gray hairs will I carry you," etc. [Isa. 46:4].[62]

The objections of the angels are apparently based upon their foreknowledge that the history of man will be characterized by violence and deceit, suffering and pain. "Who needs this *tzarah*?"[63] God repudiates this counsel by eliminating the critics and intimidating the remaining angels into acquiescence. The event of creation is shot through with ambiguities that elude rational explanation. God's goodness prompts Him to create man and endow him with freedom. But this leads to sin and corruption, for which justice will require punishment. Clearly, then, for many persons existence is not good![64] Later, when wickedness has become reality in the generation of the Deluge and the critical angels permit themselves a "We told you so!" God responds with a passage that indicates that He and He alone has the patience and tolerance to wait until human history works itself through to the desired end. The original objection, however, remains unanswered.

In a companion Midrash, God breaks a deadlock among the debating angels, symbolized by moral qualities, by hurling Truth, one of the opposing angels, to the ground. While there is a treasure of profound significance in this marvelously suggestive homily, the obvious point is again that God overcomes rational objections to the creation of man by nonrational procedures.

Another rabbinic teaching tells how originally the moon and the sun were equally large ("the two great luminaries"). But when the moon correctly pointed out that "it is impossible for two kings to use one crown," God commanded the moon to reduce itself in size and become "the lesser light." And when the moon complained over the injustice of having to be the one to suffer diminution after having made a valid point, God tries unsuccessfully to mollify her with all sorts of compensations. Finally God says, "Bring for me an offering because I reduced the size of the moon" (". . . and in your new moons ye shall present a burnt-offering *for* the Lord"). Here again, in connection with an aspect of creation, God seems to be bested in an argument over what is right. His last recourse is to ask for forgiveness.[65]

In these teachings of the rabbis, we have a reflection of Judaism's agnostic reaction to theodicy, which we have designated "mystery." There seems to be an admission here that something is not right, something is not good. There is a recognition of a tragic dimension to some aspects of life in spite of Judaism's metaphysical optimism based on an all-good God who creates a universe which He pronounces "very good."[66]

Perhaps this discussion should be taken one step further. There is a tension built into morality itself which results from an implicit conflict between two moral principles: justice and mercy. Justice implies fairness based on the principle of desert. The wicked are to be punished, and the good are to be rewarded according to the notion of "measure for measure." The rights of all are to be upheld; the needs of all are to be met. Mercy, however, implies a readiness to forgive, a willingness to give up one's rights in love for another. Mercy implies a benevolence which longs to shower goods upon all, regardless of whether they deserve it or not. We shall see in a later chapter that this is one of the fundamental problems in the relationship between Halakhah and morality. More important for now, however, are the implications of this implicit conflict as they bear upon our concept of God. For both justice and mercy are among God's attributes. "Lord . . . merciful and gracious . . . forgiving iniquity and transgression and sin . . . and will by no means clear the guilty. . . ."[67] The 103rd Psalm is a paeon to God's compassion: "For as the heaven is high above the earth, so great is His mercy toward them that fear Him. As far as the east is from the west, so far hath He removed our transgressions from us. Like as a father has compassion on his children, so has the Lord compassion upon them that fear Him." Yet in Psalm 78, where we read again that God, "being full of compassion, forgiveth iniquity," we are also told that "many a time doth He turn His anger away, and doth not stir up *all* His wrath." The element of punishment and retribution is not forgotten.

The rabbis spoke of the divine attributes, or *middot,* of justice and mercy as if they were self-subsistent powers or hypostases.[68] The form-lettered name of God, YHVH, was seen as signifying the attribute of compassion, while the name ELOHIM denoted the attribute of justice. Thus, since in the first chapter of Genesis, God is called ELOHIM, and in the second chapter He is referred to as YHVH ELOHIM, the rabbis suggested that God first attempted to create the world in accordance with the principle of strict justice and accountability but soon realized that the world could not long endure without the forgiving quality of mercy, and so the attribute of mercy was joined to the attribute of justice.[69]

The most poignant expression of the conflict between the attributes of justice and mercy is found in the rabbinic teaching that God prays, and what does He pray: "May it be My will that My mercy may subdue My wrath, and may My mercy prevail over My attribute of justice, so that I may deal with My children in the quality of mercy and enter on their behalf within the line of strict justice."[70]

Urbach points out that while the rabbis generally sought to preserve both attributes as part of the nature of God, some rabbis appeared to make the attribute of justice dominant, so that compassion could only be expected from God if *you* were compassionate.[71] Others, however, like Rabbi Akiva, spoke of God as the All-Merciful, *Rachaman,* since they believed that even suffering was not the result of God's justice but of His compassion—"scourges of love." In some Midrashim, the struggle between the two attributes becomes a struggle between the attribute of justice and God Himself, who becomes identified with mercy. Rava pointed out a number of instances in the Torah where, contrary to the accepted principle, God's name of ELOHIM is associated with mercy. Rava maintained that this is due to the merit of the righteous, who are able to transform the attribute of justice into mercy: "Blessed are the righteous, who convert the attribute of justice to that of compassion. . . . He who forbears to retaliate, i.e., lets his right go unclaimed—all his iniquities are likewise passed over . . . the attribute of justice leaves them unpunished."[72]

It therefore appears quite clear that the rabbis were profoundly aware of a double problematic at the center of the concept of a moral God. There is, on the one hand, the conflict between justice and raw experience that we called the problem of theodicy, and on the other hand, the differing requirements of justice and mercy as attributes of God. Both raise questions about the nature of God, and both must ultimately be relegated to the impenetrable mystery of God's unique and unitary nature.

5

The Qualities of Jewish Morality

We have already indicated that the basic moral principles upon which the Decalogue is based were in fact already well known and enjoyed some degree of approval long before Israel stood at Sinai.[1] This is implied by the biblical narrative itself. Judaism, however, not only assumed the widespread dissemination of the basic principles of morality but also made the normative judgment that all men are bound by these moral standards. Since the fatherhood of God implies the brotherhood of man, the prophet could ask: "Have we not all one father? Hath not one God created us? Why do we deal treacherously every man against his brothers?"[2] And when moral behavior was not forthcoming from man, the consequence was punishment: "For the earth is filled with violence through them; and, behold, I will destroy them . . ."[3] Later, in speaking of the nations of Amon and Moab, the Torah faults them for immoral behavior, "because they met you not with bread and water on the way, when you came forth out of Egypt."[4]

With this in mind, we must ask ourselves what is unique and distinctive about Jewish morality. Certainly, there are some obvious distinguishing characterizations that can be made. It would appear that Jewish morality is strongly deontological in character, emphasizing a sense of duty and obligation that embraces the concept of what is right. Furthermore it would have to be acknowledged that Jewish morality is essentially humanistic in nature, placing the highest value upon human life and personality in directions that encourage justice and righteousness, love and kindness in social relations, and humility and moderation in our personal development. But even if we add the theological component and say that we have in Jewish morality a sort of religious humanism, we are still in the realm of class-membership and general classification. We have as yet not put our finger upon what is distinctively *Jewish* about the morality of Judaism. What seems clear to the present writer is that there is no *Jewish* morality either in the sense that Judaism can be expected to offer some uniquely different definition of right and wrong or in the sense that the essentials of Jewish morality obligate Jews only.

Yet, if we are to properly understand the morality of Judaism we must take note of certain special qualities which seem to distinguish it from other systems. In terms of essential content, we find that the basic meaning of justice and righteousness, love and kindess, compassion and mercy coincide with our ordinary understanding of these terms. The morality of Judaism, however, will be found to differ in respect to certain ancillary aspects or dimensions which taken together impart an unmistakable and unique quality to Jewish morality.

Passion And A Sense Of Urgency

In a previous chapter we pointed out that in the biblical and rabbinical view, morality is the chief demand made upon man by God, whose own nature, insofar as it can be known, is moral. This conviction was supported by the historical memories of the Exodus, which seared into the national consciousness the concept of a God who hears the call of those in pain and liberates the oppressed. This imparted a very clear and overriding centrality to morality in every area of life. While attempts had been made earlier in human history to endow morality with religious sanction, it was always *wisdom,* human or divine, which was seen as its source. Just as there are wise rulers who compose good laws for their people, so might there be wise gods who recognize effective laws and urge them upon man for the benefits they bring. At Sinai, however, a new source and a new authority were revealed for morality. "Thou shalt not steal" may be good advice in order to achieve a stable and orderly society, but it must first be seen for what it is: an expression of the divine will. "In the Israelite conception, justice and morality belong to the realm of prophecy, not wisdom . . . The divine imperative from a God . . . whose will is essentially moral and good."[5]

Such a radical and unprecedented shift in the perception of the source of conventional morality resulted in a new and dramatic emphasis upon the importance and significance of morality in the destiny of the nation. This message was clearly and forcefully hammered home by the long line of Hebrew prophets.[6]

A quality that most impresses the reader of the prophetic literature is the intensity of the passion and the almost "hysterical" tone with which these messengers of God denounce the immorality of their times. As A. J. Heschel points out, there seems to be, for the contemporary reader, a disproportion between what the prophet finds and the reported reaction of God. After all, so what if "somewhere in ancient Palestine poor people have not been treated properly by the rich?"[7] Is it not incongruous that the glorious city of Jerusalem should be destroyed and an entire nation go into exile because of some minor acts of injustice? In our day we are accustomed to viewing acts of social injustice or conditions of human suffering either with the controlled detachment of the professional social worker or with the cynical, worldly-wise sense of resignation of the journalist. How are we to account for the fierce impatience, the extreme indignation, and the harsh rebuke of the Hebrew prophets? Didn't they know that there is hardly a society in the world where you don't have people who daily "trample upon the needy . . . make the ephah small and the shekel great. Deal deceitfully with false balances . . . buy the poor for silver and the needy for a pair of sandals?"[8] To us the moral state of society seems tolerable. We balance out the evil and the shady with the deeds of charity and pockets of decency. "Our standards are modest and our sense of injustice timid."[9] The prophet, however, makes no allowances for human weakness. He finds society dreadful. His ear seems constantly attuned to all of the small agonies that we tune out.

Yet for these ordinary, commonplace sins of personal greed, social inequality, deceit, and violence, the prophet, in the name of God, threatens world-shattering catastrophes:

The Lord has sworn by the pride of Jacob,
Surely I will never forget any of their deeds,

> Shall not the earth tremble on this account,
> And everyone mourn who dwells in it . . .[10]

The voice of the prophet is charged with agony and agitation.

> Woe to him who heaps up what is not his own . . .
> Woe to him who gets evil gain for his house . . .
> For the stone cries out from the wall,
> And the beam from the woodwork responds,
> Woe to him who builds a town with blood,
> And founds a city on iniquity.[11]

The only way to account for the shrillness, the passion, and the near-hysteria of the Hebrew prophets in their denunciation of immorality is to understand that the prophet looks upon the world through the perspective of God, who has a stake in the human situation, who cares for man, who in some sense is involved in the affairs of men. "For I know their sorrows."[12] If, indeed, God is mercy and love and justice, then any act of injustice anywhere must, in some sense, "affect God."[13] One poor man cries out and foundations seem to tremble. "And it shall come to pass, when he crieth unto Me, that I will hear."[14] "The prophet's word is a scream in the night, . . . while the world is at ease and asleep, the prophet feels the blast from heaven."[15] There is another insight which can assist us in understanding the dominant moral passion of the Bible. The rational bias in philosophy, which is our legacy from the ancient Greeks, has influenced us all to assign higher value to the universal over the particular, the abstract over the concrete. This has its origin in Greek ontological theory and epistemology. Thus Plato had little regard for the visual arts because their artifacts were twice removed from the Ideal Forms, and Aristotle thought more of drama than history because the latter dealt only with particular events while drama is more general, depicting types of character and kinds of events. It is for this reason that general terms like "justice," "righteousness," "ethics," and "morality" seem to possess an air of sublimity and nobility, while particular acts of morality, embedded in all the prosaic details of their concrete situation, may, by contrast, appear trivial and insignificant. Yet, when we stop to consider the nature of morality, we find that the very reverse is the truth. Justice and righteousness for all of their sonorous sound are mere concepts—empty and disembodied. Moral reality is achieved only when these moral ideals are realized in human affairs and actualized in concrete human deeds and actual human relationships. It is this emphasis on particular moral acts that characterizes the Torah approach to morality. The very first story told of Abraham after he enters into the covenant with God and becomes, as it were, the first Jew, involves an act of hospitality. Weary strangers appear at Abraham's tent, and although weak from his recent circumcision and presumably still experiencing the presence of God, the aged Patriarch breaks off the divine encounter and "runs to meet them."[16] After inviting them in, we are told, "Abraham ran to the herd and fetched a calf . . . and he took curd and milk . . . and he stood by them under the tree and they did eat."[17] This wealth of detail describing the personal devotion of the Patriarch in a series of benevolent actions reveals what is the ultimate task of the Jew and the human being: to realize abstract moral concepts in the myriad situations of everyday life. In the words of Efros,

> God knocks, in a manner not found in any other literature, on all the windows of man: know me, recognize me, admit me! Why is He so interested to be known? . . . the transcendentally ethical longs by its very nature to clothe himself in human acts and relations because these constitute his concrete existence and meaning.[18]

This thought is perhaps alluded to in the following Midrash: "'Who hath raised up one [lit. awakened] from the east, at whose steps victory [lit. righteousness] attendeth?' [Isa. 41:2]. Rabbi Reuben said: 'Even righteousness was asleep and Abraham awakened it. How was this done? Abraham opened an inn and tended to the needy.'"[19] What is most suggestive here is the notion of "righteousness being asleep." That is to say, righteousness and other moral principles "existed," in the sense that they were known and recognized and perhaps even approved as concepts. However, they were "asleep," in the sense that no great urge was felt to apply them or to carry out the principles in everyday life. With Abraham and Judaism came a new understanding of morality as the "way of the Lord," a way followed by the Lord Himself, and a new urgency, a new sanctity, a greater significance was assigned to moral actions. Righteousness, as it were, was now "awakened" from its slumbers, came alive and was now beginning to be expressed in the concrete affairs of men.[20]

The Quality Of Universality

To further understand the significance of calling the morality of Judaism universal, we must take a closer look at the concept of justice, which is one of the root concepts of morality. Generally speaking, the common notion of justice seems to involve the concept of equality. When we think of the requirements of distributive or retributive justice, we think of the scale, with its suggestion of balance and proportion. After some consideration, however, we are led to the concept of fairness. While it might be commonly thought, for example, that a system of taxation would be perfectly just if it imposed equal burdens upon all, upon reflection we realize that perfect equality leaves no room for allotting special privileges and burdens to special classes, as is often required by justice. More exactly, therefore, by justice we mean the elimination of arbitrary distinctions, of personal and subjective preferences, and the establishment of a proper balance between competing claims. This has to do with matters referring to the distribution of goods and services, compensation for loss and damage, and retribution for wrongs committed. The idea of justice really consists of two parts: "a uniform or constant feature summarized in the precept, 'treat like cases alike' (equality) and a shifting or varying criterion used in determining when for any given purpose, cases are alike or different (fairness)."[21]

Studies in the logic of morality have shown that moral judgments and moral reasoning possess what has been called the characteristic of implicit generality. This can be formulated as the generalization principle: "What is right or wrong for one person must be right or wrong for any similar person in similar circumstances," or as the generalization argument: "If everyone were to do that, the consequences would be disastrous; therefore no one ought to do that."[22] These general observations appear to be features of the structure of moral language and ultimately appeal to the canons of consistency and logic rather than morality. Some writers have therefore concluded that this observation in itself is only a fact about language and has no moral implications. M. G. Singer, however, has argued convincingly that to be inconsistent in the area of morality is to be partial and unfair, which is, in turn, to be unjust, and human beings ought not to be unjust. He claims that what we have here is a moral principle so fundamental and self-evident as to be a pervasive feature of moral language. "And it is not a fallacy to deduce a moral injunction from it."[23]

Given the generalization principle and the intrinsic universality of justice and morality, it follows that from the aspect of man as moral agent, justice *concerns all men*. From the point of view of man as object of moral concern, the principle of universality implies that justice is *due all men*. This aspect of the principle of universality has found expression in the well-known moral maxim known as the Golden Rule and in Kant's formulations of the categorical imperative.

Once we understand the essential relationship of universality to the concept of justice, we can appreciate the use of universality as a criterion by which to evaluate different systems of morality. Thus, in continuing our search for the distinguishing characteristics of the morality of Judaism, we might now suggest that the sheer extensivity of the Jewish concept of justice, its universal range and refusal to exclude various defenseless social classes from the protection of justice, constitutes one of its chief positive features.

The Torah, indeed, draws the implication of the teaching that all men are created in the image of God. False and irrelevant distinctions must not be introduced to disqualify human beings from their right to justice. For if man is made in the image of God, if he is the creation of God, then every human being is included and the entire significance of the one man is extended to embrace every man. Said Rabbi Akiva, "Beloved is man, for he was created in the image [of God]."[24] Every man is fellow man to every other man, or is "thy brother." The fatherhood of the one God implies the brotherhood of all men, which generates the concept of universal morality. It has been suggested that the well-known passage in Leviticus, usually translated "thou shalt love thy neighbor as thyself, I am the Lord,"[25] should be interpreted, "Love thy neighbor; *he is as thou [kamokha]*," and in that "as thou" lies the full meaning of the commandment.[26]

The identification of justice with God projects God's infinity and absoluteness onto the concept of justice, removing it from the category of subjective reality and relativity.[27] Justice applies to all. No man qua man is more than any other. The Torah, therefore, rejects double codes of morality— for yourself and for others, for the great and for the humble, for rulers and for the ruled, for individuals and for nations, for private life and for public life. "One law and one ordinance shall be both for you and for the stranger that sojourneth with you."[28]

The underpriviledged and the defenderless in society are singled out in the Torah for special attention. "Ye shall not afflict any widow or fatherless child . . ."[29] Sensitive to the fact that justice requires equality and rejects all favoritism, the Torah warns us not to let our desire to help the poor lead us into a situation of reverse discrimination where we do an injustice to others: "Neither shalt thou countenance a poor man in his cause" and "thou shalt not respect the person of the poor nor harm the person of the great."[30]

No less than thirty-six times does the Torah remind us of our special obligation to the alien or stranger.[31]

> And if a stranger sojourneth with thee in thy land, ye shall not do him wrong. The stranger that sojourneth with thee shall be unto you as the houseborn among you, and thou shalt love him, as thyself; for ye were strangers in the land of Egypt: I am the Lord your God.[32]

Indeed the ultimate source of the universality of Torah morality is to be found in the synthesis of two metaphysical beliefs: first, the unity of mankind as fixed by a common ancestry in Adam and a common nature grounded in the "image of God"; second, a vision of the redemption that will encompass all mankind: "For then I will turn to the peoples a pure language that they may call upon the name of the Lord to serve Him with one consent."[33]

The Problem Of The Re'ah

Some scholars have questioned the validity of the assertion that Jewish morality is indeed universal. Examining the pivotal passage in Leviticus, "And ye shall love thy neighbor [re'akha] as thyself," they ask,

"What does the Bible mean by 'neighbor' and how has the term been understood in Jewish tradition?"[34] An analysis of the biblical use of the term turns out to be inconclusive.[35] It appears that the term *re'ah* is sometimes used in contexts that clearly include non-Jews as well as Jews, while in other places the reference appears to be Jews only. More important, however, is the understanding developed in rabbinic tradition. In regard to a number of crucial laws, rabbinic tradition does restrict the meaning of *re'ah* to Jews only.

> And if one man's ox hurt the ox of his *neighbor* [*re'ehu*] . . .[36]

> And if a man came presumptuously upon his neighbor to slay him with guile . . .[37]

> . . . neither shall thou stand idly by the blood of thy *neighbor* [*re'akha*].[38]

> . . . and thou shalt love thy *neighbor* as thyself.[39]

Rabbinic interpretation as found in the Talmud and the Midrash Halakhah and in the codes understands these laws as referring only to those who were truly "thy neighbors" or "fellows"; i.e., one's fellow Jews.[40]

Does the existence of such restrictions on these moral rules disprove the universality of Jewish morality? To put it even stronger: Doesn't such apparently discriminatory treatment of non-Jews show Jewish morality to be seriously flawed? Before we turn to these specific passages and their rabbinic interpretations, let us examine the Torah for other expressions regarding behavior toward non-Jews.

We find, for example: "Thou shalt not abhor an Edomite, for he is thy brother; thou shalt not abhor a Mizri [Egyptian], because thou wast a stranger in his land."[41] In regard to the runaway slave the Torah teaches: "Thou shalt not deliver unto his master a bondsman that is escaped from his master unto thee. He shall dwell with thee, in the midst of thee, in the place which he shall choose within one of thy gates, where it liketh him best; thou shall not wrong him."[42] Jewish tradition understood this to apply even to a Canaanite slave who has fled from his Jewish master and seeks refuge with Jews in the land of Israel.

In outlining the relationship between employer and employee the

Torah states: "Thou shalt not oppress a hired servant that is poor and needy, whether he be of thy brethren or of the strangers that are in thy land within thy gates. In the same day thou shalt give him his hire."[43] The rabbis interpreted "stranger" here to mean *ger toshav,* the resident alien who has not converted to Judaism but has rejected idolatry. Maimonides, basing himself on the Talmud, rules that it is forbidden to steal from an idolator as well as from a Jew.[44] And Samuel teaches in the Talmud that it is forbidden to deceive any human being (*genevat da'at*—where no monetary loss is involved), even an idolator.[45]

To support the physical needs of a non-Jew in Israel was seen by the Torah as a Jewish obligation: "And if thy brother be waxen poor, and his means fail with thee, then thou shalt uphold him; whether a stranger or a settler shall he live with thee."[46]

The right of the non-Jew in Israel, even of the idolator, to purchase and own a Jewish slave is clearly reflected in the rabbinic interpretation of Leviticus 25:47.[47]

It remained, however, for the rabbis to make explicit the teachings embodied in the Torah's concept of man and to declare that the law of love applied to the non-Jew as well.

> Hillel said, "Be of the disciples of Aaron . . . loving thy fellow creatures [*beriyot*]."[48]

> Rabbi Joshua said, ". . . hatred of his fellow creatures drives a man out of the world."[49]

> Ben Zoma said, ". . . who is worthy of honor? He who respects his fellow creatures."[50]

> Abbaye said, ". . . man should be inventive in ways of fearing God, should be gentle of speech, should control his wrath, and promote peaceable intercourse with his brethren, with his friends, and with all men, and with even the non-Jew in the market place, in order that he may be loved above and below and be acceptable to all creatures."[51]

And in the eyes of God:

> "This is the gate of the Lord into which the righteous shall enter": not priests, Levites, or Israelites, but the righteous, though they be non-Jews.[52]

"This is the law . . . according to which *man* shall live"—man, not priest or Levite; the inference is drawn that the non-Jew, if he obeys the law, "is equal to the High Priest."[53]

The pious of all nations have a share in the world-to-come.[54]

And as the great kabbalist Rabbi Chayim Vital pointed out: "Know that love of mankind applies even to non-Jews, for it is incumbent upon one to love all of mankind, created in the image, as it is written, 'Man is beloved, because he was created in the image of God.' "[55]

Since the Torah in Genesis had already established that all men were created in God's image, and therefore that all men are moral agents and entitled to be treated as ends in themselves, it would follow that any moral rule applies to all human beings, Jews and non-Jews alike. The question that arises, therefore, is why the Torah in several of its commandments of a moral character uses ambiguous terminology (such as *re'ah*), leading the rabbis in their interpretation to restrict the application to Jews. Since we assume the unitary character of the Torah, self-contradiction prevents us from accepting any explanation suggesting an intrinsic disability in the non-Jew. We must therefore look for considerations growing out of the requirements of the general welfare or moral factors arising from the special circumstances of the particular law.

We must remind ourselves that whatever else the Torah is, it must be viewed first and foremost as a practical constitution for a particular society of living men and women at a given point in time and place. In a word, the Pentateuch must be seen within a specific historical context. The Jewish generation that received the Torah found themselves surrounded by barbaric idolaters who lacked the basic structures of law and morality. Indeed, the Sinaitic covenant, which creates a special faith-community and whose blueprint is the Torah law, was necessitated by a serious regression on the part of humanity. Reflected in the Torah, therefore, are special obligations that one has to one's own countrymen and co-religionists even as one has special obligations to members of one's own family. Given the specific historical situation to which the Mosaic code addressed itself, priority had to be given to developing cooperating, loving relationships among Jews themselves, and to overcome tribal and other parochial differences before the law of love could be realistically advocated for the non-Jew.

Furthermore, given the usual state of politics and relations with the nations on one's borders, advocacy of the law of love to all men would have inevitably included the avowed enemies of one's people. But justice as well as prudence requires that one not jeopardize the security and welfare of one's family and neighbors by embracing the enemies of one's people. Love, like any other moral principle, is not absolute and is context-dependent. For Judaism, Jewish peoplehood and the reality that is Jewish society are also positive values. In the historical context in which the Torah was promulgated, it was moral as well as wise to urge the Israelites "to love thy neighbor [re'akha] as thyself."[56] Indeed, any just moral system is predicated on a measure of reciprocity which is a realistic expectation if all individuals within the group accept the system as normative or are under equal obligation to comply. But if the Torah were, for example, to command Jews to lend money without interest to non-Jews as well as Jews and to cancel in the Sabbatical years all debts to non-Jews as well as Jews,[57] without any means of securing reciprocal treatment from non-Jews, a manifestly unjust situation would have been created. The high moral standard, therefore, was best restricted, at least initially, to the faith-community of Israel, to which the Torah was directed.[58]

Let us return now to a consideration of the specific laws mentioned above which are restricted to one's re'ah. Maimonides, following the lead of the Babylonian and Jerusalem Talmuds, explores the Mishnah's restrictive interpretation of Exodus 21:35 by pointing to the asocial behavior of the Canaanites of old. The extra payment that the Canaanite is obliged to make in the case of his ox doing damage is to be understood as a punitive measure to impress upon him the need to better restrain his animals.[59] However, as was already noted by the commentators in the Talmud, the implication here is that a non-Jew who observes the basic humanitarian Noahide laws ought to be treated the same as the Jew.[60] This received its fullest expression much later when Rabbi Menachem ha-Meiri, in the late 13th century, ruled that "nations who are disciplined by the ways of religion (such as contemporary Christians) are not to be considered idolaters and are to be considered 'your brother.'"[61]

Similarly, in connection with Exodus 21:14, the Talmud was astonished to think that the Torah would exclude the non-Jew from the law

which condemns to death a man who deliberately murders his neighbor. After all, even before the Sinai legislation, the Torah had proclaimed, "Whosoever sheddeth man's blood, by man shall his blood
be shed; for in the image of God made He man."[62] But here again the
rabbis explained that without a doubt he who deliberately kills any
human being has violated the sixth commandment and would be duly
punished by heaven. In restricting this particular law the rabbis were
responding to the general hermeneutical principle that whenever the
text permits, interpretations tending to limit the area in which the
death penalty might apply are to be favored.[63]

In interpreting the command "Thou shalt not stand idly by the
blood of thy neighbor [re'ekha],"[64] Maimonides does indeed exclude
persistently sinful Jews and idolaters, with the explanation that "none
of these is 'thy neighbor.'"[65] What is involved here is the obligation to
place oneself in a situation of *safek sakana*; i.e., to risk possible death in
order to save one's friend (*re'a*) from certain death. But perhaps such a
costly effort should be reserved only for those who are in some sense
deserving. Once the criterion shifts to one of desert, one can argue that
deserving non-Jews ought to be included. Indeed, Nachmanides, basing himself on Leviticus 25:35, rules that "We are commanded to safeguard the life of a *ger toshav,* to save him from evil such that if he is
drowning or has been buried under a heap or is sick, we are obliged to
exert all of our strength to save him, or if his life is in danger we might
violate the Sabbath to save him."[66]

In regard to Leviticus 19:18 we have two related approaches in
explaining why it is restricted to *re'akha*—"your neighbor." We have
not as yet attempted to clarify the precise meaning of this commandment in terms of what it actually requires of the individual. What is it
to "love your neighbor as yourself?" It certainly includes various positive acts of benevolence, such as providing for one's neighbor's basic
needs. We will put aside for later consideration the question whether
this commandment means that every obligation to the "other" takes
precedence over or is equal to providing for our own needs. The law
"to love," however, seems to call for a strong emotional identification
with the *re'ah,* involving empathy for the joys and tragedies, successes
and failures, of one's neighbor. But if this is the case, it would seem
reasonable to expect the recipient of such love to be worthy in some

sense. For such emotional identification would seem to go beyond the requirements of the basic respect and justice that are to be accorded all men. One would expect the individual with whom one identifies to reflect not only the minumum in terms of human qualities but some degree of achievement toward the normative and ideal. It is perhaps for this reason that Maimonides, following the rabbis, restricts this law not only to Jews but to "he who is your *re'ah* in Torah and observance of the *mitzvot*."

It would follow, therefore, that in the category of non-Jews or "son of Noah," one who is observant of *his* commandments—i.e., the seven Noahide laws—also comes under the same law of love.[67]

A somewhat different approach, articulated by Rabbi Aaron Soloveitchik, argues that "and thou shalt love thy neighbor as thyself," because it is associated with the commandment "You shall severely rebuke your neighbor" and "You shall not take vengeance nor bear any grudge against the children of your people," constitutes a degree of mutual responsibility (*arevut*) and unconditional emotional love which is appropriate only between the members of the faith-community of Israel. The love that we are required to have toward all men, *ahavat ha-briyot,* is a moral, intellectual love springing from an objective view of the person loved. Referring to the historical reality and the requirements of justice, Rabbi Soloveitchik notes, "Blind love for non-Jews (in the sense described above) would be suicidal for the Jews themselves."[68]

We conclude, therefore, that the morality of Judaism, viewed in its totality and in its theoretical structure, is universal. Its initial halakhic expression, however, is fixed in a historic national framework, and this is sometimes reflected in certain restrictive interpretations.

Yechezkel Kaufmann arrives at a similar conclusion:

> The fact is that the plain meaning of "neighbor" or "brother" in the Bible is Israelite. The law of Leviticus 19:18 was given to and framed for Israelite society. It is not a theoretical maxim, but a practical law. It demands that every man show compassion toward those among whom he lives, and help them; and the Israelite lived among Israelites.

> However, there is no reason to suppose that the Bible intended to exclude other peoples from the basic law of love. That it embraced non-Israelites too is clear from the injunction to love the alien (Lev. 19:34); the *gēr* of

the Bible does not necessarily adopt the Israelite religion; note the ground of the law: "for you were *gērīm* [surely not proselytes!] in the land of Egypt". Any alien who lived within Israelite society, then, came under the law of love.[69]

Several writers have suggested that the well-known discussion between Rabbi Akiva and Ben Azzai should be read in the light of the above problem.

> Rabbi Akiva says, "'Thou shalt love thy neighbor as thyself' is a great principle in the Torah." Ben Azzai says, "There is an even greater principle and that is: 'This is the book of the generations of Adam. In the day that God created man, in the likeness of God made He him; male and female created He them.'"[70]

Perhaps Ben Azzai feared that the passage in Leviticus could be construed as applying to fellow Jews only, which would introduce a misleading restriction. He therefore suggested "an even greater principle," a passage which reiterates the common and divine origins of all men, unmistakably implying the universality of moral obligation.[71]

The Talmud states: "the poor of the gentiles are to be supported together with the poor of Israel, the sick of the gentiles are to be visited together with the sick of Israel, and the dead of the gentiles are to be interred even as we inter the dead of Israel, in order to achieve the 'ways of peace.'"[72] The expression "for the sake of peaceful ways" should not be interpreted as practical but nonmoral advice. For, in fact, this principle iteslf constitutes one of the moral foundations undergirding the entire Torah and the manner in which it is to be interpreted. "The whole Torah exists only for the sake of the ways of peace."[73]

In the codes, it is ruled that the above is an individual and communal obligation even when the needy of the gentiles are not together with the needy of Israel.[74] Maimonides produces as a proof-text for this ruling the passage in Psalms: "The Lord is good to all, and His mercies are upon all His works." In other words, our obligation to be just and benevolent to all men rests on the foundation-stone of all Jewish morality—*imitatio dei*. As God's justice and benevolence are universal, so shall your justice and benevolence be universal.

The following was written by one of the most authoritative rabbinic figures of the last century:

> It is well known that the early as well as the later geonim wrote that we must abide by the law of the land and refrain from dealing unjustly with a non-Jew. . . . Therefore, my brethren, listen to my voice and live. Study in our Torah to love the Almighty and love people regardless of faith or nationality. . . . Follow justice and do righteousness with Jew and non-Jew alike. The people of my community know that I always caution them in my talks and warn them that there is absolutely no difference whether one does evil to a Jew or a non-Jew. It is a well-known fact that when people come to me to settle a dispute, I do not differentiate between Jew and non-Jew. For that is the law according to our holy Torah.[75]

The Talmud relates that when the Almighty announced the first two commandments of the Decalogue, the nations of the world were not impressed and commented that "He is preaching for the sake of His own honor." But when the Almighty added "Respect thy father and mother," they withdrew their criticism and acknowledged all of the commandments.[76] This teaching seems to reflect a demand for the universal in Jewish morality. The respect and regard due God is in origin no different from the respect and regard due to our parents. If the relationship of creature to creator obligates, then a similar obligation exists in connection with the other two partners in the fashioning of man—one's father and mother. If the God who demands man's respect also calls for respect for man's human parents, then it is clear that we are confronted by a moral God and not a deity seeking self-glorification. God, as it were, recognizes the generalization principle.

The Quality Of Inwardness

Another characteristic of Jewish morality becomes manifest when we focus upon the dimension of depth or inwardness. This includes what is sometimes referred to as personal morality. That is to say, Judaism is not merely concerned with actions and their consequences, with overt behavior, but seeks to penetrate the consciousness of the agent and demands good thoughts and attitudes, benevolent intentions and sincere motivation. As the rabbis expressed it: "The Merciful One requires the heart."[77] If confronted by an "either-or" choice between thought and deed, intention and action, Judaism would indeed select the deed over the thought and the consequences over the intent as the prime moral element. This is reflected in the following teachings:

He [Rabbi Chanina ben Dosa] used to say, "He whose deeds exceed his wisdom, his wisdom shall endure; but he whose wisdom exceeds his deeds, his wisdom shall not endure."[78]

Not learning but doing is the chief thing.[79]

The emphasis on deeds is also seen in the phrase which is used most frequently in rabbinic literature to designate moral virtue or the life of piety: *ma'asim tovim*—"good *deeds*." Moral value is to be found in the real world of action and consequences rather than in the amorphous realm of motives and intentions.[80]

Nevertheless, it is equally clear that the perfect moral experience is a total process in which the motivation, the sustained *kavanah* (directed consciousness), is incorporated into the fully executed action. An action subject to moral review differs from ordinary bodily movements precisely in the fact that it involves certain psychological factors described by the words "voluntary," "deliberate," "rule-guided." Hence, the Pentateuch distinguishes the murderer from the accidental homicide, condemning the first to death and providing the second with asylum.[81] The rabbis ruled, however, that good deeds performed out of ulterior motives are acceptable, because the agent, it is hoped, will ultimately learn to develop the proper motives.[82] And while God's forbearance prompts Him to exempt from punishment evil thoughts that are not carried out in action, the high moral demand of Judaism would ideally have us purify our hearts and dispositions as well as our hands.

Under certain circumstances, God credits the good intention even when one is prevented from carrying it out in practice.[83] And "he who sits and refrains from transgressing is rewarded as if he had performed a positive command." This indicates that inaction accompanied either by a struggle in which one overcomes temptation or simply by a conscious will to do what is right is judged to be of equal moral value to the actual deed.[84]

The negative commands of the Torah dealing with human relations attempt to restrain a person from harming or causing any loss to another individual. This includes his life, limbs, possessions, and even his reputation and ego.[85] The range of these rules is indicated on the second table of the Decalogue, which begins with "Thou shalt not murder" and ends with "Thou shalt not covet thy neighbor's house . . . nor anything that is thy neighbor's."[86] But coveting is hardly a crime punishable by a court of law and can hardly be considered something which in itself causes harm to one's neighbor. And indeed, in terms of the Halakhah one violates this commandment only when some particular action follows upon the "coveting." Yet Judaism, wished to penetrate to the root of the evil and in the process revealed the profound depth of its moral sensitivity. The Pentateuch, in declaring, "Thou shalt not covet" and "Thou shalt not desire," teaches us that to cast an envious eye on the possessions of our neighbor is already to cross the line between mine and thine.[87] But even if it does not bother my neighbor, Judaism would have us rid ourselves of such feelings because their very presence within a human being is destructive of human personality and pollutes the self. "Rabbi Eleazar ha-Kappar said, 'Envy, desire, and ambition drive a man out of the world,'[88] and the rabbis noted that there is a sense in which "thinking about transgressions is worse than the transgression itself."[89]

Similarly, the positive commands which reflect my obligations to my neighbor, ". . . and that thy brother may live with thee," implying that I must do all to make it practically possible for my brother to live, reach all the way to "Love thy neighbor as thyself."[90] Here too the range is from the level of deeds to the depth of the inner man; your feelings and his psychological needs.

In regard to the ritual laws, the rabbis taught that the deed was all-important, with only a minimal requirement in terms of the intent.[91] Indeed, particular virtue was seen in an act of compliance with ritual law where the natural inclinations of the agent were in direct opposition. The struggle itself and the decision to obey God are more important than the development of a disposition that would either desire or abhor the substance or the particular action (e.g., nonkosher food). We find the teaching: "Let not a person say, 'I find it impossible to eat the flesh of swine,' but rather, 'I find it very possible, what shall I do when my Father in heaven has prohibited it?'"[92] It was in regard to situations such as this that Rabbi Gamaliel taught: "Nullify thy will before His will."[93] Precisely because of the instrumental nature of the ritual commands did the rabbis find it possible to state that "a transgression for the sake of heaven is as valued as a *mitzvah* that is not performed for the sake of heaven."[94] The strong positive motivation of a Jael can overcome the negative character of the deed.

However, in respect to moral rules, we find little reason to distinguish between the relevance and importance of attitudes and intentions on the one hand and of actions and consequences on the other. This is because, first, actions subject to moral judgments must be seen as the actions of a certain individual person who is the responsible author. They are *his* actions. But since a person is not only a physical organism to whom actions can be attributed on the basis of mechanical causation, but a willing, feeling, and intending agent, it is necessary that psychological facts be included in the judgment. Second, in the Jewish view, this area of the inner man is as much the subject of morality as the public realm of act and deed. Therefore, inner experiences, such as intentions and motives, feelings and emotions, and inner structures, such as attitudes and dispositions, are to be viewed not only as aspects of action but as bona fide human experiences having moral significance in their own right. It is for this reason that Maimonides asserts in regard to moral issues that the individual who no longer has to struggle against recalcitrant desires but has trained his entire being to yearn only for the just and the good and the righteous is morally superior.[95] In regard to such situations Rabbi Gamaliel advised: "Do His will as if it were thy will."[96]

The rabbinic scheme of classification identifies a group of commandments called *lav she'ein ba ma'aseh,* negative prohibitions not involving action. Included in this category are commandments involving thoughts—remembering or forgetting, speech, hearing, sight, or simply acts of omission. These commandments are considered more stringent than those involving action.[97] Some of them refer to basic attitudes affecting our relationship to God:

> Guard yourself lest you forget . . .
>
> Do not say in your heart . . .
>
> Do not fear them . . .[98]

In the moral sphere we have the following: "You shall surely give him, and let not your heart feel badly when you give it to him."[99] Even when the proper deed is being performed and you are making a contribution to the poor, do it with a cheerful mien and a generous spirit. This demonstrates the point made earlier that the personal attitudes of the agent are of moral significance. Consider also:

> If there be among you a needy man . . . thou shalt not harden thy heart, nor shut thy hand . . .
>
> Thou shalt not take vengeance, nor bear any grudge against the children of thy people.[100]

The rabbis interpreted this to mean that a person is in violation of this prohibition if, for example, he responds positively to a request for a loan but says, "I am lending you my snow shovel because I am not like you, who, if you recall, refused to lend me yours when I asked for it last winter."[101] What is immoral is not merely making the statement but carrying the grudge. "Do not despise your brother in your heart."[102] Thinking evil was considered transgression even when it was not accompanied by specific plans or intent to act out the thought. This is seen in the following passages:

> When thou goest forth in camp . . . then thou shall keep thee from every evil thing [davar ra, lit.[102] "words" or "thought"].[103]
>
> And ye shall not go about after your own heart and after your own eyes, after which you used to go astray.[104]
>
> There are six things which the Lord hateth . . . a heart that deviseth wicked thoughts.[105]

The moral rules involving speech are many and complex and will be treated in a separate section.

Some of the Torah's severest condemnations were reserved for acts of omission—for that insidious moral paralysis which seems to infect people and stops them from stretching forth a helping hand or saying a kind word or picking up the lost object.

> Beware that there be not a base thought in thy heart.[106]

> Do not shut thy hand.[107]

> Thou shalt not see thy brother's ox driven away and hide thyself from them. . . . Thou mayest not hide thyself.[108]

Thus the individual who refuses a loan to a needy person is guilty of violating two commandments: (1) the transgression of omission, of not lending, and (2) the transgression of hardening one's heart.

Jewish moralists have been quick to point out, in considering our ongoing obligation to rescue the lives and property of others when they are in danger,[109] that we must train ourselves to make quick and effective responses to new situations and must develop ability to make realistic judgments as to what is possible.

Rabbi Jonah Gerondi makes this important practical suggestion:

> It is good and very proper that there be in every community volunteers consisting of intelligent people who should be prepared and equipped for all means of rescue work [hatzalah] in the event that any man or woman be in trouble. For behold, we are obligated to bestir ourselves for the lost ox or sheep of our neighbor and mind it until the owner claims it, how much more should we be prepared to work for the well-being of their owners themselves. As the prophet Isaiah says: ". . . bring the poor that are cast out to thy house."[110]

This extension of moral concerns in the Torah from the external public area of deeds to the subjective realm of the inner self takes us from the area of intersubjective human relationships to the area of personal morality. We have already indicated that the rabbis developed their insights on personal morality in the midrashic literature and particularly in the Mishnah tractate *Avot,* where they attempted to lay down guidelines for personality development by identifying good and bad attitudes and emotions.

> Rabbi Yochanan ben Zakkai asked his students, "go forth and see which is the good way to which a man should cleave." . . . Rabbi Eliezer said, "A good eye [kindly, free from envy]." Rabbi Eleazar said, "A good heart [unselfish love]."[111]
>
> Rabbi Eliezer said, ". . . be not easily moved to anger."[112]
>
> Rabbi Joshua said, "The evil eye, the evil inclination, and hatred of his fellow creatures drives a man out of the world."[113]
>
> Rabbi Levitas of Yavneh said, "Be exceedingly lowly of spirit . . ."[114]

The insight that the most important fortress that must be won for God is the inner citadel—the heart of man—was perceived by psalmist and sage and reiterated by the rabbis.

> Create me a clean heart, O God, and renew a steadfast spirit within me.[115]
>
> Who will ascend the mountain of the Lord? Those clean of hands and pure of heart.[116]
>
> Above all that thou guardest, keep thy heart, for out of it are the issues of life.[117]
>
> Thereupon Rabbi Yochanan ben Zakkai said to them, "I approve the words of Eleazar ben Arakh rather than your words, for in his words ['a good heart'] yours are included."[118]

The rabbis recognized quite clearly that certain character traits were basic and crucial in their influence upon the overall personality and behavior patterns of people. One such set of opposing traits is humility (*anavah*) and pride (*ga'avah*).

The Torah had already warned against pride and arrogance: ". . . lest thy heart be lifted up, and thou forget the Lord thy God,"[119] and "Everyone that is proud in heart is an abomination to the Lord."[120] The Rabbis made the judgement, on the basis of both Scripture and their own experience, that the most important single virtue

was humility, and conversely that the severest vice was pride, haughti-
ness, or arrogance.[121] Nor only was humility or meekness seen as a key
quality in achieving a proper relationship to God, a necessary condition for prophecy and for acquiring Torah knowledge, but it was considered a prerequisite for attaining a moral relationship with one's fellow creatures.[122]

According to an early work on Jewish morality, "Humility as a
mental attitude requires that a person reflect and become convinced
that he is not worthy of praise or honors, certainly that he is not
superior to his fellow creatures."[123] The opposite trait, arrogance, consists of a person attributing importance to himself for any one of a
number of possible reasons, such as his intelligence or accomplishments or beauty or distinguished lineage or material wealth.[124] This
leads him to believe that he is entitled to special privileges and honors
more so than his fellow creatures. Such an individual will find it difficult to fulfill the law of love—"Love thy neighbor as thyself"—since he
believes himself to be superior and therefore entitled to preferential
treatment.

These basic attitudes have direct and immediate expression in
terms of a person's speech (respectful and modulated tones), gait and
carriage (purposeful but unhurried), dress (modest and conservative),
and other activities, with consequences for all of his relationships with
others.[125] Thus the rabbis taught: "A person's conversation should
always be with courtesy and dignity toward others."[126] His posture
should reflect dignity and humility, and "he should not demand or
take for himself places of honor."

The insidiousness of arrogance was seen in the fact that it both
encouraged and fed upon other undesirable character traits. Whether a
person has a propensity toward anger, for example, or readily
acknowledges his mistakes, or is willing to forgive those who wronged
him is probably related to his arrogance/meekness quotient. Morover,
an egotistical person, once he is convinced of his own worth, will be
more prone to self-indulgence—catering to desires and caprices that
might lead to immorality. The rabbis cautioned against treating this
aspect of morality as merely a matter of learned behavior, of exterior
mores and manners. Acquiring a polite and decorous exterior might
hide a self-inflated pride or arrogance, but it would simply be a

means of inviting deception and cultivating hypocrisy. One's exterior must coincide with the interior, the appearance with the reality. And both must give witness to the presence of moral truth.

Maimonides taught that humility was one the exceptions to the doctrine of the mean in that this particular characteristic required that on the behavior range from arrogance to meekness, one should veer drastically to the pole of meekness.[127] In saying this, Maimonides revealed one of the basic differences between the value systems of Greece and Israel. He based himself upon the Torah's description of Moses as "very humble" and upon the rabbinic teaching, ". . . be exceedingly [very, very] lowly of spirit."[128] Yet the rabbis were keenly aware of the fact that there was an irreducible measure of self-regard that a person must retain in order to have a basic sense of self and a minimum of ego-strength. A person who convinced himself that he was full of guilt and completely worthless would be incapable of insisting on his basic rights as a rational creature or on the respect due him as a being created in the image of God. Thus several views were expressed that a student of the Torah should retain a modicum of pride.[129] And in the Bible we find the prophet reminding the first king of Israel, "Though thou be little in thine own sight, are thou not the head of the tribes of Israel?"[130]

A medieval work on *musar* points out that a person must have enough self-respect to maintain the health and cleanliness of his body, wear decent and respectable clothing, and not devalue basic pleasures of life.[131] It is also quite proper to be cognizant and proud of one's good deeds and accomplishments in Torah and to generate the self-esteem necessary to champion the cause of Judaism against its detractors.[132]

A clear difference of opinion developed among later thinkers as to the most effective strategy to be pursued in motivating an individual to reach out for the good and to refrain from doing evil. Some considered that the individual's natural pride and ego must first be shattered. Then, in complete self-abasement and dependence, he must seek out God and rebuild a proper way of life. Others, however, were persuaded that one must first develop enough self-confidence to aspire to greatness. If a man has pride in his achievements to date and confidence in his abilities, he will then be able to mature in both his relationship to God and his relationship to his fellow men.[133] Rabbi Jonah Gerondi begins his *Sha'arei ha-Avodah* with the following words:

> A man must know his own worth and recognize his own abilities and the attributes of his fathers, their greatness, importance, and love in the eyes of the Lord . . . and if he be tempted by desire to go astray . . . he should say to himself, "Is it seemly that a person with my great talents, my unusual attainments, and a son of great and eminent forebears, should contemplate doing something of this sort . . ."[134]

However, this sense of meekness or humility, which seems to be so basic to the concept of "personal morality," introduces a new consideration into the relationship between the self and the other. We suggested earlier that the moral rule "Love thy neighbor as thyself" posits a standard of impartiality and equality between the self and the other. "Do not do to your fellow man what you would not want done to yourself." Nachmanides makes it clear that this rule cannot be a requirement for the individual to become as involved with the other, and as devoted to him, as he is to himself.[135] We all obviously have certain duties to ourselves that take priority. As Rabbi Akiva said, "Thy life is prior to the life of others."[136] What the rule does require is that we cherish the person and property of the other even as we do our own, so that we do not cause any harm to him or damage to his property. The rule further implies that we must be concerned with his needs when it does not necessitate the neglect of our own. It also implies that we should desire for our fellow all that we wish for ourselves and not be envious of him.

If the Law of Love, therefore, leaves room for the self to be favored in certain key respects, the principle of humility leads us in the opposite direction, to favor the other over the self. Thus, the personal attribute of *anavah* becomes, in its behavioral aspect, the mode of *chasidut*. In judging others, I am required to give them the benefit of the doubt and judge them meritoriously, whereas in judging myself I am to be more rigorous, assuming the worst and doubting my capacities. While in regard to myself I am to flee from honor, in regard to the other I am to constantly strive to honor him. For myself I must develop a sense of trust in God and be prepared to look to Him for aid and assistance. In regard to my neighbor, however, I am urged to cultivate a sort of methodological skepticism; an attitude which says, "If I do not help him, no one else will!" A Chasidic rabbi once said that "doubt" was introduced into the world precisely for the sort of situation in which a person in need asks for help. At that moment do not offer the needy person pious hopes, telling him that "God will help" but rather, "doubt," and help him yourself! In estimating the needs of my neighbor I must consider his psychological needs as well as his basic physical needs. Thus if a wealthy friend comes upon hard times and experiences severe anguish over the loss of some of his amenities, I am morally obliged to try to restore them. However, in regard to myself, my sense of humility does not pemit self-indulgence. Personal humility requires that I cultivate an ability "to be happy with one's portion."[137]

Indeed Rabbi Amiel has pointed out that while the moral rules "Thou shalt not murder" or "Thou shalt not steal" are predicated on the principle of justice or impartiality, the rule of "Thou shalt not covet" is not.[138] For, if I truly believe myself to be entitled to all of the goods that my neighbor is blessed with, how can I not but envy and covet "his wife, his house, and all that is his?" We are led to the conclusion that in order to be able to observe the tenth commandment of the Decalogue we must achieve the attribute of humility. I must, in some sense, be prepared to apply a different standard to myself than to others.[139]

This is clearly seen in the following *Mishnah*:

> There are four characters [*middot*] among men. He who says, "What is mine is mine, and what is thine is thine," this is a middle [average, neutral] character [*beinonit*]; some say this is the character of Sodom. He who says, "What is mine is thine, and what is thine is mine," is ignorant [a boor, *am ha-aretz*]. He who says, "What is mine is thine, and what is thine is thine," is a saint [pious, *chasid*]. He who says, "What is thine is mine, and what is mine is mine," is a wicked one."[140]

This *Mishnah* will be given a comprehensive analysis in a later chapter. For now we merely wish to point out that while the *beinonit* follows the conventional mode of justice, "What is thine is thine, and what is mine is mine," the *chasid,* in his humility, adopts an attitude that seems to forfeit his own rights, relinquishing what is rightfully his own in favor of the other.

Speech Morality

Speech occupies a middle ground between thought, volition, and feeling on the one hand, and actions and deeds on the other. In comparison to the latter, verbal expression is often downgraded as "mere words" *millim b'alma,* and a person might be criticized for being "all talk and no follow-through." Speech does not appear to have the same direct impact upon one's environment as do actions. Words seem to evaporate into the air, leaving no trace. In ordinary circumstances, therefore, people are not prone to exercise the same degree of control over their speech as they do over their actions. And while the basic process of socialization insists that we learn that "there is a time to be silent and a time to speak," it is not concerned to teach us to be selective in what we speak.

Yet words are not merely sounds but vehicles of meaning, and the dramatic impact they sometimes have is due not to the sound waves they generate but to their significance as symbols. Words carry a message and are closely linked to consciousness. Speech expresses most directly our thoughts and our intentions—the content of our reflective mind. It is therefore most representative and revelatory of the self. In this sense, therefore, words even more than acts are our legitimate offspring, and we are usually obliged to take responsibility for them.

One of the most remarkable features of Jewish morality is its repeated insistence that man is morally responsible for the words he utters—that speech-acts no less than other acts are candidates for moral judgment, and that a moral code must include rules regulating speech. Judaism comes to this conclusion from two different directions.

Both in the Pentateuch and in the books of Psalms and Proverbs we find a profound awareness of the effects both for good and for evil that speech can have in human society. This awareness was further developed by the rabbis. "Death and life are in the power of the tongue."[141] Far from being "mere words," strings of vocables called sentences are projectiles carrying multiple warheads that can destroy at a distance.

Tales carried by one person to another about a third can set brother against brother, arouse hatred and enmity, and poison human relations to a point that can lead to violence and destruction. Although a man's hand can reach only so far, his words can travel to the ends of the earth and can hurt at a distance. "Their tongue is a sharpened arrow it speaketh deceit."[142] The rabbis called this evil *lishan telita'ey* ("the three-way tongue") because "it slays three persons: the speaker, the one spoken to, and the one spoken of."[143]

But over and above the devastating social consequences of evil speech, there is another reason why the rabbis viewed this vice with such horror. Judaism believes the power of speech and the capacity to form language to be a uniquely human property related to man's having been created in the image of God.[144] If the spark of divinity in man is associated with something in his spiritual makeup (mind, self-consciousness, ego, personality, freedom of will), then speech must be seen as that wondrous tool by which man can break out of his isolation, express his thoughts and feelings, and communicate with others. Even God is described as breaking forth into creativity and ultimately into revelation by means of the word: "And the Lord said . . ." What is so heinous about evil speech is that a person takes a priceless and unique gift—the divine-like power of verbal conceptual expression that can be used to build authentic relationships between man and man, and between man and God—and abuses it. The talebearer uses words to destroy relationships and to sow hatred and discord instead of love and understanding. Therefore, just as the study of Torah, which is a speech activity, is as meritorious as all of the other *mitzvot* combined, so too is the sin of slander, also a speech activity, considered as severe as all the other transgressions combined.[145]

While in terms of its immediate consequences, evil speech could be classified as social morality, an analysis of its origins and long-range effects lead one to view it as part of personal morality. The desire and for some the need to engage in *lashon ha-ra* (evil speech) is surely connected with envy and resentment and a sense of insecurity within the person. Appropriately, the rabbis saw the phenomenon of the *metzora* (one stricken with leprosy) as a form of punishment for the sin of slander.[146] But just as the *tzara'at* is an eruption in the skin of a disease which has, perhaps, a deeper source within the body, so is *lashon ha-ra* a verbal expression of the venom of misanthropy. A preoccupation with gossip and talebearing entrenches the poison ever deeper within the person and ultimately destroys him. "Envy, lust, and ambition draw a person out of this world."[147]

The rabbis considered slander to be an evil of exceptional gravity.

There are four offenses for the commission of which punishment is exacted in this world and the capital remains for the world-to-come. They are: idolatry, unchastity, bloodshed, and slander.

Whosoever speaks slander is as though he denied the fundamental principle [existence of God]. The Holy One, blessed be He, says of such a person who speaks slander, "I and he cannot dwell together in the world."[148]

A significant number of rules in the Pentateuch concern themselves with speech morality. Some are quite straightforward:

You shall not lie one to another.

You shall not curse the deaf.

You shall not go up and down as a talebearer among thy people.[149]

Other passages were seen by the rabbis as referring to speech morality. One is required generally to speak the truth. "Keep thee from a false matter."[150]

It is forbidden to issue a false report about another. "If a man take a wife . . . and bring an evil name upon her . . . the elders shall take that man and chastise him."[151] It is also forbidden to receive a false report.[152]

From the passage, "Thou shalt keep thee from every evil thing" [Hebrew *davar,* which can also be read as 'word'], the rabbis concluded that one is forbidden to speak ill of one's fellow even if what is said is true.[153]

The law of love imposes a responsibility upon the Jew not only for his fellow's material well-being but also for his religious development. Should you observe your neighbor doing something wrong you are commanded to rebuke him. However, the utmost caution must be used not to cause him any shame or embarrassment: ". . . thou shalt not hate thy brother in thy heart; thou shalt surely rebuke thy neighbor and not bear sin because of him"; i.e., do not incur any sin in the process of rebuking him.[154]

The command "And ye shall not wrong one another" was interpreted to mean," "wrongdoing through words." Thus, if a person is a penitent, do not say to him: "Remember your past deeds!" If he is a convert, do not say to him: "Remember the deeds of your father!"[155]

The rabbis taught: "A person should be prepared to throw himself into a furnace of fire rather than shame his fellow in public."[156] Indeed, the rabbis observed that if one causes a person to turn pale with embarrassment (because the blood drains from his face), this is a form of "shedding blood" and is, in a sense, tantamount to murder! The rabbis found sources in the Torah against flattery and hypocrisy, against obscene language, and in general urged upon Israel the use of clean, pleasant, and nonabrasive speech.[157]

Evidence of the moral significance of proper speech in Judaism and the far-reaching nature of its consequences is to be found in the fact that according to an authoritative work on the subject, one who engages in immoral speech is in violation of no less than seventeen negative commands and fourteen positive commands.[158]

But there is also a positive aspect to speech morality. For if words can bruise, wound, and even slay, they can also cheer and heal and console. The rabbis urged their disciples to be the first to offer greetings when meeting people and to do so cheerfully.[159] They pointed out that in times of bereavement, concern and sympathy expressed in words are a most potent means of comfort and solace. Anger can be soothed with gentle words, and reconciliation between erstwhile enemies can often be effectuated. Even humor has its proper role, and the rabbis lavished praise upon those who utilized this priceless human capacity to brighten the day and bring a smile to anxious souls.[160]

The rabbis were very much aware of the great difficulty involved in developing control over one's speech in such a manner that one would not violate the moral rules and principles involved. The tendency to blurt out a response under provocation, the ease with which words can be formed, the constant pressure to be "sociable" and to have newsy and witty tidbits to contribute to the conversation (most easily accomplished at the expense of others)—all of these prompted the rabbis to acknowledge that *lashon ha-ra* is one of those transgressions which no one can escape even on a daily basis. And as Rav put it in evaluating the incidence of certain transgressions: "Most with theft, some with sexual immorality, but all with *lashon ha-ra*."[161]

In addition to knowledge of the moral law and sensitivity to the hurt that can be caused by malicious and ill-considered speech, the rabbis counseled a general speech policy that would lean toward reticence and periods of silence.[162]

Man is responsible for his words because speech expresses his thoughts and feelings, and these constitute the very essence of man. This is reflected in the Halakhah. Generally speaking, in order for a transaction to be legally binding in Jewish law, it has to be accompanied by a formal mode of transfer. A verbal agreement is not sufficient. However, the rabbis never lost an opportunity to stress the inviolability of a person's word. One who reneges on a verbal understanding or who does not keep his promise to give a gift is called a *mechusar amanah*,[163] one lacking in trustworthiness. Actually, the entire judicial process pertaining to taking testimony from witnesses was based on trust in a man's word, since an oath was never required of them.

There are, however, areas in Judaism where a verbal utterance creates more than a moral obligation. In the words of Dr. S. Belkin, "there is probably no other legal system in the world which gives the spoken word the legal force it has in Rabbinic law."[164] In contributing to the Temple, a verbal declaration created a legal obligation and effected an immediate transfer.[165] By analogy, some authorities ruled that a simple oral pledge to give charity creates a legal transfer and obligation which can be collected from the person's estate.[166] Another area where the spoken word alone is effective is in the process called *hefker,* by which a person can renounce ownership over his property. Of course, the Torah itself had already described the institution of vows and oaths by which a person, by uttering the proper verbal formula of the *neder* (oath), can prohibit himself from benefitting from various objects, including his own property. This self-created prohibition, generated by words, carried with it the full sanctity and authority of the Halakhah: "When a man taketh a vow or sweareth an oath, to bind his soul with a bond, he shall not break his word, he shall do according to all that proceedeth out of his mouth."[167]

"Man And Beast Thou Preservest, O Lord"

The Torah's concern for animals, reflected in many specific laws in the Pentateuch, can be seen as an expression of both the universality of Jewish morality and its quality of depth. If undeserved and unnecessary pain is evil, then it should make no difference whether those suffering are human beings or animals. Common sense tells us that animals are sentient beings subject to the same physical pain that we human beings are subject to and perhaps to certain forms of psychological stress as well. It follows, therefore, that human beings are morally obliged to refrain from any act that might cause pain or discomfort to animals, have a positive obligation to relieve animals of pain, and carry a responsibility to provide for the needs of the animals that come within their orbit. Even as God's mercy and goodness extend to all creatures, so must man's. "The Lord is good to all, and His tender mercies are over all His works"; therefore, "A righteous man regardeth the life of his beast."[168]

Animals are a form of life, and life in all of its forms, plant and animal as well as human, is a source of value. The "living God" points man in the direction of value and bids him: ". . . and ye shall choose life!" In the course of creation, animals received a special blessing from God, and after the deluge, God established His covenant specifically with them.[169] The psalmist praises God for His concern for the beast: "He giveth to the beast his food, and to the young ravens which cry."[170] This is in no way in conflict with the principle implicit in the Torah that man is the ultimate purpose of creation and that the lower forms serve man in certain specified but regulated ways.

Judaism's concern for animals is prompted not only by moral regard for the beast per se but also by consideration of the consequences of tender concern for animals and of cruelty toward animals for the personality of man as a moral agent. Here we are again involved in the dimension of depth and the area of personal morality. The human self is a unitary entity whose attitudes and dispositions bring about actions and are in turn shaped by actions. To cultivate the moral traits of mercy and kindness requires a total transformation of the self, with no residual pockets of meanness or callousness. This can best be exemplified by the astonishing story told about Rabbi Judah the Prince:

> Rabbi Judah was sitting and studying the Torah in front of the Babylonian synagogue in Sepphoris, when a calf passed before him on its way to the slaughter and began to cry out as though pleading, "Save me!" Said he to it, "What can I do for you? For this you were created." As a punishment for his heartlessness, he suffered toothache for thirteen years. One day, a weasel ran past his daughter, who was about to kill it, when he said to her, "My daughter, let it be, for it is written, 'and his tender mercies are over all His works.'" Because the rabbi prevented an act of cruelty, he was once again restored to health.[171]

At first glance this talmudic teaching has disturbing implications. Are we to infer from it that cattle ought not to be slaughtered and that household pests (rodents, insects) ought not to be killed? This very question was asked of one of the Geonim, who responded by saying that creatures that are not harmful ought not to be killed. In regard to the calf on its way to slaughter, the Gaon wrote that the act of slaughtering for food is entirely lawful and moral, but in the unusual situation of Rabbi Judah, where to the rabbi and bystanders the behavior of the animal had all the appearance and the dramatic quality of a personal plea for intercession and succor, the appeal should not have been ignored. Rabbi Judah was punished because, instead of rationalizing the situation and stifling his emotions, he should have indulged his feelings of compassion so as to at least delay the slaughter for a few days. "Those who saw Rebbe [Rabbi Judah] surrender the animal and took no pity on it, despite its seeking protection, would become hardhearted in their relations both to man and beast."[172]

This incident beautifully portrays the moral sensitivity of Judaism to the question of the care and treatment of animals. Within the context of the dependent relationship of animals and their subservience to man, man must concern himself not only with the pain and needs of the animal but also with the consequence of this relationship upon his own character and personality.

In considering the implications of Torah legislation concerning animals, Jewish tradition concluded that *Tza'ar ba'alei chayyim de-*

oraita—the prevention of suffering by animals is a biblical law.[173] As such, the Halakhah permitted certain forms of assistance to animals in distress on the Sabbath even though the measures involved were forbidden by rabbinic ordinance. The reason given was, of course, that biblical law supercedes rabbinic law.[174] The rabbis pointed in particular to the following laws in the Pentateuch:

> If thou see the ass of him that hateth thee lying under its burden, thou shalt forbear to pass by him; thou shalt surely release it with him.[175]

> Thou shalt not see thy brother's ass or his ox fallen down by the way and hide thyself from them; thou shalt surely help him to lift them up again.[176]

Not only is it forbidden to directly inflict pain upon an animal but if you come upon an animal in distress due to its owner's greed or stupidity, even if the owner be your enemy, you are morally obliged by the Torah to come forward and become involved in bringing relief to the beast. Helping to reload the animal ("Thou shalt surely help him to lift them up again") is also of benefit to the beast as the load should be more evenly distributed. A code of Jewish law bids the Jew to take measures early to prevent possible mistreatment of animals:

> If horses are pulling a wagon and they come to a bad spot or to a steep mountain and they cannot go on without help, one is bound to help, even where the driver is a non-Jew, in order to avoid pain to living things, lest the driver beat them excessively to make them pull beyond their strength.[177]

Over and beyond the prevention of outright physical pain, certain commands in the Torah regarding animals seem to be concerned about more subtle forms of stress and discomfort. Thus in connection with the laws of sacrifices we read: "When a bullock or a sheep or a goat is brought forth, then it should be seven days under the dam; from the eighth day and thenceforth it may be accepted for an offering."[178] Although different reasons can be found for this law, the Midrash perceived in it a further manifestation of God's mercy.[179] An animal's tenderness and concern for its offspring has long been an admired object of simple observation. To cause an immediate separation between the offspring and the mother, thus interrupting the nursing process, is to cause cruel and unnecessary pain.

Related to this law is the command: "And whether it be cow or ewe, ye shall not kill it and its young both in one day."[180] Maimonides explains that the purpose of this prohibition is:

> in order that people should be restrained and prevented from killing the two together in such a manner that the young is slain in the sight of the mother; for the pain of the animals under such circumstances is very great. There is no difference in this case between the pain of men and the pain of other living beings, since the love and tenderness of the mother for her young ones is not produced by reasoning but by imagination, and this faculty exists not only in men but in most living beings.[181]

Since the Torah is sensitive to the parent-offspring relationship among animals, it is not surprising that it is also concerned about the birds. Our ordinary observation amply attests to the remarkable tenderness with which the mother bird attends to her brood. And so indeed we have the unusual command in the Pentateuch:

> If a bird's nest chance to be before thee in the way, in any tree or on the ground with young ones or eggs, and the dam sitting upon the young; thou shalt in any wise let the dam go, but the young thou mayest take unto thyself, that it may be well with thee . . .[182]

Thus the Torah permits the young to be taken only after the mother has been sent away so as not to perceive what is happening. Maimonides again explains the law in humanitarian terms:

> When the mother is sent away she does not see the taking of her young ones and does not feel any pain. In most cases, however, the commandment will cause man to leave the whole nest untouched because the eggs and the young are as a rule unfit for food. If the law provides that such grief should not be caused to cattle or birds, how much more careful must we be that we should not cause grief to our fellow men.[183]

Still another set of laws in the Torah reveal an even more remarkable sensitivity to the feeling of animals.

Thou shalt not muzzle the ox when he treadeth out the corn.[184]

Thou shalt not plow with an ox and an ass together.[185]

Obviously the point of the first law is not merely to remind the owner of the ox that he has an obligation to feed his animal. In the special circumstances brought about by the work being done for the owner, the ox is surrounded by food. Having aroused the animal's desire for food, it would be cruel to frustrate that desire by muzzling the ox as it works amidst the corn. The rabbis rightfully connected this law with the command to the employer regarding his hired servant: ". . . in the same day shalt thou give him his hire."[186] The owner who muzzles his ox during the threshing may have every intention of generously feeding the animal after the threshing. The Torah, however, would condemn the timing. Justice and righteousness require that the ox be permitted to eat now during the threshing rather than later. Similarly, there is something appropriate about paying one's worker immediately after his work is done, as it is his by right. The rabbis broadened the principle of "muzzling" to include any number of situations wherein the owner is responsible for removing any hindrance or obstacle which frustrates the animal and impedes his feeding.[187]

The Pentateuch itself does not give any reason for the prohibition against plowing with an ox and ass together. Conceivably it belongs to the group of laws which oppose the mixing of diverse kinds, as we have in connection with sha'atnez and kelayim.[188] Indeed, Maimonides sees the prohibition against working animals of two different species together as a preventive against their having intercourse.[189] It is more likely, however, that the reason for this law is the general principle of tza'ar ba'alei chayyim: the prevention of pain to animals. For an animal to have to live or work together with others not of its own species is in itself a source of uneasiness and anxiety. Or as Ibn Ezra points out, yoking two animals of unequal strength together is to certainly cause pain to the weaker animal and frustration to the stronger one.[190]

In declaring the Sabbath to be a day of rest, the Torah included not only "thou, thy son, thy daughter, thy man and woman servants" but also "thy cattle."[191] Not being a moral agent, the animal obviously was not "commanded" and therefore cannot be said to have an obligation to rest on the Sabbath. Instead the Jew is instructed to have his animal rest. The Halakhah fully developed this aspect along with all the other Sabbath laws, stipulating in great detail what might be considered a "burden" that the animal is forbidden to carry, and what is a part of its accepted equipment. The principle was very clearly accepted that having the animal rest on the Sabbath was not merely to ensure the owner's rest but was an end to be pursued for its own sake. This Sabbath law must be considered in conjunction with the exemptions in the Sabbath restrictions mentioned earlier in order to alleviate *tza'ar ba'alei chayyim*. Together, they spell out the Torah's understanding of the relationship between man and animal and their roles as creatures of God. God has created a universe which is good. The living God, the God of all life, brought into existence many forms of life. During the same period of creation (on the sixth day) the beasts and the birds preceded man into existence and were blessed, and a covenant was entered into which implies a commitment by the Creator to sustain and preserve His creatures. For thousands of years, man and the domesticated beast lived and worked closely together. For much of his food, clothing, work, and transportation man depended upon the beast. Although subservient to man, the beast, as a sentient, mobile form of life, is a source of value and has rights.[192] Man, as a moral agent, has the obligation in all of his many dealings with animals to "do them good and not evil"; therefore, rabbinic ordinances on the Sabbath must give way to this biblical imperative. The observance of the Sabbath, however, is the collective testimony of the Jewish people bearing witness to God as the one and only creator and to the universe as the work of His hands. Not only must the Jew, therefore, cease from his labors, but the animal as the junior partner in the work and toil which builds society, must also rest. The animal as well as man has a share in the cosmic drama in which "the breath of all that lives shall praise Thy name, O Lord our God."

From the following passage, the rabbis inferred that a man must first feed his animals and then himself: "And I will give grass in thy fields for thy cattle, and thou shalt eat and be satisfied."[193] The authorities have pointed to the biblical story of Rebecca, where it appears that where drink is involved, man comes before the beast. For Rebecca said, "Drink, and then I will also give your camels to drink."[194] Rabbi Jacob Emden was once asked whether the priority to feed one's domestic animals applied to pet dogs and cats as well? In an interesting responsum he argued that since dogs and cats (in his day) seem to enjoy a certain independence of movement and can forage for themselves, the full obligation of the law to feed animals first may not apply to them as it does for farm animals. Nevertheless, he concludes, "one who wishes a righteous act should first feed his dog and cat before partaking of food himself."[195]

In some instances the Pentateuch prescribes the death sentence for animals. Thus we read: "If an ox gore a man or a woman that they die, the ox shall surely be stoned and its flesh shall not be eaten."[196] This, of course, should not be interpreted as retribution or punishment, but as the removal of a man-killer so as to prevent a recurrence of the tragedy. Indeed, rabbinic interpretation held that the animal could be executed only where it could be shown before a duly constituted court that the animal had killed intentionally.[197] Thus Judaism insisted that animals be treated with justice as well as with compassion.

More difficult to explain, however, is the following law: "If a man lie with a beast, he shall surely be put to death, and ye shall slay the beast."[198]. Already, the Mishnah asked, "True, the man has sinned, but wherein has the animal offended?" Perhaps the most acceptable explanation is one offered by the rabbis: "Scripture ordered that it should be stoned so that the animal should not pass through the streets whilst people say, 'This is the animal on account of which so-and-so was stoned.'"[199] That is to say, if the unfortunate beast is permitted to remain in the community, it serves as a constant reminder of the ugly incident, with its implied shame and indignity for man.

It is evident from the laws just reviewed that the primary apprehension of the Torah was that man, in continuous interaction with the beast as a defenseless source of food and energy, would in his greed tend to exploit the animal, overwork it, beat it in anger, and generally mistreat it. Another area to which the rabbis extended this concern was man's utilization of the beast as a source of sport and entertainment. Thus they castigated those who hunt beasts with the aid of bloodhounds and who attend the stadium as "sitting in the seat of the scornful."[200] In a revealing passage Josephus, the first-century Jewish historian, describes the attitudes of his countrymen.

Herod also got together a great quantity of wild beasts and of lions in very great abundance and of such other beasts as were either of uncommon strength or were of such a sort that were rarely seen. These were trained either to fight with one another or with men, who were condemned to death. And truly, foreigners were greatly surprised and delighted . . . but to the Jews it was a palpable breaking up of the customs for which they had so great a veneration.[201]

In a world in which bullfights attract thousands of spectators and cockfighting has its fervent followers, the Jewish concern for animals shines forth as an inspiring instance of the depth of Jewish moral sensitivity. A more recent summation of the Jewish attitude toward hunting is found in a responsum by Rabbi Ezekiel Landau.

Question: I have been favored by God with a large estate consisting of villages and forests, the latter swarming with wild animals. Is it permitted me to hunt these animals as a mere pastime? Will such activity violate the law against perpetrating cruelty to animals?

Answer: Rabbi Moses Isserles in his Responsa has already considered this problem. He showed that the law against cruelty to animals applies in every case except where an animal is killed outright, or killed for a material benefit to man. So much for the legal aspect of the problem. But I am surprised that you were moved to ask such a question. In the Torah the sport of hunting is imputed only to fierce characters like Nimrod and Esau, never to any of the Patriarchs or their descendants. . . . I cannot comprehend how a Jew could ever dream of killing animals merely for the pleasure of hunting when he has no immediate need for the bodies of the creatures. . . . Some have tried to justify the hunting of wild beasts on the ground that they are dangerous to man, basing their view on the dictum of Rabbi Eliezer, "Whoever is early in destroying them does a meritorious act" (Sanhedrin 15b). This option is incorrect. First, because Rabbi Eliezer's view is not accepted; second, because (as Resh Lakish explained) Rabbi Eliezer referred only to animals that have already shown their ferocity toward man. Some have advanced the argument that we may not kill those beasts that have owners, since they are under care and to some extend tamed, but that we may slay ownerless beasts, since they are in a ferocious state liable to do harm—that we may kill them even on the Sabbath. This argument is erroneous, and does not touch our case. We may kill wild animals found in places inhabited by man, where the beasts constitute a menace to man. But it is certainly no act of merit to pursue wild beasts in their haunts. It is rather a lustful occupation.

A distinction is made for the man who makes his livelihood by hunting, and selling the furs and skins of his quarry. His work is proper, for the animal world has been subordinated to man to provide for his needs. A man may take the life of clean animals for food, or unclean animals for their furs and hides. But when the act of killing is prompted by that of sport, it is downright cruelty.[202]

In comparing the attitude of the Torah toward animals with some of the teachings found in other cultures and civilizations, it appears that Judaism "struck a golden mean"[203] between the extreme cruelty of the Roman and early Christian world on the one hand and the veneration of animals found in some Eastern religions, such as Brahmanism and the Jainism, on the other. As indicated earlier, the Torah set forth very clearly the place of animals in the scheme of creation: "Use but not abuse"; concern for the animal's needs and prevention of cruelty even while working with the animal. While the beast may be slaughtered for its meat, the Talmud, on the basis of biblical references and oral tradition, developed a highly detailed set of rules as to how the animal is to be slaughtered. The complex laws of *shechitah* seem to have as their rationale the provision of a means of death for the animal that will be as swift and as painless as possible, with a loss of consciousness coming almost immediately.[204] Indeed, one of the earliest regulations concerning the use of the animal for food was given to Noah, in which it was forbidden to devour a limb torn from a living animal.[205] The right of man to make use of the animal for medical purposes was affirmed by later rabbinic authorities. Some questions remain, however, in cases where the pain to the animal may be intense and prolonged and the experimentation involved may be highly theoretical, without any direct implications for medical advance.[206]

We have noticed how in every step of the theological drama of the universe—in creation and in revelation—the animal kingdom is remembered, with its role defined and its interest safeguarded. It is to be expected, therefore, that in the final process of redemption, the animal would be remembered as well. Thus in his vision of the Messianic age, the prophet Isaiah sees the elimination of the predatory instinct and the concomitant extension of peace and its blessing also to the animals.

> The wolf and the lamb shall feed together, and the lion shall eat straw like the ox; and dust shall be the serpent's food. They shall not hunt nor destroy in all My holy mountain, saith the Lord.[207]

And in "the end of days," the animals will have nothing to fear from man:

> And in that day I will make a covenant for them with the beasts of the field, and with the fowls of the heavens, and with the creeping things of the ground; and I will break the bow and the sword and the battle out of the land, and will make them to lie down safely.[208]

In this section we have attempted to show how Judaism's attitude toward animals provides evidence of the extensivity as well as the intensivity of its moral concerns. Perhaps all of this is summed up in a remarkable passage in the Book of Psalms:

> Thy righteousness is like the mighty moutains;
> Thy judgments are like the great deep;
> Man and beast thou preservest, O Lord.[209]

The psalmist extolls the justice and righteousness of God in the only terms that are appropriate. The only praise of righteousness, God's or anyone else's is to say that it is truly just. But this appears to be a truism. Therefore, using spatial analogies, the psalmist attributes to God's righteousness and justice the dimensions of height and depth: they are as elevated, as high, as the "mighty mountains," and as deep as the *tehom* itself! They are subject to no false barriers and to no artificial restrictions. And the proof is: "man and beast Thou preservest O Lord."

Concern For Human Dignity

We have been attempting in this chapter to indicate some of the distinctive qualities of the morality of Judaism. Many of these, as we have seen, are expressions of the unusual extent to which the basic moral sensitivity and moral judgment are applied, whether it be to the alien or to the animal or to vague emotions within one's own heart. In this final section we wish to turn our attention to another sensitivity of Jewish morality, which we shall call a concern for the dignity of the person.

In rabbinic literature we encounter the concept as a fully developed halakhic and aggadic category called *kavod ha-beriyot* or *kavod ha-adam*—respect or honor or dignity due to the individual. In the Pentateuch, while we find a command to "respect" (give *kavod* to) one's parents, we do not find a specific command to respect one's fellow human being. However, the concept is reflected in certain laws in the Torah. Thus, we have the following: "When thou dost lend thy neighbor any manner of loan, thou shalt not go into the house to fetch his pledge. Thou shalt stand without, and the man to whom thou dost lend shall bring forth the pledge without, unto thee."[210] The creditor's right to the pledge does not entitle him to invade the privacy of his neighbor's home. Being in the relationship of debtor to creditor has already placed him in a position of subservience, with an attendant loss of pride. To bring this uncomfortable relationship into the inner sanctuary of his individuality, i.e., his home, is to cause him further embarrassment. "Thou shalt stand without . . . and the man shall bring the pledge unto thee."

The rabbis built on this insight, warning that in the process of helping someone one must be extremely careful not to humiliate or to embarrass. "A rabbi saw a man give a *zuz* to a poor man publicly. He said to him, 'Better had you given him nothing than to give him and put him to shame.'" That is why the rabbis taught that the preferred charity is practiced secretly: "Where a person gives a donation without knowing who receives it, and a person receives it without knowing who donated it."[211] And Maimonides sums up: "A man ought to be especially heedful of his behavior toward widows and orphans, for their souls are exceedingly depressed and their spirits low, even if they are wealthy. How are we to conduct ourselves toward them? One must not speak to them otherwise than tenderly. One must show them unvarying courtesy [*derekh kavod*]; not hurt them physically with hard toil nor wound their feelings with harsh speech . . ."[212]

In another direction the rabbis developed the concept of privacy, accepting the principle that "Damage caused to one by the sight of another is real damage."[213] Thus, looking through one's window into the courtyard of another or watching from one's roof the activities on the roof of an adjoining house was considered a breach of privacy and constituted an act of damages. As pointed out in a recent study, the Halakhah in its principle of *hezek re'iyah* included a prohibition of "all forms of surveillance—natural, mechanical, and electric, visual and aural."[214] In a remarkable instance of moral sensitivity as well as a response to a practical problem, Rabbi Gershom enacted a *takkanah* protecting the privacy of letters and prohibiting the reading of another's mail.

Rabbinic interpretation of another law in the Pentateuch yielded a special category of damages called *boshet,* "shame" or "indignity." Thus, we find the law:

> When men strive together, one with another, and the wife of the one draweth near to deliver her husband out of the hand of him that smiteth him, and putteth forth her hand and taketh him by the secrets; then thou shalt cut off her hand, thine eye shall have no pity.[215]

Interpreting the "cutting off of the hand" as monetary payment, the rabbis concluded that the woman was to pay for the embarrassment and indignity which she caused. This was formulated in the Mishnah thus:

> If a man wounds his fellow man he becomes thereby culpable on five accounts: for injury, for pain, for healing, for loss of time, and for indignity inflicted. . . . How is one compensated for indignity inflicted? All according to the man who inflicts the indignity and the man who suffers the indignity.[216]

The rabbis in the Talmud go on to demonstrate how the nature and extent of dignity/indignity is different for different people and depends upon any number of factors, including the social status, age, and sex of the individual involved, and the place, the time, and the public nature of the incident.[217] However, while the upper reaches of the dignity/indignity quotient may be relative (and indeed there are special requirements for the *kavod* of God, the Torah, one's rabbi, one's parents, and one's wife), there are basic minimum requirements for *kavod ha-beriyot* or *kavod ha-adam* that are the right of every human being qua human being. "Let the honor [dignity] of your fellow man be as dear to you as your own."[219]

Another source of the Pentateuch that shows concern for what we are calling "human dignity" is to be found in the rabbinic inference from the command, "Thou shalt not see thy brother's ox or his sheep driven away and hide thyself from them; thou shalt surely bring them back unto thy brother."[220] The rabbis infer that there is a circumstance when one may "hide himself" from the obligation to chase after his neighbor's ox, and that is if he is "an elder or scholar," because such activity would be beneath his dignity. The accepted interpretation here is that since an elder or a scholar would not suffer this indignity even if his own property were involved, he need not act differently to save another's property.[221]

The Torah's concern for the dignity of man even went so far as to include the dignity of thieves and cowards. For example, the law specifies that he who steals a sheep must pay a fine of four times the value of the sheep, while he who steals an ox must pay five times the value of his theft. Rabbi Yochanan ben Zakkai explained why this is so: the one who stole the sheep had to undergo the embarrassment of carrying it off in his arms, and the Torah compensates him for this indignity, but the one who stole the ox was spared such embarrassment because he could simply lead the ox by its tether.[222] Rabbi Yochanan further interpreted the exemption under which various individuals could return home from military service, such as "he who built a house and he who was engaged to a woman," as respectable cover-ups for those who were returning because they were actually "afraid and soft-hearted." "Come and see to what extent the Omnipresent had compassion upon the dignity of man."[223] In a similar vein the rabbis wondered why the Pentateuch, in describing the place for the sin-offering on the altar, says, "in the place where the burnt-offering is killed shall the sin-offering be killed," [224] instead of simply giving a geographic location, such as "in the north." Their explanation was that the Torah wished to save the sinner any embarrassment so that onlookers would think he was offering a burnt-offering rather than a sin-offering.

The term *kavod* seems to be used in the Torah to signify different things. Sometimes, particularly in connection with God, *kavod,* translated as "majesty" or "glory," seems to refer to the outward manifestations or visible expressed effulgence associated with Divinity. Examples of this use are such passages as "The *kavod* of Thy kingdom" and "the entire earth is filled with His *kavod.*" Yet even in this usage, the word *kavod* does not simply refer to some sort of "light" or celestial clouds.[225] To perceive the *kavod* of the Lord is certainly to experience inwardly some appreciation of that which is the distinctive essence of God insofar as it is given to man to experience. Therefore, when used in connection with man, as in the rabbinic phrase, *kavod ha-beriyot,* it naturally slides into meaning "worth" or "value" or "dignity," which is tied in to man's individuality or selfhood and equated with his inner personality. In many passages in the Book of Psalms, the word *kavod* refers to man's self or soul.[226] As such, man's *kavod,* or dignity, comes to mean his intrinsic value, not as a means to an end but as something absolute in and of himself. But in Judaism man is so endowed because he was created "in the image God," which according to Nachmanides means, "as it is written, '. . . and thou has crowned him with *kavod* and glory'" which refers to man's intelligent, wise, and resourceful station.[227] Man's dignity is therefore to be equated with his freedom, his creativity, his responsibility and his self-consciousness. *Kavod* is indeed something that is felt subjectively by man within himself.[227] Man must have a sense of self-respect. Self-abased people who lose their sense of dignity begin to lose their humanity and are disqualified by Halakhah from giving testimony.[228] However, when a man takes into consideration the dignity of others, there develop objective criteria of behavior which symbolically reflect appreciation of the other's *kavod* (dignity) and become the means of according him *kavod,* now understood as "honor."[229] The individual who develops a passion for these "symbols" of *kavod* and "pursues them" for his own glory is developing a bad character trait which the rabbis warned against.[230]

The relationship between the dignity and privacy lies in the fact that a person's dignity refers to his individuality and uniqueness. To uncover another person, to publicly disclose all of his "secrets," to "strip" another person physically or psychologically, is to inflict indignity and a shame upon him, because with nothing hidden and everything exposed, he loses his individuality. Thus the *kavod* of a Torah scroll requires that it be "hidden" from view in the ark when not being read. Norman Lamm points out that there are two aspects of deity: one is God's knowability and relatedness to man; the other, His transcendence and unknowability.[231] From the point of view of man, God's *kavod* requires a respectful distance and regard for the divine privacy. "But as God reveals and conceals, so man discloses and withholds his own personality." Formed in the image of God, man also desires to remain in part unknown, and thus preserve his dignity.

The relationship between the dignity of man and the *kavod* of God is sharply expressed in a remarkable homily quoted by Rashi on the biblical passage which states that the body of a man sentenced to death should be buried the same day, because "he that is hanged is a reproach to God."[232] Said Rabbi Meir: "This may be compared to two twin brothers in one city. One became king and the other became a brigand. The latter was caught and hanged, and all who passed by exclaimed, 'The king is hanging!'"[233] It follows, therefore, that to inflict indignity upon man is ultimately to dishonor God.

The range of *halakhot* in which the principle of *kavod ha-beriyot* or *kavod ha-tzibbur* (dignity of the community) plays a role is a wide one.[234] It includes interrupting the recitation of the *Shema* or setting aside the laws of mourning in order to return a greeting and is also reflected in the rules pertaining to the *met mitzvah* (abandoned corpse), the burial of which is given such overriding importance that it must be performed even by a *kohen* (priest), despite the fact that involvement with a corpse violates the special priestly laws of ritual purity. Further examples include the laws regarding the proper conduct of services so as not to affront the dignity of the congregation and the harsh punishment meted out to one who would violate the honor of a woman.

A remarkable sensitivity to the special needs of women in terms of their appearance was expressed by Rabbi Akiva in his ruling that even during their "unclean period" wives may use cosmetics and wear colorful clothing. Similarly, newly married women were permitted to wash on Yom Kippur, contrary to the general prohibition.[235] Moreover, as the Talmud relates, when it became apparent that certain burial and mourning practices followed by the rich were so lavish as to embarrass the poor, a series of changes were enacted to simplify the procedures and make them uniform for all classes.[236]

Let us briefly summarize the conclusions of this chapter. In terms of the essential meanings of the basic moral concepts found in the Torah, such as *tzedek, mishpat, chesed, rachamim, tov* and *ra,* we discover no surprises, no radical divergence from what is generally understood by those terms. What is distinct and unique about the morality of Judaism are certain qualities that result from the ways in which these concepts are applied and realized; the universality of their application; the passion and earnestness with which they are urged, the depths of feeling and intent which are regarded as morally relevant; the profound regard for the moral implications of speech; the tender concern for animal life; the keen sensitivity to the intangibles of human dignity.

It must have been a profound awareness of these qualities which led the psalmist to proclaim:

He declareth His word unto Jacob,
His statutes and His ordinances to Israel.
He hath not dealt so with any nation;
And as for His ordinances, they have not known them, Hallelujah.[237]

6

Morality and Halakhah

In order to properly examine the relationship between Halakhah and morality in Judaism, it is necessary that we back up a bit. For the Jew, the effective source of the basic rules he is to follow in his behavior is the word of God as found in the Torah. These include moral imperatives, ritual commands, and civil laws. The exegetical process called *midrash* was utilized by the rabbis to "unpack" all of the implications of the written text, to introduce oral traditions, to resolve disagreements, and to arrive at definitive rulings. The corpus of final and accepted rulings in all questions of Jewish law came to be known as Halakhah. The word comes from the root meaning "to walk" or "to go" and denotes a "way" or "norm" and "procedure."[1] As we indicated earlier, those moral rules in the Pentateuch which are particular and specific were explicated, elaborated, and developed by the halakhic process in the same manner as were the ritual laws.[2] Indeed, not only was the logic the same, but often the very same concept would have application in both a problem of morality and a matter regarding Temple procedure.[3] All of this, of course, is as expected. Moral rules are *mitzvot,* and therefore are authoritative in terms of their source and obligatory from the point of view of the agent. Moral rules in both their positive and negative forms are meant to be observed in real life and ought to be presented in the form of clear guidelines for behavior. This is what Halakhah is designed to do. Hence, it is to be expected that the Jewish moral code will be treated by and will find its final form in, the Halakhah.

Another reason for the very close relationship between law and morality in Judaism is the historical fact that "Jewish jurisprudence is a national jurisprudence" whose main development took place on alien soil and one of whose objectives was to preserve the identity of the people and ensure its survival.[4] But the survival of the Jewish people, in the light of its transcendent destiny resulting from its covenant with God, constituted a weighty moral consideration which penetrated the Halakhah at many different points, shaping and influencing the law.[5] Moreover, since for a good part of its development, Jewish law lacked the power to introduce coercive measures and enforce the law, it had to depend upon the free consent of the people. This voluntary aspect further enhanced its distinctive moral character.

Is There A Morality Independent Of Halakhah?

Further consideration of our material, however, leads to the conclusion that while much of the moral content of Judaism is incorporated in the Halakhah and there finds its fullest realization, certain special areas of experience, for reasons we shall attempt to discover, seem to lie outside the sphere of the Halakhah. The clearest evidence of this is to be found in the concept of *lifnim mi-shurat ha-din,* usually rendered "beyond the line of the law" or "beyond the measure of the law" or "beyond the strict law." Thus, we find the teachings of Rabbi Yochanan: "Jerusalem was destroyed because they based their judgments solely upon Torah law and did not act *lifnim mi-shurat ha-din.*"[6] On other occasions, the Talmud, in conscious contrast to the *din* (law), speaks of a higher standard of behavior which it calls "the standard of saintliness" or the rabbis may sometimes note, "the spirit of the sages is pleased with him."[7]

As we shall see in examining some specific examples, it appears that there is a sense in which the *din* (law), which may be equated with the Halakhah, is not self-sufficient. It is conceivable that a person could carry out all the requirements of the *din* and yet fall short of his moral obligations.[8] There are some for whom this conclusion is not very palatable, for reasons that have to do primarily with ideology and apologetics. It has become rather popular over the last few decades to describe the essence of traditional Judaism as halakhic Judaism, with emphasis upon the unique role and overriding primacy of the Halakhah. It is to Halakhah, say these publicists, that we are to look if we wish to find the philosophy of Judaism, the aesthetics of Judaism, and certainly the morality of Judaism.[9] This is an exaggeration and, in a sense, a distortion. Yet there are those who become so convinced of the all-pervasive role of Halakhah in Judaism that they would strive very hard to make sure that everything a Jew is supposed to do and believe, be it law, morality, custom, philosophy, or even dimly perceived ideals, somehow belongs under the heading of Halakhah. And I suppose you can stretch the term Halakhah until it covers anything you want it to cover.[10] But to do this is to reduce the issue of the relationship between Halakhah and morality to a semantic question. And this is to obfuscate when we should be trying to elucidate.

The fundamental and universally accepted distinction between Halakhah and Aggadah[11] leads us, of necessity, to the conclusion that Halakhah is not an umbrella term which includes all Torah material but rather, in both content and form, is generally to be equated with what we would otherwise call "law," the Hebrew term *din*. Therefore, the repeated distinction made by the rabbis between *din* and *lifnim mi-shurat ha-din* raises two questions for us: what this difference consists of, and why the Halakhah could not handle all of the pronouncements of Jewish morality. What is this area of Jewish morality which the rabbis referred to as *lifnim mi-shurat ha-din* or *midat chasidut,* "the ways of saintliness"?

Lifnim Mi-Shurat Ha-Din

Let us first consider the question of the authority or source of obligation of these wider and more vague areas of Jewish morality. We find that the rabbis had a proof-text or biblical source upon which to append their notion of *lifnim mi-shurat ha-din*:

"And thou shalt show them the way they shall walk therein and the actions which they shall do." Rabbi Eliezer of Modi'in says: "and the actions" refers to *din* proper; "and they shall do" refers to *lifnim mi-shurat ha-din*.[12]

Thus, the Torah itself urges us to conduct ourselves beyond the measure of the law. Indeed, Rabbi Isaac of Corbeil lists the obligation of *lifnim mi-shurat ha-din* as one of the 613 commandments.[13] Another passage associated with a broad moral imperative reaching into *lifnim mi-shurat ha-din* is the command, "And you shall do what is upright and good in the eyes of the Lord."[14] Yet another source is the verse, "In order that you may walk in the path of the goodly."[15] Regardless of how we interpret these passages, their character remains that of imperatives rooted in the Torah. If, then, both the *din* and the *lifnim mi-shurat ha-din* have their source in the Torah, in what do they differ? One approach might be to suggest that they differ only in the form in which they are presented in the Torah; i.e., the former are given as particular rules amenable to legal treatment while the latter are received as very general principles or maxims which each individual must apply to his own situation.[16] This, in turn, gives rise to a difference in the method used in achieving compliance. Where you have *din* you can have enforcement by the courts, but moral principles outside of the Halakhah must wait upon voluntary observance by the individual.

Before we can comment upon this approach, we must explore the possibility that the *din* and the *lifnim mi-shurat ha-din* differ in the degree of obligation which they enjoy. Can we look upon the *lifnim mi-shurat ha-din* as referring to a corpus of morality within Judaism that might be designated as supererogatory or optional? That is to say, are there any moral actions for which one is not faulted if they are left undone but for which one receives, so to speak, special credit if they are performed? A more thoughtful definition of a supererogatory action, suggested by Alan Donagan, is "an action which promotes an end which is morally obligatory to promote but in a way which is not obligatory because it demands too much of the agent."[17]

Are The Teachings In Avot Supererogatory?

In his introduction to his commentary on the Mishnah tractate *Avoth*, the Maharal (Rabbi Judah Loew of Prague) offers the following interpretation of the three different views offered in the Talmud as to how one may become a *chasid,* or saintly person:[18] The first view, in which man's relationship to his fellow is held to be paramount, says:

"Let him fulfill all matters pertaining to damages." Thus one is entitled to be called a *chasid* if he performs acts of kindness and charity and is most conscientious to see that no hurt or harm comes to his neighbor. The second view, in which man's relationship to God is paramount, says: "Let him fulfill matters pertaining to blessings." Thus one cultivates the essence of *chasidut* (saintliness) by constantly pronouncing the name of God in all of the different situations of life. The third view says: "Let him fulfill matters pertaining to *Avot*." In this view, a person becomes a *chasid* by being perfect within himself and by cultivating moral character traits. Maharal goes on to say that the material in *Avot* is *musar* and *derekh eretz*—i.e., patterns of behavior that our own reason urges upon us.

From this it might appear that the Maharal regarded efforts at personal morality, the development of proper dispositions and character traits, as being outside the framework of *mitzvot* and *averot* (transgressions) and "merely" the promptings of conscience and common sense. However, a close reading of the Maharal makes it clear that even though he held that the *mili di-avot* are not presented in the form of positive or negative commandments, he did not see this as completely negating their obligatory character. For the Maharal, this means that the status of *chasid* is conferred upon one who develops his character in accordance with the teachings of *Avot* inasmuch as they represent *lifnim mi-shurat ha-din*. Therefore, the area of *lifnim mi-shurat ha-din* is to be identified with the area of personal morality or perfection of the self.

As we indicated in an earlier chapter, the Pentateuch and the prophets thought of morality in terms of particular actions to be done or avoided and demanded adherence to certain general rules of behavior.[19] Even when a degree of abstraction is achieved, it is still pegged to behavior and is presented as a goal of action: "And you shall do the upright and the good"; and "Righteousness, righteousness you shall pursue." It was in the Book of Proverbs and in the rabbinic teachings as formulated in the Mishnah tractate *Avot* and in other rabbinic literature that the emphasis is first placed upon personal character development and the attainment of certain inner dispositions that could lead to proper responses and moral behavior. Thus, for example, a person who curbed his appetite for food and drink and learned to eat sparingly would not only avoid the excesses of gluttony and inebriation but would find it easier to discipline himself against the temptation of eating forbidden foods or appropriating what belongs to others. Developing proper character and cultivating proper attitudes, therefore, start the battle for morality at a much earlier phase and can often act as a preventive of serious moral transgression. This is reflected in the teaching: "Think about these three things and *you will not come into the hands* of transgression";[20] i.e., you will not come under their power.

There are some authorities who maintain that the material in *Avot* does not occupy a special status but can be understood as part of the oral development and explication of the *mitzvot* found in the Torah, such as "Love thy fellow as thyself" and its rabbinic formulation, "Do unto others as you would have others do unto you."[21] As for the source for the obligation to develop decent character traits, this can be found in the Torah command "And you shall walk in His ways," which the rabbis interpreted to mean: "As He is merciful, so shall you be merciful," construed as a built-in character trait. Others hold that the teachings in *Avot* are not explanations of *mitzvot* found in the Torah but oral traditions of teachings revealed independently to Moses at Sinai. Hence *Avot* begins with a preface which recounts the Sinaitic order of transmission: "Moses received the Torah from Sinai . . .";[22] for these authorities, the teachings in *Avot* are as obligatory as the other *mitzvot*.

For the Maharal, as we have seen, the cultivation of moral dispositions is not directly commanded in the Torah, is not part of the Torah's system of *mitzvot* and *averot,* and is recommended by human reason. While there is, of course, a sense in which "reason" ought to be obeyed, since that which is rational ultimately reflects the will of our Creator, nevertheless there might be grounds, on the basis of Maharal's comments, to consider the "path of saintliness" which leads through personal morality as, in some sense, supererogatory and constituting extra piety. For, after all, it is conceivable that a person in his actual behavior may conform to the moral demands of the Torah without restructuring his personality traits. Thus, for example, although a person may easily and frequently become angry, he may exercise strong control over his speech and actions so that no harm comes of it.

Ibn Paquda, Maimonides, And The Morally Optional

There is a view of man's obligations under the Torah, found in the writing of Bachya ibn Paquda, which leaves no room for the morally optional.[23] In examining the nature of the service that man is duty-bound to render God, his creator and benefactor, Bachya initially speaks of a threefold division of human activities: those that are commanded, those that are prohibited, and those that are permitted. The commanded and prohibited are, of course, all of those beliefs and emotions, speech acts, and deeds, whether by commission or omission, which are the subject of specific rules in the Torah. But when he begins to examine the area of the permitted, which covers all of the practical activities involved in preserving one's health, managing one's affairs, and transacting business and basic social activities, Bachya makes some further distinctions depending on the manner in which these aforementioned activities are performed. If, for example, one provides for one's basic needs in a way which can be regarded as adequate and sufficient, and one does this for the sake of God, then one has actually fulfilled a divine command. For man has been told, ". . . be fruitful and multiply, replenish the earth and subdue it," and, "Good is the man who . . . guideth his affairs with discretion."[24] However, should one go about these practical affairs in a manner which is extravagant and excessive; should one overindulge in the pleasures of life and the pursuit of riches, against which we have been warned that they may lead to transgression and immorality, then one is doing what has been forbidden. For the Torah warns us: "Be not among wine-bibbers, among greedy eaters of meat," and, "In the multitude of words there wanteth not sin," and, "Labor not to be rich."[25] Should a person deny himself what is necessary in any of these, but if his motive is neither piety nor a desire for closer communion with God, then he too is doing that which is prohibited. Bachya therefore concludes that in reality all human actions fall into two classes only: those that are commanded and those that are prohibited.

It is clear that Bachya is able to arrive at such a conclusion only because he succeeds in finding some very broad, general imperatives, such as "Know him in all thy ways,"[26] that makes it possible to view any action (like playing golf!), if done "for the sake of heaven," as the fulfillment of a divine command. It is doubtful however, whether the many passages in the Book of Proverbs which are based on wisdom and the "blessing" to primal man to "subdue" the environment can be viewed as "commandments" in the strict sense.

In considering the view of Maimonides, it appears at first glance that he too is suggesting that the "way of saintliness," or *lifnim mi-shurat ha-din,* lies beyond the halakhic imperative.[27] Maimonides identifies the *derekh ha-shem*—the "path of God"—and the command "And you shall walk in His ways" with the "median way," or "middle path," between two extremes; he also calls this "the way of the wise." The *chasid,* however, is one who veers away from the median toward one of the extremes. But Maimonides cites no scriptural source to indicate that the way of the *chasid* is normative and obligatory upon all. Surely, there can be no higher level of morality than to go in the *derekh ha-Shem*; in other words, the principle of *imitatio dei,* already identified by Maimonides with the median way. In the light of Maimonides' teaching elsewhere, it appears that the way of the *chasid,* which veers away from median morality, was understood by Maimonides to constitute remedial effort or a sort of moral therapy.[28] That is to say, to develop any of the *middot,* such as humility or control of anger or generosity, in a way that deviates from the mean is justifiable only when a particular individual must compensate for some natural excess or deficiency. Veering away from the median in the opposite direction of his weakness will train his faculty and ultimately restore the proper balance. To engage in such therapy is temporarily proper and right for such an individual. Generally, however, for Maimonides, there is only one correct moral response for every situation, obligatory upon every individual in a similar situation, and its source and authority is that it represents the "way of God."

Degrees Of Obligation

A remark made by Tosafot, however, may give us a clue as to the possible area for supererogatory or optional morality within Judaism.[29] Noticing that the Talmud, in discussing cases of *lifnim mi-shurat ha-din,* sometimes refers to the passage "which they shall do," sometimes to the passage "and you shall walk in the path of good men," and sometimes makes no scriptural reference at all, Tosafot suggests the following distinctions. In those cases where the Talmud explicitly mentions "which they shall do," we can infer that there is an *obligation* for the individual to act *lifnim mi-shurat ha-din*. This is because in these particular cases, had there been others in identical situations, they would be legally obligated to pay. It is only because the particular individuals involved have a special privileged status relative to the situation (Rav Chiyya because he was a moneychanger, and Rabbi Ishmael because he was a sage)[30] that they are legally absolved from payment. It is at this point that the Torah, by its teaching "which they shall do," morally obligates such individuals to relinquish their special exemption and return to the norm of the law (*din*).

In the case of Rav Judah and Mar Samuel, the person who finds the purse after the owner despaired of finding it, may legally keep it.[31] However, if subsequently the owner comes and identifies the purse, it should be returned, *lifnim mi-shurat ha-din*. Here, no passage is referred to, continues Tosafot, because this case, unlike the previous two, does not depend upon the special status of the individual involved. All who find a purse under these circumstances may keep it. Nevertheless, there still exists here some degree of moral obligation stemming from *lifnim mi-shurat ha-din,* because returning the purse involves no real loss on the part of the finder.

However, in the case where a passage from the prophetic writings is cited, such as, "So that you may walk in the path of good men," we are not dealing with what can be called a moral *obligation.* For here Rabbah bar Rav Huna suffered a severe monetary loss because of the carelessness or even neglect of the porters.[32] Yet on the basis of this passage in Proverbs, which calls for compassion, Rabbah is told to return the porters' garments, which he seized, and to pay their wages, because he could well afford it and the porters were poor and hungry. What Tosafot is suggesting is that a person has a moral obligation to renounce certain advantages of the law that would result in bringing him new possessions. However, he cannot have an obligation to give up what is and what has been his. In short, acts of benevolence, *tzedakot* and *gemilut chasadim,* when performed, are acts of great moral value and significance. However, a person cannot be said to have a moral obligation to seek out and perform such acts in the absence of a situation which demonstrates a need and creates a moral challenge and demand. In the absence of such a situation, the individual who stands on his legal rights cannot be said to have violated any moral principle. Thus, the Mishnah lists "acts of loving-kindness" among those things that have no "measure."[33] And Bertinoro explains that acts of kindness performed personally with our bodies, such as visiting the sick and burying the dead, have no "measure," whereas contributions of money to feed the hungry and redeem captives, when *opportunities to do these mitzvot come into our purview,* have a "measure"—as the rabbis have said, "not more than a fifth [of his profit]."[34] While one has a moral obligation to respond to a present and perceptible need, one does not have a moral obligation to spend all of one's time seeking out people in need. In this sense, *gemilut chasadim* may be considered supererogatory, since one who indeed goes out of his way to find opportunities for benevolence is certainly following the path of saintliness. (See the accompanying chart, which shows the relationship between those rules which are included in *din,* those that are *lifnim mi-shurat ha-din,* and those that are actually supererogatory.)

Principles Now—Details Will Follow

From several well-known comments by Nachmanides we can gain an insight into another aspect of the relationship between Halakhah and morality.[35] He makes it rather clear that regarding both personal and social morality, the particular commands of the Torah are not sufficient to cover all situations and all circumstances. There are lacunae, interstices, and ever-new possibilities created by technology. The "literalist" or "legalist," who considers everything to be permitted unless he can be shown "where it is written in black on white" that it is forbidden, can indeed operate quite extensively within the area technically permitted by the Torah and yet simply be a boor.[36] One can become a glutton on kosher food, lustfully overindulge in permitted sexual relations, and waste hours in small talk that is not *lashon ha-ra* but trivial and banal. Hence, the need for the general exhortation "You shall be holy," which the rabbis interpreted as, "Sanctify yourself in that which is permitted."[37] But the command "And you shall do the

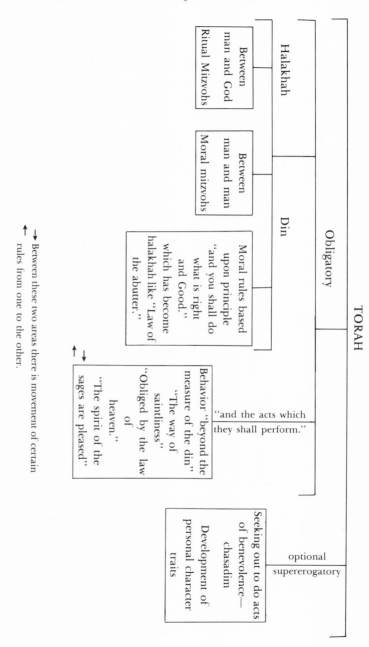

right and the good" is for the social morality of the Torah what the command "You shall be holy" is for the personal morality of the Torah. In man's relationship to his fellow man, the complexity of life is too great and varied to enable a single document or legal system to spell out in terms of particular rules all of the possible "do's" and "don'ts." Hence, the Torah's guidance had to include a general teaching, "And thou shall do the right and the good," which Nachmanides identified with the *lifnim mi-shurat ha-din.* Here is his comment in full:

> And our rabbis have a fine interpretation of this. They said: "This refers to compromise and *lifnim mi-shurat ha-din.*" The intent of this is that, initially, He had said that you should observe the laws and statutes which He had commanded you. Now He says, with respect to what He had not commanded, that you should likewise take heed to do the good and the right in His eyes, for He loves the good and the right. And this is a great matter. For it is impossible to mention in the Torah all of a person's actions toward his neighbors and acquaintances, all of his commercial activities, and all social and political institutions. So after He had mentioned many of them such as "Thou shalt not go about as a talebearer, thou shalt not take vengeance nor bear any grudge, thou shalt not stand idly by the blood of thy fellow, thou shalt not curse the deaf, thou shalt rise up before age," and the like, he resumes to say generally that one should do the good and the right in all matters, to the point that there are included in this "compromise" and *lifnim mi-shurat ha-din.*

According to Nachmanides, therefore, the obligation to be moral even to the extent of *lifnim mi-shurat ha-din* is clearly rooted in the Torah. The area of *lifnim mi-shurat ha-din,* in both its personal and social aspects, differs from the other Torah imperatives only in respect to the form in which these teachings are given to us. Much of the morality of the Torah is given in the form of specific rules—positive and negative *mitzvot,* such as "Thou shalt not curse the deaf" and "Thou shalt rise up before age," where the application to the concrete situation is usually clear and uncomplicated. However, the area of *lifnim mi-shurat ha-din* was indicated to us by a broad principle, "And thou shalt do the right and the good." The task of specifying the precise action mandated or prohibited by this vague principle is obviously not a simple one. This inferential process, and the uncertainty that often goes with it, tends to put a distance, at least in the mind of the agent, between the contemplated action and its source in the Torah. The "boor" may think he is operating with Torah license because his particular actions are not explicitly forbidden by the Torah. Actually, they are included in the admonitions: "Ye shall be holy" and "You shall do the right and the good."

"The Right" And "The Good" As Specific Halakhot

There are two very interesting instances in the Talmud where the ever-seminal principle of "Thou shalt do the right and the good" actually gave rise to two specific, permanent laws. These are known as the "return of the assessed property" and "the law of the neighbor" or "the law of the abutter."

1. According to talmudic law, if a debtor does not pay his debt, the creditor may obtain a writ of seizure from the court and take possession of landed property owned by the debtor even if it is in the possession of someone who purchased it after the loan was made. After the property is assessed, it is assigned to the creditor and it becomes his. Nevertheless, on the basis of "the upright and the good," the sages ruled that if the debtor or the purchaser find the means of repaying the creditor the original loan, the assessed property reverts to its previous owners.[38]
2. A person who has land bordering on the land of the seller enjoys the right of preemption with regard to the land that is for sale. If the seller proceeds to sell it to another, the person whose land borders the land for sale can displace the buyer by paying him the same price he paid to the seller.[39]

The intrusion of moral considerations and their effect on the law in these cases is quite remarkable, as pointed out by Silberg:

> Here in this seemingly weak law, the Sages proceeded (as it were) beyond the law, and applied a legal construction which has no precedent in other areas of the law: they made the buyer—against his will—into the agent of the person with right of preemption, so that his act of closing the deal

with the buyer automatically transferred the property to the person with the right of preemption:[40]

"For we have already shown that the acquisition by the buyer has also acquired the land for the person with the right of preemption, and no other formal act of acquisition is necessary. . . . Though the seller did not intend to transfer it to anyone other than the buyer and he protests that he did not transfer it to the person with the right of preemption, but only to the buyer, and the buyer protests similarly that the acquisition was meant only for himself, we say—for the sake of doing what is upright and good—that the acquisition which occurred effected an acquisition for the neighbor . . ."[41]

For both of these laws, the source and origin in the Torah is nothing more specific than the general rule to do "the right and the good." Yet both were absorbed into the legal system, and the machinery of the law is used to bring about the desired end. These are "laws" in the important sense that there is an obligation to perform and it is enforced by the courts. In the case of the law of the neighbor, the neighbor sues the buyer in court and the court will order the buyer to transfer to the neighbor the field which he, the neighbor, has, in effect, "purchased." In these two instances, the *lifnim mi-shurat ha-din* has been completely absorbed by the *din*.

Since the moral demand in both of these cases involves important questions of property ownership which affect a person's livelihood and apply to frequently recurring situations in the life of society, it is to be expected that such considerations can best be handled by the Halakhah and incorporated into the *din*. In both cases, the Halakhah compels the appropriate party (the seller in one instance and the creditor in the other) to do what is morally right. In doing so, neither party incurs any damage to himself. In this instance, the role of the general moral principle that "you shall do what is right and good" was to serve as the source for certain ordinances that have since become part of the Halakhah.

Maimonides, after describing the law of the neighbor, concludes by enumerating certain other categories of priority where a seller of property has to choose among several possible buyers.[42] Neither is a *bar metzra* (abutter) in the original sense. Thus, Maimonides suggests, a buyer from the city is to be favored over someone from the country-side, a scholar over a neighbor, a scholar over a relative, a neighbor over a relative. However, rules Maimonides, in any of these cases, should any of the less-favored buyers preempt the purchase, the sale stands. This is because this last schedule of priorities was understood by the sages to constitute not *din* but the "way of saintliness." But this raises the following question: Why is it that the original law of *bar metzra,* although based on the general moral principle of "what is right and good," was completely absorbed into the structure of *din* with its power of enforcement, while some of these other closely related cases, which are also based on moral considerations, remained in the realm of saintliness?

In this connection, the comments of the *Maggid Mishneh* are worth noting:

> The point of *dina de-bar metzrah* is that our perfect Torah has laid down [general] principles concerning the development of man's character and his conduct in the world; as, in stating, "Ye shall be holy," meaning, as they [i.e., the rabbis] said, "Sanctify yourself with respect to that which is permitted you"—that one should not be swept away by the pursuit of lusts. Likewise, it is said, "And thou shalt do the right and the good," meaning that one's interpersonal conduct should be good and just. With regard to all this, it would not have been proper to command [about] details. For the Torah's commands apply at all times, in every period, and under all circumstances, whereas man's characteristics and his behavior vary, depending upon the time and the individual. The rabbis [therefore] set down some relevant details subsumed under these principles, some of which they made [the equivalent of] absolute *din* and others [only] ante facto and by way of *chasidut*—all [however] ordained by them. And it is with reference to this that they said, "The words of consorts [i.e., the rabbis] are more beloved than the wine of Torah, as stated, 'For thy love is better than wine.'"[43]

It seems clear that the author of the *Maggid Mishneh* is addressing himself to the question we have just posed. He acknowledges that some particulars subsumed under the principle of "the right and the good" were made the equivalent of *din* while others remained "the way of *chasidut*," but he does not tell us why. Two possible explanations may be offered. Since the priority of the *bar metzra* was considered a *takkanah,* (rabbinic enactment),[44] the usual procedure would be to restrict its application only to those cases that fully qualified under the explicit provisions of the *takkanah*; i.e., one who actually owned property bordering on the one to be sold. The additional categories mentioned by Maimonides, while similar in certain respects, are not specifically included in the *takkanah* and therefore remain in the penumbra of "saintliness." Another explanation may lie in the differences in substance between the various groupings. The category of the *bar metzra* is based upon an objective, easily recognizable fact which confers upon the *bar metzra* a clear interest in the property in question which the other would-be buyers do not have. Furthermore, to deny the *bar metzra* his claim would be to commit a real injustice. The just and fair effects of the *takkanah* are thus manifest. The other priorities mentioned by Maimonides, however, are more vague. While the reasons for these priorities might be clear in principle, such as the higher value placed on Torah scholarship or the townsman's claim to proximity, to ignore these priorities does not appear to necessarily involve actual injustice. Furthermore, in particular cases, where a comparative judgment would have to be made, there might be other considerations favoring the other buyer which might tend to overweigh these priorities.

Should Morality Be Enforced?

In returning to the question as to why certain areas of morality remained outside of the Halakhah, we might examine the element of enforcement or coercion. In our original comparison between law and morality we noticed that in every system of law it is expected that various agencies utilizing methods of sanctions will be established to enforce the law and, if necessary, to compel individuals to abide by its provisions. Morality, however, not only does not provide for enforcement but seeks, as an ideal, the free-willed compliance of moral agents as an uncoerced voluntary act. Since moral standards are those by which we are judged as human beings and for which we are held responsible, it follows that a moral action should be *my* action, an expression of *my* will and *my* intent. Thus, a moral action preferably should be a voluntary one in order to preserve a maximum of moral value.

Why then were certain moral rules incorporated into the Halakhah and given over to the courts to enforce while others were left to voluntary observance? The obvious answer is that the moral rules like "Thou shalt not murder" and "Thou shalt not steal" were considered so essential to the well-being of society that society, unable to wait for or rely upon voluntary compliance, gave them the character of law so that they could be enforced by the courts.[45] Another possibility is that many of the negative moral rules forbidding individuals to do certain acts are seen from the side of the other as rights that must not be interfered with. You must not steal because the other person has a right to his property. Hence, it is appropriate that society protect the rights of individuals by imposing sanctions and providing enforcements. In this light, we can understand why the courts carried out the sanction of flogging only in connection with negative commands and not in relation to positive commands.[46] If, however, some of the positive moral commands reflect the attitude of *chasidut,* which often involves "showing kindness to those who have no claim whatever upon us,"[47] then there is no corresponding right on the other side. It therefore does not seem appropriate to compel anyone to show this sort of kindness.

In examining those rules that were given over to the courts for enforcement and those that were not, we notice changes taking place in both directions.[48] That is to say, not all rules remained fixed in their respective categories. Let us consider the moral obligation to come to the aid of the poor. Originally, the many exhortations to this effect in the Pentateuch were undoubtedly not enforced by the courts but were left to the moral conscience of the people. In a primarily agrarian economy, where the land had originally been distributed on an equitable basis, such problems of poverty that developed were adequately handled by the practice of "gifts to the poor"; the gleanings of the edges, the forgotten sheaves and tithes for the poor all of which were voluntarily observed. In the Second Temple period, however, after the social disruptions of the Exile and the rise of an urban poor, these voluntary methods proved inadequate. At that point, the social conditions required that the giving of charity be organized differently and more effectively, which meant that the state or the courts had to step in and use stronger methods to obtain compliance. The conditions of Jewish life in the Diaspora, where the commandments of the agricultural "gifts to the poor" did not apply, also reinforced the need to introduce more effective organization in bringing relief to the poor. And so we find the ruling in the Talmud that a community has the right to compel its members to give *tzedakah,* which can be legislated as a form of a tax. The difference in perspective accompanying the change in which giving to the poor is transformed from a matter of personal conscience to an act required and enforced by law is as follows: In the moral perspective, the agent looks upon the act of helping the needy as something he personally and morally ought to do. The poor man's outstretched hand is merely the occasion that presents the agent with his moral opportunity. Of course, as a moral act, it has greater moral worth when it is done voluntarily. However, in the social-legal perspective, the focus is not on the agent but on the unfair and intolerable situation of the poor. Their needs ought to be alleviated. In this perspective, *who* gives the money is unimportant. If a legal process will bring in the funds and do the job quickly and effectively, so be it! On this view, the moral value of bringing quick relief to the suffering of the needy is deemed more significant than the moral value involved in making it possible for the agent to contribute voluntarily.

In this manner we can understand the underlying dynamic by which imperatives that were once voluntary moral rules became laws enforceable by the institutions of society. A similar evolution occurred in regard to the father's obligation to feed his children and the children's obligation to support their parents. Both were originally moral and voluntary and later became laws enforceable by the Jewish community.[49]

Another group of moral offenses that became actionable by the courts is indicated by the talmudic statement: *kofin al midat sodom,* "we coerce over a trait of Sodom."[50] This refers to a person who is so mean as to deny benefit to others even where no gain is involved thereby for himself. Thus a person can be compelled to share in the cost of a court document that serves both parties, even though he might argue that he prefers a special document all for himself. Similarly, since it involves no loss or expense on his part, an individual can be compelled to participate in making an *eruv chatzerot* (a symbolic merging of privately owned "domains"—e.g., fronting on a common courtyard—to permit certain types of carrying between them on the Sabbath).[51]

Although in the talmudic literature there is an obvious effort to clearly distinguish between the requirements of *din* and those of *lifnim mi-shurat ha-din,* in the writings of the later commentators, and particularly in the responsa literature, we find a tendency to incorporate these "extra-legal" considerations into the Halakhic process itself so that these moral imperatives become actionable by the courts. Although we do not find complete agreement on this point among either the earlier or the later authorities, nevertheless, there does seem to be a consensus in the direction of incorporating the "extra legal" into the judicial process:[52] "And this is the practice in every court of justice in Israel—to compel the right and proper matter even though it is not required by the *din.*"[53] Elon concludes: "The respondant in his responsum, the decisor in his book of rulings, and the court of law in its judgment—all of them included the moral imperative—to the extent that it was involved in the question before them—as a part of their responsa and rulings."[54]

As we will show later on, there originally developed a moral standard outside of the Halakhah mainly because of certain built-in characteristics of the halakhic process; i.e., its formal nature and its tendency to "quantification." But this was true in the talmudic period, when the emphasis was upon legislation; i.e., formulating the law in its general and abstract character. However, in the later period, and particularly in connection with the responsa literature, we are primarily confronted by particular cases regarding an individual or community, and the responsum, while making law, was in the first instance received as a directive to be applied in the concrete and immediate situation. As such, moral considerations could not be ignored. The inquirer sought the guidance of the Torah and wished to know what he, as a Jew, was to do in his particular situation. But whether the source is *din, lifnim mi-shurat ha-din,* or saintliness, it is all prescribed by the Torah and ought to be put into practice. Therefore, not only was he instructed in the finer points of morality, but whatever pressures were available to the courts were utilized in order to achieve compliance.[55]

An example of a law that evolved in the opposite direction—from law to morality—involving the command to "be fruitful and multiply." After an initial period in which the natural rewards of large families must have made fulfillment of this *mitzvah* a matter of course, there apparently followed a period in which society felt compelled to intervene. Thus, we find the law that a man who has been married for ten years and is childless is compelled to divorce his wife. One of the authorities adds that a young man who has reached the age of twenty and refuses to marry may be compelled by the courts to do so.[56] However, a more recent decisor points out that in his day all attempts to coerce the childless to divorce or the single to marry and to prevent marriages to women who cannot bear were discontinued.[57] These matters once again became moral issues for the individual conscience.

The Inner Tension Between Din And Rachamim

However, a real understanding of the relationship between Halakhah and morality must begin with an awareness of what must be seen as a basic conflict between their fundamental principles.[58] The Halakhah in its aspect of law and in regulating relations between man and man is based upon the concept of justice and equality. It therefore stresses the notion of "What is mine is mine, and what is thine is thine." In its social aspects, it emphasizes negative rules or prohibitions because it assumes that individuals come endowed with life and possessions and rights. It therefore strives to prevent the proper order of society from being disturbed and the rights of individuals from being violated.[59] The point of conflict with the broader concept of morality can be understood in the disparity between "Thou shalt not favor a poor man in judgment" and "Make right the poor and the indigent."[60] In considering a judgment between two individuals, the Halakhah requires that we ignore the fact that one is poor and the other rich and make every effort to decide the case with objectivity and in accordance with the general rules governing possession or damages or rights or responsibilities. But what of our obligation to help the needy, to have compassion upon the poor, and to unselfishly give of ourselves and our fortunes in our love for others? The answer is that you may indeed voluntarily relinquish what is your own. In judgment, however, the judge may not be charitable with the money of others. The case must be decided on its merits.[61]

The basic disparsity between *din* (morality in its aspect of justice) and morality as benevolence is reflected in an important *Mishnah*: "There are four attitudes among men: He who says, 'Mine is mine and thine is thine,' is a median [middle-of-the-road] attitude, but others say it is the attitude of Sodom. He who says, 'Mine is thine and thine is thine' is a *chasid* . . ."[62]

How do we account for the wide gap in the sage's evaluation of the one who takes the position of "Mine is mine and thine is thine"? Ostensibly it does appear to be a morally correct position—the attitude of a law-abiding citizen who desires only what is rightfully his and respects the property and rights of others. The answer is that from the point of view of *din,* it is quite an acceptable position. But as a total moral philosophy it omits the dimension of benevolence; it breeds an intolerable selfishness, and if unrelieved by compassion can only result in a value system reminiscent of wicked Sodom. But saying this does not resolve the conflict or tension between *din* and *rachamim*—justice and mercy. So long as the *din* compels us to approve the attitude of "Mine is mine and thine is thine," so long as we must uphold the right of the rich man to take the poor man to a *din Torah* and insist on what is rightfully his, the tension and the conflict remain. For as we indicated earlier, the courts will enforce the right of the individual to keep or get back what is his (justice), but the courts generally will not compel an individual to give up what is his own in an act of loving-kindness (*chesed*). There is the danger that an individual who commits himself to the ideal of justice for himself as well as for others may not find it easy to do himself the "injustice" of sharing what he has with others.[63]

From a discussion recorded in the Talmud, it appears quite clear that the rabbis were aware of the inner tension between justice and righteousness, *mishpat* and *tzedakah*. The question debated by Rabbi Elazar and Rabbi Yehoshua was whether the judges in cases of conflicting monetary claims should seek a compromise settlement, *bitzua,* in which everyone loses a little, or render judgment according to the *din,* in which one loses all and one wins all.[64] The latter approach has, of course, the virtue that it can be regarded in a sense as a "true" judgment.

. . . which is justice that includes *shalom* [peace]? This is compromise . . . wherever there is *mishpat,* there is no *tzedakah*; wherever there is *tzedakah,* there is no *mishpat*. Which is justice [*mishpat*] that incorporates within it *tzedakah*—this is compromise.

Tzedakah here is understood as referring to compassion and mercy, while the concept of *shalom* is understood in this context as soothing outraged feelings and overcoming the pain of monetary loss. Now, a compromise will often distribute the goods in question along lines which the *din* does not approve of as just or deserving. And these latter are, of course, moral values. It is for this reason that Rabbi Elazar says: *yikov ha-din et ha-har*—"Let the *din* prevail regardless!" However, Rabbi Yehoshua is of the opinion that the moral values of *tzedakah* and *shalom* are, in some sense, higher and ought to be realized by the judicial process. A compromise settlement is a combination of *mishpat* and *tzedakah* because instead of its being pure *chasidut,* in which one side relinquishes his rights in a burst of altruism, objective outsiders mediate an arrangement which includes elements of fairness as well as compassion. The judge is therefore urged to seek *bitzua* even though its terms are not identical with those called for by the *din*.

An insightful attempt to reconcile the two moral standards of *mishpat* and *chesed* is found in an interpretation offered by Rabbi Jacob ben Asher in the introduction to his volume on *Choshen Mishpat.* He draws our attention to the divergent statements of Simeon the Just and Rabban Simeon ben Gamaliel as to what constitutes the moral underpining of the world:

> He [Simeon the Just] was wont to say, "The world stands on three things: on the Torah, on divine service [worship], and on acts of loving-kindness."

> Rabbi Simeon ben Gamaliel says, "The world endures because of three things: truth, law [*din*], and peace."[65]

Rabbi Jacob ben Asher sees the moral education of man as developing in two stages. At first, stable conditions of justice and order must be instituted in society so that the lives and possessions of people and their families are protected against violence and capriciousness. The proper instrument by which to achieve such stability in this first stage is the law and the institutions that pronounce and enforce the law. Hence, Rabban Simeon ben Gamaliel teaches that the necessary conditions for the continued existence of society are truth, law, and peace. The ultimate goals of society, however, go beyond the law and enter the area of personal morality. Here the burden is upon the individual to transcend his self, reaching out to the other to give of himself and of what is legally and rightfully his own. It is to this second stage, in which the standard of *chesed* must dominate, that Simeon the Just refers when he states that the world stands on Torah, divine service, and acts of loving-kindness. These are the goals of man in society which aim at the self-transcendence of the individual through acts of *chesed*.

The Consequences Of Legal Formalism

It turns out, therefore, that while it may be correct to say that Halakhah and morality are complementary, their relationship is much more complex than that. There is, as we have seen, an inner conflict between some of their essential components; between *mishpat* or *din* on the one hand and *chesed, shalom,* and *tzedakah* on the other. This can be better appreciated when we examine a characteristic of the Halakhah which has been called its "legal formalism" or emphasis upon "quantification."[66]

We have already noted that the codes of law found in the Torah were primarily designed not as broad principles to be interpreted by judges but as practical rules of behavior to be studied and applied by ordinary men and women in the normal course of their everyday lives.[67] Only when the law as written does not give clear guidance in the particular case in question or when rival claims raise issues of interpretation should we go to court:

> If there arise a matter too hard for thee in judgment . . . between plea and plea . . . then shalt thou go to the priests and the Levites and to the judge that shall be in those days, and thou shalt inquire, and they shall instruct thee the judgment, and thou shalt do in accordance with what they instruct thee.[68]

In the words of Moshe Silberg: "In modern jurisprudence the judge is sovereign over the law, while in Jewish jurisprudence, the judge is the servant of the law.[69] Keeping this in mind, the rabbis, in explaining many of the laws both ritual and moral, strove to be as precise as possible and to give fixed measures and delineations to their concepts. Consider the following illustration as found in the Mishnah:

> As long as she remains in her father's household she can always collect her settlement stipulated in the *ketubah* . . . the sages say: "As long as she is in her husband's household, but if she is in her father's household she collects the settlement in the *ketubah* up to twenty-five years."

> [Gemarah] Said Abbaye to Rav Joseph: "If she came on the final day before sunset, she collects the settlement; if after sunset, she forfeits it!" He answered: "Yes: all the measures laid down by the sages are thus. In a pool of water of forty *se'ah* one may immerse himself; in forty *se'ah,* minus the smallest measure, he may not."[70]

The question before the Mishnah is, How much time does a widow have to claim the settlement provided by her late husband under the *ketubah?* If a prolonged period of time passes and she does nothing, does this silence imply renunciation and forfeiture on her part? The sages rule that where the woman remains in her late husband's household, the harmonious relationship she has developed with its members may explain her reticence in claiming the settlement. Hence, her claim remains alive indefinitely. However, if she has returned to her father's household, then a silence of twenty-five years may be taken as renunciation, and after that period she has forfeited her right to the sum mentioned in the *ketubbah.* Abbaye's question points up a curious consequence of quantifying a psychological presumption. Since up to the very last moment of the last day of that time period, we presume that she has not waived her claim, does she really have enough time in that split second to make the proper renunciation? Rabbi Joseph's reply is, of course, that this is a to-be-expected consequence of a common characteristic of the Halakhah, as seen by analogy with the laws of the *mikveh.* The precise minimum measure of forty *se'ah* for a proper *mikveh* is based upon an estimate of the amount of water necessary for an average person to immerse himself so that his entire body is covered by water. Once a precise, objective measure has been established, the objective standard takes over and the rationale is ignored. So that if a very short person immerses himself in a *mikveh* of forty *se'ah* minus a drop, the immersion is invalid even though his body is entirely covered by the water.

Another illustration of how the Halakhah will often formulate a law that turns on the existence of an empirical consideration expressed in a precise, objective measure is the following: "A bird found within fifty cubits of a nest belongs to the owner of the nest; if outside the fifty cubits, it belongs to the finder."[71]

The question involved here is whether the finder may assume that the bird is ownerless and keep it or whether it belongs to the owner of the nest and thus must be returned to him. Basing themselves upon the empirical generalization that "a hopping bird does not hop more than fifty cubits," the rabbis formulated the law in very clear and exact terms. In the discussion that follows in the Talmud, Rabbi Jeremiah raises a question which again points up the possible illogical consequences of such exactitude: "What if one of the bird's legs is inside the fifty-cubit radius and the other outside?"

If we now examine some of the cases where the Talmud refers to the standard of *lifnim mi-shurat ha'din* or to "the standard of saintliness," or to a type of behavior with which "the spirit of the sages is pleased," we will find that these moral considerations are invoked outside the framework of the *din* because the *din* itself, operating on the basis of objective, quantified, general standards, is compelled to ignore the moral factor present in the particular reality of this individual instance.

1. The father of Samuel found donkeys in the desert over twelve months after they had been lost.[72] According to the *din*, when an object has been lost for twelve months, one can assume that the owner, despairing of ever finding it, has in effect renounced ownership and thus that the finder may keep the object. The father of Samuel, however, acting *lifnim mi-shurat ha-din*, returned the donkeys to their owner. While it is undoubtedly true as a general psychological rule that after a while the owner of a lost object "despairs" and no longer expects its return, the fixing of a precise time period, no matter what it be, has only a general probabilistic "truth" and in some particular

instance may, in fact, not be true at all. Thus, while the law gives the father of Samuel the right to keep the donkeys, he was sensitive to the moral stain of taking what belongs to someone else and could legitimately ask: "But what if the owner of these particular beasts did not despair of the return of his animals even after twelve months?" The Halakhah, in seeking a just rule for a class of situations, formulated the law in terms of a quantified measure of time based on a true psychological principle. In a particular case, however, it may not coincide with the moral response. In such cases, the Torah urges the individual to go beyond the law and do what is morally right.

Another law involving a time limit based on a psychological presumption pertains to coins worn thin through use to the point where they are no longer acceptable as currency. If someone who receives such a coin notices its poor condition, he may return it, and the one who gave it is obliged to replace it. The Mishnah considers the question of how long the recipient has to return the coin and rules that in cities where moneychangers who are experts can be found, the time-limit for returning the coin is only as long as it takes to consult the moneychangers. In villages, however, the recipient has until the eve of the Sabbath, when purchasing the items he needs for the Sabbath should have made him conscious of his coins. Then, surprisingly, the Mishnah goes on to say, "if the one who passed it [the coin] recognizes it, he should accept it even after twelve months."[73] In the Gemara this is challenged as contradictory to the law as laid down both for the city and the village, where the recipient has at most only until the eve of the Sabbath. The answer given by Rav Chisda is, "The standard of saintliness is referred to here."

Here again, the *din* is based upon fair, cogent, and realistic considerations that probably obtain in most cases. The hazard of receiving defective coins is well-known, and if one is in doubt, the *din* provides time to consult. But if in a concrete situation you are confronted with a defective coin which you recognize as being one you passed, even if twelves months have elapsed, you are not morally justified in arguing: "But where were you all of this time?" In this particular instance, who knows what factors prevented the recipient from making his claim earlier? And so the standard of saintliness, to which every person ought to aspire, would have the giver accept the coin in return.

2. A ruling involving a lost purse leads the Gemara to the distinction between *din* and *lifnim mi-shurat ha-din.* Mar Samuel was of the opinion that a purse found in a busy marketplace may be kept, since the owners must surely despair of its ever being returned. Yet, he says, if a person comes and identifies it, it should be returned, in response to the moral imperative "to go beyond the line of the law."[74] Here again, the *din* and the *lifnim mi-shurat ha-din* run on separate tracks because of the former's dependence upon probabilistic generalizations.

3. Jewish law insists that a transaction is legally valid only if it is accompanied by an appropriate, recognized act of acquisition (*kinyan*), such as "pulling" or "lifting." A vague agreement based on the spoken word is not considered binding. Yet we are told: "All movable property is acquired through 'pulling,' but one who keeps his word, the spirit of the sages is pleased with him."[75]

Considering all of the possible problems and abuses that can arise in the course of complex commercial transactions involving the transfer of goods and materials, it is undoubtedly fair and practical that the law insist that no transactions be considered valid and binding unless accepted procedures are followed. However, Judaism stresses the sanctity of the spoken word and teaches that individuals should live up to their word, keeping their promises and announced intentions, since these confer a moral obligation. Therefore, while a person who has given his word to sell is not legally obligated, the morality of Judaism would urge him to keep his word so that the spirit of the sages may be pleased with him.

4. Sometimes the Halakhah itself, in attending to both ritual as well as moral considerations, gives rise to situations in which what is permitted by the *din* diverges from the truly moral. A person whose house caught on fire during the Sabbath can save edibles sufficient for his Sabbath meals but not more. The rabbis feared that a blanket permission to save all of the contents of the house would get the owner so involved in the rescue operation that he would begin to extinguish the fire, and this is forbidden on the Sabbath. However, in order to increase the number of items saved, the homeowner may announce to others: "Come and rescue for yourselves." He is, in effect, renouncing ownership of what he cannot save and urging his neighbors to help themselves. However, says the Mishnah, "If they are wise they make an accounting with him after the Sabbath."[76]

Here again, it is the standard of saintliness that is in question. One is supposed to understand that the unfortunate homeowner's invitation to others to "rescue for themselves" was a desparate measure induced by his own helplessness under the *din*. Technically, he did renounce ownership, so that legally what the neighbors rescue belongs to them. But a *chasid* would hardly want to take advantage of another person's misfortune. Let the *chasid,* therefore, return the salvaged items after the Sabbath. But, of course, he can claim and accept compensation for his rescue efforts.

5. Sometimes, in expounding the laws of damages, the Talmud describes a case where the individual who caused the damages could not be made to pay according to the *din* because of some indirection in the chain of cause-and-effect leading from the individual's act to the ensuing damages.[77] In such cases, the usual rabbinic expression is: "Not liable by human laws but guilty before heaven." In other words, while the courts cannot compel him to pay for the damages, he does have a moral obligation to make restitution.

What causes a gap to open up between the legal and the moral in these cases is the need to operate in the legal sphere with a clear and, of necessity, delineated concept of causality that entails liability. The ways in which a person can "cause" harm to another person or his property, or be said to be responsible for such harm, are so complex and devious that all of the possibilities cannot be brought under a law.[78] Thus there develops an area of causal connections that is beyond the definition of causality adopted by the law but that must be seen morally as generating consequences for which one is responsible and for which one should compensate those harmed.

Morality As An Operating Principle Within The Halakhah

However, it is precisely because of the legalistic nature of the Halakhah, which formulates its teachings in terms of general rules and abstract principles designed to apply to a broad class of cases, that we from time to time, in particular situations, encounter internal conflicts between the moral demands of the Torah ethos and the constraints of the objective requirements of the Halakhah. Torah has to be applied to a constantly changing world in which both the physical environment and human behavior patterns take unexpected turns. As a result, Jewish life sometimes finds itself with a fixed Halakhah which, either because of what it is doing or because of what it is unable to do, has unjust and immoral consequences for particular people in particular circumstances.[79] When confronted by such situations in the past, the Torah leaders, sitting either as a judicial body or as the organized *Kehilah,* found *within* the halakhic system the authority and the technical means to remedy the situation, eliminate the abuse, and right the wrong. In this way the moral component made its demand heard and was given expression, so that harmony could be restored within the total system.

According to the law in the Torah, two witnesses are required to establish a fact before the courts.[80] Situations arose, however, as a result either of war or of accident, where a husband disappeared and was presumed dead, yet there were no witnesses to testify to his death.[81] In such cases, the rabbis legislated what was known as *takkanot agunot,* which permitted the wife to remarry on the basis of her own testimony or on that of one witness.[82] The reason behind this enactment was explicitly declared to be a moral one: "In order to save the woman from the status of *agunah,* the rabbis dealt leniently with her."[83] Clearly, the rabbis were able to find the authority to set aside a law in the written Torah because of an equally important concern of the Torah: the painful situation of women in such circumstances. Obviously, this original enactment falls short of solving all the problems arising out of the *agunah* situation, a type of case that continues to challenge rabbinic ingenuity and to trouble the rabbinic moral conscience in our own day.[84]

Another classic case is the famous *prosbul* of Hillel. According to the Torah, the Sabbatical year cancels any debt resulting from a loan.[85] In the days of Hillel, contrary to the warning of the Torah "not to close their hands to their destitute brother," people stopped lending money in anticipation of the Sabbatical year. Hillel's *takkanah,* designed to remedy this situation, had the creditor assign his notes to the court before the Sabbatical year, which made them no longer liable for cancellation.[86] While scholars continued to debate the grounds for the *prosbul* for a long time afterwards, the fact is that the rabbis, through halakhic engineering, were able to obviate a social problem that had become acute in their day—ironically enough, a problem precipitated by a Halakhah that has as its goal the creation of a social condition of justice and equity.[87]

In yet another enactment designed to prevent a seller of goods from taking advantage of a purchaser, the rabbis ruled, contrary to the Torah as written, which implies that the transfer of money is sufficient to close a transaction, that a recognized act of *kinyan,* such as "pulling," would be required in order to finalize the transfer of ownership.[88] Until the act of *kinyan* occurs, no purchase has taken place. Under the old arrangement, once the transfer of money took place, the seller would cease to concern himself with the care and protection of the goods, which might still be in his possession.

Problems arising out of the illegitimacy of offspring is another area where morality seems to clash with Halakhah. The bastard or *mamzer,* according to the Torah, is the offspring of forbidden relations and is excluded from intermarrying within the community—unto all generations. Of course, the institution of *mamzerut* (bastardy) itself raises a moral question. Is this not a case of children being punished for the sins of the parents, which the Torah rcognizes as unjust? Rabbi Emanuel Rackman points out that the *halakhah* of bastardy was considered a means of protecting the moral standards of the community and safeguarding the sanctity of the Jewish family.[89] The concept of illegitimacy of offspring was designed as a deterrent to immoral acts by others. But in any system of law rules that have long-range and overall beneficial consequences for the group may sometimes have harmful effects on innocent individuals. In such clashes between two different moral claims—between the individual and society—commonsense can surely appreciate the interests of society.

The rabbis were often courageous in their efforts to minimize the pain resulting from this sort of problem. In regard to a family suspected of including *mamzerim,* the rabbis adapted the principle that "Once a *mamzer* is absorbed into a family he is absorbed." Thus they prohibited revealing information about a family's history of *mamzerut* if the reputation of the family involved was generally good. The Talmud records that Rabbi Yochanan swore that he knew *mamzerim* were present in a certain family yet did not divulge his information, saying, "What can I do? Some of the great men of the generation are among them."[90] Here again, an approach based on the law itself would tend to ignore the human situation in which it operates and would wage a forceful inquiry to ferret out the *mamzer* and publicize the information lest he intermarry with some unsuspecting Israelite. Only a keen moral sensitivity to the pain and suffering this might cause can explain the hesitancy of the rabbis to carry out the full implications of the Halakhah.

In our day, both in the United States and in Israel, some of the most heated and protracted controversies have erupted over cases such as the ones above, in which halakhic situations involving acute moral dilemmas seem to go unresolved. Many of them have involved women whose status in cases of divorce and *chalitzah* (release from the obligation of levirate marriage) leaves them vulnerable to blackmail and extortion or, in the case of the *agunah,* consigns them to a sort of limbo in which they cannot remarry. Other difficult cases that have been much publicized involve *mamzerim,* the question of "Who is a Jew?" and the status of non-Orthodox conversions. In reporting these issues, the secular press in Israel perceived the rabbinic establishment as largely oblivious to the human aspect and expressive of an overly rigid Halakhah.

Obviously, every legal system will in certain circumstances cause hardship to some or will not immediately answer to the needs of others. As a general criticism, therefore, this cannot be counted as a weakness of the system. The issue that has arisen, however, particularly within the circle of those who live by the Halakhah, is whether or not there is more that can be done by the rabbinic authorities, operating within the system of the Halakhah, to alleviate some of the harsh consequences of the existing procedures. Responsible and respected voices have been heard over the past few years within the Orthodox community, answering the above question in the affirmative. Unfortunately, there has been little really serious and substantive discussion of the issues, because a consensus of present-day recognized rabbinic authorities look upon these explicit appeals to human need as constituting extraneous pressures and improper intrusions upon the halakhic process. The so-called liberals, however, insist that these contemporary problems are precisely the kind of halakhic situations that were successfully dealt with by rabbis in the past who saw the moral factor or the element of social justice as a legitimate component of the halakhic process and responded by utilizing the mechanisms available to them within the system.

What emerges from our study is the conclusion that morality is not only a specific subject area treated by the Halakhah but the overriding ethos of the entire Torah, guiding halakhic development in certain directions, through a variety of broad, yet clear principles even as it urges the individual to look beyond the *din* and walk the high ground of saintliness.

A rather unusual function was assigned by the rabbis to the passage in Proverbs that reads: "Her ways are ways of pleasantness and all her paths are peace."[91] The subject here is wisdom, which the rabbis understood as referring to the Torah as a whole. Sometimes this passage was interpreted to mean that those who observe the Torah can expect blessing and pleasantness to follow or that scholars should behave in such a way as to ensure peace and harmony among people.[92] What is of greater interest, however, is the use to which this passage is sometimes put as a decisive factor in determining the Halakhah; as an overarching norm which can be appealed to in deciding matters of Jewish law.[93] It would, therefore, appear that just as the explication and development of the Halakhah was in part guided by rational principles (such as *umedana* and *chazakah*) or logical rules of inference (such as *kal va-chomer* and *binyan av*), so too was it shaped by the moral principle that "Her ways are ways of pleasantness." Evidently, the rabbis understood the references to the "ways" and "paths" of Torah as descriptions of the fundamental structures, or a priori categories, to which halakhic development must conform.

A few examples of how this passage was employed will suffice:

1. In commanding the four types of plant species to be taken on the Festival of Sukkot, the Torah stipulates, "And ye shall take you on the first day, the fruit of goodly trees, branches of palm trees [*kapot temarim*], and boughs of thick trees [*anaf etz avot*], and willows of the brook, and ye shall rejoice before the Lord your God seven days."[94] In considering the various species that might be referred to by *anaf etz avot,* the Talmud rejects one because it is not "thick" and a second because its boughs do not cover the trunk. A third candidate, however, which is in accord with the textual requirements, is rejected by the Tal-

mud because its needlelike burrs will prick the hands of the worshipper, and after all, we are taught, "Her ways are ways of pleasantness."[95] In a similar discussion, the Talmud rejects a prickly candidate for *kapot temarim* (branches of palm trees) for the same reason—"ways of pleasantness."

2. In the matter of levirate marriage we are told, "If brothers dwell together, and one of them die and have no child, the wife of the dead shall not be married abroad to one not of his kin; her husband's brother shall go in unto her and take her to him to wife and perform the duty of a husband's brother unto her."[96]

The law is clear that the wife of the deceased falls to her husband's brother only if there was no son. But what if there was a son at the time of his death but the child dies shortly thereafter? The Talmud rules that the woman remains free of the levirate obligation. Whereupon Rabbi Judah, employing a *kal va-chomer,* infers from the case of a woman married to a *Kohen* that in the case of the death of the son, whose presence had bestowed a certain privilege, one reverts to the previous status that would have obtained if there was no son. The Talmud replies by applying the principle of "Her ways are ways of pleasantness."[97] That is to say, were the law to follow Rabbi Judah, then, if this woman had remarried while her son was alive and now required *chalitzah* from her first husband's brother because the son had died, a point of potential friction would arise which could sour this woman's marriage, contrary to the promise of "Her ways are ways of pleasantness."[98]

An unusual nuance is given to this principle by Rabbi Solomon Luria: ". . . that the words of Torah must all be pleasant and of equal consequences; the matter may not be crooked, that one person be joyous and another one have pain."[99] It is interesting to note that in this case the moral norm of "Her ways are ways of pleasantness" is powerful enough to turn aside a conclusion reached by the use of the logically compelling *kal va'chomer.*

3. A fascinating instance of the use of this norm in the posttalmudic literature is found in a ruling by Rabbi Joel Sirkes. The Halakhah states that if a convert dies without having had any issue after his conversion, his property and possessions are considered *hefker* (ownerless) and can be appropriated by whosoever desires. Rabbi

Asher ben Jehiel had been asked whether those who appropriate the property of the convert have an obligation to provide for his burial. He replied that Jewish law knows of no prior attachment of a person's property for burial purposes, and since these individuals acquired his property from *hefker,* they have no more obligation regarding the burial of the convert than any other Jew. The Tur and Rabbi Joseph Karo accepted the ruling of the Rosh (Rabbi Asher ben Jehiel). In opposition to them, Rabbi Sirkes argued that the spectacle of certain individuals taking off with the money of the deceased while others have to contribute for his burial expenses will certainly generate strife and bitterness. But the ways of our Torah are "ways of pleasantness." Hence, Rabbi Sirkes ruled that before any of the property of the deceased convert can be appropriated, adequate resources should be set aside for his burial needs.[100]

In analyzing the various enactments enumerated in the Talmud as having been legislated in response to three moral principles—"Her ways are ways of peace," "In order to prevent animosity" (*mi-penai eivah*), and "That they may not quarrel" (*delo laisai lintzuyai*)[101]—Eliezer Berkovits maintains that these moral principles, although seemingly similar in intent, were applied by the rabbis to different kinds of situations.[102]

1. *Mi-penai eivah* applies in instances where two people enjoy a personal relationship and one turns to the other with a personal request that is appropriate under the circumstances. In accordance with this principle, the other person should accede to the request even if the *din* does not require him to do so.
2. *Delo laisai lintzuyai* applies in situations where a question of ownership may lead to a dispute between individuals. In accordance with this principle, steps should be taken to clarify the question at issue so as to prevent a quarrel from developing.
3. "Her ways are ways of peace" applies in situations where certain types of behavior may offend the dignity of one's fellow man.
4. "Her ways are ways of peace" also applies in instances where laws of the Torah in matters of social welfare and acts of kindness that pertain only to relations between Jews are extended to non-Jews as well.

In giving the source for the rule that the saving of life supercedes the Sabbath laws, Maimonides comments:

It is written: "Ye shall therefore keep My statutes . . . which if a man do them he shall live by them." "That he shall live by them and not that he shall die by them." This teaches us that the judgments of the Torah are not meant to bring vengeance into the world, but are intended to secure compassion, kindness, and peace in the world.[103]

7

The Self and the Other

What Does The Law Of Love Imply?

In order to fully understand the relationship between the self and the other in the moral system of Judaism, we must first submit to careful scrutiny the two classic formulations of the general principle of man's duty to his fellow man. The first, of course, is "And thou shalt love thy fellow man as thyself."[1] We have already discussed some specific aspects of this Torah command, but now we will submit it to a thoroughgoing analysis. The second is the formulation apparently given to the command by Hillel in his famous response to the would-be convert's request for a concise expression of the essence of Judaism: "That which thou despisest, do not do to thy fellow man."[2]

Maimonides in his treatment of this *mitzvah* speaks exclusively of behavioral rather than emotional implications. Although the Torah here speaks only of "love," which is a human feeling, the rabbis, either on the basis of grammatical considerations or because of the psychological difficulty of legislating emotions, saw the fulfillment of this command as primarily involving certain kinds of behavior;[3] "Therefore," says Maimonides, "he should speak of him [his fellow man] positively and have compassion upon his possessions."[4] But, of course, to do this presupposes a positive attitude and feeling toward the other, which is why this *mitzvah* first appears in the *De'ot* section of Maimonides' code, which deals essentially with personal morality and proper character

201

traits. In another section, Maimonides speaks of the many direct personal acts of benevolence that one is obliged to perform for one's fellow man, such as visiting the sick, consoling the bereaved, burying the dead, dowering the bride, escorting travelers, and rejoicing bride and groom. And while he points out that these enactments are rabbinic, he adds that they nevertheless "are included in the command 'Love thy fellow man as thyself'; all things that you want others to do for you, do them for your brother."[5]

It would appear from Maimonides' treatment of this command that he considered it both as a particular moral *rule* with a specific content which of itself called for certain kinds of behavior and at the same time as a functional *principle*; i.e., serving to generate moral rules and involved in determining the range of their application. This latter function as a principle is implied by Hillel's characterization ("this is the entire Torah") as well as by Rabbi Akiva's description of the command as "a great principle [*kelal*] of the Torah."[6]

Nachmanides explicitly rejects the idea that the Torah would require a person to love the other with the same love that one has for oneself. He believes this to be psychologically unrealistic as well as morally incorrect because it is inconsistent with the teaching of Rabbi Akiva, ". . . *thy* life comes first."[7] Nevertheless, he points out, there is a sense in which a person's love for the other can be required to be on the same level as love of self or even to surpass it. There are some, says Nachmanides, who have a benevolent attitude toward their friends and acquaintances, wishing them well but only in a certain area and up to a certain point. They would like their friends, for example, to be financially comfortable but certainly not richer than themselves, for at that point they would grow envious even though their friends' blessing would not be at their expense. "Love thy fellow man as thyself" bids the individual to identify so intensely with the other that all envy passes from his heart. Even as we desire only the best and the maximum for our children and experience only joy when they surpass us in wisdom or wealth or achievement, so should be our attitude toward our fellow men.

Another commentator sees the qualifier "as thyself" as referring to the ordinary social behavior that you would expect from your friends in the course of a normal relationship rather than anything heroic or extraordinary.[8] He therefore sees this rule as implying the following traits: (1) that the relationship be honest and not deceitful; (2) that you constantly treat him with respect and dignity; (3) that you stay constantly in touch and inquire about his well-being; (4) that you participate in his joys and sorrows; (5) that you always welcome him with good cheer when he visits you; (6) that you always judge him charitably; (7) that you be prepared to do him small favors should the need arise and volunteer to make small loans to help him out; and (8) that you never adopt superior airs or act arrogantly toward him. It is on this most elemental social level of treating and being treated as a person that the deep mutuality of human relationship expressed in "as thyself" is first experienced. Instead of viewing this rule as a meta-ethical principle undergirding Jewish moral theory as a whole, this interpretation sees it as limited to the concrete context of a man and his friend. But then again, morality must surely start here if it is to exist anywhere.

Certainly the word *kamokha,* "as thyself," is crucial for an understanding of this rule. If the Torah, in its command to love, is calling for specific acts rather than feelings, then the "as thyself" of the imperative "Love thy neighbor as thyself" can be interpreted as referring to the kinds of actions you would like done or not done to yourself, which in turn becomes a criterion of the way you should treat the other. On this view, we are not being told about the intensity of the love emotion but rather are being given a guide as to how we ought to behave. If, for example, you wish to be helped when in need or not to be hurt by others, then treat the other in like manner. Hillel evidently interpreted the *kamokha* in this way as referring to *kinds of actions,* but for reasons we shall soon discuss, he chose to formulate the maxim in negative terms: "That which thou despisest, do not do to thy fellow man."

In the New Testament the positive formulation is given: "Do unto others as you would have others do unto you." If the Torah is indeed talking about *love,* then the positive formulation is quite appropriate, inasmuch as love usually translates into positive acts of benevolence. This is how the law of love in Leviticus evolved into the Golden Rule. If the "as thyself" is referring to love, then we are being commanded to love the other as we *in fact* do love ourselves. But the natural love of self is completely overwhelming and egotistical. If this is how we must love the other, then it implies complete benevolence, altruism, and even self-sacrifice.

Another possible interpretation is to view the *kamokha* as referring not to kinds of action but rather to the mediated character of the love or the mutual nature of the relationship as a whole. On this view, the *kamokha* acts restrictively, for what we are then saying is as follows: "Love thy fellow man as you (ought to) love yourself." Just as your love for yourself, normatively considered, is limited by the interests of others, so that it would be wrong to act for your own benefit where harm would result for others, so too should your love for your fellow man be limited to situations where no harm would come to yourself. Such an interpretation would be compatible with the ruling of Rabbi Akiva, ". . . *thy* life comes first."[9]

A third interpretation, already mentioned in an earlier chapter, translates *kamokha* as "*because* he is like you."[10] According to this we are being given the *reason* for loving our fellow man. There is a certain sameness, a certain kinship, an underlying unity which embraces all men. He, like you, is a center of value. There are no relevant differences between you (neither social standing nor color of skin, etc.) that would justify treating him differently than you expect to be treated. Indeed, that may very well be the significance of the "signature" that concludes the passage: "I am the Lord." That is to say, "I am the Lord who created both of you and has endowed all men with a 'spark of the divine,' i.e., constituted you as persons; therefore it is right that you love each other."[11] The fatherhood of God implies the brotherhood of man.

The "Deep Beauty" Of The Golden Rule

The special character of the Golden Rule as a universal meta-ethical principle has been recognized in the general philosophical literature. This principle does not take sides in a world of contending values but simply lays down a formal rule of procedure—a mode of behaving, not a goal of action.

> Now the deep beauty of the golden rule is that instead of attacking the will that is in other men, it offers their will a new dimension. Do as you *would* have others . . . as *you* would have others do. It bids you expand

your vision, see yourself in new relationship. It bids you transcend your insulation, see yourself in the place of others, see others in your place. It bids you test your values or at least your way of pursuing them. If you would disapprove that another should treat you as you treat him, the situation being reversed, is not that a sign that by the standard of your own values, you are mistreating him? . . . This is the only rule that stands by itself in the light of its own reason.[12]

The Malbim in his commentary notes that "Love thy fellow man . . ." requires that we treat our fellow men the way we wish to be treated and then observes that the philosophers (i.e., Kant) have already explained that the supreme principle which is the root of ethics (the categorical imperative) is that a person should will that whatever he does should become a universal law. That is to say, if he is tempted to do an act which is beneficial to himself but will have harmful consequences for others, he should ask himself whether he would like this mode of behavior to be practiced by everyone. But if it was, then he in turn might be on the "receiving end" and would suffer something he clearly would not want. The Malbim remarks, "And through this he too will avoid causing harm to his fellow." From this and from the discussion which follows, it seems that the Malbim understood the universalization of our proposed policies to work by getting the agent to believe that his action might stimulate others to act likewise, in which case he, the agent, will ultimately suffer. Therefore, fear and self-interest will cause the agent to refrain from his contemplated immoral act. This is not, of course, what "the philosophers" had in mind.

It is important to understand the relationship between the law of love in the Torah, its formulation as the Golden Rule by the rabbis, and the principle of universalizability embodied in Kant's categorical imperative: "Act only on that maxim through which you can at the same time *will* that it shall become a universal law." There are obvious similarities between all three, but they are not identical.

The Torah commands us to treat our fellow man with love and then defines or qualifies that behavior by referring to the way we love ourselves. Thus stated, the relationship between love of the other and love of self is simply that the latter acts as the criterion for the former. However, my *obligation* to treat the other with love derives from the authority of the moral system of Judaism and from my awareness that man is a center of intrinsic value and therefore must always be treated as an end. But once the command to love is transposed into a form of the Golden Rule which can be read as a self-subsistent moral principle, there is at least a suggestion that contained herein is not merely a criterion but the reason for its own compliance, or as MacIver put it: ". . . stands by itself in the light of its own reason." Such a consideration is based upon what is sometimes called the generalization principle: "If I judge my action to be right for myself, I implicitly judge it to be right for any other person whose nature and circumstances do not differ from my own in certain important respects."[13] Thus, to make the moral judgment that it is wrong to smoke is the equivalent of saying, "No smoking anywhere, at any time, by anyone, please." The generality of the judgment is also reflected in the fact that such a statement is precedent-forming and henceforth obligates the speaker. That is to say, if the speaker is subsequently caught smoking, he can be rightfully accused of inconsistency and immoral behavior. This implicit generality seems to be a feature of the logic of moral language; part of the grammar of ethical discourse. Once we accept this notion of the implicit generality of moral judgment, we can understand the use of the "reversibility test"; i.e., if there is certain behavior which you judge immoral when it hurts you, it ought to be equally immoral when it is hurting others.[14] This follows because by pronouncing the action wrong in one particular situation, you have committed yourself, whether you know it or not, to the action being wrong in all "similar" situations. (The fact that in the one case *you* are being hurt, while in the other case *someone else* is being hurt, clearly is not a "relevant difference.") Every moral judgment commits you to a principle. Therefore, "Do unto others as you would have others do unto you." If you do not, you have violated the law of contradiction and your behavior cannot be considered rational.

The principle of generalization is the heart and basis of Kant's categorical imperative although it is not identical with it. Kant's formulation requires not only the condition of reversibility but also the ability to will the maxim of my action to be a universal law. The latter condition is a much broader one and would render immoral, actions such as those which could not be universalized because they would causally lead to disasters (e.g., if nobody paid their debts, I couldn't get away with not paying since nobody would lend money).

It is clear, however, that Kant held this formal principle to be, in some sense, dictated by reason. In traditional usage, reason refers to man's cognitive power and includes: (1) the power of entertaining concepts such as "triangle," "justice," "mankind," etc. (which Kant called the faculty of "understanding"): (2) the power of applying concepts to given objects (the power of judgment), such as, "The invasion of Afghanistan by Russia is an act of injustice"; and (3) the power of making mediate inferences (the power of reasoning). Although these activities are theoretical, the knowledge reason generates is a precondition for action. All of our actions and decisions take place within determinate situations which vary according to the extent of our knowledge of the physical world, of human nature, and of cause-and-effect relationships. Kant believed that reason also has a practical function. By this he meant that our volition, or our willing, has a rational aspect. Only a rational being, says Kant, has the power of acting in accordance with principles. Just as theoretical reason knows individual objects as instances of a concept, so are we able to will our individual actions as instances of a concept or a rule. Thus, a principle of action, in order to be rational, must have universality as its formal character in the dual sense that it is applicable to different situations of the same kind and valid not merely for this agent but for all similar rational agents. This points up the difference between doing something out of inclination and doing something because I morally ought to do it. In the former case, I may decide not to do the action in similar circumstances next time, without inconsistency, simply because I am not inclined to do so. In the latter case, however, a moral judgment commits me to the general principle behind the action. It is this same generalization principle that makes possible both the giving of reasons for moral decisions and the varieties of inferential reasoning that takes place in moral decision-making so as to make morality teachable.

We must ask, however, why it is that moral language happens to have this characteristic of generality. Upon reflection it appears that implicit in the demand for generalization and universalizability is a moral principle which can be referred to as the principle of impartiality. This can be expressed as, "One ought not to make exceptions in one's own favor." Thus, there is something unfair or partial about refusing to treat others in a way you wish to be treated yourself. It turns out, therefore, that to be inconsistent in the area of practical reason is to be immoral. This enables us to really appreciate the "deep beauty" of the Golden Rule and perhaps helps to explain why Hillel, in responding to the question of the convert, did not simply repeat the command of the Torah, "Love thy fellow man as thyself," but replied as he did. By presenting the essence of Judaism in the form of the Golden Rule he was not only describing it but justifying it; not only stating that the core of the Torah was proper human relationship but demonstrating that to behave otherwise is both unreasonable and morally wrong.[15]

Why Be Negative When You Can Be Positive?

One of the more tantalizing questions in this matter is why Hillel chose to express the Golden Rule in its negative form rather than in its positive form. We have already indicated that in the New Testament this essential teaching of Judaism is given in its positive form: "All things that you wish others to do to you, do for them, this is the law and the prophets."[16] Is there any significance to this difference? Christian theologians in the past popularized the polemical view that it demonstrated the superiority of Christian ethics over Jewish ethics in that the positive version called for a true outpouring of love and benevolence while the negative version simply requires that you cause your fellow man no harm or embarrassment.[17] But, of course, this is incorrect, because Judaism abounds in positive expressions of man's obligation to man, from the original law of love in Leviticus to Hillel's own "Love all creatures."[18] It should also be remembered that although it may be in the negative form, the Golden Rule imposes positive obligations as well. Thus, if another person is in need and we are in a position to help him, it is our duty to do so, since if we were in need ourselves, we would *not like* to be ignored.

Scholars have offered a variety of explanations for Hillel's negative formulation of the Golden Rule. One writer opines that the entire issue has been overstated, and that "his negative formulation is hardly more than a random choice of terminology and may have been prompted by his desire to express the concept in terms of a popular proverb."[19] Another writer, offering a contextual explanation, suggests that Hillel was addressing a convert who was entering Judaism from an alien way of life and thus had to forget a good deal of the "old" before we could embrace the "new."[20] Hence, Hillel thought it wise to stress the negative; i.e., "Depart from evil. . . ,"[21] you must unlearn many old habits, there are things you must *not* do to others. But, of course, Hillel did add, "the rest is commentary, go and learn." In other words, after you learn to "depart from evil" we will go on in the next lesson to take up the positive—how to "do good."

I am persuaded, however, together with Achad ha-Am[22] and the Maharsha (Rabbi Samuel Eliezer Edels), that there are substantive reasons for Hillel's choice of a negative formulation. I believe it can be shown that the negative form is more precise and more effective as a moral principle. In the general literature, the positive form of the Golden Rule has usually been considered more conducive to absurdities than its negative counterpart. Since it starts out with the present contents of the individual's mind and sets no restrictions, it gives no hint as to the kind of person you should be before you start transferring your inclinations to others. Does it, for example, enjoin the masochist to become a sadist? (It is proper for me to beat you because I want you to beat me.) It has been argued that the positive form of the Golden Rule can give no guidance in our complex society where people are so heterogeneous. What I want others to do for me might be quite different from what they want me to do for them. This type of criticism, however, seems to miss an essential point of the positive form of the rule. I am not supposed to regard the other as possessed of *my* desires, passions, and temperaments, but as possessed of *his*. I must imaginatively enter into his situation and, given his framework of needs and circumstances, do for him as I would for myself. The rabbis seemed to be aware of this weakness and at one point warned, "So you may not say, 'As I was offended, let him be offended; as I was disgraced, let him be disgraced.'"[23]

Another type of criticism, equally unjustified, is voiced by Sidgwick: "This formula [the positive version of the Golden Rule] is obviously imprecise: for one might wish for another's cooperation in sin and be willing to reciprocate for it."[24] If by "sin" he means some offense against our fellow man, it is hard to see that this reflects a weakness in the Golden Rule. It merely means that the agent is willing to observe the rule in one area (offering reciprocal cooperation in regard to a particular project) but is violating it in another (in his choice of projects). Thus, if there is, indeed, honor among thieves, what is to be deplored is not the precept which enjoins us to honor our fellow man but the refusal of some to apply the precept universally.

There is, however, a crucial ambiguity that appears to infect the positive version of the Golden Rule. The question we must ask is: Does this rule lay down a constant obligation to seek out acts of goodness to perform for my fellow man, or is it an elliptical way of saying, "When contemplating an action, do only that which in similar circumstances you would like done to yourself"? If the latter interpretation is adopted, then you really have the equivalent of the negative version, so that the two can easily be combined into a more complete, precisely stated version of the Golden Rule: "Whatever I judge reasonable or unreasonable that another should do for me, by the same judgment I declare reasonable or unreasonable whether I, in like case, should do it for him." If, however, we favor the former interpretation, we emerge not with the rule of fairness or consistency but with the principle of benevolence or universal love, which states: "Every rational creature ought in its sphere and station, according to its respective powers and faculties, to do all the good it can to its fellows." Because Achad ha-Am interpreted the positive version of the Golden Rule in this manner, he argued that it was nothing more than "inverted egoism" and that "it simply takes the circle of egoism and replaces the 'self' by the 'other' in its center." Since what the self wishes for itself has no limits, if you oblige a person to do this for others, "you are inclining the scales of justice to the side of the other and against the self."[25] This leads to a sort of "moral fanaticism"[26] in which we constantly have a moral obligation to maximize goodness in the world. But if the Golden Rule is indeed urging upon us such extreme altruism, then it no longer "stands in the light of its own reason." For we can no longer appeal to the rule of consistency since the "as you love yourself" refers, on this view, not to normative behavior but to natural man's unbridled egoism, which could hardly serve as a model to be universalized.

It may, therefore, be concluded that the negative formulation of the Golden Rule, as compared to the positive version, is a much more precise expression of a basic moral principle in Judaism that appeals to consistency and fairness, and at the same time can function as a criterion for judging the moral correctness of individual actions. Our discussion, however, has brought to our attention the rule of benevolence and the question whether there are limits to the love that man should extend to his fellow man.

To Hate Or Not To Hate

Within the heart of man the issue is not merely "to love or not to love" but also "to love or to hate," for the repertoire of human feelings includes the very fierce and destructive negative emotion of hatred. Like its opposite, "love," the feeling of hatred has its roots in biology and represents man's natural response to certain negative aspects of his situation which evoke in him fear or resentment or revulsion. Like the other emotions, hatred is clearly not all of one piece and is experienced as an entire range of feelings of varying intensity and nuances, from a mild dislike to a cold abhorrence to a raging, passionate detestation. But if hatred, like the other emotions, arises naturally in man, and God created man, then the emotion as such must be accepted as part of the *grand design* and as playing a needed and legitimate role within the life of man. The morality of Judaism does not condemn the emotion of hatred per se as evil but questions the uses to which it is put or who or what becomes the object of hate.

Does the prompting of Jewish morality to love one's fellow man, as contained in the overlapping commands to "Love thy fellow man," and "Love the stranger," and "Love humanity," effectively preclude the legitimation of any sort of hatred for any man? It is interesting to note that Christianity imputes to the "Old Dispensation" the actual teaching of hatred of one's enemies: "You have heard that it was said, 'You shall love your neighbor and hate your enemy,' . . . But I say to you, Love your enemies and pray for those who persecute you."[27]

The first point that must be made is that the original command to love one's fellow occurs in a set of sentences in which we are explicitly commanded not to hate: "Thou shalt not hate thy brother in thy heart; thou shalt surely rebuke thy neighbor and not bear sin because of him; thou shalt not take vengeance nor bear any grudges against the children of thy people, but thou shalt love thy fellow as thyself, I am the Lord."[28]

While each of these commands is usually considered a separate injunction, they can be read in sequence as advice on how to approach one's enemy, personal or religious. A person has caused you harm or has offended you and the resentment has built up into hatred. You watch your neighbor mindlessly violating the sancta of Judaism and your indignation turns to hatred. The teaching of the Torah is: Do not permit the hatred to fester in your heart. Hate is toxic and if stored within tends to corrode the entire personality. Work through your hatred by "rebuking your neighbor." *Tokhachah* (reproof) is a process of confrontation and communication. Confront your neighbor and tell him how you have been hurt. Ask him why he is doing what to you appears to be wrong. Try to get him to see how wrong it is. Perhaps you can get him to change. In any event, "Do not bear sin upon him"; i.e., separate the sin, the evil deed, from the person.[29] As a result of your own verbalization, in which you clarify the true source of the wrong, the hatred can now be vented upon the evil deed rather than the person or can be confined to the evil within the person.

The Talmud relates the following story:

> There were some lawless men living in the neighborhood of Rabbi Meir and they used to vex him sorely. Once Rabbi Meir prayed that they should perish. His wife Beruriah exclaimed: "What is in your mind? Is it because it is written: 'Let sinners cease out of the earth'? But the text can be read to mean: 'Let *sins* cease out of the earth—and when *sins* shall cease, then the wicked shall be no more.' Rather should you pray that they repent and be no more wicked." Rabbi Meir offered prayer on their behalf and they repented.[30]

Having treated the emotion of hatred, the Torah goes on to say that certainly, in no way, should these feelings be permitted to manifest themselves in overt acts of vengeance. On the contrary, you must treat the person you once hated the way you treat yourself—with forgiveness, with indulgence, and with *actions* denoting benevolence and love.

The fact is that we do find two sources in the Torah which appear to advocate hatred. There is, first, the passage in Psalms: "Do not I hate them, O Lord, that hate Thee? And do not I strive with those that rise up against Thee? I hate them with intense hatred; I count them mine enemies."[31] There are some who interpret this as referring to wicked individuals who publicly violate the laws of the Torah and do not respond to efforts of *tokhachah*. The Talmud sees this passage as referring to "heretics and disbelievers" and was so accepted by Maimonides.[32]

Then there is the interesting discussion in the Talmud concerning the passage: "If thou meet thy enemy's ox or his ass going astray, thou shalt surely bring it back to him again." While the Torah commands you to be good to this person and to retrieve his animal, nevertheless there seems to be a tacit acceptance and legitimation of his status as "your enemy."

Rabbi Samuel concludes that "your enemy" in this passage refers to someone whom you are "permitted to hate" because you personally witnessed him transgressing (since you are only one witness, this makes him "your enemy" but not a "public enemy"). Presumably, this is a case where he persists in transgressing even after he has been warned and admonished.[33]

Recent rabbinic authorities perceive radical changes as having taken place in the human situation which in large measure render even this opportunity to hate inoperable today. Rabbi Meir Simchah of Dvinsk, for example, points to the fact that the same law which in the Book of Exodus is formulated in terms of "thy enemy" is in the Book of Deuteronomy expressed in terms of "thy brother": "Thou shalt not see thy brother's ass or his ox fallen down by the way, and hide thyself from them; thou shalt surely help him to lift them up again." Says the rabbi, if the use of the term "thy enemy" implies an acceptance by the Torah of that relationship, giving permission to hate someone who committed a transgression, that was understandable in the Book of Exodus, which addressed the Jewish people prior to the sin of the worship of the golden calf. At that point in their history, after the revelation at Mount Sinai, the Jewish people were on a high moral and spiritual plane, far from sin and aspiring to become the ideal "kingdom of priests and a holy nation." Within a context of striving and high expectations, it may be appropriate to look upon your neighbor who transgresses as "your enemy." However, after the sin of the golden calf, which constituted a major setback in the spiritual development of the people, sin and transgression became much more pervasive. Under these changed circumstances, it would have been wrong and unseemly for someone who himself was probably stained with sin to hate someone else because of his transgression. Therefore, in the Book of Deuteronomy, which speaks to the people after their fall from Sinaitic innocence, the permission to hate the transgressor is withdrawn and the law to assist is given in terms of "thy brother" rather than "thy enemy."[34]

Two remarkable and extremely significant principles related to this issue are found in the writings of the *Chazon Ish* (Rabbi Abraham Karelitz). One of them is built upon the observation of the talmudic sages that already in their generation no one knew how to admonish or rebuke.[35] *Tokhachah* was viewed as a very complex and very difficult art whose purpose was to extricate the transgressor from the grip of sin, giving him a glimpse of the right side of the question, and restoring to him some modicum of freedom of choice. Only after experiencing such *tokhachah* can a person be held responsible for his deed. Such a task obviously involves great psychological insight and human sympathy which few have. But if *tokhachah* is today a forgotten skill and the Halakhah permits hatred only after *tokhachah,* then every transgressor today is technically in a state of *before tokhachah,* which is to say that he is included in the obligation to "Love your fellow man as yourself."

In terms of the heretic and the harsh behavior toward him suggested by the Talmud,[36] the *Chazon Ish* states that such laws prescribing physical violence do not apply today. In order to be justified, to be properly understood, and to have the desired results, such a policy presupposes a widespread acceptance of the principles of religious faith empirically supported by a rather visible Providence. However, in our day of *hester panim,* in which the Divine Presence is hidden, and as a result faith everywhere is weakened, such behavior would be terribly misunderstood, counterproductive, and simply not justified. Instead, we are to try to draw all men to us with gentle words in peace and love.[37]

Rabbi Jacob Emden bases his approach upon the sweeping nature of the teaching to "Love humanity [*beriyot*]," which the rabbis saw as the special attribute of Aaron but identified as an essential aspect of the Torah way of life. By embracing all men, even idolaters, as candidates for our love, the rabbis emphasized the overriding nature of the imperative. All references to hate, therefore, must be interpreted as being directed at anything except human beings. Hate the deed but not the agent. Hate the evil consequences but not the person. In commenting upon the sequence of attributes: "He loves the Omnipresent; He loves humanity," Rabbi Emden states that often it is precisely a man's love for God which brings him to hate people when he sees them disobeying the word of God. For "those who love God detest evil." One must learn to depersonalize the evil and, in this context, disassociate the deed from the perpetrator, so that our essential love can remain unimpaired.[38]

We may, therefore, conclude that in Jewish morality in its fully developed form, we can find no justification for hating either a personal enemy or a religious enemy (whether from the same religion or from another religion). In a choice between coming to the aid of your friend or of your enemy, the Talmud gives priority to the enemy in order that you may overcome your natural antipathy.[39] And the Book of Proverbs teaches: "Rejoice not when thine enemy falleth, and let not thine heart be glad when he stumbleth."[40]

The Lesson Of The Good Samaritan

Judaism, however, is the religion of the Jewish people and only of the Jewish people. And as we have already noted, Jewish survival places high on our scale of moral values. The Jew loves his fellow man, but he also loves his people and his homeland, and it is morally right that he love all of them. The *political* enemy of the Jew, therefore, cannot easily be dismissed.[41] It is worthy noting in this connection that Christianity in its original formulations lacked a political and social dimension and focused only on the morality of the individual. The parable of the Good Samaritan is another instance of the Christian attempt to demonstrate the limitations of Jewish morality and the superiority of the teachings of Jesus.[42] It will be remebered that a "lawyer" had asked what he must do to inherit eternal life and then himself refers to the command to love God and to love one's neighbor as oneself. But when the lawyer asks Jesus, "And who is my neighbor?" Jesus replies with the story of the beaten, half-dead person by the road who is ignored by a passing priest and Levite, but is tenderly helped and cared for by a Samaritan. Jesus asks, "Which of these three do you think proved 'neighbor' to the man?" The point that would have to be granted by all is that there can be bad Jews and good non-Jews. And that the law of love applies to all. But why does Jesus speak of a Samaritan? Why not a pagan or an Essene? The answer is that the New Testament had another implication in mind. The Samaritans were primarily political enemies of the Jewish people. To urge upon Jews in first-century Judea that the real key to eternal life is to broaden the application of "Love thy neighbor" to include the Samaritans and the Romans, or possibly to start with the Samaritans and the Romans, is comparable to urging Israelis today that their primary moral problem is to begin to learn to love the Arabs. Of course, one ought to love Arabs, Samaritans, and ancient Romans together with all people. But to push such a program at a time when these people are your political enemies, actively engaged in the destruction of your people and the conquest of your land, betrays a colossal insensitivity to the national and political concerns of the Jewish people then and now.

However, one does not carry the label "political enemy" forever. The Torah teaches us to forgive and forget: "Thou shalt not abhor an Egyptian, because you wast a stranger in his land."[43] And on the Festival that celebrates our birthday—the liberation of the Jewish people from Egyptian bondage—we do not recite the full Hallel service of jubilant praise during most of the days, out of a sense of sorrow for the Egyptian dead!

Morality is the science of choosing between alternatives—the available alternatives as permitted by the situation. Sometimes, through no fault of our own, situations "nasty and brutish" are imposed upon us. The Jews of Europe during the Holocaust had to deal with the most agonizing of moral questions: whether to flee, to abandon loved ones, to destroy oneself, to renounce God? Sometimes we work our own way into situations "nasty and brutish" while in the pursuit of legitimate and even moral ends. One has a right to engage in business, build an industry, and employ workers, although in the process one runs into a pack of horrendous moral questions regarding decent working conditions, fair wages, inferior products, disposal of polluting wastes. And so it is for the Jews of Israel. A nation, particularly a persecuted and rejected nation, has a right to return and resettle its land. The Zionist effort, in conception, was legitimate and eminently worthwhile. Up to the moment it proclaimed its state, it succeeded without displacing a single Arab. The situation that developed in the course of resisting Arab attack has indeed become increasingly "nasty and brutish": four wars, displaced persons, armies of occupation, terrorism and counterterrorism. The moral questions that such a situation gives rise to are indeed immense. Particularly for Jews, moral problems arising out of the use of power and out of a responsibility for the body politic are rather new: the effect of a people's army on Israeli society, time spent away from family by reservists, women in the army, accidents during training due to carelessness, looting, overreacting to demonstrators, collective punishment—all of these pose profound moral challenges that must surely strain the integrity and moral fiber of the individual. Some Israeli and American Jews, however, seem to suggest that simply being in such a situation is somehow corrupting and shameful. This would be valid if Israel had aspired to rule over a million Arabs and if the Basle Program had included a desire to develop "the most powerful military machine in the Middle East." The fact is that Israel, like Joshua of old, "called out in peace" at each major turn of events. In her four wars, Israel acted only after being threatened and attacked. Jewish morality teaches, "If someone comes to kill you, rise up and kill him first,"[44] and thus the preemptive strike is pronounced both prudential and moral. Had Israel lost any of her four wars, she would have had the moral problems our people faced in the Holocaust. Because Israel was successful in defending herself, she has now a different set of moral problems. But facing challenges in the pursuit of legitimate ends are neither corrupting nor shameful. Lack of moral knowledge or of the strength to respond in a morally correct way is.

Judaism has never run from the possibility of war in spite of a keen awareness of the horror of the death and destruction that come with it. Those things that are worth living for are also worth dying for. And there will always be someone who will want to deprive you of what you cherish: wife, family, freedom, home. But there is a morality of war, a right and a wrong way among the particular alternatives forced upon you. The Torah does teach: "And your camps shall be holy,"[45] and the Jewish State has developed a concept of *tohar ha-neshek*—"the purity of arms"—an ongoing exploration of the application of the moral principles of Judaism to the horrifying but real circumstances of war and terrorism in Israel today. Thus, rabbinic journals have been discussing, in great seriousness and in great detail, the moral issues involved in actions like the Kibya reprisal raid, the Entebbe rescue, and the incursions into southern Lebanon.[46] The context in which these problems has to be seen was well stated by Harold Fisch:

> The moral problem is not whether to enter the battle or not: this is not the moral choice which is open to us. The choice is not even whether we should remain in Israel or not. This is no longer an open issue. The only issue is how to carry on the battle, how to remain in our land under conditions which force us into war, how under these conditions to do what must be done and still be true to our Jewish heritage.[47]

Judaism teaches that man has duties to himself as well as to others. Man is directed to provide for his own needs, to keep himself in good health physically and mentally, and to seek medical aid when ill. He is also forbidden to harm himself and certainly to take his own life.[48] But man is also commanded to love his fellow man as himself, to respect his person and property, to aid him in need, and to rescue him when he is in danger. This last duty is based upon the command, "Thou shalt not stand idly by the blood of thy fellow,"[49] which according to the Talmud means that if you see someone drowning or being attacked by wild beasts or by robbers, you are obliged to go to his rescue. Whatever effort is needed to rescue the individual, including the hiring of help, is included in the obligation. There are some authorities who rule that even if a person has to give away all of his fortune to save the life of another, he is obliged to do so. If his efforts succeed, he may, of course, claim compensation from the person he saved.[50]

Our Duty Toward The Other

The issue we must now turn to is the relationship between our duty to ourselves and our duty to others. Are they both of equal weight and importance, or does one duty have priority when their demands are mutually exclusive?

In considering these two basic duties, to the self and to the other, our moral intuitions react to them quite differently. I am instinctively suspicious of duties to the self because they are duties to *my* self. Usually, in speaking of my own needs and concerns for my own life and health, I do not use the language of morality (ought, duty, obligation) because I do not have to. To do what is obviously for my own self-preservation, self-interest, benefit, and pleasure flows immediately and spontaneously in response to my natural desires. In fact, "duty," "obligation," and "ought" resound most characteristically when they are used to refer to actions which are opposed by inclination and desire. Too often in situations involving moral questions, self-interest turns easily into selfishness and egoism, prompting a person to trample on the rights of others and to ignore his duty to his fellow man.

Let us attempt to understand the basis in the morality of Judaism for the duty toward self. Actually this duty builds up in a two-step process beginning with the fundamental principle of Jewish morality: the intrinsic worth of every human being as a person "created in the image of God." Now, I am a person *no less* than the other individual over against me. Therefore, for the same reasons that I must "love" and respect my fellow man as *tzelem elohim* must I respect and "love" the *tzelem elohim* that is within me. In adopting this attitude I must transcend the personal perspective and adopt an objective view. This notion of the essential equality of all persons in respect to their innate and irreducible value is reflected in the Torah's formulation: ". . . and you shall love your fellow man as [you love] yourself." Not only is the love of self offered here as a criterion of how one ought to love one's fellow man, but it may be seen as implicitly legitimizing that self-love. Are we to conclude, therefore, that the duty toward self and the duty toward the other are of equal weight?

In discussing the duty to rescue a person in danger, the question is raised as to whether one is obliged to risk one's life in order to rescue the other. While opinion is divided, there are authorities who rule that the mere existence of danger or the *possibility* that in rescuing the other one might lose one's life is *not* sufficient to absolve one from the duty toward the other.[51] The fact that I have an obligation to *risk* my own life in order to save another person from *certain* death is consistent with the principle that duty to self and duty to the other are of equal importance. Would Judaism, however, require that a person give up his life so that another might live?

In order to answer this question we must first consider the famous case of the two men traveling in the desert.

> "That thy brother may live with thee." This is what Ben Petura taught: Two men are journeying through the desert and one of them has a single jug of water. If one of them drinks it, he alone will get back to civilization. But if both of them drink it, both of them will die. Ben Petura taught that they should both drink and die rather than one of them should behold his companion's death, as it is said, "That thy brother may live with thee." Until Rabbi Akiva came and taught, . . . "that thy brother may live *with thee*"; your own life comes before the life of your fellow man.[52]

Ben Petura evidently holds that a man's duty to his fellow man is as important as his duty to himself, but not more so. Hence, the man with the water has the moral right neither to drink it all himself nor to offer it all to his fellow traveler. There is no alternative but that they both drink and both die.[53] Others have attempted to explain the position of Ben Petura in terms of the significance of the immediate and the importance of the life of the moment (*chayyei sha'ah*), as short as it may be. B is dying of thirst; his danger is now. A is in no danger now. His problem will come later. Ben Petura holds that A's concern for what will be tomorrow cannot cancel out his obligation to help B in his present plight. "Let not one of them behold his companion's death." There is something immoral, even obscene, in watching your companion die of thirst while you nurse the water for your later need.[54]

An alternative interpretation focuses on the inequality of their positions. A, by virtue of his having partaken of the water, is in possession of temporary existence. B, who is about to die of thirst, stands to lose even his existence of the moment. Ben Petura rules that the concern of A for a more permanent lease on life cannot justify his refusal to equalize their positions by affording B a similar existence for the moment. Something of the same issue may be involved in the question whether a person ought to *risk* his life in order to save another person from *certain* death. Does the immediate existential prospect of certain death to a human being create an obligation to help so strong that it overrides the *possibility* that in the process of rescue I may lose my own life?

Another interpretation puts it this way: one would have to give one's life for the commandments were it not for the general principle "and you shall *live* by them." In other words, the Torah was given to enhance, enrich, and prolong life, not to act as a cause of death. In our case, however, where the other person's life is in danger and we are confronted by the commandment "Do not stand idly by the blood of your fellow," we are no longer constrained by the principle "and you shall *live* by them" in observing this commandment, because by doing so we are actually making it possible for someone to live.[55]

Rabbi Akiva, however, is of the opinion that in a clash between these two duties the self has priority: "Your life comes before the life of your fellow man." More than that, Rabbi Akiva believes that the ultimate consequence of an act and its effect on our lives are determinative of the moral character of that act. Thus, as heartless as it may seem at the time, Rabbi Akiva teaches that A should withold the water from B so that he (A) may survive. "Your own life comes before the life of your fellow man."

As Achad ha-Am correctly saw it:

> All men including the self are under obligation to develop their lives and their faculties to the limit of their capacity and at the same time each is under obligation to assist his neighbor's self-development so far as he can. But just as I have no right to ruin another man's life for the sake of my own, so I have no right to ruin my own life for the sake of another's. Both of us are men and both our lives have the same value before the throne of justice.[56]

In the same vein, we have a law which limits the altruism of individuals in the giving of charity: "they ordained at Usha that if a man spends liberally on charity, he must not spend more than a fifth [of his possessions] lest he himself become dependent upon his fellow men."[57]

Another case reported in the Talmud is that of a person who is threatened with death unless he takes another's life. Here the situation is in reverse, because the question now is, Can he save his own life at the expense of another? Rabbah ruled: "Who shall say that your blood is redder than his? Perhaps his blood is redder than yours."[58] In other words, you have no right to kill the other person. The point is not that we do not happen to know in this particular case whose life is more valuable but that when it comes to taking a life, every individual is to be seen, in principle, as possessing supreme value.

Nor does Judaism play the "numbers" game. Even where the lives of many or of an entire community are threatened unless one of them is handed over to be killed, and even if he is singled out by name, the entire group must be sacrificed rather than hand over an innocent person to death. And as Dr. Belkin observes: "What makes this Halakhah even more striking is the fact that under Jewish law surrendering an innocent man to be killed by others does not constitute an act of murder."[59] However, after considerable discussion, the Halakhah remains that if the attackers demand an individual by name (as in the case of Sheba ben Bichri), and if he has been condemned to die by the civil authorities (even if the judgment is not in accordance with Jewish law), he may then be handed over to the attackers so that the rest of the company may be saved. How can this ruling be reconciled with the general principle that you cannot buy a life with a life even where many lives are involved? It is, of course, true that if the individual in question is not surrendered he will die anyway, but that consideration obtained even in the case where the individual was not named, and we ruled there that he is not to be handed over to die.

Several theories have been offered to explain this Halakhah. One view sees the individual in the classic category of the *rodef* (pursuer). Since, as a result of violating the laws of the civil authorities, this individual is a wanted man, he is unjustifiably endangering the entire community by seeking refuge among them. Now, just as the Halakhah bids us rescue the pursued even at the expense of killing the *rodef*, so too here, the "wanted man" (*rodef*) may be handed over to the authorities in order to save the rest of the group. Others point out that since this unfortunate individual has been sentenced to die as a result of some action of his own, and since no matter what we do, he will die, we are, in effect, handing over a "dead man."[60]

This ruling by Jewish morality, which weaves a painful path

between life and life and between the lives of the many and the life of the individual, is perceived thus by a recent writer:

> Common morality is outraged by the consequentialist position that, as long as human beings can remain alive, the lesser of two evils is always to be chosen. Its defenders maintain, on the contrary, that there are minimum conditions for a life worthy of a human being, and that nobody may purchase anything—not even the lives of a whole community—by sacrificing those conditions. A community that surrenders its members at the whims of tyrants ceases to be anything properly called by that name; and individuals willing to accept benefits at the price of crimes committed upon other individuals degrade their humanity. Common morality allows a certain room for compliance with tyrannical external force, when resistence has become impossible; but there is a line that must be drawn beyond which compliance is excluded, and the example of rabbinic teaching is a guide in drawing it.[61]

"But Thy Life Comes First"

To return to the case of the travelers in the desert, the Maharsha points out that it is an essential fact for Rabbi Akiva that one of the men is in rightful possession of the water. By the act of drinking his own water, this person is fulfilling his moral duty to preserve his life. He is "harming" the other only by his inaction. Were the water owned jointly by the travelers, it would certainly not be morally right for either of them to seize the water for himself. If one of them were to seize the water, he would, in effect, be discharging his moral duty to himself, but by the very same action he would also be altering the giveness of the other's situation and depriving him of his share of the water. Thus, while Rabbi Akiva agrees that one person may not save himself at the expense of another person's life, he is saying that in this case one may ignore another person's need because there is no way to morally help him. While, as we have seen, Rabbi Akiva derives the concept of the primacy of self from a biblical passage, we might still inquire as to the moral justification behind this principle.

There is a group of laws in the Halakhah in which certain priorities are listed that seem to favor not only the self before the other, but also various ingroups before the outgroups. Thus:

> "If thou lend money to any of My people that is poor with thee." If the choice in lending money is between "my people" and a non-Jew, "my people" has preference . . . between the poor members of your family and the poor people of your town, the former have preference; between the poor of your own town and the poor of another town, the poor of your town have preference.[62]

> If townspeople have a well and it is a question whether they or strangers have first call on it, they come before the strangers.[63]

> If one has a choice between recovering one's own property or that of one's father or teacher, one's own property comes first. If one has a choice of liberating oneself from prison or redeeming one's father or teacher, one's own redemption comes first . . .[64]

What we are observing here is the operation of a sensitivity which says that it is morally obligatory upon a person in some contexts to place the interests of his own family or of any group with which he is associated over the interests of others.[65] This is so because morality, which deals with the appropriate behavior between persons, must not only take into consideration the essential value of the individual, but must also determine the particular relationship that exists between the individuals involved. And human relationships are varied and complex. There are parents and children, debtors and creditors, subjects and sovereign, brothers and sisters, neighbors, professional associates, countrymen, etc., and all sorts of combinations and permutations thereof. But each relationship sets up special expectations and imposes special moral obligations upon those who stand in that relationship. Thus the Mishnah rules that in a choice of benefiting father or teacher, teacher comes first, because he has done more for you.[66] Or consider the behavior expected of the owner of a Hebrew slave. On the basis of the passage, ". . . because it shall be good for him with thee. . . ," the Talmud rules that if the owner has only one pillow, he must give it to the slave. Clearly, it is the nature of the particular relationship, master to slave, with the subservient condition of the slave (rather than the general principle of man's obligation to man), that creates a moral obligation for the owner to sacrifice his own comfort for the sake of the slave.[67] Similarly, the loyalty one owes to members of one's group, be it family, neighborhood, or country, is based upon a tacit "social contract" that converts all such close social groupings into mutual-aid societies of a sort. A family, for example, could not live in such close proximity, could not accomplish what it does for the individual, without a good deal of trust, cooperation, self-sacrifice, and benevolent activity on the part of all the members. The same analysis holds for other group memberships, with varying degrees of loyalty depending upon the intimacy of the ties. This loyalty, which is partially based on the moral sentiment of gratitude, is expressed in the priorities given to the group when alternatives are involved.

This same kind of reasoning can be seen as the basis for the priority given by Judaism to the self over the other. "Man is 'related' to himself." Because man is so "close" to himself in terms of knowing his own needs, having a natural concern for himself, and usually being in the best position to help himself, he has certain duties to himself. "For if I am not for myself, who will be for me?" Man's proximity to himself creates a certain dependence, so that if he does not give himself priority, he will truly end up deprived and disadvantaged. Therefore, "your life comes first, and what is yours comes before what belongs to other men."

In recent discussions of the Ben Petura-Akiva controversy, some rather fanciful interpretations have been offered as to the issues between them. One writer suggested that Rabbi Akiva only means to say that there is no obligation for both to die, but if the man with the water wanted to give it all to his friend, this would be a special act of piety (*midat chasidut*), and that "Ben Petura too would not object if one allowed his friend to drink and survive."[68] It is difficult to believe that in considering such a tragic situation, in which all he can suggest is, "Let them both drink and die," Ben Petura would not have alluded to another more lofty moral option if he indeed believed that one existed; i.e., that one of the men give up the water and sacrifice himself so that at least one may live. Another writer insists that these two sages are not discussing morals at all, but rather meta-ethics. Ben Petura is saying "that *each* of the two men ought to be ready to sacrifice himself rather than one see that the other die."[69] Even as a homiletic *derash* such an interpretation is not very plausible. What blinds both of these scholars to the meaning of the controversy, and what drives them to these strained interpretations, is their obvious desire to read into Jewish morality an acceptance of a high regard for self-sacrifice. Both men seem to be impressed by the statement, "Greater love hath no man than this, that a man lay down his life for his friend,"[70] and would like to find a basis for it in Judaism.

It seems clear, however, that for Judaism the view of Rabbi Akiva prevails, which is that in a clash of duties between self and the other, "Your own life comes first."[71] Perhaps the reason why the codes "are strangely silent" on this controversy between Ben Petura and Rabbi Akiva is that the identical ruling is reflected in the law, "Do not stand idly by the blood of your fellow man," which is restricted to *risking* one's life for the other, but not sacrificing it.[72]

"Greater Love Hath No Man"

The question that arises at this point, however, is that while it is generally acknowledged that according to Judaism it is not *mandatory* that an individual give his life for the other, is it *permissible* for him to do so should he desire? Is one free to choose to sacrifice one's own life to save another's? If a man decides to give his life for his friend, believing, for example, that his friend's life is of greater value because he has a wife and family, while he is single, would Judaism frown upon his action or "look upon it as an act of special piety"?[73]

Some have argued that Judaism would approve of such an act and consider it an act of selfless love. Rabbi Kook, without making any definitive ruling, sketches the background considerations justifying such a view. From his discussion it would appear that the key issue determining this question is the following: In the case which came before Rabbah, mentioned earlier, it was decided that although it is permissible to transgress the laws of the Torah in order to preserve one's life, this cannot apply to the sin of murder. For then a life is lost either way, and who is to say "whose blood is redder," or which life is of greater value? But does it really make a difference, in this respect, if instead of taking someone else's life to save my own, I take my own life in order to save another! Suicide is a grave sin according to Judaism. I am not the master of my life and may not surrender my soul at will. And if the rhetorical question of "whose blood is redder" really means that no human being can know which life is of greater value, then I too have no right to judge my life to be inferior to that of the other.[74] Jacobs, in arguing against Achad ha-Am, attempts to distinguish between Rabbah's case and a case of self-sacrifice by saying: "Rabbah deals with murder and as Rashi points out, it is forbidden to commit a crime in order to save a life, if life must be lost in committing the crime. But the sacrifice of one's life for another is no crime, for suicide is only an offense because a life is lost, not because *my* life is lost"![75] Of course, we have noted quite the contrary. To preserve my own life is a duty, and a stronger duty than to preserve my neighbor's life, precisely because it is *my* life and I am, so to speak, my closest relative. It does not seem to me to be the case, therefore, "that a man who gives his life for his friend is a saint and would be recognized as such by Judaism."

I would think, however, that the rare instances of heroic acts where an individual is carried aloft by a love for God and for Israel, as personified by his fellow man, and sacrifices his own life to save the other must be classified as a sort of *averah lishmah*—"sin for the sake of God." Normative Jewish morality cannot approve of it. Yet we cannot help but stand back in admiration and wonder at such great love and devotion. It is a case of the splendor of the sentiment eclipsing the logic and bursting through the confines of the system.[76]

While it appears that Judaism frowns upon self-sacrifice for the sake of the other, it does elevate two values above the worth of the individual human being. Self-preservation is not the supreme law in Judaism. "There are reasons for life more vital than living."[77] These values are God and the collectivity of Israel, called *Kelal Yisrael*. God, of course, ranks higher than human life. Theoretically, the love and devotion that man owes his creator should include a readiness to serve Him with one's very life. "'And you shall love the Lord your God with all your heart and with all your soul . . .' even if He takes your soul."[78] This was implied in the command to Abraham to sacrifice "his only son whom he loves" to God and is the underlying thought behind the symbolism of the Temple service involving animal sacrifice.

Love Of God and Sanctification Of The Name

Practically speaking, however, what are God's needs or concerns in the mundane world which would require devotion unto the point of death? The human being, as a moral agent, is an entity of supreme value for God in the world. Why should He desire anyone's death? The Torah itself is considered another great composition and invest-ment by God. Are Jews obliged to observe and defend the Torah even at the expense of their lives? The rabbis ruled unanimously that gener-ally it is permitted to transgress a Torah law in order to save a life. Certainly no Jew is required to give his life in pursuit of any of the positive commands of the Torah. But even in the connection with the negative commands (except for the special cases soon to be noted), all that is necessary to save a person's life may be done even if it involves violation of the Sabbath laws or eating on the Yom Kippur fast-day. This ruling is based on the passage "Ye shall therefore keep My statutes and Mine ordinances, which if a man do, he shall live by them," to which the rabbis commented, *"live* by them and *not die because of them."*[79] The Torah is understood as a gift from God to aid man in his struggle with life. The goal of Torah is life-enhancing, and in the last analysis the Torah is here to serve Israel and to serve man. Man, there-fore, need not, nay, must not, sacrifice his life for the command-ments.[80]

There are, however, exceptions. That is to say, there are situations when the Jew is obliged to give his life rather than worship idols, com-mit adultery or incest, or commit murder.[81] This must be understood as a function of the Jew's duty to "hallow God" or "to sanctify the Holy Name" (*kiddush ha-shem*). This is a most paradoxical aspect of Jewish theology. On the one hand, men struggle to attain a state of holiness, which they can only do by imitating God and by observing God's commandments. "Ye shall be holy, for I the Lord your God am holy."[82] Yet there is a sense in which God has a "need" to be hallowed by His people, Israel. "I will be hallowed among the children of Israel; I am the Lord who hallows you."[83] The rabbis developed this concept into the twin notions of *kiddush ha-shem,* "sanctification of the name," and its opposite, *chillul ha-shem,* "desecration of the name." This idea is, in turn, rooted in the concept of "witnessing," or "testifying"—

applied in the Pentateuch to the Tabernacle, the Tablets, and sometimes to the Torah itself, which "witnesses" for God against the Jewish
people as to the provisions of the covenant as well as to its being in
force.[84] But the prophets already spoke of Israel being a "witness" for
God. "You are My witnesses, saith the Lord, and My servant whom I
have chosen."[85] Because Israel is known as God's people and as the
people of the Torah, their survival, their devotion, and their moral
stature, if they are impressive, are a vindication of God, a public
demonstration of His wisdom and goodness. On the one hand, should
Israel misbehave, or abandon the Torah, or suffer greatly, then this has
a negative implication about God. There results a desecration of His
name. God, it would appear, is judged in the world by the behavior
and general situation of His people. This concept is expressed thus by
the rabbis:

> "He is a witness, whether he has seen or has known. If he does not utter
> it, then he shall bear his iniquity." "He is a witness" . . . this refers to
> Israel. "Whether he has seen" . . . as it is written: "Thou hast been
> brought to see and known that the Lord, He is God, there is none beside
> Him." "Or hath known" . . . as it is written: "And thou shalt *know* this
> day and lay it to thy heart that the Lord, He is God." "If he doth not utter
> it, he shall bear his iniquity" . . . if you do not utter My divinity to the
> gentile world, I will exact punishment from you.[86]

The individual sanctifies the name of God when he performs an
unusual act of love or generosity that calls forth admiration for the Jew
and for the God of the Jews. Also an extraordinary act of devotion is
considered a *kiddush ha-shem* inasmuch as it evokes admiration for the
God who can inspire such devotion.[87] Thus understood, sanctification
and desecration will depend to a great extent on the public character of
the act in question. Hence, the talmudic law as formulated by Maimonides is as follows:

> All the members of the House of Israel are commanded to sanctify the
> great name of God, as it is said, "But I will be hallowed among the chil-
> dren of Israel" [Lev. 22:32]. They are furthermore cautioned not to pro-
> fane it, as it is said, "Neither shall you profane My holy name" [Lev.
> 22:32]. How are these precepts to be applied? Should an idolater arise

and coerce an Israelite to violate any one of the commandments mentioned in the Torah under the threat that otherwise he would put him to death, the Israelite is to commit the transgression rather than suffer death; for concerning the commandments it is said, "which, if a man do them, he shall live by them" [Lev. 18:5]: "Live by them, and not die by them." And if he suffered death rather than commit a transgression, he himself is to blame for his death.

This rule applies to all the commandments, except the prohibitions of idolatry, unchastity, and murder. With regard to these: if an Israelite should be told: "Transgress one of them or else you will be put to death," he should suffer death rather than transgress. The above distinction only holds good if the idolater's motive is personal advantage: for example, if he forces an Israelite to build him a house or cook for him on the Sabbath, or forces a Jewess to cohabit with him, and so on; but if his purpose is to compel the Israelite to violate the ordinances of his religion, then if this took place privately and ten fellow Israelites were not present, he should commit the transgression rather than suffer death. But if the attempt to coerce the Israelite to transgress was made in the presence of ten Israelites, he should suffer death and not transgress, even if it was only one of the remaining commandments that the idolater wished him to violate.

All the foregoing applies to a time free from religious persecution. But in a period when there is such persecution, such as when a wicked king arises, like Nebuchadnezzar and his confederates, and issues decrees against Israel, with the purpose of abolishing their religion or one of the precepts, then it is the Israelite's duty to suffer death and not violate any one, even of the remaining commandments, whether the coercion takes place in the presence of ten Israelites or in the presence of idolaters.

When one is enjoined to transgress rather than be slain, and suffers death rather than transgress, he is to blame for his death. Where one is enjoined to die rather than transgress, and suffers death so as not to transgress, he sanctifies the name of God. If he does so in the presence of ten Israelites, he sanctifies the name of God publicly.[88]

One of the commentators argues that even regarding the three cardinal sins, martyrdom is not called for unless the action takes place publicly in the presence of ten Israelites.[89] Maimonides himself, however, states: "Concerning where one is enjoined to die rather than transgress and suffers death as not to transgress, he sanctifies the name of God. If he does so in the presence of ten Israelites, he sanctified the name of God publicly." This clearly implies that for Maimonides there is a *kiddush ha-shem* even if the act takes place privately. And if the only one who knows about it is the one non-Jew who is carrying out the cruel threat, it is still *kiddush ha-shem*—a demonstration before a representative of the non-Jewish world of the Jew's devotion and loyalty to the word of God. Where a Jewish public is present, *kiddush ha-shem* takes on a somewhat different character, serving to strengthen the weak-hearted among the Jewish people and as an inspiration for faith and courage.

Given a situation where the rabbis have ruled, "Transgress and do not be killed," does the indivudual have the right nevertheless to refuse to transgress and to undergo martyrdom? Maimonides is clear: "When one is enjoined to transgress rather than be slain, and he suffers death rather than transgress, he is to blame for his death."[90] This is another application of the principle we have already examined—that a man's life is not his personal property to dispose of as he sees fit, even if it is offered as a supreme sacrifice for the sake of *kiddush ha-shem*. It is interesting to note, however, that Tosafot disagrees and maintains that a person may go beyond the requirements of the law in this context and offer his life to God.[91]

The reason why we have greater leniency in regard to self-sacrifice in the matter of *kiddush ha-shem* than we do in the case of giving one's life to help another is that in the latter situation we are dealing with equal values; the blood of the individuals is of equal redness. When we weigh the consequences of such an act in terms of loss and gain we arrive at a stand-off. We have gained a life and lost a life. We remain, therefore, with the ruling: "Your life comes first." In regard to *kiddush ha-shem,* however, there is general acknowledgment that we are confronted by a supreme value. God, the creator, can legitimately call upon the services of His creatures. In terms of the overall telos and hierarchy of final ends, the status of God's name in the world and the realization of His Kingdom rank highest.[92] In this context, therefore, we find authorities taking the position that although the law does not require it, a person who, motivated by love of God, gives his life for *kiddush ha-shem,* is praiseworthy.

Our Duty Toward Kelal Yisrael

Another value which stands higher in Judaism than the life of the individual is the welfare of *Kelal Yisrael*—the collectivity of the Jewish people. By this we do not simply mean a number of individuals, for we have already indicated that the life of a single person encompasses within itself the equivalence of all life. By *Kelal Yisrael* we mean either the majority of the Jewish people in existence at that time or the Jewish community residing in the land of Israel.[93] Throughout the narrative portion of the Torah we find instances of men and women who risk their lives against heavy odds and sometimes give their lives in order to destroy the enemies of their people. When David goes out to fight Goliath in single combat, his chances are not too bright. Jael and Esther risk their lives for their people, and Deborah praises the two tribes which, in the cruel battle against the enemy, "jeopardized their lives unto death in the high places of the field."[94]

The obligation to defend the Jewish people with one's life is, of course, the basis of the law of the *milchemet mitzvah,* the "war of obligation," which is defined by Maimonides as including "rescue of Israel from an enemy that comes upon them."[95] In such a war, where the existence of the Jewish people as such is threatened, there are no exemptions and all are required to participate. It has been pointed out that in this respect the *mitzvah* of a "war of obligation" is unique.[96] Whereas in regard to the three cardinal sins, one is obliged to choose death when the choice is between death and an active transgression, in regard to war, we are required to risk death in preference to sitting back and doing nothing. But it can be argued that risking one's life in a war of defense of one's country is not completely altruistic self-sacrifice, since one is, at least in part, defending oneself and one's loved ones as well.

Recent discussions of the subject have produced different opinions as to whether one has an obligation to sacrifice oneself for the community.[97] A variety of sources have been offered in support of the different viewpoints. However, Rabbi Kook makes it clear that we are dealing here with a separate line of Jewish legal authority known as *mishpat ha-melukha,* special mandate given to the king, or to any other ruling body that the people freely accept upon themselves, to legislate and carry out policies for the welfare and security of the nation.[98] Such an authority has the right to demand obedience on pain of death and to impose sanctions by extrajudicial processes. But these enactments are considered temporary emergency measures justified by the conditions at the time and are not permanent additions to Jewish law.

It has been said that Judaism did not recognize the "state" or "society" or "city" as an entity with abstract or metaphysical significance or as having some special authority over the individual. This is reflected in the Jewish law of fines, both those mentioned in the Pentateuch and those instituted by the rabbis, which were never paid to the courts or to the community or to the state, but only to the individual against whom the wrong was committed.

In the words of Dr. Belkin:

> Nowhere in tannaitic sources do we find acceptance of the concept that the group, by virtue of its numbers, can create an abstract "society" which has authority over the individual. The only source of authority recognized by the Rabbis was the court which interpreted the Torah and rendered decisions applicable to the life of the individual as well as to the life of the group. No group or society, simply by virtue of its numbers, could exercise any authority independent of the individuals who composed it, nor is any authority ever granted to the group over the individual.

> The only state the Rabbis were conscious of was the divine state of God as revealed in the Torah and interpreted and transmitted by the oral traditions. Any crime committed by an individual was never thought of as an offense against the community or state. It was looked upon as an offense against the individual who suffered by the act and as a serious sin against the theocracy of Judaism which united all Israelites in the "religious nationality" of Judaism.[99]

We do have instances in the Book of Deuteronomy where punishments were given for a certain group of transgressios and the explanation offered seems to suggest not so much retributive or expiatory considerations as primarily utilitarian or deterrent ones. Thus, we find, "And thou shalt stone him . . . and all Israel shall hear, and fear, and shall do no more such wickedness"; "And all the people shall hear, and fear, and do no more presumptuously"; ". . . so that thou shall put evil away from you, and all Israel shall hear, and fear."[100] Nachmanides makes it clear that these locutions indicate that the harshness of the penalty in these cases is not generated by the mere grievousness of the sin, but by the need to have the punishment act as a deterrent against future occurrences.[101] This introduces into the Torah's concept of justice an element of consequentialism. That is to say, one justifies punishment not only by the fact that the agent deserves it, but by the beneficial consequences the punishment will have on others. This would seem to imply that the welfare of society as a whole is to be viewed as a positive moral value for which the interests of the individual may sometimes be sacrificed.

Judah Halevi gives a more conventional explanation in terms of an organismic theory of society: "For the relation of the individual is as the relation of the single limb to the body. Should the arm, in case bleeding is required, refuse its blood, the whole body, the arm included, would suffer. It is, therefore, the duty of the individual to bear hardship or even death for the sake of the welfare of the commonwealth."[102]

In the Aggadah, the rabbis spoke approvingly of individuals like Aaron and Phinehas who, in order to save the Jewish people from sin and punishment, performed actions in which they risked their entire spiritual future. Aaron implicated himself in the sin of the making of the golden calf rather than resist the efforts of the people outright, because he feared they would kill him as they had killed Hur, and he said, "Let the stink be rather in me"; i.e., better that I sin in the making of an idol than Israel sin in the murder of a high priest. Similarly, Phinehas, in addition to risking his life by taking action against the sinners, presumed to question the severity of the punishment meted out by God upon the people, although by so doing he was jeopardizing his position in the world-to-come.[103]

It should be remembered, however, that the ultimate reason why the individual is encouraged to give his life for *Kelal Yisrael* is not for the conventional consideration suggested by Halevi. The collectivity known as *Kelal Yisrael* or *Knesset Yisrael* is an entity that was brought into existence by the Lord of history to play a certain role and to bring about specific goals in that history. This is essentially what is meant by the "covenant" and the concept of the "chosen people." The entire point of the Book of Genesis is to focus on the Patriarchs as progenitors of a new people yet to be formed, and in backward perspective to see them as the most promising remnant of a human history that goes back to creation itself. Thus the rabbis found myriad ways of saying that the entire work of creation was only for the sake of Israel and the Torah and that great day when Israel would accept and fulfill the Torah. If, therefore, *Knesset Yisrael,* its existence now and in the future, is a unique and indispensable instrument for the realization of God's goals in creation-history, then it acquires a value which stands higher than the worth of any individual. In essence, the collectivity of Israel is worth sacrificing for, not because the many is higher than the one or because it is an obligation which grows out of a social contract or because the best interests of the self are ultimately to be identified with the common welfare, but because Israel, as the people of God, partakes of the supreme value which attaches to *kiddush ha-shem* and the realization of God's purposes in history.

An interesting question surfaces in considering a possible conflict between the demands of *kiddush ha-shem* and the survival of the Jewish people as a whole. Suppose the possibility of the entire Jewish people being assembled together and given the choice between idolatry— renouncing the God of Israel—and annihilation! What is their obligation? *Kiddush ha-shem* requires that they accept martyrdom! Yet in this particular case, it would mean the destruction of the entire Kelal Yisrael, the indispensable instrument of the ultimate *kiddush ha-shem* at the end of time. Which stands higher?

There is a suggestion which seems to be in line with the talmudic sentiment that the obligation for *kiddush ha-shem* in the here-and-now is an overriding imperative which devolves even upon the entire House of Israel.[104] (Note the language in Maimonides: "*Kol beit Yisrael*—all the members of the House of Israel [or 'the entire House of Israel']—at once . . . are commanded to sanctify the great name of God . . .".) Moral problems must be dealt with within the parameters given to us by our system as they relate to our concrete situation. Our understanding of the theological significance of *Kelal Yisrael* remains valid. Our concern for the survival of the Jewish people, therefore, is a valid concern. However, ultimate responsibility for Jewish survival is not ours.[105] The problem of the ultimate fulfillment of God's purposes and promises in history must, when the chips are down, be left to Him.

Freedom and Responsibility

The concept of individual responsibility goes back to the very beginnings of man's intellectual history. It is roughly the notion that certain states of affairs can be attributed to the actions of human beings, for which they can be held accountable in various ways. To be responsible for a certain action means that you can be rewarded or punished for it, praised or blamed. It is, in a very specific sense "your" action, for whose consequences you, rather than anyone else, have to answer.

As early as Aristotle, some of the main components of this concept were already articulated and established as fundamental considerations of moral and legal theory. Thus, Aristotle distinguished between intentional and unintentional acts. It is not sufficient, for example, if a certain accident can be traced to the movement of your arm. In order to fix responsibility we would want to know whether there were certain mental elements involved. Did you "will," or "intend," to move your arm; was it the deliberate effort of a person consciously bent on doing something, or was it a reflex movement over which you had no control? It would seem that indispensable to the concept of responsibility is some link between mind and body.

Aristotle also speaks of those situations in which a person would be excused of the responsibility, such as where the agent lacked certain relevant knowledge or where the cause of the movement came from outside the agent—that is to say, where someone is literally forced to do something by someone else. What is most interesting about this early discussion of responsibility is the untroubled assumption that except for certain special circumstances, which relieve people of responsibility, human beings, most of the time, *are* responsible for their actions; i.e., the conditions exist for the ascription of responsibility.[1] There was never any doubt in Aristotle's mind that the necessity which exists in nature, determining the way things happen, does not exist in relation to man. There is no necessity about human actions; they could have happened otherwise. Man makes his own choices. Our common moral sense seems to acknowledge the need for some such freedom as a condition for responsibility but also seems quite certain that man possesses such freedom.

When we turn to Judaism, we find that the concept of responsibility plays a most significant and vital role in its understanding of man. In the Torah, the first human beings are given a single command; they disobey it and are punished for their disobedience. But this entire process presupposes that man is the sort of being who possesses the freedom to choose to obey or disobey and thus deserves to be punished, which means that he is a responsible agent.[2] Regardless of whether we are dealing with "sin" as sheer disobedience to God, as in the case of primal man, or as moral evil, as in the case of Cain's murder of his brother, "sin is never a tragic necessity; it is always the fruit of will and its guilt is always deserved. . . . Because man can choose to do good, he is answerable for his evil-doing."[3] Furthermore, in the Torah, "sin never acts automatically; God always intervenes between sin and punishment." Since "it is not the sin that brings the affliction but the will of God," all punishment is deserved.[4]

Responsibility In The Biblical Account Of Primal Man

The tragedy of man's initial sin lies not only in his disobedience of God, but in his typical and pitiful attempt to evade responsibility, to push the blame on to the other. The man says: "The woman whom thou gavest to be with me, she gave me of the tree, and I did eat." And the woman says: "The serpent beguiled me, and I did eat."[5]

The story of Cain and Abel contains an even more pointed lesson in human responsibility. When God "accepts" the offering of Abel, but not the offering of Cain, we are told that "Cain was very angry and his countenance fell."[6] It would appear that Cain found himself assailed by very powerful destabilizing emotions. After all, he and not his brother had taken the initiative in doing what he thought was a proper act of thanksgiving by bringing some of the fruits of his farming efforts as an offering to God. Crest fallen and bewildered, he had watched his brother's offering being accepted but not his own. A fury of envy and resentment filled his heart, focusing on the handiest target—his brother Abel!

But before anything serious happens, God appears to Cain, to engage in a conversation which appears to have an informative as well as a preventive purpose. "And the Lord said unto Cain: 'Why art thou angry, and why is thy countenance fallen?'"[7]

Of course, God knew the answer to that question. But did Cain? At this very early stage of human history, man did not understand his own emotions. He had no conception of their obscure origins, no comprehension of the tortuous paths they cut through the personality, and no explanation for the explosive nature of their expression. Cain felt himself driven by powerful emotional forces he did not understand. God's initial advice to Cain was: "Don't simply accept the emotions as given. Try to understand them. Stop to analyze your feelings. Cain, *why* are you angry? To the extent that you understand the source of your feelings, to that extent will you be able to rationally direct them."

The Lord's statement continues: "If thou doest well [good], shall it not be lifted up?" That is to say, "Cain, get a grip on yourself! All is not lost. The future is still before you. If you react properly you will be all right. The path to God is still open. Your 'fallen countenance,' your injured pride, will be lifted up."

"But if thou doest not well, sin croucheth at the door, and unto thee is its desire . . ." In other words, "Cain, if you vent your emotions, things will cool down. But if you permit yourself to become obsessed by your feelings, which right now are just so much heat, they will become a means by which sin will penetrate your personality with the possibility of tragic consequences."

"But thou mayest rule over it . . ." "Remember, Cain, that you can understand and control your emotions. Don't be overwhelmed by their apparent power. You are in command. Exert your willpower. You can rule over it!"

We all know the story's sad ending. "And it came to pass, when they were in the field, that Cain rose up against Abel his brother, and slew him."[8] The rabbis, however, infer from Cain's subsequent conversation with God that he ultimately accepted responsibility for himself, exercised his freedom, repented, and was forgiven.[9]

Freedom Of Will In The Torah

While the concept of freedom is found in the Torah primarily as an implicit presupposition of human responsibility, there are some rather explicit references to this principle in addition to the assurance to Cain, "And thou mayest rule over it."

Moses concludes his farewell address to the people of Israel with the ringing: "I call heaven and earth to witness against you this day, that I have set before thee life and death, the blessing and the curse; therefore choose life, that thou mayest live, thou and thy seed."[10]

God Himself does not interfere in the human choice and takes no responsibility for the consequences that follow: "Out of the mouth of the Most High proceedeth not evil and good."[11] But God is not "neutral" in terms of the human struggle. To be good is to want to do good for others. So that God wants to see man choose the good. "Oh that they would have such a heart as this always, to fear Me and keep all My commandments, that it might be well with them, and their children for ever."[12]

Some specific laws of the Torah distinguish sharply between intentional and unintentional acts. When there is evidence of intention such as prior enmity, lying in ambush, or other signs of premeditation, and if there are two witnesses to the act, we have a case of murder and the penalty is death. "Whosoever killeth a person, the murderer shall be put to death at the mouth of witnesses."[13] For an act of unintentional manslaughter, the Torah prescribed the penalty of exile in one of the cities of refuge. This was a rather unusual institution, consisting of a group of six easily accessible cities settled by the Levites, where the hapless manslayer could live in comfortable and sympathetic surroundings "until the death of the high priest."[14] The system of "cities of refuge" seems to have served several different purposes. First, it was clearly a protective measure designed to guard against the blood-avenger.[15] According to S. D. Luzzatto, at this point in history, the blood feud was considered a sacred obligation by every family and clan. This procedure, by placing the manslayer into protective custody, assuaged the outraged feelings of the family of the victim with the thought that the slayer of their kinsman was being "punished." Others saw in the exile an expiation or therapeutic purpose to ease the burden of guilt from the shoulders of one who, after all, had been instrumental in the death of a human being.

Not All Are Held Responsible

Throughout the Talmud there is general recognition of the principle that certain individuals, by virtue of physical or mental impairment, cannot function as moral agents. That is to say, there are people who are not capable of apprehending moral distinctions or the moral quality of an act. The Talmud groups together the *cheresh,* the *shoteh,* and the *katan*—the deaf-mute, the person of the unsound mind, and the minor—as persons of limited liability and legal capacity.[16] Generally speaking, they are not liable for their torts or punishable for their offenses. The Talmud also speaks of the *shikor,* the drunkard, as being in this class but distinguishes between degrees of intoxication.[17] The drunkard generally is considered liable for any damages and legally competent to carry out business transactions and acts of marriage and divorce.[18] For certain religious actions, like rendering Torah rulings, prayer, and Temple service, the ingestion of an amount of alchohol sufficient to cause a degree of incoherence in one's speech renders one unfit. However, when one reaches the level called "drunk as Lot," then in terms of responsibility one receives the status of *shoteh*—one of "unsound mind."[19] It will be recalled that in the biblical story, Lot in his intoxicated state was completely unaware of what was happening, oblivious to his surroundings and certainly to the moral significance of what he was doing. In trying to express the precise disability of the *shoteh-shikor,* the sources speak of a loss of *da'at* ("mind," "cognition," "intelligence"), by which they apparently mean the inability to make the proper judgments, to relate decisions to the information available, to foresee the consequences of acts, and to exert willpower to resist various pressures and impulses.[20] There is, however, a difference between the *shikor* and the *shoteh* which finds expression in the rulings of the rabbis. The *shoteh* is not morally responsible for being a *shoteh,* while the *shikor* usually gets into his condition through a series of voluntary acts. In a number of situations the rabbis dealt sternly with cases of injury or death in which drunkenness was involved. They justified their rulings on the basis of the need for deterrent measures in view of the social situation of the times.[21]

The rabbis also acknowledged that a person is responsible for his actions only if he does them of his own free will. If he is compelled to commit an unlawful act, he is neither legally nor morally responsible. This is reflected in the law of the Torah regarding a man who rapes a betrothed woman: ". . . the man only shall die. But unto the woman thou shalt do nothing; there is in the damsel no sin worthy of death; for as when a man riseth against his neighbor and slayeth him, even so is this matter."[22] The Torah equates an act performed under physical duress with an act performed under threat of death. Interestingly enough, however, the Talmud does not consider a threat to one's money as duress and thus such a threat does not justify committing an unlawful act.[23]

While inadvertence and compulsion were certainly considered excusing conditions where criminal actions, such as "injury to another," were concerned, there was a tendency in the Talmud to consider man's responsibility for damages as almost absolute: "A man is always forewarned [*mu'ad,* 'responsible'], whether he acts inadvertently or willfully, whether he is awake or asleep. If he blinded his neighbor's eye or broke his vessel, he must repay in full."[24] The Talmud adds that he must do so even if he acted under compulsion. Dr. Belkin explains that in the case of injury to another person one not only causes damage (*nezek*) but also commits a crime against the human personality.[25] As Maimonides states:

> If one commits injury against another person, he may not be compared to one who damages another's property. For in the latter case, atonement is effected for him as soon as he makes the required compensation. But if one wounds another, atonement is not effected for him even if he paid all

the five courses of payment [pain, cost of healing, loss of earnings, humiliation] or even if he has sacrificed the rams of Nebaioth, for his sin is not forgiven until he begs forgiveness of the injured person and is forgiven by him.[26]

This latter component is mitigated by inadvertence or compulsion. However, for that portion of the compensation which is "damages" (nezek) and is not considered a criminal offense, man is always responsible, so that it is not affected by intention or willfulness. Later authorities, however, qualified the absolute liability suggested by the Mishnah by limiting it to the premises of the injured party and also by introducing a new category of "complete accident."[27]

In the Aggadah as well, the rabbis made clear their awareness of the importance of human freedom and responsibility. One of the more popular aphorisms was the pithy, "All is in the hands of heaven except the fear of heaven."[28] Much in a man's circumstances is determined by forces outside of his control. However, his basic attitude toward life, which includes and is formed by his relationship to God, is decided by himself. Elsewhere in the Talmud, it is put thusly: "The angel appointed over conception . . . takes a seminal drop, sets it before the Holy One, blessed be He, and asks, 'Sovereign of the Universe, what is to become of this drop? Is it to develop into a person strong or weak, wise or foolish, rich or poor?' But no mention is made of its becoming wicked or righteous."[29] This is left to the person himself.

As we noted earlier, primal man already tried to evade responsibility by somehow suggesting that others were involved in his transgression. Yet for the rabbis, the very teaching that mankind had a common ancestor provided important support for the notion of individual responsibility. "Why have all men come from one ancestor? Because of the righteous and the wicked; that the righteous should not say, 'We are the descendants of a righteous ancestor,' and the wicked say, 'We are the descendants of a wicked ancestor.'"[30] Indeed, Josephus, who was determined to impress his Roman contemporaries by portraying the various Jewish sects of his time as distinguished by philosophical differences, notes that a characteristic feature of the Pharisaic philosophy was the insistence upon the essential freedom of man, so that he is able to act responsibly while at the same time a large area is reserved for the workings of Providence.[31] The rabbis also sensed an attempt to evade responsibility in the remark of the hapless brothers of Joesph: "And their heart failed them, and they turned trembling one to another, saying: 'What is this that God hath done to us?'"[32] "Thus it is written: 'The foolishness of man perverteth his way; and against the Lord does he fret.'" Often man is himself responsible for the trouble he is in, yet in his blind rage he will try to hang it on God.[33]

God's Omnipotence And Man's Freedom Of Action

It is perhaps appropriate at this point that we make mention of an important historical fact: "The philosophical problem of free will makes its first large-scale appearance in a religious context."[34] In the beginning the reflecting individual had no reason to question the evidence of his own personal, subjective experience that he indeed was making choices in matters both very trivial and very momentous.[35] This is why, as we have seen, Aristotle had only to work out the various conditions under which responsibility obtains while assuming without any question the principle of human freedom, which undergirds the concept of responsibility. The first major threat to the concept of human freedom, oddly enough, was seen as coming from the belief in one omnipotent, omniscient God who is concerned with human affairs. If the relationship between man and God is viewed on the model of a king and his subjects, a master and his slaves, then it might be imagined that God, having His own goals and purposes, would do everything in His power, which in this case is absolute, to achieve His ends. Early Protestant thinkers were overwhelmed with a sense of God's power and found notions of man's freedom almost presumptuous.

> This . . . is . . . wholesome for Christians to know: that God . . . foresees, purposes and does all things according to His immutable, eternal, and infallible will. By this thunderbolt "Free will" is thrown prostrate and utterly dashed to pieces. Those . . . who . . . assert "Free will" must either deny this thunderbolt, or pretend not to see it, or push it from them. . . . From which it follows . . . friend Erasmus . . . that all things which we do,

although they may appear to us to be done mutably and contingently . . .
are yet in reality done necessarily and immutably with respect to the will
of God. For the will of God is effective and cannot be hindered.

. . . And as His will cannot be hindered, the work itself cannot be hindered from being done in the place, at the time, in the measure, and by
whom He foresees and wills. . . . If it [free will] be ascribed unto men it is
not . . . properly ascribed . . . wherefore it becomes Theologians to
refrain from the use of this term altogether whenever they wish to speak
of human ability.[36]

The first question that arose was, Does God manipulate the environment in such a way as to thwart the consequences of certain human
actions when they are against His interests? Thus, God might have
been expected, in some way, to rescue Abel from the onslaught of
Cain[37] and Isaac from being deceived by Jacob and Rebecca. Such a
procedure would interfere with man's ability to achieve certain consequences but not with his freedom of choice or freedom of action. It is
clear from human experience that in this sense man has a considerable,
if limited, freedom. Medieval Jewish thinkers called this the realm of
the possible, or the "contingent."[38] The limits on man's freedom to
carry out his desires that are imposed by the physical environment are
constantly being eroded by the expansion of scientific knowledge and
technology. In general, God abides by the principle that "The heavens
are heavens unto God, and the earth has He given to the sons of
man,"[39] and He does not interfere even if man decides to roam
through the heavens. Yet biblical and rabbinic literature abound with
accounts of God intervening, either overtly or through "behind-the-
scenes" manipulation, to subvert the best-laid plans of certain men.
The conspiracies of his brothers to destroy Joseph turn out altogether
different than planned: ". . . ye meant evil against me; but God meant
it for good."[40] David, throughout a harrowing life full of narrow
escapes, carried an abiding faith that it was God who saved him from
all of his enemies. Also, the overt interventions of God to save Israel by
means of "signs and wonders" called miracles, whether from Pharaoh
or Sennacherib, are, of course, limitations placed upon man's freedom
of achievement. The many questions that the concepts of general
providence and special providence give rise to are discussed by Mai-

monides and others and need not detain us here.[41] The point is that according to Judaism, God is active in human affairs.

However, the limitation on human freedom that might be expected from a belief in Providence was more than balanced by the rabbinic teaching: "In the way in which a man wishes to walk, he is guided."[42] This is interpreted to mean that there is a sense in which the external environment is plastic to man's moral thrust. Nature generally will neither frustrate your good intentions nor save you from your evil desires. God has, as it were, instructed the world outside of you to cooperate with your moral choices. What this implies is that your moral choices are very real, for their consequences will truly be played out, so that the responsibility is awesome indeed. "If one goes to defile himself, openings are made for him; and he who goes to purify himself, he is helped."[43]

As part of his effort to preserve the integrity of the concept of human freedom, Maimonides virtually single-handedly fought the influence of astrology in his day and completely denied its having any effect whatsoever on the character or affairs of men. He carefully distinguished between the science of astronomy, which he praised for its accuracy and practical benefits, and the speculations of astrology, which he labeled "foolishness" and false.[44]

But what of the inner workings of the mind? Does God interfere with the mechanisms of volition and the decision-making process that is within man? One would think that to do so would surely compromise the integrity of man's freedom and the inviolability of his very selfhood! Yet the Torah records several instances of what is described as God "hardening the heart" of an individual or a nation.[45] The classic case of this is, of course, the Pharaoh of the Exodus. Time after time, God hurls devastating plagues upon Pharaoh and Egypt, but no sooner is the plague removed in response to Pharaoh's plea, than he reverts to his stubbornness and refuses to let the Israelites go. But if Pharaoh's stubbornness is due to God's "hardening of the heart," and not to his own volition, how can he continue to be punished for his refusal? In response to this problem, Maimonides develops a new doctrine to the effect that sometimes, in punishment for a particularly grievous transgression, God may indeed remove a person's freedom, making it impossible for him to repent. Nevertheless, the blows he continues to receive are deserved because of the evils he performed while he still had his freedom.[46]

A number of other writers, however, are uncomfortable with the idea that God should ever deprive any person of his power or interfere with his freedom.[47] Therefore, they interpret the "hardening of the heart" to the contrary; not as interfering with his volitions but actually as making it possible for Pharaoh to carry out his true inclinations. The earlier plagues had created personal and social pressures which Pharaoh would have found hard to withstand. One more blow and Pharaoh would have released the Israelites, although he did not really want to and was thoroughly unrepentant of the cruelties he had committed. Thus, the "hardening" did not constitute the actual decision but merely was an artificial stiffening to offset the coercive effects of the plagues so that Pharaoh could again do what he wanted to do.

The most serious aspect of the problem that the concept of God poses for the notion of free will is associated with the implications of God's attribute of omniscience. If God is all-knowing, then it would seem that God knows beforehand everything that ever happens in the world. Thus, before a person makes a choice among the alternatives before him, God already knows which alternative he will choose. How then can the person's choice be free? Can the person choose anything except that which God already knows he will choose? God's foreknowledge can never be mistaken and has no gaps in it. But if the person had no choice, how can he be held responsible for his actions? The problem can be stated in the form of a dilemma: If God's knowledge is perfect then man is not free; if man is free then God's knowledge is not perfect.

The rabbis in the Talmud were aware of the difficulty of reconciling man's freedom with God's omniscience but did not offer any solution. What they did was simply to reassert the two principles involved: "Everything is foreseen, yet permission is given,"[48] as if to say that the principles of divine omniscience and human freedom of the will are both basic to Judaism and must be firmly held in spite of the apparent contradiction. Throughout the Middle Ages, this problem was intensely debated by the theologians of the three monotheistic religions. Maimonides offered a solution which at first glance seems to add nothing to the talmudic aphorism quoted above and seems to be a mere flight into agnosticism. He points out that all of God's attributes are identical with His essence, which is unknowable.[49] God's knowledge, therefore, is completely unlike human knowledge and is also unknowable. But the contradiction between God's omniscience and human freedom arises out of our thinking of God's knowledge as being similar to human knowledge, only more perfect. In truth, says Maimonides, it is completely different and beyond our comprehension. On the face of it, Maimonides seems to have replaced a paradox with a mystery! That is to say, we now have no reason to believe that the two principles are contradictory because we really do not know what it means to say that God is all-knowing. Basing themselves on some remarks made by Maimonides elsewhere, some writers have suggested a more plausible interpretation of Maimonides' theory. In the *Guide,* Maimonides lists a number of ways in which God's knowledge is said to be different from man's knowledge.[50] God's knowledge is one, yet it embraces many different kinds of objects; it applies to things not in existence; it comprehends the infinite; it remains unchanged though it knows changeable things. "God's certain knowledge of one of two eventualities does not determine the future occurrence of the one eventuality." And in spite of the talk of "unknowability," Maimonides does attempt to give some understanding of how God's knowledge "works" and how it can have the unusual properties mentioned. God's knowledge, unlike our own, is not derived from things. God does not reach outside of Himself to learn. "God fully knows His unchangeable essence and has thus a knowledge of all that results from any of His acts." What remains to be drawn are the implications of this insight for the concept of time. Let us rethink the dilemma and note the pivotal role played by the time factor. "... *before* a person makes a choice, God *already* knows [*beforehand*] which alternatives he will choose ..." Eliminate the time factor and you seem to eliminate the problem. For coincidental or contemporaneous knowledge does not seem to conflict with free choice. My knowledge of your choices *as* you make them (assuming my ability to have such knowledge) poses no problem. It is foreknowledge that seems to create the conflict. If I know today the choice you will make tomorrow, my knowledge must be based on the conditions that exist today, which, if the knowledge is correct, have already determined what you are going to choose tomorrow. Whenever we have knowledge of the future, there must be a causal connection between the future event and our belief. If I know today what you will do tomorrow, then if what you do is causally determined, you obviously cannot fail to do it. In short, you have no free choice.

However, there is no "before" or "after" for God. He is called in the Torah, *Eheyeh-Asher-Eheyeh,* "I am that I am," eternal present, was, is, and will be, collapsed in absolute being that stands above time. We must imagine a God before whom all of time lies rolled out so that He knows it all in an eternal present. Thus, while from the point of view of man, who is locked into the sequence of time, God knows *beforehand* what I am about to do, for God all of the future is *now,* so that in a sense, God is always watching man as he makes his choices.[51] Recently, this point was formulated in the following way: "We can see then that the whole problem created by, 'If God knew yesterday what I will do tomorrow. . . .' cannot arise on the view that God is outside of time. It turns out to mean, 'If God knew while He was living through yesterday what I will do tomorrow . . .' and this is illegitimate since God did not live through yesterday."[52]

In the general philosophical literature there has been a renewed interest in the problem of the compatibility of God's foreknowledge and free choice. While some arguments have been offered against the "outside-of-time" solution suggested here, they have not, in my judgment, been successful.[53] One writer, however, has maintained that it should not be necessary to argue that God is "outside of time" so long as we hold that God knows the future intuitively not inferentially.[54] There is general agreement that were God's foreknowledge to be inferential foreknowledge, where He deduces what is going to happen in the future from what is happening in the present by use of causal laws, then, of course, free will would be ruled out. But if God simply "peers into the future," seeing it immediately rather than deducing it, then His knowing the future is the way we know the present and does not preclude free choice on the part of man. This is indeed the crux of the matter. In essence, we have here only one solution. Talk of God being "outside of time" and the approach of Maimonides that "God knows everything because He knows Himself" are merely different ways of explaining how it is that God has the kind of intuitive knowledge in which He can see the future as an eternal present.[55]

Freedom As The Ground For The Call To Repentance

While, as we have seen, the concept of free will is a "great principle and pillar of the Torah and the *mitzvah*," its most dramatic expression in Judaism is undoubtedly to be found in the concept of repentance, called *teshuvah,* or "return." This is the call that issues forth repeatedly from the Torah: "Return, O Israel, unto the Lord thy God, for thou hast stumbled in thine iniquity. Take with you words and return unto the Lord."[56] No matter how far Israel may stray, he will ultimately return. "In thy distress, when all of these things are come upon thee, in the end of days, thou wilt return to the Lord your God . . . for the Lord thy God is a merciful God . . ."[57] And speaking of repentance, the Torah assures us, "For this commandment which I command thee this day, it is not too hard for thee, neither is it far off . . . but the word is very nigh unto thee, in thy mouth and in thy heart, that thou mayest do it."[58]

In innumerable teachings, and in a variety of ways, the rabbis reinforced and elaborated this basic teaching of the Torah and the prophets that the gates of repentance are always open, that God is anxious for man to repent, and that it is never too late.[59] Clearly, it is one thing to believe that man has freedom of will and, in an open field of alternatives, can respond to moral imperatives. It is quite another, however, to believe that man who has sinned, who has sullied his soul, and who has beclouded his reason by succumbing to the temptations of lust and pride, can ever extricate himself from the clutches of entrenched sin that has become habit. Does not the sinner cease to be called a "child of God"? The answer of the Torah is a thundering no! The sinner can return. "Let the wicked forsake his way, and the man of iniquity his thoughts, and let him return unto the Lord, and He will have compassion upon him, and to our God, for He will abundantly pardon."[60]

Teshuvah means "penance" and "return," but more important, it implies reconciliation with God. But this reconciliation is not the work of "grace" or a divine act of deliverance.[61] *Teshuvah* begins with a decision made by man. Just as the Torah attributes sin to man, regarding it as *his* sin, so is it *his* teshuvah. Man can and must make the first move. "Return unto Me, and I will return unto you."[62]

In Judaism, sin and evil come without any metaphysical credentials. Their weight or power is in direct proportion to man's weakness
and imputations. If man runs to do the bidding of the *yetzer ha-ra* (the
evil inclination), it can become as massive as a mountain. If man
chooses to ignore its importuning, it is as thin and negligible as a hair.
The essential steps of repentance are, "that the sinner give up the sin,
remove it from his mind, and resolve in his heart not to repeat the evil
action again; so also must he regret his past and give expression
with his lips to his thoughts."[63] Once man turns to God in this manner,
his acceptance is immediate.

In one of his lectures, Rabbi J. B. Soloveitchik points to the fact
that Maimonides chooses to treat the principle of freedom of the will
not in the section called *yesodai ha-Torah,* which deals with the basic
principles of Judaism, but rather in his section on *teshuvah.*[64] Most
curious, however, is the fact that instead of beginning the section with
this principle, which is presupposed by the entire concept of repentance, it first appears in chapter five. In a brilliant analysis, Rabbi Soloveitchik shows how the kinds of repentance considered in the first four
chapters of the section on *teshuvah* may not involve the deliberation
and free expression of man's volition. A person may go through all the
steps of *teshuvah* described above simply because he has become old
and feeble and no longer has the strength or inclination to sin. Or
again, a person may awaken after a night of dissipation with the
"morning-after" blues. Often a revulsion will set in; a disgust and dis-
illusionment with the past that will cause the sinner to forsake his
ways.[65] Admittedly, this sort of repentance is not of the highest quality.
True, in both cases, the individual has abandoned his immoral
behavior and resolves to improve in the future. However, this has
come about because the person has merely followed the path of least
resistance or strongest desire. No decisional struggle was involved, no
overcoming of pressures. After chapter five, in which he introduces the
concept of freedom of the will, Maimonides returns to the subject of
repentance, but now with an altogether different type of *teshuvah.* Maimonides now speaks of the need to repent immediately, without waiting for old age or for other drastic changes in one's situation. More
importantly, we are now told that man has an obligation to repent not
merely for evil acts but also for immoral character traits, such as envy
and anger, hatred, and lust for money and honor. And then, in a flight

of sheer poetry, Maimonides goes on to describe the transformation that *teshuvah* can bring about:

> How exalted is the degree of repentance? Just last night a certain individual was separated from the Lord, God of Israel, as it is said, "Your iniquities were making a separation between you and your God" [Isa. 59:2]. He cries aloud and is not answered, as it is said, "Yea, when you make many prayers, I will not hear" [ibid. 1:15]. He fulfills religious precepts and they are flung back in his face, as it is said, "Who has required this at your hand to tread My courts?" [ibid. 1:12]; "Oh, that there were even one among you that would shut the doors, that you might not kindle fire on My altar in vain; I have no pleasure in you, says the Lord of hosts, neither will I accept an offering at your hand" [Mal. 1:10]; "Add your burnt-offerings to your sacrifice and eat flesh" [Jer. 7:21]. Today, the same individual [having repented] is closely attached to the Divine Presence, as it is said, "And you that cleave to the Lord your God are alive, every one of you, this day" [Deut. 4:4]. He cries and is immediately answered, as it is said, "And it shall come to pass that before they call I will answer" [Isa. 65:24]. He fulfills religious precepts and they are accepted with pleasure and with joy, as it is said, "For God has already accepted your works" [Eccles. 9:7]. Yet more, they are eagerly desired, as it is said, "Then shall the offering of Judah and Jerusalem be pleasant to the Lord as in the days of old and as in ancient years" [Mal. 3:4].[66]

This is the sort of *teshuvah* that can only be brought about by a man exercising his freedom of will—a sudden and radical transformation because this man chooses to change. But this free decision, which can be called "repentance out of love," results not merely in the performance of a single act, but in a restructuring of one's entire personality—a remaking of one's value system, an overhauling of one's character traits. In this section, Maimonides also refers to the repentance of redemption, of which Rabbi Soloveitchik observes, "The individual sinner also repents in this manner; becomes his own King-Messiah and redeems himself from the imprisonment and exile of sin."

Is God "Tilting" Toward Human Salvation?

While the concept of free will in Judaism emerges strong and unimpaired from the various encounters with conflicting considerations that

we have examined, there is yet another area in the rabbinic concept of
the relationship between God and man that seems to impinge on
human freedom. However, here the impingement seems to be of a
gentle, poetic nature rather than rigorously philosophic. I have reference to a consideration which emanates from God's goodness and love
of man. While God has given man glorious freedom and awesome
responsibility and does not interfere with that freedom, nevertheless, as
we mentioned earlier, God is not neutral as to the outcome. God has
invested heavily on the side of the good. While He offers man "life and
the good" and also "death and evil," God always leads with the
"good" and then, from the sidelines, as it were, cheers man on and
urges him, "And you shall choose life." Note also the difference in
God's response to man's choices: He who chooses evil, doors are
opened, i.e., no obstacles are placed in his path. Whereas, he who
comes to be purified—he is assisted; i.e., he is met with positive aid
and encouragement.

The pristine moment of choice, however, which alone confers
upon man his awful responsibility, must take place amidst an exquisite
balance of good and evil forces, so that man indeed remains free to
choose. The need to maintain a fine balance within every person
between the pressures for good and the pressures for evil explains a
number of rabbinic teachings concerning the *yetzer ha-ra,* the evil
inclination. The *yetzer ha-ra* was considered to be more powerful than
the *yetzer tov.* To begin with, the former is with a person from the very
beginning, while the good inclination emerges in the individual at
maturity. Secondly, the evil inclination uses all sorts of sly stratagems
and devious indirections to entrap the individial. The rabbis concluded
that man would never be able to overcome the evil inclination were it
not for the help that God gives him.[67] But again, this must be interpreted to mean that *after* man makes the first move, takes the first step,
God's help can be expected.

Each person gets the *yetzer ha-ra* he can handle. "Whoever is greater
than his fellow, his evil inclination is likewise greater."[68] Also, the
teaching that the embryo is sworn before birth "to be righteous and
not wicked," may also be interpreted as the bestowal of an extra
measure of "conscience" to help offset the special powers of the *yetzer
ha-ra.* This consideration may also be a factor in governing the occur-

rence of miracle-like events. Experiences which the Torah calls "signs and wonders," whose agency is somehow attributed to God, generally have the effect of convincing those who witness them of the existence of God and His involvement in human affairs. Conceivably a person could be profoundly committed to evil and deeply opposed to God and all that He represents and yet, after witnessing an overt miracle, feel himself intellectually compelled to proclaim: "The Lord, He is God!" But the effect of miracle-like events on the spectator is relative to his degree of scientific knowledge and level of general cultural sophistication. In ancient times, when divinity was universally perceived in every tree and in every storm, miraculous events did not have a coercive effect on the free choice of individuals. Israel's early history attests to that. Yet the rabbis observed that in the period of Mordecai and Esther and the events of Purim, overt miracles were no longer in evidence and could no longer be expected.[69] Perhaps this is because as man develops, and his understanding of the world about him is based increasingly on causal laws, the occurrence of supernatural events which could only be explained by being attributed directly to God assumes a coercive character. It is probably for the same reason that there could never be a valid, intellectually-compelling "proof" for the existence of God. Since the initial turning to God and acceptance of His sovereignty must also be an act of free will, this too ought not to be intellectually forced upon a person.

What is difficult to understand, however, are any number of prayers in the Jewish liturgy in which Israel appears to beseech God for items that clearly are supposed to be achieved by man himself through the exercise of his own free will. Consider the following examples:

Prayer after the last of the early morning blessings:[70]
". . . O lead us not into sin or transgression, iniquity, temptation, or disgrace; let not the evil inclination have sway over us . . ."

Ahavah Rabbah prayer prior to the Shema:
". . . put it into our hearts to understand and to discern . . . to do and to fulfill in love all the words of instruction in Thy Torah . . . let our hearts cleave to Thy commandments and unify our hearts to love and reverence Thy name . . ."

Blessing for repentance in the Shemoneh Esreh:
"Cause us to return, our Father, unto Thy Torah; draw us near, our King, unto Thy service; and bring us back in perfect repentance unto Thy presence. Blessed art Thou, O Lord, who delights in repentance."

Prayer on the New Month
". . . O grant us a life marked by the fear of heaven and the dread of sin . . . a life of love of Torah and fear of heaven . . ."

One is tempted to suggest that when man pours out his heart to God in unrestrained expression, his feelings overflow the constraints of philosphy. True, man has been given freedom, but in his lonely hour, beset by his awesome responsibilities, man reaches out for the security of our Father in Heaven, and in defiance of the distinctions of theory, asks God to help him in his choices. Others say that we pray to God not to interfere with the inner mechanisms of choice but to modify in certain helpful ways our outer circumstances. Thus, for example, some people claim that if they did not have so many financial problems, they would find it easier to make certain proper moral choices. Others argue that poor health makes it difficult for them to make the right decisions. Perhaps our prayers ought to be understood as asking for assistance from God in ways which would indirectly make it easier for our hearts to cleave unto His commandments and lessen the power of the evil inclination.

It is interesting to note that in the blessing for repentance quoted above, the concluding benediction, which always sums up the essence of the blessing, describes God as simply "delighting in repentance." In other words, while in our passionate entreaties we ask God to actively bring us to repentance, when we sum up and express God's operational connection with repentance, it is in terms of a "hands-off," "delighting in repentance." In short, it is man who must do the repenting.[71]

The Incompatibility Of Freedom And Determinism

In our own day, the concept of human freedom is threatened not so much by anything to do with God but rather by a certain popular way of looking at the world that is called determinism. This theory has been generated by the successful development of the natural sciences since the sixteenth century. A basic assumption of the evolving sciences was the concept of universal causation, which is that every event has a cause. Of course, it may be impossible to prove that this theory is true. But wherever science has examined the world—be it medicine or weather prediction, immense celestial phenomena or atomic physics—the assumption has proven correct and fruitful. Whatever happens at some specific moment is the outcome of something that happened at a prior moment; i.e., the present is always *determined* by antecedent conditions. Another assumption of the sciences is that the events occur in orderly patterns which can be formulated as causal or empirical laws. On the basis of knowledge of the causal laws and the antecedent conditions, accurate predictions can be made. The theory of determinism is a combination of universal causation and total predictability. Most people seem to accept a theory very much like determinism in their daily lives. Regardless of whether we are dealing with inanimate objects or living organisms, people or the weather, we are constantly mapping the future or exploring the past on the basis of the causal laws that govern all things. Now if we apply the principle of determinism to human behavior we get the following:

> Given the motives which are present to an individual's mind, and given likewise the character and disposition of the individual, the manner in which he will act might be unerringly inferred; that if we knew the person thoroughly, and knew all the inducements which are acting upon him, we could foretell his conduct with as much certainty as we can predict any physical event. . . . No one who believed that he knew thoroughly the circumstances of any case, and the characters of the different persons concerned, would hesitate to foretell how all of them would act. Whatever degree of doubt he may in fact feel, arises from the uncertainty whether he really knows the circumstances, or the character of some one or other of the persons, with the degree of accuracy required; but by no means from thinking that if he did know these things, there could be any uncertainty what the conduct would be.[72]

But why not take it a step further? Not only could a man's conduct be predicted but every impulse, every desire, the length of time he takes to deliberate, and the choice he finally makes—all are caused by antecedent conditions and are in principle, predictable. All of this is further complicated by new advances in psychology and psychoanalysis, which tell us that "our very acts of volition and the entire train of deliberations leading up to them are but facades for the expression of unconscious wishes or rather unconscious compromises and defenses."[73] What remains, then, of man's freedom?

The force and momentum of the ground swell of opinion in favor of determinism, with the blessings of science behind it, is so strong that people long ago might have concluded that free will is an illusion and that the mind of man, like the rest of nature, is locked into a causal nexus that permits of no exceptions and no escape. There are two vital phenomena in human experience, however, which again and again call men back to the concept of freedom and compel him to question the assumptions of determinism. These are: (1) the implications of the concept of responsibility, and (2) the feeling of freedom that man experiences in his own self. Let us examine these two considerations in detail, beginning with the concept of responsibility.

We stated at the outset of this chapter that responsibility means to be answerable or accountable to some moral tribunal, with liability for punishment if found guilty. We are accountable only for what is ours, for what can be imputed to us. If we were to reflect for a bit on the conditions that must obtain before we can hold someone responsible, we would probably come up with the following:[74]

A. I must remain throughout the self-same person. Thus, "I was not myself" is an excusing condition.

B. The deed must be mine. The deed must issue from my will—which rules out acts wherein I am forced or compelled.

C. I must be a moral agent with knowledge and intelligence. I must be capable of apprehending moral distinctions and must have sufficient knowledge to be able to project the consequences at least to some extent of my deed. This would tend to rule out children, madmen, etc.

Condition B rules out any force or compulsion and requires that the action be my own; i.e., freely performed. Let us analyze this a bit further. Why would the ordinary person consider an individual who had been compelled to perform an immoral act as not a fit subject upon whom to pass moral judgment; to praise or blame? Because you cannot be held responsible for an act you could not help performing. If a person could not have acted otherwise than he did, which means that he had no genuine alternatives, no open possibilities, then moral praise or blame seems futile and out of place. It appears that when we say a certain person morally ought to have done a certain deed, we imply that in our opinion he could have done that deed. In short, the moral "ought" implies "can." This appears to be a necessary condition of every moral judgment. "He could have acted otherwise." But what does this mean? This establishes the point that the condition "He could have acted otherwise" must provide at least "freedom in *action*"—"He could have *acted* otherwise *if* he had so chosen."

This, however, does not appear to be a sufficient condition for responsibility, because we can then ask, "*Could* he have chosen otherwise?" If the answer is, "Not if all things remained the same," then he still had no alternative. Therefore, the requirement for responsibility would appear to be the categorical, "He could have chosen otherwise, everything in the universe prior to his choice, including his own character as so far formed, being the same." This can be called "freedom in choice," or following Campbell, "contra-causal freedom."[75]

Is "Soft-Determinism" The Answer?

The concept of moral responsibility is considered so vital and necessary to our society that many contemporary philosophers, in spite of their abiding conviction of the truth of determinism, are not willing to abandon the concept of responsibility. They have, therefore, developed an approach called "soft-determinism," which attempts to show that freedom and determinism are compatible. "Soft-determinists" accept the concept that "ought implies can" but maintain that the only freedom required is freedom in action. In the words of W. T. Stace: "Acts freely done are all caused by desires or motives or by some sort of internal psychological states of the agents involved. The unfree acts are all caused by physical force or conditions outside the agent."[76]

Let us now critically evaluate the attempts of the soft-determinists to preserve the notion of responsibility by reconciling the concept of determinism with an emasculated concept of freedom. Their program consists of two parts: (1) an explication of the concept of responsibility, and (2) an analysis of sentences of the type, "He could have acted otherwise."

Schlick begins by asking, "What is the aim of fixing responsibility?"[77] He sees the answer strictly in terms of reward and punishment. To him the question "Who is responsible?" is the same as the question, "Who, in a given case, is to be punished?" What we are looking for, therefore, is some agent upon whose motives we can bring to bear the appropriate educative influences so that, in similar situations in the future, his strongest motive will impel him to refrain from rather than repeat the act. Given this analysis, the only conditions under which it would not be appropriate to reward or punish or, which is the same thing for Schlick, under which a person should not be responsible, are conditions of external constraint or, for example, of insanity, since punishment could not have its desired effect on the motives of an insane person. With this analysis, in terms of reward and punishment, Schlick maintains that the entire meaning of responsibility is completely and fully explicated. It follows from this that freedom of choice is not a requirement of responsibility, so that determinism is not in conflict with morality. The only reason why it should ever have been thought so is because of an unsophisticated confusion between the prescriptive laws of man and the descriptive laws of nature, as the results of which it was erroneously believed that the element of compulsion involved in the former is somehow also involved in the latter.

In evaluating this viewpoint, a number of weaknesses soon become apparent. It does not, in a number of ways, seem to conform to what we mean by moral responsibility in ordinary linguistic usage.

1. If Schlick is right, shouldn't we consider animals to be morally responsible, since reward and punishment can influence their future behavior? It is well known that we do not.
2. Often in historical writings we tend to attribute moral responsibility for certain present situations to people long dead. This is not meaningful, according to Schlick's analysis.
3. Often we will judge the degree of a man's moral responsibility to be

lessened if we know, for example, that his formative years were spent in a bad environment. Yet if, according to Schlick, all that is involved is whether we can affect his future motives, then considering bad environment an excusing condition again makes no sense.[78]

4. Schlick's strict exclusive identification of moral responsibility with punishment is open to serious question. Sometimes we may think a person morally commendable and yet feel we must "punish" him because of the socially injurious nature of his sincere but muddle-headed behavior. Again, it seems clear, contrary to Schlick, that we often do answer such questions as "Ought (or ought not) that person to have done what he did?" not with the purpose in mind of praising or blaming, so that it may act as a preventive for the future, but quite simply to react in moral judgment to what is a right act or a wrong act.[79]

5. It is by no means clear that the retributive elements in punishment are not part of the ordinary understanding of this term. If they are, then Schlick's analysis ignores them completely.

6. Finally, as Hart argues, it does not follow, simply because the threat of punishment is useless in a particular case, that his punishment will also be unnecessary to maintain the efficacy of threats for others at its highest. We might be better off if the law contained no explicit exemptions, as they are hard to prove and people might decide to break the law in the hope of falsely claiming these exemptions if caught. Thus, on the basis of Schlick's analysis, we would be hard put to defend our preference for a legal system that requires mental conditions for responsibility over a system of strict liability or social control—such as brainwashing.[80]

Let us now turn to the linguistic portion of the soft-determinist position. As indicated earlier, there is general agreement that "ought" implies "can." Disagreement, however, arises when we ask to understand the meaning of "can" or "could have" in such sentences as "I could have acted otherwise." A suggestion that goes back to G. E. Moore holds that "A could have acted otherwise" is to be analyzed as "A could have acted otherwise if he had willed or chosen otherwise." Nowell-Smith develops Moore's suggestion into a doctrine, asserting that sentences in the form of "I can . . ." or "I could have . . ." are to be analyzed or are to be completed by adding "if" clauses and are to be considered suppressed hypothetical statements.[81]

J. L. Austin, in a well-known paper, shows that these assertions are incorrect.[82] First he demonstrates that the "if" of "I can if I choose" cannot be the "if" of causal condition. He also maintains that the "if" of "I can if I choose," along with other such uses of "if," is simply the linking of a positive and complete assertion that "I can" with the question of whether I choose to. The "if" is the "if" of doubt and hesitation and not the "if" of condition. Austin argues further that such sentences as "I could have acted otherwise" do not always require an "if" clause to complete them. "Could have" can be viewed as a past-indicative rather than a past-subjunctive or conditional. He distinguishes between the assertion that "I could have" always *means* "I could have if I had chosen" and the assertion that "I could have" must always be *analyzed* as "I could have if I had chosen." But even the latter claim is not very plausible in the light of the criticisms just advanced. Often we do wish to assert that, "I did choose and I did try, but I failed. Yet somehow I feel I could have done it with the conditions being exactly as they were."

In his book *Ethics,* Nowell-Smith presents the following unlikely analysis of the sentence, "Smith could have read Book E last night": ". . . he would have read it, if there had been a copy, if he had not been struck blind . . . and if he had wanted to read it more than he wanted to read anything else."[83] But surely this is not what we mean when we say, "Smith could have read it last night." There is a difference between a statement which implies or asserts that certain conditions *were* fulfilled and a *conditional* statement, which is a statement about what would have happened *if* this condition had been fulfilled. Certainly, to establish the truth of such a past-indicative we would have to establish that certain conditions were satisfied. But this does not make it a conditional assertion. Grammatically speaking, therefore, "cans are not constitutionally iffy"—so that when we say, "A could have acted otherwise," we assert this categorically. Both the physical act and its determining choice were causally contingent, and it was within A's power to do so.

If the program of the soft-determinists stands refuted, then we come back to the conditions implied by the unabridged concept of responsibility. As stated in the strange-sounding but precise language of the professional philosopher: "In order for an act A to be imputed to person P, then at the time when A is performed, the performance of an act non-A is not incompatible with the total state of the universe—including the psychic state of P at time T." This means that P could have chosen to do otherwise and implies that there are exceptions to the rule that my wants are always necessarily connected to antecedent events which are not my wants. In short, this requirement is incompatible with determinism.

Our Consciousness Of Having Free Will

The second area of human experience that is said to nourish a belief in human freedom is the distinctive feeling of freedom which individuals experience at various moments in their lives. This phenomenon is sometimes referred to as an intuition of freedom or as a consciousness of free will or as a sense of self-determination. Very often in life we find ourselves choosing among alternatives, some of which are in varying degrees attractive to us and some of which appear to make some moral claim. In the experience of choosing we intuit directly that it is our choice that determines what shall be done.

One writer points out that rather than speak of a feeling in this regard, we ought to speak of an experience, because choice is not something we are conscious of but rather something we consciously do. In the act of choosing we take up the point of view of an agent. The element of freedom in selecting is actually an integral part of the primitive experience.

> To select alternative X is to take X rather than Y, otherwise it is not selecting but merely following the one open path. In order to take X rather than Y, both X and Y must be given for selection. This is to say that the practical stance is a necessary condition of choice. The experience of choice then presents a claim of being a true selecting among alternatives which are given as genuine possibilities to be selected among. What more could a claim of freely selecting involve than this claim of truly selecting among true possibilities? . . . a selecting I am accomplishing and hence dependent upon my agency.[84]

Other writers find evidence for human freedom in man's consciousness of sometimes exerting effort of will, which they distinguish from the simple act of choosing. The "will" must not be thought of as some separate faculty of the self engaged in a struggle with the other faculties of components of the self, but rather as an activity of the total person considered as a complex activity-unit. These writers are also careful to separate effort of will from muscular effort and intellectual effort. Characteristically, we become aware of an effort of wills in those situations where our desires tend to lead us toward one object while our sense of duty points us in another direction. "In such situations where there is conflict between one's desire and one's willing, the human self may become conscious of making an effort of will since we are going in the line of greater resistance."[85] Ordinarily, we say that the self *has* a desire but that the self *makes* the effort. This gives expression to the other aspects of the experience, which are (1) that we feel the self to be the source of the effort, as emanating from a decision to exert the effort, and (2) that we know we can withhold the exertion or make the exertion in varying degrees.

The ordinary person has no difficulty in distinguishing sharply between those situations in life where he had no real choice—where events pressed themselves upon him and his decision "was really the only thing he could have done"—and those where we are "vividly alive to real alternatives for creative actualization."[86] Says Ferré:

> Even afterward, therefore, when the deliberation is over, the choice made and the chosen course of action initiated to the exclusion of its alternatives, my experience forbids me to deny that I might have created differently, even under exactly the same kinds of relevant external and internal motivational conditions. To withdraw this claim would be to forfeit my data for the sake of a theory.[87]

The determinist does not deny that many people have such feelings. He claims, however, that it is all an illusion. As Freud put it, "The truth is that you have an illusion of psychic freedom within you which you do not want to give up . . . but this belief is quite unscientific."[88] Pavlov agreed: "It is true that persons have the subjective feeling of freedom . . . there is an immediate impression, hard to surmount, of some voluntary freedom of action, of some spontaneity, but this is illusory."[89] We are told to ignore the feelings and realize that we are not free in this sense.

> The average man knows that he chooses and he thinks his choice is free. But that is a delusion; his choice is not free. He can choose and he does choose. But he can only choose as his heredity and his environment cause him to choose. There is a cause for every wish, a cause for every choice; and every cause of every wish and choice arise from temperament which is heredity or from training which is environment. And these have fixed his choices before he makes them.[90]

It is generally agreed that often in life we experience a feeling of involuntariness, of things happening despite ourselves. Here we feel ourselves caught in the grip of forces external to our real self. In response to this the determinist takes what seems to be a somewhat unreasonable position. If a feeling of involuntariness accompanies an act, he tells us, it is always veridical, never illusory, and we may infer the reality from the appearance. If, however, we have a feeling of voluntariness, it does not tell us the truth about the act according to the determinist, and if we infer anything about reality from the feeling, we are under an illusion. No matter that both experiences are equally clear and strong. But on what grounds does the determinist make such a distinction? Usually when we decide that something is an optical illusion, we do so only after we confront one experience with a number of other experiences with which it is incompatible. But in our case no one has offered any evidence that would enable us to sense directly the illusory character of our sense of freedom. It is only his commitment to the metaphysical theory of universal causation that serves as a basis for the determinist.[91]

Freedom, Yes! Random Chance, No!

We mentioned earlier that one of the necessary conditions of responsibility involves the concept that the agent must retain throughout the selfsame identity. The self, in some sense, must be seen as an abiding continuant. This is the basis for the quite correct insight of Hume and

others that there are aspects to responsibility which actually pre-
suppose constant conjunction and regularity of sequence and, to a certain extent, predictability in the behavior of moral agents. Our reliance
on the characters of other people as trustworthy implies that we believe
their actions to be on the part of the same continuing character we
have seen at work before. Confidence in a person's constancy of
character is certainly a tribute to his moral worth and not a detraction
from it. The emphasis which we place on habit formation in moral
training also implies that the more we behave in a certain way, the
more likely it is that we will continue to behave that way. As David
Ross, who himself accepted the implications of determinism, noted
rather ruefully: "It seems to me that something like half of our ordinary thinking on moral questions implies a belief in the undeterminacy
of the will and something like half, a belief in its determination."[92]

It, therefore, must be granted to the determinist, as one of the
requirements of moral agency, that there are wide areas of human conduct within which free will as a rule is not exercised and human behavior flows in its predictable course.[93] The Talmud in general and the
halakhic process in particular are replete with instances where assumptions are made as to how people will behave in certain situations. "If a
person transgresses and repeats the transgression, it becomes as if permissible to him," and "If a person had the opportunity to sin once and
again and resists the temptation, he is assured not to sin." Most revealing is the rabbinic discussion on the question of the law of the "rebel-
lious son."[94] The harsh punishment ordained by the Torah was
explained on the basis of a projection of this person's future. Although
at the moment he is guilty of disobeying his parents and of stealing in
order to satisfy his appetites, transgressions which hardly justify the
death penalty, the Torah judged him according to the way he will end
up. A person such as this, it said, will in the end kill people to get what
he wants. There are also a number of halakhic principles based on
assumptions of psychological regularity which the rabbis relied upon
in establishing the law.

Free will does not operate in a vacuum. It operates only within the
limits and possibilities of my given wants, abilities, understanding, and
environment. "All free will is freedom within limits of a person's
inborn capabilities and of the world in which he lives."[95] Ample room

can thus be provided for the social sciences and for all those activities which rely on predictability in human affairs.

The one area that must be reserved for the possibility of contra-causal freedom is in the moral realm: "situations in which the agent is aware of a conflict between strongest desire and duty," or situations where the agent believes that his essential character or integrity as a self hangs on his decision.

At this point we find ourselves in a rather unhappy position. On the one hand we have shown the need to have the kind of freedom in which he can go against the network of causes playing upon him, including those of his formed character. Yet if the "free" choice does not flow from the agent's character, then what is it if not a "random" act, an act of "chance"? But in that case how can it be considered *that person's* choice at all? How can the act be attributed to that person?

In now seems that the concept of responsibility itself contains two apparently contradictory conditions:

A. That I remain throughout the selfsame person.
B. That I could have acted and chosen otherwise.

These, reduced to more precisely stated proportions, come to the following:

1. At the time when act A is performed, the performance of an act non-A is not incompatible with the total state of the universe, including the psychic state of the agent at time T.

2. The reason for A shall not in every case be derivable from the agent's character as so far formed.

3. There is a reason for A, in some sense, that rules out randomness.

By these last two items we mean that there must be some meaningful way to talk of an act of the self even though, in an important sense, it is not an expression of the self's character. The meaningfulness and certainly the real possibility of this have been denied by many writers. Thus, W. I. Matson argues: "Assuming there be such a difference making property in the agent, it surely makes sense to ask, 'Is this property innate or acquired?' If acquired, where did the ability to acquire this property come from? If innate, is the agent responsible for what he was born with?"[96]

Judaism's answer is, of course, that this "difference-making" property in man is indeed innate, being a capacity to choose—the freedom which is part of what it is to have been created in the image of God. Man is indeed not responsible for having the capacity to choose, but he is responsible for how he uses this capacity—for the choices he makes.

Man As A "Prime Mover"

We have reached a critical juncture in our discussion of the free-will problem. To take the next step in the direction in which the argument points is to cross over into an unfamiliar world of uncaused causes, real self-starters, introducers of new energy, creative activity. The determinist must turn aside at this point and take any other road except this one. His naturalistic, scientific orientation forecloses for him any option in which man is seen as a creature unique in the universe. For we have come to the crux of the issue. To say that man possesses contra-causal or categorical freedom is to say that on some occasions, man can make a choice which could not have been predicted because it goes against the entire lineup of causal conditions existing at the time. But what *causes* man to make that particular choice at that time? Our answer has to be a bold, unblushing: "Nothing—at least not in the conventional sense!"

> In order to explicate and clarify this concept of "categorical freedom" libertarians have distinguished the concepts of "agent causation" and "event causation." While event causes merely transmit change, agent causes genuinely originate it: event causes on this view are the links in causal series; agent causes are the absolute originators of such series. Thus a group of conditions, of which at least one must itself be an event or constitute some kind of change, may bring about some other change—as the movement of a match will under certain conditions cause its ignition. However, whatever events figure in the cause do themselves have a cause in their turn; they are mere links, or parts of links in a causal series. Certain substances, however, can initiate change in an absolute

sense; that is, they are capable of originating a change that does not itself issue from some other change. This is a capacity that some philosophers would attribute to God alone and that other philosophers would describe as a philosopher's fiction; however, it is the libertarian view that man possess this power. This ability is alternatively described as the "power of absolute self-origination," as a "creative power," as the "power of agency" and, perhaps best, as "the ability to act as a prime mover."[97]

But this is exactly the teaching of Judaism and a partial yet felicitous explication of the concept of man "created in the image of God." For men too can create, as it were, *yesh me-ayin,* "out of nothing." Man is a member of both the higher and lower orders of the universe, and the point of intersection is his psyche.[98] While the self-conscious portion of self faces outward, plugging into the empirical web of causality, the essential grounds of his selfhood, whose depths man can never glimpse, backs up into the mysterious realm of the spirit. And it is from there that the self, by choosing or deciding, can creatively introduce new energy and crucially modify the balance of power in his own personality.

Let us imagine how this might work in a concrete case. We read in Genesis how Joseph was doing well as the overseer of his master's estates in Egypt but is confronted by a problem when his master's wife "casts her eyes" upon him and repeatedly makes improper advances. Then, one day when they are alone, "she caught him by his garment, saying, 'Lie with me.' And he left his garment in her hand and fled."[99] In this account there is no indication that Joseph experienced any struggle. He rejects her offers from the very beginning and maintains this position until the end. The rabbis, however quite realistically suggest that as a normal young man, Joseph must have been sorely tempted and did undergo a fierce struggle. But what ultimately saved him from succumbing was the appearance in his mind of the image of his father, the aged Jacob. This cooled his passion and he fled. How would we analyze this situation in the light of our theory of contra-causal freedom? After all, the rabbis saw this as a great moral deed and entered Joseph into the gallery of biblical heroes as *Yoseph ha-Tzaddik*—"Joseph the Righteous one."

As we examine the character and consciousness of Joseph at that moment we find that the two considerations in his mind urging him to flee are: (1) his sense of loyalty to his master, and (2) his commitment to the way of God, the moral values taught to him by his father. However, the collective strength of these inhibitory factors must surely have been puny as compared to the attraction and allure of this woman and her promise of sexual favors. Any prediction based on the present reality must maintain that Joseph will succumb. Our determinist will say that Joseph must succumb. But what happens? Out of the freedom which Joseph possesses as a human being, he, the complete unitary self that is Joseph, decides to resist and exerts his will, which as William James points out, works by "attending to a different object and holding it fast before the mind."[100] The essential achievement of the volition is to gain possession of the field of thought and keep the attention strained on that one idea or object; to keep affirming and adopting it so that it doesn't slip away. The longer it can be kept before the mind, the stronger does this idea grow in power and influence. Now, we know that Joseph had had a loving relationship with his father, Jacob. But that was a while back in Canaan. Besides, Jacob had felt abandoned by his family and had not been thinking of them much lately. But now, confronted by this moral crisis, Joseph decides to conjure up in his mind the thought and image of his father. He exerts his will to keep that idea in place until it grows and begins to crowd out the fantasies aroused by his master's wife. Joseph thinks, "What would my father want me to do? What would my father think of me if I succumbed? How important is my relationship to this man and what he represents?" Soon the grip of the emotions has been broken and Joseph finds the strength to flee.

But even if our account be true and man is indeed a "prime mover," were an omniscient psychologist to come immediately *after* the event and examine the contents of Joseph's mind, he would find no evidence of any miraculous self-origination. He would report as follows: "Gentlemen, I find everything quite in order and rather pedestrian. We find in Joseph quite a strong attachment to his father; in fact he is obsessed with a sort of 'father image.' The reason it hasn't been much in evidence prior to this crisis is that it was repressed into the subconscious. Obviously, Joseph fled because he was following what was his strongest motivation."[101]

It is interesting to note in this regard the similarity between the self-originating choice of a moral agent and an event attributed to God, usually called a miracle, about which the following has been said: "A miracle is emphatically not an event without cause or without results. Its cause is the activity of God; its results follow according to natural law. In the forward direction (i.e., during the time which follows its occurrence) it is interlocked with all nature just like any other event. Its pecularity is that it is not that way interlocked backwards, interlocked with the previous history of nature."[102] In a similar manner, after the free choice has been made, a natural explanation will always be found because in order for the choice to realize itself it must interlock with nature. Before the choice, it could have been otherwise.

Earlier, we referred to an act of free will as a truly creative act. What is it we are creating? The very important answer is that man is creating himself. A person's character is never complete. Until a person's very last breath, his self is constantly in the process of developing and changing. At every age and at every stage of development, an individual's own personality, as so far formed with its habits and attitudes, restricts the range of choice and influences further development. The self, however, can sit in judgment on his own personality as so far formed and can disapprove and can decide to change it.

Character-building may be the most important area of human creativity. Noting a difference in the wording of the Rosh Hashanah, law which says to "make [yourselves] an offering" instead of the usual "bring an offering," the rabbis interpreted God to be saying: "On Rosh Hashanah I consider it as if you are making yourselves."[103] It has been noted that the "I"—the human self—is most intermittent and erratic. It is elusive and transitory. No other organism known to man can recite the apparently simple first-person pronoun "I" and comprehend its significance. Both the divine *Anokhi* and the human "I" are best known by their actions. But from the outside we only see activity without an actor. Both create worlds, and both are mysterious sources of self-creation. The "I" must always create itself. Kant showed that all proofs of God's existence are flawed, and Descartes was unsuccessful in proving the existence of the "I". As pure subjectivity, both can only be known from within. But the human "I" does appear in response to the moral challenge of a given situation. Only in the moment of moral decision, when the "I" makes a choice, engages in a struggle, and assumes responsibility, it is, through and through, "I"; is it all self, spiritual and free.[104]

But if the exercise of free will is the kind of creative activity we have been describing, then Campbell is quite correct in pointing out that "there is then absolutely no other way save an intuition of practical self-consciousness, in which we can become aware of it. Only from the inside, from the standpoint of the agent's living experience can such 'activity' possibly be apprehended."[105]

Human Selfhood: Intersection Between God And Nature

The significance of free will for Judaism extends far beyond the moral sphere. The fact is that the free-will controversy touches upon the fundamental philosophical issue that separates the religious person's outlook from the orientation of the naturalism and scientism that reign in the academic circles of contemporary society. The latter are committed to the notion that nature or the empirical realm is the whole of reality, assuming with a "perfect faith" that all of the regularities, uniformities, and causal relationships that are observed to operate today have ever been thus and will ever be thus. This, of course, safely eliminates any non-natural entities, such as God and soul and such strange events as miracles and free will. The religionist believes that the natural world is only a partial system within a larger reality which impinges upon nature at certain points, and although science has looked within nature and reports no traces of God, and seems to agree with Laplace, who stated that he had no need for "God" in his hypothesis, the points of intersection between the partial system of nature and the larger reality continue to merit our attention and interest. These points of intersection would be the original act of God in bringing the world into being,[106] events in history that are attributed to the "direct" agency of God,[107] and those aspects of human selfhood that exhibit qualities that might be traceable to man's origin as "image of God."

In the second chapter, we described how the Genesis account of the creation of man is telling us that man somehow stands apart from the rest of nature and in terms of origin, nature, and destiny is related to a moral God. Developments in the nineteenth-century biology, as typified by Darwin, tended to deny the uniqueness of man's status. Distinctions between human and animal characteristics were minimized, with Darwin claiming that even man's moral sense had originated by natural selection. But, of course, it can be questioned whether man's evolutionary origin necessarily determines his nature and significance. To say that it does would appear to be an instance of committing the "genetic fallacy." Over the course of time, almost every development which from one perspective seemed to suggest that man is not unique, and that he is totally explainable on the basis of a gradual continuum differing only in degree from the simple forms of life to the complex, was counterbalanced by an opposite view which found some new reason to believe that man was still *sui generis*.

Thus, the development of the computer, with its "memory bank" and its impressive ability to "think," to play a good game of chess, and even to modify its own programs in the light of past performance, has led some to speculate that minds are not very different from machines. So that man is not unique, after all. Yet the same developments have led others to point to capabilities of the mind that mechanization does not seem able to imitate. For example, little progress has been made in developing a machine that can recognize patterns.[108] Furthermore, those who attempt to equate minds and machines can do so only after dismissing the notion of "consciousness" and the subjective aspects of such mental states as "loving," "willing," and making free choices. Finally, the computer seems to be incapable of originality, and even if it is self-correcting it does so by following rules it was "told to follow."[109]

From another direction, scientific research into the physiology of the brain has produced much compelling evidence for the view that mind rests upon a physiological basis. For example, electrical stimulation of particular areas of the brain produces feelings of happiness, anxiety, or anger. The influence of drugs on mental experience seems to suggest a strong chemical influence on the makeup and control of human personality. Experiments with rats suggest that there are centers of pleasure in the brain (limbic areas) whose stimulation an animal finds almost irresistible. When a rat has learned that pressing a lever in his cage provides such a stimulation, the rat will forgo food and drink and press the lever at the incredible rate of 8,000 times an hour until it falls dead from total exhaustion. If we extrapolate this insight for human beings, it would suggest that the pleasure motive must be a truly overwhelming one, raising questions about the possibility of moral choices. These discoveries remind us of the ancient but influential theory of psychological hedonism; that man is capable of acting only out of a desire for pleasure.

Yet, out of the same research comes a surprising observation that seems to reinstate a notion of the uniqueness of man precisely in this area of experiencing pleasure. We are told that neural pathways exist between the cortical thinking regions of the brain and the limbic system, and that nerve impulses flow downward from the higher to the lower region. Thus, distinctively human behavior could now be characterized as motivated by activation of the limbic pleasure regions of the brain that is caused not primarily by the sense organs, but as a result of the activity of the brain's thinking regions. "Only in the *human* brain can thinking activate the limbic pleasure areas."[110] Human beings can derive pleasure from chess, from doing philosophy, from a sense of doing their duty, from studying the Torah. It turns out that Mill was right all along. Pleasures differ not only quantitatively but also on the basis of quality. There are higher and lower pleasures. Mill may not have had any real justification for thinking so, but today physiological grounds exist for such ranking.

An insight such as this helps to place two aspects of Judaism into clearer perspective. The first is that Judaism was never fearful or suspicious of pleasure. It recognized its powerful and all-pervasive role in human existence. Its strategy, however, was to harness and channel sensory pleasures in support of higher Jewish values. Thus sensory pleasures are brought into the divine worship. There is the sanctification over wine, the rule that "there is no joy except in the accompaniment of meat and wine," and the entire concept of *oneg shabbat* and *simchat yom tov,* the joy and pleasure of the Sabbath and the festivals. Secondly, the rabbis defined each of the higher intellectual and emotional values of Judaism as a special sort of pleasure. In the world-to-come, which is described as "delightful," the righteous *enjoy* the divine splendor. We pray to God that we may find the words of His Torah *pleasant,* since a man studies only that Torah which his "heart desires." Prophecy rests upon a person only when he is in a state of joy, while the highest religious experience is enjoying the *simchah shel mitzvah,* the "joy of the commandments."

In recent years, the behaviorist approach in psychology has grown in popularity, mainly as a result of the work of B. F. Skinner. In a recent work, he argues that the real problems of society can only be solved by what he calls "behavioral technology," a sort of conditioning in which desirable behavior is made to pay off.[111] Skinner maintains that behavior is not determined from within but rather from without, by changing the environment. Man's behavior, he claims, is completely predictable, and the knowledge already exists for a science of control. His conclusion is that man can no longer afford the illusion of freedom and the anarchy and disasters that it has spawned.

It is perhaps not completely coincidental that the most devastating critique of Skinner's book was written by Noam Chomsky, whose work in linguistics had led him to a rather unconventional conclusion.[112] In the course of his work, Chomsky has been tremendously impressed by the complexity of human language. He finds it remarkable that a child can "learn" to speak a language; to understand the grammar "on relatively slight exposure and without specific training." Chomsky denies that there exists a "learning theory" that can account for the acquisition of language skills through experience. Instead, Chomsky prefers what he calls the "innateness hypothesis," which holds that one of the faculties of the mind, common to the species, is a faculty of language that "provides a sensory system for the preliminary analysis of linguistic data and a schematism that determines a certain class of grammars." If so, then it would seem that the language faculty is unique to human beings. "It is a reasonable surmise, I think, that there is no structure similar to the Universal Grammar in non-human organisms and that the capacity for free, appropriate, and creative use of language as an expression of thought with the means provided by the language faculty is also a distinctive feature of the human species having no significant analogue elsewhere."[113]

This will come as no surprise to students of Judaism, who will recall that the words in Genesis, "And man became a living soul," are translated by the Targum as "a speaking spirit."[114]

But if man is free and creative in this unique and radical sense, then it means that we do not live in a closed or block universe. The selfhood of man, grounded in contra-causal freedom, is perhaps the most revealing point of intersection of all. If man understands that he can act in self-originating creativity and weave new and unexpected additions to the unhemmed fringes of his personality, then he might be more receptive to the notion of a God who is the uncaused cause of the universe and who mysteriously has input into nature and history not only "then" but "now" and is the creator par excellence.[115] Even as we know ourselves to be free and to act responsibly, so might we be encouraged to seek out "He before whom we are destined to give a judgment and a reckoning."[116]

9
Systemic Aspects of Jewish Morality

In this final chapter we shall attempt to delineate some of the inner structures of Jewish morality in order to demonstrate that Judaism includes not merely a set of moral rules but a moral system as well. It has been said, that a moral system should have at least the following three properties in order to be so designated.[1]

1. The moral rules and principles that are included should be *integrated*; i.e., every part should be related to every other part directly or indirectly.
2. No part of the morals within the system may be incompatible with any other part. If they appear to be so, the system must provide a mechanism by which the incompatibility is resolved and the individual in that situation is able to find guidance as how to behave. In short, to be a system, the morals therein must be *consistent*.
3. The set of morals in question should be *comprehensive*. That is to say, the system should contain rules covering every moral situation or should provide a way of generating a correct moral judgment and guidance for whatever problems might arise in the future.

I believe it can be shown that the morality of Judaism, to a very great degree, does constitute a system in the sense defined above. Let us begin with the property we have called "integration."

The Logic That Integrates

There are different ways in which the moral teachings of Judaism may be said to be related to each other. One can point out that all the teachings emanate from the same source—a certain body of writings that are considered authoritative. It can also be suggested that the morality of Judaism aims at certain end-goals—certain valued conditions, such as peace and harmony, which these rules and principles are expected to bring about. In the one case, the teachings are integrated by a common origin, in the other, by a common purpose. There is, however, a more important sense in which the moral teachings of Judaism are related to each other, and that is by means of the "connective tissue" of logical relations. We will attempt to show (1) that the moral rules found in the Pentateuch are largely deducible from the moral principles in the Pentateuch, and (2) that the rabbis, in interpreting and explicating the teachings of the Torah in order to further develop the morality of Judaism, utilized methods that were, by and large, of a logical and rational nature.

In the moral system of Judaism the primary literary source of moral principles, many moral rules, as well as some individual moral judgments is, of course, the written Torah. We have already described the form in which they are found and where.[2] Vindication of the acceptance of the Torah itself as a source of binding moral teachings would in one sense rest upon acceptance of the theological underpinnings of Judaism, but in another sense might be said to depend upon our intuitive grasp of the moral nature of God and His demands.[3] It is, however, of the utmost importance for a correct understanding of the nature of Jewish Halakhah and morality to comprehend this seemingly paradoxical phenomenon of a thoroughly rational, man-directed halakhic process operating on a revealed corpus of *mitzvot* of divine origin. While the discussions raged among the talmudic rabbis and the medieval authorities as to whether there are "reasons" for all the commandments and what they might be, the undeniable fact is that the process by which we explicate and fulfill the precepts both ritual and moral—the process of exegesis and interpretation which is the oral law and its development—is a thoroughly rational one conducted by human beings in accordance with accepted rules and procedures.[4] No contradiction was seen between the principle that "The Torah is *from* heaven" (*Torah min ha-shamayim*) with its implication of the divine origin of the commandments, and the principle that "The Torah is not *in* heaven" (*Lo ba-shamayim hi*), which was understood to mean that no superhuman, extrarational interference will be countenanced in the unfolding of the halakhic process.[5] In the words of Joseph Albo: "The Law of God cannot be perfect so as to be adequate for all times, because the ever-new details of human relations, their customs and their acts are too numerous to be embraced in a book. Therefore Moses was given orally certain general principles, only briefly alluded to in the Torah, by means of which the wise men in every generation may work out the details as they appear."[6]

What facilitates the integration of a set of morals is the recognition that differences exist in the extent of the generality of the maxims or judgments that are employed in moral discourse. First, there are singular moral judgments; for example, "Simon ought to return the money he borrowed." Second, there are moral rules, such as "One ought to keep one's promises." Finally, there are ultimate moral principles, such as "One ought to do that which promotes the welfare of society." In the instances given above it becomes an easy matter to integrate the three moral statements by simply showing that they are related by the logical process of subsumption. The singular moral judgment can be justified by showing that it is covered by the moral rule. And the moral rule, in turn, can be justified by deducing it from the moral principle.

1. One ought to keep promises (major premise—rule).
2. Simon promised to return the money (minor premise—factual statement).
Simon ought to return the money (conclusion—singular moral judgment).

1. One ought to do that which promises the welfare of society (major premise—principle).
2. Promise-keeping promotes the welfare of society (minor premise—factual statement.
One ought to keep one's promises (conclusion—rule).

In terms of justification, the sequence would always be "upward" from singular moral judgments to rules to principles. However, in terms of generating responses to new and changing moral situations, the direction would tend to be "downward" from principles to rules to individual moral judgments.

An important difference has been noted between moral rules and moral principles. Moral rules are propositions to the effect that a certain kind of action is generally right or generally wrong. Because of their degree of specificity, moral rules are not invariant. They cannot be regarded as universally valid. As J. S. Mill once said, "It is not the fault of any creed, but of the complicated nature of human affairs that rules of conduct cannot be framed as to require no exceptions."[7] Moral principles, however, are more abstract and therefore can be regarded as holding in all circumstances and allowing no exceptions. While it is possible for moral rules within a particular moral system to conflict, so that the system must provide a resolution, it is impossible for moral principles to conflict.[8]

Self-Evident Sevarah As a Source Of Principle

We have already indicated in an earlier chapter that the Torah contains several moral principles of a general nature and that these were recognized as such by the rabbis.[9] From the talmudic discussions, however, it is clear that another source for principles both logical and moral was recognized as being of equal authority to the text of Scripture. This was called *sevarah,* or that which appears self-evident to human reason. How do we explain the occurrence of this belief in the Talmud? The association of Torah with *chakhmah* as "wisdom" in all books of the Bible served to generate the notion in the minds of the rabbis that Torah as the revealed will of God is identical with that wisdom which appears to man as self-evident truth or as empirically grounded insight into human experience.[10] While reason and logic play an indirect and supporting role in the employment of almost all of the methods of halakhic exegesis, there are occasions where the Amoraim, in particular, appeal to *sevarah,* "self-evident reason" or "common sense," as a direct and immediate source of a particular halakhah without further recourse to a text or other hermeneutical rules. Moreover, any statutes or *halakhah* whose source was in *sevarah* was regarded as being Torah itself; as enjoying full scriptural authority.[11] Many times in the course of a discussion in the Talmud, the rabbi would exclaim: "If we have a *sevarah,* why do we need a text?"[12] Thus, while *midrash,* as a method of exegesis, "unpacked" the hidden content of Torah by interpreting the words and sentences of the text, *sevarah* was believed to achieve the same because at a certain level there was complete congruence between the clear reason of man and the purpose and spirit of the Torah.[13]

To say that a moral or logical principle is known by intuition or is self-evident is to say that it is its own evidence. "What this amounts to is the double claim that we can recognize the truth of the principle simply by reflecting on the full meaning of the principle itself and that we do not need any further evidence to know that the principle is true."[14]

Examples of the use of *sevarah* are the following: The Talmud asks: "How do we know that the onus of proof falls on the plaintiff rather than the defendent?" In other words, what is the source of the established legal principle that he who wishes to remove something from someone's possession has the burden of proof? When a proof-text is offered, Rav Ashi asks, "Why is a text required? Is it not a *sevarah?* One who is in pain visits the house of the doctors."[15] Just as it is appropriate that the patient seek out the physician and not the reverse, so is it proper that he who has claims on property in the possession of his neighbor prove his claim rather than the defendant.

We have already referred to the principle of the Torah that where a human life is in jeopardy all of the *mitzvot* of the Torah may be set aside except for the prohibitions against idolatry, incest and adultery, and murder. In other words, a Jew is obliged to forfeit his life rather than be guilty of violating any of these three injunctions. In responding to the question of the source of the law regarding forfeiture of life rather than murder, the Talmud answers that it is a *sevarah*: "How do you know your blood is redder? Perhaps his blood is redder."[16] While one may transgress the Torah in order to save a life, it makes no sense to apply this rule to the case of murder, since to do so is to cause a life to be lost anyway. But what the *sevarah* adds is that all human lives are to be considered equally precious.

A third illustration is to be found in the Mishnah: "If a woman says, 'I was a married woman but now I am divorced,' she is believed, for the mouth that prohibits is the mouth that permits." This principle is described by the Talmud as a *sevarah,* a self-evident truth that enjoys universal assent.[17] Since we would have no grounds for forbidding her to marry were it not for her own acknowledgment that she was married, we are logically compelled to believe her again when she says she has been divorced and is thus free to remarry.[18]

From The General To The Particular, And Vice Versa

Let us return to the words of Albo quoted earlier that "the wise men in every generation" are expected "to work out the details" from the given general principles. As we have already illustrated, the way to show a "natural" connection between rules and principles is to demonstrate that the former can be deduced from the latter. Arguments by subsumption are the simplest and most common argument patterns found in moral discourse. We can, therefore, expect to find that subsumption, which is based upon deductive reasoning, will be one of the ways by which the particulars were generated from the general principles contained in Scripture.

A clear example of the attribution of deductive reasoning to the rabbis is the following statement by Maimonides:

> The following positive commands were ordained by the rabbis: visiting the sick, comforting the mourners, joining a funeral procession, dowering a bride, escorting departing guests, performing for the dead the last tender offices, acting as pallbearer, going before the bier, making lamentation [for the dead], digging a grave and burying the body, causing the bride and the bridegroom to rejoice, providing them with all their needs [for the wedding]. These constitute deeds of loving-kindness performed in person and for which no fixed measure is prescribed. *Although all these commands are only on rabbinical authority, they are implied in the precept: "And you shall love your neighbor as yourself"* [Lev. 19:18]; that is: what you would have others do to you, do to him who is your brother in the Law and in the performance of the commandments.[19]

The seven rabbinic rules enumerated by Maimonides involve the most important and traumatic occasions in the life of the individual, occasions when the concern and help of one's fellow is most needed and appreciated. Indeed, these are the areas which in Jewish communities evolved from opportunities for individual acts of *chesed* to organized volunteer groups and on to established communal institutions which created new standards in social welfare. But while one finds in the Torah individuals and even God Himself performing such acts of loving-kindness, nowhere in the written text are these activities given as moral imperatives applying to all people. What the rabbis did then, according to Maimonides, was to note that the principle of "Love thy neighbor as thyself" implied specific duties for man in these various areas. Since these particular occasions of sickness, death, marriage, and security were so vital and prevalent, and since the needs were generally so uniform, the rabbis formulated specific rules as to what and how it was to be done.

The deductive form is quite simple:

1. Do onto others as you would have others do onto you.
2. If you were sick, you would wish to be attended.
3. Therefore, attend those who are sick.

An illustration of the use of simple deductive logic in applying the Halakhah to a contemporary problem is the question of the Jewish attitude toward cigarette smoking.[20] Ignoring the actual authorities who may have pronounced on the subject, the underlying logic is quite simple. First we must locate the relevant general principle: "take heed to thyself, and take care of thy life, and . . . take good care of your lives."[21] This plainly enjoins us from intentionally placing ourselves in situations which can endanger our lives. Next we must ascertain the facts: "The surgeon-general has determined that cigarette smoking is dangerous to your health." Although cigarettes are nowhere mentioned in the Bible, we must conclude that Jewish morality forbids us to smoke. While the general principle has always been known, it has been necessary in every generation to update, by means of our expanding knowledge and experience, the kinds of things that are dangerous. Thus, Maimonides, for his day, lists the following:

One may not put his mouth to a flowing channel of water and drink . . . lest he swallow a leech.

One should not put small coins into his mouth.

One should not walk over a shaking bridge or enter a ruin.[22]

The Rema adds, "It is prohibited to rely on a miracle," and Maimonides rules, "If one says, 'If I want to put myself in danger, what concern is it to others?' disciplinary measures may be taken."[23]

In terms of actual historical development, however, it is perhaps closer to the truth to say that the specific rules found in the Pentateuch were interpreted by the rabbis in such a way as to become in themselves veritable "principles" capable of generating further rules.[24] This was done by employing the traditional methods of exegesis known as the Thirteen Middot, which we shall soon examine. Thus, for example, on the basis of the single reference in the Torah to the "ravished maiden"—"And to the woman nothing shall be done"—the rabbis inferred the fundamental principle that "Victims of coercion are held blameless by the Torah." Or, again, in the view of the rabbis, the scattered rules in the Torah regarding an ox that gores or an uncovered cistern became the basis for the "four main categories of damages."[25] Just as the biblical heroes, Abraham, Isaac, Jacob, Moses, et al, although appearing as individuals, serve as models and furnish us with functioning standards of moral behavior, so too may "striking events" or the concrete cases spelled out in the biblical codes "rise in memory to provide a touchstone for anything resembling it."[26]

Finding The Facts That Will Confirm The Hypothesis

There were other occasions when the rabbis had a strong sense of the Torah being committed to certain principles yet could find no explicit statement to that effect. For example, anyone who reads the Torah must receive the impression that the Torah is concerned about the welfare of animals and would consider it immoral to give them unnecessary pain. Yet while many *mitzvot* involve animals, nowhere is it immediately clear that the reason for the legislation is concern for the beast rather than concern for the owner or some ritualistic consideration.

What the rabbis did, therefore, was to fashion a reasonable hypothesis that would logically connect the principle they wished to prove with a number of factual statements, so that if the factual statements were true, the hypothesis would be true. For example, we suspect that our classmate Simon is ill but we have received no specific information about his health. What we can do is to develop a hypothetical argument along the following lines: "If Simon were ill, then he would be absent from school, he probably would have informed his teachers of that fact, he would have consulted his doctor, acquaintances would have reported that he looked unwell lately, etc." Then, if we check out these facts and find that he was indeed absent from school, . . . etc., we can conclude that the hypothesis stands confirmed, so that we can assume that Simon is ill.

This form of reasoning, sometimes called the hypothetical confirmatory argument, always follows the following pattern, where H stands for the hypothesis and E for the facts that the hypothesis is supposed to explain (*Explanandum*).

1. If H then E (If the hypothesis is true then the following conditions should obtain)
2. E (These conditions do obtain.)
   _____
   H (conclusion: The hypothesis is true.)

While a hypothetical confirmatory argument is closely related to analogical arguments, the special function of the former is to adduce facts to confirm the particular hypothesis. The more facts cited, the stronger the argument becomes.[27]

In one instance, the Talmud concludes that the practice of returning lost objects on the basis of certain descriptive or identifying characteristics (*simonim*) given by the alleged owner is *de-oraita*; i.e., of scriptural origin.[28] They derive this from the passage in the Torah which in speaking of the individual who finds a lost animal adds: "And if thy brother be not nigh unto thee, and thou know him not, then thou shalt bring it home to thy house, and it shall be with thee until thy brother *seek it,* and thou shalt restore it to him."[29] Since it is obvious in the given situation that the object cannot be returned to its owner until he seeks it, the rabbis interpreted the phrase to refer to the finder's "seeking out," or interrogating, the alleged owner. That is to say, in order to make sure that the claimant is indeed the owner, the finder may ask for identifying marks (*simonim*). Thus, by assuming a certain belief on the part of the Torah, we can make sense of a difficult expression.

In the discussion alluded to earlier, involving the question whether pain suffered by animals is *de-oraita,* the argument is similarly to the effect that the Torah accepts the principle that we have a moral obligation to alleviate the pain of an animal.[30]

> H. 1. If the Torah holds that an animal's pain is a moral concern, then (1) the rule to help unload an animal should have priority over the obligation to help load. (2) It should make no difference whether the owner is a friend or an enemy, a Jew or non-Jew. (3) Unloading should be done without reward, while for loading he may ask for compensation.
> E. 2. The Torah rules are such that (1) the rule to help unload . . . (2) it makes no difference . . . (3) unloading is to be done without reward . . .
>
> ---
>
> H. *Tza'ar ba'alei chayyim de-oraita*
> The Torah believes pain of animals to be a moral concern.

It would appear that this is also the general meaning of the claim that "Doing things because of the principle 'Thy ways are ways of peace' is *de-oraita*"; i.e., that the entire underlying purpose of the Torah seems to be to establish harmonious and peaceful relations among men.[31] If this cannot be assumed then much in the Torah makes no sense.

Midrash Which Confirms And Midrash Which Creates

From a historical perspective, the first step in going beyond the explicit injunctions found in the Pentateuch was connected with the basic effort to understand and interpret the words of Scripture in accordance with an elaborate method of exegesis and inference known as *midrash*—in this context, *midrash halakhah*. Since in most of its expressions, Jewish morality was treated as part of Halakhah, it is to be expected that the exegetical apparatus or means of derivation generally used in the Halakhah were the same used to explicate the moral teachings. The process of *midrash* has also been referred to as hermeneutics, which is defined as "the science of interpretation or of explaining the meaning of an author's words according to certain rules."[32]

In its fully developed form, this process of *midrash* served two different functions.[33] At times, the midrashic process which connects a newly elaborated Halakhah to a particular passage was formal only. Known as *asmakhta,* its purpose was not to generate law but to provide a biblical anchor, or textual framework, for an already existing Halakhah known from the oral tradition. This was done as a mnemonic device to make it easier to study and to remember and also to point up the inseparable link between the oral law and the written law. But on other and more important occasions, throughout the history of the development of the Halakhah, the *midrash* functioned as the instrument for the creation of new Halakhah. In every period, the rabbis were confronted by problems arising out of ambiguities or apparent contradictions in the text or by questions posed by changing social conditions. Responding to these problems by midrashic interpretation of the written Torah was much preferred by the rabbis to any alternative method, since the method of *midrash* produced Halakhah that was not an "addition" to what exists in the Torah but rather an unpacking of what had always been implicit in it. The "natural" relationship of particular to universal preserved the integrity of the concept of the unity of the Halakhah, old and new.

These two types of *midrash,* the *midrash* which creates and the *midrash* which confirms or sustains, are recognizable by their different literary styles.[34] The *midrash* which confirms is satisfied to tie the already-known Halakhah to the Torah text by the most gossamer of threads; a hint, a sign, an allusion is already sufficient. Although admittedly artificial, the formal connection was adequate for its purpose. By contrast, the *midrash* which creates will draw the Halakhah out of the very interior of the biblical verse, showing by logical arguments how the derived Halakhah embodies the very spirit of the written word.

Consider the following example of how interpreting existing texts can lead to differing views resulting in new Halakhah. In Deuteronomy we have the sublime teaching instructing the creditor how he is to behave regarding the surety he may have taken from the poor:

> And if he be a poor man, thou shalt not sleep with his pledge; thou shalt surely restore to him the pledge when the sun goeth down, that he may sleep in his garment, and bless thee; and it shall be righteousness unto thee before the Lord thy God.[35]

> Thou shalt not . . . take the widow's raiment to pledge.[36]

It appears from these passages that from a widow one may not take a pledge at all, while from a poor man one may take a pledge but must return it before nightfall. Regarding the defining characteristics of the "widow" referred to in this law, we find a dispute between Rabbi Judah and Rabbi Simeon.[37] Rabbi Judah says that a pledge may not be taken from a widow regardless of whether she is rich or poor. Rabbi Simeon, however, maintains that from a rich widow one may take a pledge but not from a poor widow, because in the process of returning it to her each evening and retrieving it each morning, "one will give her a bad reputation in her neighborhood." In explaining the difference of opinion, the Talmud points out that Rabbi Simeon emphasized the evident rationale of the law. Since we see that the pledge must be returned each evening if the borrower is poor, it may be surmised that from a poor widow no pledge should be taken, since the creditor's daily comings and goings will embarrass her. It follows, therefore, that if the widow is rich, a pledge may be taken and need not be returned each evening. Rabbi Judah, however, believes that we must be bound by the actual terms used by the Torah. A "widow" is a woman whose husband has died. Since the Torah prohibits the taking of a pledge from a "widow" without further qualification, it includes both rich and poor. It might, of course, be reasoned that perhaps a widow is to be considered psychologically and emotionally deprived and merits special treatment regardless of her financial situation. In any event, it seems clear that differing methods of interpretation may result in different conclusions as to what is morally right in a particular situation.

The Method Of Categorization

The casuistic character of the Halakhah sometimes adds a dimension of complexity to the process of reasoning that takes one from general moral principle to the determination of a ruling in a particular case. Let us, for example, consider the problem of abortion. While the Torah itself does not directly pronounce on the subject, there are some implications which together with certain rabbinic teachings lay down the following as given:

1. Killing a fetus is not considered murder. The punishment prescribed is monetary compensation.[38]
2. A fetus may be destroyed in order to save the life of a mother endangered by childbirth. Once the greater part of the child is born, one may not harm it, as one may not set aside one person's life for that of another.[39]
3. A further distinction is introduced, apropos to the rules of ritual uncleanliness, between a fetus during the first forty days after gestation, when it is considered "mere fluid," and the fetus after forty days, when a miscarriage will in some respects be considered similar to a regular birth.[40]

Two opposing inferences may be drawn from the first and second teachings regarding the status of a fetus. One is that prior to birth, a fetus is in some sense not to be regarded as a full living person. Yet there is an implication that in the absence of danger to the mother, a fetus ought not to be destroyed. The first teaching does not imply that a fetus may be indiscriminately destroyed, only that killing it is not a capital crime.

What emerges from the above is that while it would appear to be morally wrong to kill a fetus in the absence of danger to the mother, the underlying rationale is not clear. It is at this point that different rabbinic authorities offer different theories to explain the status of the fetus by suggesting different principles under which destroying a fetus is to be subsumed.

Thus, there are some who maintain that the prohibition of destroy-

ing a fetus is biblical, while others argue it is only rabbinic. Some claim
that the fetus, certainly after the first forty days of fertilization, must be
seen as possessing some degree of life, so that to destroy it is to be
guilty of some form of homicide. Others, however, argue that the element of homicide is largely ruled out by the first and second teachings,
which indicate that the fetus is not considered a *nefesh,* a living person.
Instead, they say, the fetus may not be destroyed because it constitutes
potential life, and thus this prohibition is related to onanism, which forbids the destruction or wasting of male seed. Still others relate it to the
prohibition against unlawful wounding or injury of both the fetus and
the mother.[41]

The important point to note is that while these different theories or
categorizations contribute to the complexity and uncertainty of the
question, their very diversity provides a certain flexibility for rabbis
faced by moral dilemmas in a concrete situation. Different consequences flow from these different categorizations.[42] Thus, if one does
not consider destruction of the fetus homicide, then one may rule that
an individual need not sacrifice his life rather than perform an abortion. But again, if feticide is prohibited because it is a form of "destroying seed," then it follows that abortion for convenience is immoral
even within the forty days of fertilization. On the other hand, if in feticide one is not dealing with the question of homicide but with these
other factors, or if the prohibition, whatever it is, is rabbinic rather
than biblical, then in considering cases of therapeutic abortion, where
the issue is not the mother's life but her physical health or even her
psychological well-being, one may find a basis to permit abortion. It is
reported, for example, that a prominent rabbinic authority in Israel
permits the performance of an abortion within the first three months
of pregnancy when there are valid grounds to fear that the child will be
born deformed or abnormal.

Another example of the consequences of this method of categorization may be found in the approach developed by the rabbinic authorities in the Middle Ages toward Jews who inform against their people to
the gentile authorities. It should be kept in mind that under the then-
existing conditions, a Jewish informer constituted a formidable danger
to the entire Jewish community. The civil authorities were often only
too eager to accept any calumny against the Jews, as it would give them

an excuse to persecute and to plunder. In several responsa, some of the leading rabbinic scholars traced the reasoning by which they justified their ruling that a known informer (having on at least three occasions caused a Jew or his property harm) may be put to death by the Jewish community.[43]

But how could this be done, when after the dissolution of the Sanhedrin, capital punishment was no longer within the province of the rabbinical court, and the traditional modes of execution were no longer operative? The answer is that the rabbis found a different principle under which to act—a different category in which to place the informer; namely, the law of the rodef, the "pursuer." This law states that if A is pursuing B to kill him, either directly or indirectly, anyone may save B even at the cost of A's life. This is inferred from the biblical law that a betrothed woman may be saved from rape at the cost of the assailant's life.[44]

The traditional capital charge with its formal court proceedings applied to acts that had already been committed; when the person himself had committed the murder and only when a human life had been taken. By contrast, the rule of the *rodef* applies to individuals before they have committed the crime and are only threatening. In other words, we are dealing here with prevention rather than punishment. The law of the *rodef* applies to crimes that are indirectly caused, even if the action is directed only against the property of the victim, as we shall see in the case of the informer. This kind of sentence does not depend upon properly constituted courts and formal rules of procedure, but any person who is witness to such a pursuit is obligated to take action. In the words of the Rosh:

> The sages have equated the person who would inform against his fellow Jew in order to help the gentile government confiscate that fellow's property, with the person who pursues another to kill him. Once Jewish property falls into gentile hands, they have no pity. Today they take part of it; tomorrow the whole of it, finally they deliver the Jew himself to the executioner—perhaps when faced by death he will confess he has no more wealth! Therefore, one who informs against a Jew's property is deemed to be a *rodef* and can be put to death.

In the case before the Rosh, which took place in Seville in 1312, a certain Jew had terrorized the Jewish community by his defamations before the ruler, Don Pedro III. Although warned several times to desist, he refused and continued to inform. Drawing upon a parallel case in the Talmud, the Rosh agreed to this extraordinary procedure as a measurse to curb lawless acts: "This is done as a deterrent against the proliferation of informers and to rescue all Israel—the victims, from his power."[45]

Logic And Hermeneutics In The Thirteen Middot Of Rabbi Ishmael

From the very beginnings of the halakhic process, various methods of interpretation were used. These were organized systematically by exegesis into thirteen, sometimes called the thirteen hermeneutical rules.[46] To the extent that the methods of interpretation (*middot*) employed in the Halakhah are logical, drawing inferences from the words and statements of the text and from the intentions hidden in the expressions and allusions of the words, we can say that the inferences of the *middot* are, in a sense, words of the lawgiver himself.[47] The process of *midrash*, however, particularly as applied to the nonhalakhic portions of the Torah, suggests a broader and less exact process. The rabbis already indicated that there are "seventy faces to the Torah" and that different people can perceive different nuances in the same expression. The varieties of translations themselves give ample witness to the conceptual possibilities inherent in the text. While the Aggadah can tolerate a multiplicity of views, the Halakhah seeks a resolution in terms of a single acceptable mode of behavior—a path that many can traverse without deviating to the right or to the left. Hence, a word *middah* (pl. *middot*) whch implies a measure or a precise demarcation.

The following are the thirteen *middot* of Rabbi Ishmael:

1. Inference from minor to major, or from major to minor.
2. Inference from similarity of phrases in texts.
3. A comprehensive principle derived from one text, or from two related texts.
4. A general proposition followed by a specifying particular.
5. A particular term followed by a general proposition.

6. A general law limited by a specific application, and then treated again in general terms, must be interpreted according to the tenor of the specific limitation.
7. A general proposition requiring a particular or specific term to explain it, and conversely, a particular term requiring a general one to complement it.
8. When a subject included in a general proposition is afterwards particularly excepted to give information concerning it, the exception is made not for that one instance alone, but to apply to the general proposition as a whole.
9. Whenever anything is first included in a general proposition and is then excepted to prove another similar proposition, this specifying alleviates and does not aggravate the law's restriction.
10. But when anything is first included in a general proposition and is then excepted to state a case that is not a similar proposition, such specifying alleviates in some respects, and in others aggravates, the law's restriction.
11. Anything included in a general proposition and afterwards excepted to determine a new matter, cannot be applied to the general proposition unless this be expressly done in the text.
12. An interpretation deduced from the text or from subsequent terms of the text.
13. In like manner when two texts contradict each other, the meaning can be determined only when a third text is found which harmonizes them.[48]

Actually, all thirteen methods are instances of two basic types of *midrash,* the explicatory midrash and the analogizing midrash.[49] The first strives to explain, clarify, and interpret particular texts or laws from within themselves. The second involves an argument from analogy in a broad sense, in which different laws or subject matters are likened to each other, resulting in an extension of the law into new areas. Analogical arguments are based on the inference that if one individual or class shares one or more properties with a second individual or class, certain other properties of the first are also shared by the second. The last ten *middot* of Rabbi Ishmael's group fit into the first category but can then be organized into four subgroups. The second category is exemplified by the first three *middot,* which we will consider later on.

The Explicatory Midrash

The fifth *middah,* called *perat u-kelal,* works as follows: "A particular term followed by a general proposition, then the general proposition is seen as adding to the particular term"; i.e., the particular terms are seen merely as examples, while the law in question is seen as applying to all particulars that fit into the general proposition, mentioned or not.

Consider the laws of the *shomrim* (bailees): "If a man deliver unto his neighbor an ass, or an ox, or a sheep, or any beast, to keep, and it die, or be hurt, or driven away, no man seeing it; the oath of the Lord shall be between them, to see whether he has not put his hand unto his neighbor's goods . . ."[50] Sometimes the *shomer* is held responsible for the damages and other times he is not held responsible but has to take an oath that he has not caused the damage. What are the items given to the bailee to be kept which are covered by these laws? If we examine the passage above, we see that the Torah first enumerates various particular items: "ass, ox, sheep," and then follows with a general term: "or any beast." Since this is an instance of *perat* (particular) followed by *kelal* (general), we infer that the law applies to all manner of living creatures that may be given into his safekeeping.

The eighth through the eleventh *middot* are somewhat different than the one just considered. Although here too we are dealing with the relationship between general and particular terms, the question of sequence is irrelevant.[51] For here we are dealing with cases where the entire imperative is repeated again in connection with the particular. Since the particular is included in the general proposition, why was it singled out for special mention?

Let us examine the following precept:

Thou shalt not see thy brother's ox or his sheep driven away, and hide thyself from them; thou shalt surely bring them back unto thy brother. And if thy brother be not nigh unto thee, and thou know him not, then thou shalt bring it home to thy house, and it shall be with thee until thy brother require it, and thou shalt restore it to him. And so shalt thou do with his ass; and so shalt thou do with his garment; and so shalt thou do with every lost thing of thy brother's, which he hath lost, and thou hast found; thou mayest not hide thyself.[52]

In the last verse we have the general directive, "And so shalt thou do with every lost thing of thy brother's," which would, of course, include his ass and his garment. Why then does the Torah repeat the "And so shalt thou do" in connection with these two particulars? The rabbis explain that from this we infer that just as a garment is an object which has both recognizable characteristics (simonim) and claimants (i.e., is not ownerless), so too only in respect to those objects which have both recognizable features and claimants is one obliged to announce one's find.[53]

The twelfth middah has an interesting application in the case of the Decalogue. How should we interpret "Thou shalt not steal"?[54] Does it refer only to stealing objects or property, or does it perhaps include stealing human beings, which we call "kidnapping"? Let us examine the broader text in which this precept was placed. If "Thou shalt not steal" is grouped together with "Thou shalt not murder" and "Thou shalt not commit adultery," both of which carry the death penalty, then it might be inferred that this injunction as well refers to a kind of stealing that carries the death penalty; i.e., kidnapping. For we read in Exodus, "And he that stealeth a man and selleth him, or if he be found in his hand, he shall surely be put to death." By the same reasoning, in the passage "Ye shall not steal, neither shall ye deal falsely, nor lie one to another," the prohibition "Ye shall not steal," according to the associated items, should be interpreted as referring to the stealing of objects.[55]

The thirteenth and last middah is straightforward enough: "When two texts contradict each other, the meaning can be determined only when a third text is found which harmonizes them." There are many instances in the Torah where passages from two different portions, or two passages in the same portion, or even two parts of the same passage appear to contradict each other. What we are being taught here goes beyond the simple finding of a deciding third text. A broad philosophical approach is being suggested. When we discover two texts in conflict, we are not to select one over the other or to decide that a corruption has entered one of the texts, but rather we are to examine the entire subject in all of its occurrences and find a way of reconciling or harmonizing the conflicting passages. What makes this a reasonable procedure is the a priori assumption that the Torah as a whole possesses a unitary character whose explicit rules are the facade of an underlying structure that is coherent and consistent.[56]

For example, consider the following two passages from the Torah:

> Thou shalt not oppress thy neighbor nor rob him; the wages of a hired servant shall not abide with thee all night until the morning.[57]

> Thou shalt not oppress a hired servant that is poor and needy, whether he be of thy brethren or of thy strangers that are in thy land within thy gates. In the same day, thou shalt give him his hire; neither shall the sun go down upon it, for he is poor and setteth his heart upon it, lest he cry against thee unto the Lord and it be a sin in thee.[58]

As we compare these texts, a discrepancy becomes apparent almost immediately. According to the last passage we must pay the worker upon completion of his day's work and not delay even to the setting of the sun. The first passage, however, speaks of not delaying until the next morning and makes no reference to paying that same day! The rabbis reconciled the two passages by interpreting the first as referring to a day-laborer and the second to a night-laborer, with the Torah in both cases giving the employer a fair and practical twelve-hour period in which to pay his employee his wages.[59] Thus in the first text we are told not to delay his payment beyond the next morning while the second text warns us not to delay beyond the setting of the sun of the following day.

An instance of conflicting passages in the same portion is the following:

> 1. If thou *meet* thine enemy's ox or ass going astray, thou shalt surely bring it back to him again.

> 2. "If thou *see* the ass of him that hateth thee, lying under its burden . . ."[60]

"Meeting" a lost animal implies an actual physical encounter. If this is the standard to be used, then it would seem that one does not have the obligation to concern oneself with a lost animal unless one actually bumps into it! On the other hand, the second passage suggests that my orbit of obligation extends as far as the eye can see! "If *thou* see . . ." But again, in the spirit of the principle which requires that each word and sentence of the Torah be acknowledged for its contribution to the truth, the rabbis harmonized these rules by limiting the area of the finder's responsibility to a distance of a *ris,* which is about two-fifteenths of a mile.

Elon draws our attention to a type of inferential argument employed by the rabbis that is not included in Rabbi Ishmael's inventory of thirteen. He calls this argument "interpretatio logica," pointing out that while it is essentially an explicatory *midrash,* it often results in new *halakhot* and judicial principles.[61]

Consider the following law:

> But if the man find the damsel that is betrothed in the field, and the man take hold of her, and lie with her, then the man only that lay with her shall die. But unto the damsel thou shalt do nothing; there is in the damsel no sin worthy of death; for as when a man riseth against his neighbor and slayeth him, even so is this matter. For he found her in the field; the betrothed damsel cried, and there was none to save her.[62]

In a previous passage, the Torah had ruled that if this takes place in the city, both are punishable. In elucidating the law, the rabbis state that the references to "city" and "field" are to be understood as representing locations which can shed light on whether the woman resisted or not. The decisive factor is not the geography but whether or not there were people around who could have heard her cries and saved her.[63] If there were, and she did not call out, then even in the field she is guilty. But if there was no one around, then she is blameless even if it took place in the city.

If we consider the logical process involved in the *midrash* we can see that it consists of two steps. The first involves a rational reconstruction of the law in which we cut through the particulars and intuit the morally relevant factor determining the woman's moral status. Once that factor has been isolated, we can form a universal proposition and by simple deduction apply the law to new cases.

Another law involving similar reasoning is the following: "No man shall take the mill or the upper millstone to pledge; for he taketh a man's life to pledge."[64] The last clause in this passage makes it clear that the prohibition should not be limited to an "upper millstone." We are obliged to understand why this particular object was singled out for such a law. The rabbis rightfully concluded that the "upper millstone" is meant as an example of an object used for the manufacture of food. Therefore this law prohibits taking any similar object as a pledge.[65]

The Analogizing Midrash

Pressure to interpret the Torah text often came not only from problems presented by the text but from the insistent realities of life itself. Sometimes circumstances would raise certain questions that were not all answerable from the text even after it had been expanded by the explicatory *midrash*. Here then was a need to be filled by the analogizing *midrash*: a method of inferential reasoning by which different subject matters would be deemed similar in some sense, so that a property possessed by one could be inferred as applying to the other. This second major category of *midrash* is represented by the first three *middot* of Rabbi Ishmael.

1. *Kal va-chomer*—inference from minor to major based on logic.
2. *Gezerah shavah*—inference from similarity of phrases based on formal similarity.
3. *Binyan av*—inference based on substantive similarity.

Elon points out that there is another analogolical device often used in the Talmud, simply referred to as *hekaish,* in which a rule applying in one matter is inferred to apply to another matter as well.[66] But on what grounds are the two matters equalized? In the case of the simple *hekaish,* it is on the grounds that the Torah itself has somehow linked the two subjects. An illustration of this type of *hekaish* may be found in the law of the betrothed maiden who is raped, which we have referred to above and which the Torah compares to murder. Since the innocence of the woman seems self-evident and is clearly stated, what are we to infer from the fact that the Torah compares these two situations?

> The law of the murderer is likened to the law of the betrothed woman. Just as the betrothed woman may be saved from rape even if it means taking the life of the rapist, so too may we take the life of the *rodef* [pursuer] who seeks to kill someone (and if there is no other way to save the victim). And the law of the betrothed woman is likened to the law of the murderer. Just as in the case of murder, a person must suffer himself to be killed rather than transgress, so too in the case of the betrothed woman.[67]

Of all the hermeneutical rules listed by Rabbi Ishmael, the *kal va-chomer* seems to be the one most grounded in logic rather than in literary exegesis. The rabbi pointed out that there are at least ten informal instances of the use of *kal va-chomer* to be found in the dialogue and teachings of the Torah.[68] As the term itself indicates, the *kal va-chomer* seems to involve a type of inference which goes from minor to major or sometimes from major to minor. An example of a *kal va-chomer* used in the Bible is the argument made by the brothers to Joseph: "Behold, the money which we found in our sacks, we brought to thee again out of the land of Canaan: how then should we steal out of thy lord's house silver and gold?"[69] An illustration of a *kal va-chomer* found in the Talmud is the following:

> If then in regard to such a light precept [sending forth the mother bird], which concerns a matter that is worth but an *issar,* the Torah has said, "that it may be well with thee, and thou mayest prolong thy days," how much more so in regard to the weightier precepts of the Torah [i.e., precepts which require greater effort or expense].[70]

The crucial factor in this form of reasoning seems to be the relationship which holds between the elements involved. One seems to be "greater" or "more severe" than the other, or conversely one seems to be "lighter" or "less" than the other. At times this relationship is assumed to be self-evident and is not spelled out in the exchange. At other times, when the *kal va-chomer* is employed in a more formal manner, the ways in which one element is perceived to be the "major" and the other the "minor" are stated by reference to certain specific properties. The latter form has been called the complex type of *kal va-chomer* and can be rendered symbolically thus:[71]

1. If A, which lacks Y, has X, then B, which has Y, certainly has X.

But what type of logical inference is this? There is an intuitive cogency to this form of argument when used in terms of everyday life. Thus, in questioning whether I can lift a certain object, it makes sense to say, "If that ten-year-old child can lift it, I certainly can lift it." Or in trying to determine whether a particular expenditure is within my means, I am told, "But if people on welfare can afford a color TV, you certainly can!" What provides the inferential power in a *kal va-chomer* that enables us to learn something new about B that we did not know before?

The view that the *kal va-chomer* is to be identified with the traditional logical form known as the Aristotelian syllogism has been criticized on both historical and analytic grounds.[72] Historically it is pointed out that the use of the *kal va-chomer* in the Pentateuch precludes the possibility of its users having been influenced by Aristotelian logic. However, in terms of the underlying structure of the *kal va-chomer,* the matter is not so simple. Jacobs argues that the syllogism and the *kal va-chomer* are fundamentally different forms of reasoning on the basis of the following considerations. First, the element of "how much more so" is lacking in the syllogism. Second, the syllogism is tautologous, while the *kal va-chomer* is not. Third, the syllogism deals with class membership or class inclusion, while the *kal va-chomer* speaks of possessing certain properties. Even if we should grant Jacobs his distinctions, he does not leave us any wiser as to the true nature of the *kal va-chomer*. If we accept his criticism, then we know that a *kal va-chomer* is not a syllogism of the type known as "in Barbara." But then, what form of reasoning is it?[73]

Actually, Jacob's analysis is highly questionable. While the *kal va-chomer* may not be identical with the Aristotelian syllogism, it nevetheless can be seen as a form of deductive reasoning. As such it would also be tautologous. But all that means is that given the premises, the conclusion follows necessarily, which is the price you pay in deduction for the certainty it yields. Another writer, in speaking of the *kal va-chomer,* states: "It has quite a logical foundation being a kind of syllogism, an inference *a fortiori.*"[74] At another point, this same writer says, "The argument *a fortiori* termed *kal va-chomer* is a kind of argument from analogy."[75] However, in describing the principle underlying the inferential force of the *kal va-chomer* he seems to suggest that its foundation is not so much logic as an assumption about the nature of the Torah:

> The Law is assumed to have the tendency to proportionate its effect to the importance of the cases referred to, so as to be more rigorous and restrictive in important cases and more lenient and permissive in comparatively unimportant matters. Hence, if a certain rigorous restriction of the law is found regarding a matter of minor importance, we may infer that the same restriction is the more applicable to that which is of major importance.[76]

But if the *kal va-chomer* rests on an assumption about the law, then it is hardly "a kind of syllogism." And if it is the latter, it could hardly be "a kind of argument from analogy."

In order to truly understand the *kal-vachomer,* let us begin by carefully examining its structure. As may be surmised from (1) the key feature seems to be that B is "greater" or "more severe" than A by virtue of some property that B has in greater strength or quantity than A. It would therefore appear that we have here a relational argument (sometimes called *a fortiori*) which takes this form:

2. If A is greater than B, and B is greater than C, then A is greater than C.

This holds for relationships which are transitive and asymmetrical. Let us consider the example given before: "If a child can lift that object, then you, a healthy adult, should certainly be able to lift it!" Can this be made to fit into the pattern of (2)?

3. If A (adult) is stronger than B (child), and B is "stronger than" the object X (i.e., can lift it up), then A is "stronger than" object X.

Only by such forced and artificial reformulation of the property assigned to B as a relationship remotely resembling the relation "stronger than" in the first premise, are we able to think at all of the *kal va-chomer* as a relational argument. What we must do, therefore, is to add another premise that connects the relation "more than" with whatever property we are trying to attribute in the conclusion. Sometimes, in a simple *kal va-chomer,* this is not overtly expressed but is assumed. Thus in the case of (3), the additional premise which we intuitively grasp is that weight-lifting capacity depends upon and increases proportionately with physical strength, so that if A is greater than B in terms of physical strength, the same relationship will hold in terms of weight-lifting ability. A *kal va-chomer,* therefore, is more like what is sometimes called a *sorite,* a form of reasoning in which more than one deductive step has been compacted into one argument. Let us break up our *kal va-chomer* into two separate deductive steps:

I.

1. Weight-lifting capacity (WLC) and physical strength (PS) are related in such a way that if A is greater than B in regard to PS, then A is greater than B in regard to WLC.
2. A is greater than B in PS.

(conclusion) A is greater than B in WLC

This last conclusion is the equivalent of the following, which serves as the major premise of our second step:

II.

1. For any object X, if B can lift X, then A can lift X.
2. B can lift X.

(conclusion) A can (certainly) lift X.

Both of these steps follow the elementary rule of valid implication known as *modus ponens.* Let us see whether this analysis can hold for the *kal va-chomer* mentioned in the *Mishnah* referred to earlier. Here too we must try to articulate the unspoken premise that enables us to translate the given relationship of "more severe than" into terms of the property whose presence we seek to prove.

I.

1. Effort and expense in performance of *mitzvot* are related to divine reward in such a way that if *mitzvah* A is greater than *mitzvah* B in terms of effort and expense, then *mitzvah* A is greater than *mitzvah* B in terms of divine reward to be received.

2. There are certain "weightier *mitzvot*" (WM) in the Torah that are greater than the *mitzvah* of sending forth the mother bird (SFM) in terms of effort and expense.

(conclusion) The WM are greater than the SFM in terms of divine reward.

II.

1. If there is some reward X which is to be received for performing the *mitzvah* of SFM, then it is to be received for performing the WM.

2. Well-being and longevity are to be received for performing the *mitzvah* of SFM.

(conclusion) Well-being and longevity will (certainly) be received by those who perform the WM.[77]

Not all the instances of *kal va-chomer* offered in the Talmud are accepted as valid and correct. A refutation of a *kal va-chomer* is called a *pirkha*. The *kal va-chomer* can be refuted either by showing that B, which was assumed in the premise to be "less severe," is in fact "more severe" in virtue of some new factor that is introduced or by questioning the premise that connects the relation of "more severe than" with the property we are trying to establish in the conclusion. This can be done by showing that there is another element C which is similar to B but does not have the property in question.[78]

It would therefore appear that the *kal va-chomer* is a type of inference based on deductive logic which can usually be reformulated into one of more implicative and relational arguments.

The *middah* known as *gezerah shavah,* or inference from a similarity of phrases in texts, was originally applied to two subject matters that were identical or similar in context. However, later this was expanded to apply to items that simply shared linguistic affinity of certain words.[79] Some authorities tried to limit the use of the *gezerah shavah* to texts where the phrase or words to be used for the *gezerah shavah* were considered superfluous. Since this particular exegetical rule is least anchored in logic, the rabbis decided to restrict its use by ruling that no one can apply a *gezerah shavah* in explicating the Torah unless he has received a tradition to that effect from his teachers.[80]

Binyan Av And Induction

Rabbi Ishmael's third *middah,* described as "a comprehensive principle derived from one text or from two related texts," is called *binyan av.* This method consists of deriving a general principle from a single instance or from two or more texts in which an underlying common property is seen as the causative factor and henceforth is adopted as the determining principle that fixes the law. As it were, a general principle is "built up" (*binyan*) from the particulars given. An example of the *binyan av* derived from two texts is the following from the law of the *eved kena'ani* (Canaanite servant):

> If a man will smite the eye of his servant, or the eye of his maid-servant, and will destroy it, he should give him his freedom because of the eye and if the tooth of his servant, or the tooth of his maid-servant, he will cause to fall, he should give him his liberty because of the tooth.[81]

Had the Torah referred only to the eye of the servant, we should have limited our application of this law to the specific occurrence of damage to this particular organ. Since, however, the Torah exemplifies the law in two texts with reference to both eye and tooth, we are led to abstract common properties from these different parts of the body that we can generalize into a principle that will explain and govern the law in question.[82] The rabbis conclude that the law before us awards freedom to a servant upon whom deliberate and visible damage has been done to an organ or extremity which is not replaceable. As a result of applying this general principle, the rabbis were able to list twenty-four different damages for which the servant must be set free.[83]

Inasmuch as *binyan av* seems to be a process of reasoning by which we proceed from the particular to the general, it would appear to be in some way similar to the process of induction. However, the thrust is quite different. As applied by science to empirical phenomena, the force of the inductive process is to provide us with confidence that a causal relationship seen to hold in a number of particular instances will continue to hold in similar circumstances in the future. In the case of *binyan av,* the difficult task is to isolate and ascertain the causal factor from amidst a plethora of different possibilities. Once this has been done, the justification for applying it to future cases is no problem. Unlike the situation in the physical sciences, in the Torah we are dealing with prescriptive law rather than with descriptive law. The unity and the rational underpinnings of the Torah are presuppositions which we bring to our study of Jewish law and morality.

Binyan av does appear to bear a similarity to Mill's "method of agreement," which is defined as: "If two or more instances of the phenomenon under investigation have only one circumstance in common, the circumstance in which alone all the instances agree, is the cause (or the effect) of the phenomenon."[84] This is beautifully illustrated by the more complex *binyan av* (four texts) that is generated from the "four main divisions of damages," given in the Torah in the form of four specific cases: an ox that gores or kicks, an open pit or cistern into which an animal falls, grazing animals, and a moving fire.[85] Here again we are mystified by what appears to be an overabundance of illustrative material of the different forces for whose damages a person is held accountable. The same question arises: Are the things for which an individual is to be held responsible limited to the specifics enumerated, or are these particular cases merely varied illustrations of some single underlying concept that determines responsibility on the part of the owner? After considerable discussion the rabbis concluded that the single decisive factor which all of these items embody is that "they tend to cause damages."[86] In considering new cases this becomes the operative factor. If you are the owner of anything that "tends to cause damages," you are obligated to take precautions and are therefore responsible for whatever damages it may cause.

In comparing these different exegetical or hermeneutical *middot,* it would seem that a derivation based upon a *hekaish* suggested by the Torah is most authoritative and is the equivalent of being written in the Torah itself. Similarly, if the *gezerah shavah* can, indeed, only be applied if sanctioned by a direct tradition, this would place its derivations in the foremost ranks of the oral law. Since the *kal va-chomer* and the *bin-yan av* are both primarily logical in character, insights derived by their use may be regarded as having been "unpacked" from the Torah and therefore partake of its authority.[87]

Methods Which Reach Into The Present

It has been shown that the selfsame methods of inference and exegesis employed by the Tanaaim and Amoraim of the Talmud were also used by the post-talmudic authorities to extend and elaborate the judicial and moral rules of the Torah. An interesting example is the prohibition against moving the boundary markers of one's neighbor's field. This is expressed in the Pentateuch in the form of two prohibitions:

> Thou shalt not remove thy neighbor's landmark, which they of old time have set . . .[88]
>
> Cursed be he that removeth his neighbor's landmark.[89]

In ancient times, the precise and permanent fixing of land boundaries was always a difficult and problematic matter and was therefore a tempting opportunity for those with larceny in their hearts.[90] In later periods, the need arose to give legal recognition to certain abstract rights of an economic and commercial nature. Thus, if someone was already operating a particular business in a certain area, was it morally right for another person to open the same type of business in close proximity when it was likely that such a move would cause grave financial harm to the already established business? This too seems to involve the concept of intruding into another person's "territory."

In the Talmud generally, we find an acceptance of the idea of free and unrestricted competition among craftsmen and merchants.[91] We do find a general moral exhortation against impairing another person's source of livelihood,[92] but it was never, in the Talmud, embodied into law with specific sanctions. During the Middle Ages, when economic opportunities for Jews became severely limited, the problem of what constituted fair and unfair competition and what were the legitimate rights of established businesses and traditional monopolies became acute. Rabbinic authorities saw the analogy between encroaching upon someone's geographic domain and moving into someone's economic sphere. And so we find an interesting responsum written by Rabbi Solomon Luria in the sixteenth century in Poland in the case of a person who lost the lucrative concession of a custom post due to a neighbor who offered a larger sum to the ruler.[93] Luria ruled that the defendant either restore the customs post to the first individual or compensate him for the damages, although this appeared to be a case of *gerama,* or indirect damage for which there is no liability. In his decision he referred to the view of an earlier authority (Roke'ach) that anyone encroaching upon another's source of livelihood is in violation of the injunction: "Cursed is he who removes his neighbor's landmark." Luria asks how a *mitzvah* whose plain meaning refers to stealing property in the land of Israel can be seen as applying to interference with a person's livelihood in Poland. His explanation is that Roke'ach's ruling reflects a tradition which perceived in the curse, if narrowly interpreted, a needless repetition of the prohibition against *hassagat gevul* (encroachment). In other words, acceptance of the principle of the unity of the Torah, with its implication of the inadmissibility of unexplained repetition, warranted the ruling of the Roke'ach that this passage in Deuteronomy can be broadly interpreted to cover infringement of another's livelihood.

Over the centuries, rabbinic authorities employed this broader understanding of *hassagat gevul* to evolve standards in matters relating to tenancy rights, trespass among craftsmen, including the office of rabbi, as well as the entire issue of copyright and reprinting rights. As Elon concludes, "The doctrine of *hassagat gevul* strikingly illustrates one of the paths for the development of Jewish law, namely extension of the content of a legal principle beyond its original confines, in a search for solutions to problems arising through changes in social and economic conditions."[94]

Another illustration of an important area of moral instruction that developed out of a broad rabbinic interpretation of the biblical text is the injunction against *genevat da'at*—deliberately creating a false impression in a person's mind even where no monetary loss is involved. It is interesting to observe how the various texts bearing on theft or stealing were variously interpreted so as to give broad coverage.

1. "Thou shalt not steal" (*lo tignov*) refers to stealing people.[95]

2. "nor rob him" (*lo tigzol*) refers to taking another's possessions openly by use of force.[96]

3. "you shall not steal" refers to theft of objects by stealth.[97]

4. "and if thou sell . . . or buy . . . ye shall not wrong [*onoah*] one another"[98] refers to cheating in price in which the seller overcharges or the buyer underpays or in regard to weight, measure, or quality of goods. In all cases of *onoah* there is monetary damage although the buyer gives his money voluntarily.

In considering the concept of "stealing" (*genevah*), the rabbis perceived the unqualified nature of the injunction and realized that "stealing the mind" of a person—replacing truth with falsehood in his consciousness—constituted a greivous deprivation even where there is no monetary damage.[99] They understood that the "psychological anguish" suffered by the victim and his loss of peace of mind was probably more damaging than monetary loss. Thus, if the seller creates an impression in the mind of the buyer that the object is other than it in fact is, he is in violation of this moral-legal rule even if the price he asks and gets is proper. This injuction applies even if a person "steals" for a joke and later returns the "stolen" item. Therefore, Samuel teaches, "It is forbidden to 'steal the minds' of people [deceive them], even of an idolater."[100]

This principle has important implications for an entire complex of current moral issues in the area of misleading advertising and packaging of products. *Genevat da'at* also raises some very sensitive questions in interpersonal relationship regarding the moral probity of encouraging people to believe that you love them when you really do not or to believe that you have done them some favor when in reality it was not you at all. According to many authorities the injunction against *genevat da-at* is considered *de-oraita,* of biblical origin; i.e., it is perceived to be implicit in the general concept of *genevah*; part of the meaning of *lo tignovu*.[101]

Just as the Amoraim regarded the *halakhot* in the Mishnah and tannaitic sources as material to be interpreted according to the traditional thirteen hermeneutical *middot,* so too did the later authorities regard all of the talmudic literature as well as any rulings of earlier post-talmudic rabbis as material to be similarly interpreted.[102] Thus, in the case of a teacher who missed school for an extended period because of illness, Rabbi Meir of Rothenburg, in the thirteenth century, ruled that no reduction was to be made in his salary. He derived that ruling from a *kal va-chomer* based on the principle that all of the rights of the *eved ivri* (Hebrew servant) as found in the Talmud are to be applied to the ordinary hired worker: "If the *eved ivri,* who in submitting himself to his type of servitude is in violation of Torah values, nevertheless is given certain rights, then certainly the ordinary employee of today, whose employment is not in violation of the Torah, should surely be given those rights."[103]

A responsum by another thirteenth-century rabbi, Asher ben Jehiel (the Rosh), illustrates how the traditional *middot* of *hekaish* and *kal va-chomer* were applied to the talmudic material by a medieval authority. Involved in this case was an attempt to avoid the repayment of a legitimate debt by recourse to legal fictions and technicalities,.

The entire responsum follows:

> You asked about Reuben, who borrowed money from Simeon without giving him a written note or receipt. Thereafter Reuben gave away all his property to Levi, in order to avoid having to pay his debt to Simeon. For Reuben knows that in the absense of a written contract, the lender cannot collect from property that belonged to the borrower at the time the debt was incurred, but was subsequently sold or given away as a gift.

> It seems to me that in this case we follow our estimation of Reuben's obvious motives [this judicial assumption is called an *umedana,* literally: a measurement]. And on that basis we must conclude that after all Reuben's strenuous efforts he has accomplished nothing at all. His case is similar to that of a critically ill man who assigned all his property to another person. Subsequently, he recovered and sought the return of his estate. We declare the gift void because of our *umedana*: we appraise his intention as having been that the gift was to take place only in the event of his death, which then seemed imminent, and since he recovered and his intention was not fulfilled, the transfer of the property is invalid.

> Another such case is that of a man who left his home for overseas and then heard that his only son had died. Whereupon he assigned all his property to a stranger. Later, his son appeared and claimed his father's estate. The Talmud records the opinion of one teacher who denies the son his father's estate and holds the transfer of property as legal and valid.

However, R. Simeon ben Menasya, whose opinion remains Halakhah, declares the father's gift void because of *umedana*: we consider it obvious that had the father known his son was alive, he would never have given away all his money to a stranger. There are many other such illustrations of the sages' deciding an issue upon the basis of *umedana*.

Now there is hardly a stronger *umedana* than the case under discussion. Reuben, who gave away all his money, obviously had no intention of supporting himself thereafter by begging from house to house. His intention is so obvious as to be self-evident: he seeks to circumvent the law and avoid payment of his debt to Simeon.

But we cannot permit his dishonest scheme to succeed. His deviousness will not help him. Proof comes from the Talmud, *Bava Metzia* 108a. A man who wishes to sell his land must give his immediate neighbors the right of first refusal. They have priority in purchasing from him the land at the same price he would receive from a stranger. This is a moral consideration, for a stranger could buy land elsewhere without injury, whereas the neighbor who wishes to acquire more land would suffer inconvenience if his new lot were not adjacent to his present one. This moral point has the force of law, on the basis of the verse, "You shall do what is right and good in the eyes of the Lord" [Deut. 6:18].

Now the Talmud considers the following problem. If a man bought a lot which was surrounded on all sides by other lots belonging to the same seller, the sale is valid only if the land purchased was either far superior or far inferior to the surrounding land; for then we assume that he had no plans to acquire the adjacent property in addition to his present purchase. However, if the lot was essentially of the same quality as the land around it, then we assume [*umedana*] that the buyer was seeking to circumvent the law of the neighbor's priority. He felt that if the seller would place all his lands for sale on the open market, and he would ask to purchase them, the neighbors would object and assert their rights of first refusal by buying the land themselves. His plan, therefore, is to buy into the area by initially purchasing this lot surrounded on all sides by the seller's other lots. The neighbors can register no objection because this first plot is not adjacent to any of their land.

But then he becomes a "neighbor" to the seller's other property, equally with the original neighbors—so that when the seller is ready to dispose of the remainder of his property, he may acquire it without having to receive permission from them. Since we assume this to be an attempt at deception, we frustrate his designs by allowing the original neighbors to assert their right of first refusal upon the sale of the first lot. Such is the decision of the Talmud.

Now if we employ umedana *appraising a man's motives as devious, and deny him the legal means to act on them, in the case cited by the Talmud—then most certainly do we do so in the case under discussion here. For the underlying principle in the Talmud's case, that of a neighbor's prior rights, is only a rabbinical decree derived from the verse "You shall do what is right and good,"* etc. Even though the principle is only one of rabbinical law, the sages went to great lengths to uphold it against circumvention. *Surely, then, in our case, which involves not merely a rabbinical decree but an attempt to rob by deception and to violate a biblical precept by not paying a creditor, we must use every means to thwart his plans.* We must therefore allow Simeon to collect from Levi the money owed by Reuben.

Another precedent is the case of a slave owned by two partners jointly. If one partner frees his half, the sages force the other partner to do likewise, so as to avoid the anomaly of a man who is half-slave and half-free—and is therefore forbidden to marry either a bondswoman or a freewoman. Now the Talmud in *Gittin* 40a records the case of one partner who emancipated his share in a slave. The other partner, afraid that the rabbis would force him to do the same and thus cause him to lose his investment, promptly sold his half to his minor son. His plan was obvious; the rabbinical courts could not force the new half-owner, the minor son, to liberate his share of the slave. Rav Joseph ben Rava consulted Rav Papa, and the latter replied: pay him back in kind, i.e., declare his gift to his minor son as null and void, and then force him to liberate his share of the slave.

From all this we see that when one attempts to circumvent the law, the talmudic sages opposed him and sought to nullify his actions. *We must therefore compare all new cases to theirs, and learn from their precedents. For the sages of the talmud did not record in advance all possibilities of future circumvention.* Clearly, in our case, where we are dealing with a major law—the payment of a debt—there is hardly a greater *umedana* revealing the underhandedness of Reuben.

I have seen a similar decsion in a responsum by my teacher [Rabbi Meir of Rothenburg] concerning real-estate transactions which specified conditions seeking to undermine the *ketubbah* [marriage document] rights of the wife of one of the principals. The law grants a woman, upon her marriage, certain rights, which are recorded in the *ketubbah*. These assure her first claim, for specified amounts, on the property of her husband in case of his death or their divorce. Now the buyer wants to purchase the real estate on condition that it not be subject to his wife's *ketubbah,* so that, for instance, should he divorce her, she could not collect from this property. In a second such instance, a man bought a parcel of land and arranged for the contract to be written in his brother's name, again so as to deprive his wife of her *ketubbah* in the case of his death or their divorce. In both cases, our teacher and rabbi—Meir, of blessed memory—ruled that the wife may indeed sue for her *ketubbah* from this property. In appraising their motives [*umedana*], we find that both were obvious attempts to circumvent the rabbinical decree of *ketubbah,* and we therefore disqualify the conditions attached to the sale.

Peace to you and your study of Torah, in accordance with the wishes of Asher son of Rabbi Yehiel; may the memory of the righteous be a blessing.[104]

In the italicized passages, we clearly see how the Rosh employed a *kal va-chomer* to infer a judgment from a talmudic precedent and how he "compares" his case to earlier ones (*hekaish*) in order to deal with a comtemporary social abuse.

A striking example of a late medieval sage applying the *middah* of *kelal u-perat u-kelal* (the sixth of the thirteen *middot*) to a written responsum by an earlier rabbi is the ruling of Rabbi Judah Mintz regarding the vital question of the extent of the power and authority of the Jewish community in coercing minority elements to support its public institutions. The Talmud had always maintained the right of the community to do this in regard to building a synagogue or purchasing a scroll of the Torah for public reading. Questions arose, however, about less central institutions, such as public bakeries, communal kitchens for the poor, and certain peripheral structures, for which individual members of the community, arguing that they had no need for the intended benefit and would not use it, could and did refuse to contribute.[105]

Rabbi Mintz referred to an earlier responsum of Rabbi Meir of Rothenberg in which the latter, ruling on a similar case, expressed himself first in general terms, then listed specific applications, and then again spoke in general terms. From this Rabbi Mintz concluded that in deciding the range of institutions over which the majority of the community or their duly appointed representatives can exercise coercive power, we are not limited to the instances specifically mentioned in the Talmud or even in later responsa. Any project which the majority of the community decides is of use and benefit to the community may be imposed upon the total community, with all obliged to support it, be it practical or charitable, a religious or a social need.

Takkanot And Gezerot: Instances Of Means-Ends Connectives

It has been suggested that moral systems that are essentially teleological—emphasizing value phenomena, such as the "good"—tend to organize themselves on the basis of means-end categories, while deontological systems—dominated by the conception of moral law and stressing obligation phenomena—lend themselves more to deductive procedures.[106] The morality of Judaism, which seems to be a composite system incorporating both teleological and deontological elements, utilizes both types of logic in these different domains of moral phenomena. We have already discussed the role of deductive reasoning. In another important area of Jewish moral development, however, the internal structure is formed by lines of means-ends connectives. Let us now turn our attention to this area: the very extensive legislative activity of the rabbis, resulting in *takkanot* (enactments) and *gezerot* (safeguards).

We have already indicated that the supreme source of legislation for the Jew is the written law found in the Pentateuch. Hence, the primary task of human reason was to "unpack" all of the implications of these written rules and principles, employing the special hermeneutical *middot* and other exegetical methods. The written Torah itself, however, seems to delegate some of its authority to the "judge that will be in those days."[107] "According to the law which they will teach thee, and according to the judgment which they will tell thee, thou shalt do; thou shalt not turn aside from the sentence which they shall declare unto thee, to the right nor to the left."[108] Others see the following passage as significant: "Ask thy father, and he will declare unto thee, thine elders, and they will tell thee."[109] These passages were understood not merely as upholding the authority of the rabbis as interpreters of the written law, but also as conferring upon them an authority for independent legislation of a certain type—that is to say, authority to establish policies whose consequences will be the realization in society of the moral values of the Torah. Maimonides characterizes *gezerot* and *takkanot* as follows:

> *Gezerot* are decrees ordained by the prophets and sages of every generation in order to make a protective fence around the Torah. This was commanded by God and is what is meant by the general statement, "And you shall keep My charge," which was interpreted to mean, "Provide protection for My observances." The sages called these *gezerot,* or "protective measures." Another category consists of laws based on empirical investigation regarding the social behavior of individuals . . . or matters which are helpful to society with respect to observance of the Torah . . . These are called *takkanot*.[110]

The *gezerot* seem primarily to involve prohibitions or negative commands and served to extend the domain of the forbidden into the heretofore-permitted areas as a rabbinc safeguard for what was biblically prohibited. Thus, for example, the rabbis forbade marriages between the relatives of more distant consanguinity than those prohibited by the Torah itself.[111] The *takkanot* usually consisted of positive actions enacted by the authorities of every generation from Moses on down, including prophet, sage, rabbinic court, and general community, and addressed themselves to specific situations where the good and moral welfare of society were involved. While the authority of the rabbis to issue *takkanot* and *gezerot* was grounded, as we have seen, in the written Torah, the logic employed in both types of ordinances was of a means-ends relationship.

We earlier alluded to the following passage as containing one of the general moral principles of the Torah: "Ye shall diligently keep the commandments of the Lord your God, and His testimonies, and His statutes, which He hath commanded thee. And thou shalt do that which is right and good in the sight of the Lord . . ."[112]

As noted by Nachmanides, the command to do "what is right and good" must be seen in contrast to the preceding verse, which urges us to "keep the commandments." That is to say, where your situation is governed by specific commandments and statutes, by all means observe the commandments! But even where no particular precept or specific rule is relevant to your situation, you must nevertheless deliberate and determine on your own that which is "right and good in the sight of the Lord" and do it. Thus, for the authorities in every generation, the "right and good" constitute the end goals, which may be reached by different means, depending upon the changing circumstances of man's environment. The rabbis, therefore, in legislating the *takkanot* of the abutter, which gives the owner of an adjoining property the first right to purchase the field, consciously saw themselves as guiding people to do the right and the good.[113] That a rule such as this is intended to be a means to a just and moral end is clearly seen in the way it responds to changing circumstances. Should the individual who wishes to purchase the field be able to demonstrate that he desparately needs that field for his livelihood, then the rights of the abutter cannot be exercised. Or should the situation be such that the general welfare calls for housing rather than for putting more fields under cultivation, then here too the law of the abutter does not apply.[114]

Jewish tradition dates a number of *takkanot* to the earliest periods of Jewish history and ascribes them to ancient biblical leaders. Joshua, who led the Jewish people into the land of Israel, is appropriately named as the author of ten *takkanot* that sought to regulate human rights in areas where the private and public sectors seem to interact. Thus, the following were enacted:

- Small domesticated animals can be grazed on private lands planted with tall trees, but not larger animals. On private lands given to low planting, permission for any sort of grazing must first be secured from the owners.

- Although Lake Tiberius (Kinneret) was included in the portion of the tribe of Naphtali, anyone could fish there provided he did not use apparatus that might obstruct the passage of boats.

- When a public road becomes impassable for reasons of mud or water, travelers may detour along the side of the road even though it means traversing private property.[115]

Ezra and the men of the Great Assembly are reputed to be the authors of ten *takkanot*, among which is one that permits peddlers of jewelry and cosmetics to sell their wares in the villages so that the women may remain "beloved" by their husbands.[116]

Simeon ben Shetach enacted certain safeguards for a woman's *ketubbah* in case of divorce; namely, that all of her husband's property stands as guarantor for the amount of the *ketubbah*. If a husband who divorces his wife has no ready cash, he must be prepared to sell his property in order to pay for the *ketubbah*.[117]

Hillel the Elder is, of course, known for the famous *takkanah* of *prosbul*. This was a response to a social and economic problem which arose during the period of the Second Temple as a consequence of the seventh-year release of debts. As the time of the release approached, people hesitated to lend money, because it could not be recovered. This was, of course, in direct violation of the warning of the Torah, which had anticipated this kind of reaction: "Beware that there not be a base thought in thy heart, saying: 'The seventh year, the year of release, is at hand.'"[118] The *prosbul* worked as follows: Before the Sabbatical year, the creditor assigned his claim to the court in a document. This had the effect of instituting an action to recover a debt. The court considered the debt secured by land owned by the debtor (or the creditor could transfer land to the debtor for this purpose). Since secured debts were not affected by the Sabbatical year, the debt was not canceled.[119] "This takana of Hillel was indeed a measure, 'for the improvement of the social order' (*le tikkun haolom*), for it benefitted both rich and poor since it protected the wealthy against loss and aided the needy in obtaining loans."[120]

Rabbi Gamaliel the Elder was considered the central figure in establishing *takkanot agunot*, legislation enabling a woman to remarry after her husband's death had been reported. The Torah requires the testimony of two witnesses in order to judiciously establish a fact. It would follow, therefore, that before a woman could be declared a widow, and thus be enabled to remarry, there would have to be two witnesses testifying to the death of her husband.[121] Often, however, such witnesses could not be found. This created the distressful problem of the *agunah*, the abandoned wife who could not remarry even though she was living alone and her husband was in all probability dead. The *takkanot agunot* provided that proof of the death of an absent husband was deemed sufficient if only one witness testified, even if that one witness was the wife herself. The rabbis felt that the testimony of the wife could be relied upon because she would realize the grave consequences she was exposing herself to by remarrying if her husband was still alive, for in that case she would be guilty of adultery and the children of her second marriage would be *mamzerim*.[122]

Another *takkanah* attributed to the school of Hillel provided that where the stolen object was not easily accessible, the robber could return its monetary value instead of the object itself. This was designed to make it easier for the robber to repent and make restitution.[123]

The Torah itself holds man accountable for any damages he might cause either intentionally or unintentionally. However, this seems limited to damages that are visible; i.e., recognizable changes brought about in the object. No warrant was found in the Torah to hold people accountable for damages that were invisible; e.g., rendering one's neighbor's vessel ritually unclean (*tameh*). In a *takkanah* motivated by the *tikkun haolam,* the rabbis extended man's liability to cover intangible damages caused intentionally.[124]

After the talmudic period, as the result of far-reaching political and social changes and the further dispersal of the Jewish people, the hegemony of the Babylonian centers of Jewish learning came to an end. In its place we have the development of a number of different geographic centers with the basic unit-structure being the community. The rabbinic authority to enact subsidiary legislation in the form of *takkanot* passes from the single center which legislated for all Jewry to the individual autonomous Jewish community. Of cousre, several communities might come together to issue a joint *takkanah* or by recognizing some noted rabbinic personality among them. It is for this reason that after the tenth century we do not find any *takkanot* that applied to Jews worldwide. Even the famous *takkanot* of Rabbenu Gershom, which included the prohibition against polygamy and the prohibition against opening a letter addressed to someone else, were not considered binding on significant segments of Oriental Jewry until recent times.[125]

Side by side with the *takkanot* emanating from the rabbinic authority of the *bet din* (rabbinical court), there developed, in social and economic areas, *takkanot ha-kehillot,* legislation emanating from the *tzibbur*—the social polity or its appointed or elected lay representatives.

> Wherever the majority agrees, enacts a policy, and accepts it upon them-
> selves, the views of individuals may be ignored. For the individual in every
> community must respond to the enactments of the majority in the same
> manner as all Israel regarded the enactments of the Sanhedrin. If they
> [the majority] choose to legislate, their enactments are authoritative and
> all who violate them may be punished.[126]

Regardless of the form it may take, the *takkanah* remains essentially
a rabbinic construct connected to the Torah at two points: at its source,
where the Torah commands us to obey the rabbis "in your day," and in
terms of its consequences, i.e., since the *takkanah* is designed to bring
about, in its time, place, and situation, the Torah values of justice,
equity, and peace.

Assumptions Based On Empirical Generalizations

The successful use of the *takkanah* seen as policies designed as means to
bring about certain moral ends, presupposes the use of inductive
logic. That is to say, the authors of the *takkanah* must have inferred, on
the basis of actual experience, that policies of type A will lead to consequences of type B. As Edel points out, "A morality that speaks of
resolving problems or satisfying needs can be inductive only to the
extent to which there is dependable achievable knowledge of needs and
problems and modes of satisfaction."[127] There are indeed many areas
of Jewish morality where the rabbis drew moral conclusions from
premises that involved beliefs about the physical universe and assumptions about human psychology derived from empirical observation
and inductive reasoning.[128]

First among these premises is the concept of *chazakah,* which functions as a sort of legal presumption in which it is assumed that the
object remains in the state it was last ascertained to be unless there is
reason to believe that some change took place. Thus, if a messenger
delivers a bill of divorce to a woman from a sick husband, we consider
the divorce valid. We do so because we assume the husband to have
been alive at the time of the delivery since that is the condition in which
he was last known to be (*chezkat chei*).[129]

Sometimes the concept of *chazakah* takes the form of a specific generalization about human behavior, such as:

1. *Chazakah* (there is a presumption), that an agent carries out his mandate.[130]
2. *Chazakah,* that a person does not pay his debt before its due date.[131]
3. *Chazakah,* that a person does not exert himself to prepare a meal and then spoil it.[132]
4. *Chazakah,* that a person does not drink from a cup unless he examines it first.[133]

The concept of *rov,* the "majority" of instances, was also relied upon by the rabbis in many areas of Halakhah. Thus, unless you have evidence to the contrary, you may assume that "most animals" (of the proper species) are kosher" i.e., have no blemishes which can render them unfit to eat, and that "most eggs do not have blood spots."

There is yet another category of strictly psychological assumptions that the rabbis utilized in deciding various matters. These they called *umedana*—beliefs as to what people's true intentions might be under certain circumstances. Clearly there could always be exceptions. The rabbis, however, felt that the probabilities of their generalizations were high enough to rationally base the law upon them.[134]

Many of these generalizations show a high regard for the basic decency and sense of justice that govern people's behavior.

> . . . that a woman does not have the impudence to declare falsely in her husband's presence that he divorced her.[135]

> . . . that a *chaver* [a member of group that has undertaken to observe special laws of the tithes and purity] does not allow anything which was untithed to leave his hands.[136]

> . . . that no man affixes his signature to a document unless he knows the contents thereof.[137]

We have attempted to point out the different kinds of logical reasoning used by the rabbis in all generations which tend to relate the teachings of Jewish morality to each other and give the totality of the teachings the character of an integrated system. In summary, then, these logical methods include: subsumption–deduction; hypothetical confirmatory arguments; argument by analogy; legislative enactments linked to moral ends; and amplification of principles to cover new situations by the process of categorization.

Is There An Ultimate Moral Principle?

We have succeeded so far in tracing the vertical relationships between rules and principles. Let us now turn our attention briefly to the horizontal relationship between the moral principles and seek to discover whether they are in turn related to any supreme or ultimate moral principle.

Of course, the morality of Judaism derives its initial unity from the belief that "it is all given by one shepherd"; i.e., that these teachings have the selfsame source in God. In order, however, to exhibit the systematic character of Jewish morality, we must structure this point in a more formal way. By way of illustration let us start with these general principles found in the Torah.

P1   Love thy neighbor as thyself
P2   Righteousness, righteousness shalt thou pursue
P3   And thou shalt do what is right and good

From our discussion earlier, it is evident that Rabbi Akiva was quite correct in calling P1 a "great principle of the Torah." Its acceptance logically entails a commitment to many of the moral rules of the Torah. Let us now construe P1 in its positive form so that it logically subsumes those moral *mitzvot* that require us to perform acts of benevolence to our fellow men. A partial list of these follows:

R1   To give gifts to the poor
R2   To lend money without interest
R3   To return lost articles or animals to their rightful owners
R4   To return lost articles to their rightful owners
R5   To stand up in respect for the aged
R6   To love the stranger

R7 To build a parapet around one's roof
R8 To visit the sick (rabbinic *mitzvah*)
R9 To bury the dead
R10 To gladden the heart of the bride and groom (rabbinic *mitzvah*)
R11 To extend hospitality (rabbinic *mitzvah*)
R12 To make peace between people (rabbinic *mitzvah*)

The principle "To pursue righteousness" (P2) should be understood as calling primarily for nonmalfeasance; i.e., not to hurt anyone, unjustifiably, in any way, and also to foster those conditions in which the maximum extent of distributive, and retributive justice can be arranged. This would include the following rules of the Torah:

R13 Not to murder
R14 Not to kidnap
R15 Not to steal or rob
R16 Not to deceive
R17 Not to take interest
R18 Not to curse the deaf or cause the blind to stumble
R19 Not to move a boundary stone
R20 Not to bear false witness
R21 Not to lie
R22 Not to have false weights
R23 Not to take graft
R24 Not to publicly shame the other
R25 Not to bear tales or slander the other
R26 Not to covet
R27 Not to oppress underprivileged members of society: orphans, widows, strangers
R28 To create conditions under which those who are deserving will be punished

Let us also assume that our third principle, P3, directs us to abide by the "higher morality" of *lifnim mi-shurat ha-din,* which we can take to mean acts of benevolence that go beyond the requirements of the Halakhah or as programs of personal morality involving the development of inner discipline and good character traits.

While these three principles would appear to be able to generate most of the moral rules in our system, there would appear to be a need for a fourth principle, sometimes called the principle of fidelity. This involves our sense of obligation to keep our promises and to live up to commitments implicit or explicit. It does not appear to be the case that the moral principle of fidelity is derivable from P1 or P2. In one sense, one *can* justify the obligation to keep a promise on the grounds that it is not just to disappoint the expectations of the promisee (P2). But the fact is that we still feel a moral obligation to keep our promises to those long dead and to honor our commitments to God, situations which do not seem to be easily covered by P1 or P2.

Some moralists have claimed that the duty of keeping promises is to be classified under the principle of veracity, since both are fulfilled by "effecting a correspondence between words and facts."[138] In the case of ordinary truth-telling we do so by bringing our statements in line with the facts, whereas in the case of promise-keeping we do so by making fact correspond to our statements. However, if this is the derivation of the principle of fidelity, then we should feel the same moral obligation to carry out our statement about the future even when they are not made in the form of a promise but merely as an assertion. The duty to act in good faith, however, seems to be based not simply on a desire to achieve conformity between my deeds and my assertions but upon some notion of a commitment or a pledge that is generated by my words.

We must therefore introduce another principle (P4) to cover the requirements of fidelity. We shall base it upon the following passages: "That which is gone out of thy lips, thou shalt observe and do . . ."; ". . . he shall do according to all that proceedeth out of his mouth."[139] Although both of these passages are parts of commandments that seem to be talking about formal vows and oaths made to God, Maimonides sees in these imperatives a general obligation to keep one's promises to one's fellow man, honor one's word and carrying out one's pledge even if expressed in an informal way.[140] Some moral rules found in the Torah that could be subsumed under P4 would be:

R29 To provide for one's wife and children

R30 To pay one's worker on time
R31 To pay pledges made to the Temple
R32 To remain faithful to the covenant with God

What remains unaccounted for, howevewr, is the commonsense intuition that benefits ought to be requited—the principle we call gratitude. This tells us that receiving goods or services imposes some sort of moral obligation to express thankfulness, to repay the benefits, to have a special affection or kindly feelings, and even to have a sense of "owing" something to one's benefactor. A cursory consideration of the notion of gratitude seems to suggest some connection with the principle of justice. As with the concept of justice, we seem to be talking about a sense of balance, a standard of "measure for measure," of fairness. Indeed, Sidgwick has pointed out that if we universalize the principle of gratitude we get the common view of justice:

> If we take the proposition that "good done to any individual ought to be requited by him" and leave out the relation to the individual in either term of the proposition we seem to have an equally strong conviction of the truth of the more general statement "that good deeds ought to be requited" or "that men ought to be rewarded in proportion to their deserts" which is the principle of distributive justice.[141]

It does not appear, however, that we can do the reverse: derive the concept of gratitude from the concept of justice. For while the latter can teach us that "men ought to be rewarded in proportion to their deserts," it does not contain the element contributed by the principle of gratitude, which is that I, the recipient of the benefit, have special obligation to reward *my* benefactor. Although the Torah, in many instances, assumes the existence and binding nature of the moral obligation of gratitude, we do not find an explicit general principle of this kind. We would, therefore, have to justify its inclusion in our system on the basis of *sevarah,* as a self-evident moral intuition (P5). The moral rules that could be subsumed under P5 would be;

R33 Respect your father and mother.

R34 Bringing of the First Fruits
R35 Reciting blessings before and sometimes after pleasurable experiences (rabbinic *mitzvah*)

> (While these last two are rituals and relate to God, they appear to be based upon the principle of gratitude.)

The question that arises next is how to relate principles P1 to P5 to each other and possibly to some ultimate principle. This brings us back to the question we raised at the outset: What does it mean in terms of structure to say of Jewish morality that "it was all given by one shepherd"? We could say that at this point the integrative character of the system of Jewish morality must be transposed from terms of logic into terms of authority. Principles P1 through P4 are found in the Torah which is accepted by Jews as expressing the will of God, and therefore ought to be obeyed as a religious obligation. Principle P5 is declared self-evidently true by our reason, which is also given to us by God. But on this view principles P1 through P5 must be seen as the ultimate *moral* principles of our system inasmuch as they are not derivable from any other more general *moral* principle.

It is possible, however, to interpret "it is all given by one shepherd" in quasi-moral terms. The "one shepherd" happens to be the moral God of Israel. Principles P1 to P5 emanate from God as divine imperatives, but our primary response is not simply to an *authority* but to one whom we sense to be absolute goodness. On this premise, we can enthrone an ultimate moral principle at the apex of our moral system from which principles P1 to P5 can be generated. This is the teaching, "And you shall walk in His ways . . ." ("to keep the ways of God, to do righteousness and justice").[142] Thus, *imitatio dei* becomes the categorical imperative of Judaism. We are to love our neighbors because God loves us. We are to pursue justice and righteousness because God is just and righteous. We are to do what is right and good because God has mercy on all His creatures. We are to keep our promises because God keeps His.

Two alternative models, therefore, emerge as depicting the moral system of Judaism:

(1) **WILL OF GOD**

	TORAH			HUMAN REASON
BENEVOLENCE	JUSTICE	SUPEREROGATORY	FIDELITY	GRATITUDE
P1	P2	P3	P4	P5
R1–R12	R13–R24	PERSONAL MORALITY	R25–R28	R29–R31

(2) **THE ULTIMATE MORAL PRINCIPLE**
"AND YOU SHALL WALK IN HIS WAYS"

P1	P2	P3	P4	P5
R1–R12	R13–R24	P.M.	R25–R28	R29–R31

Providing For Consistency

One of the most important requirements of a moral system is that it offer a decision procedure to be followed when there is a conflict between the various moral rules. Thus, if a woman is drowning and calls for help, should the man on shore respond when he realizes that to save her he will have to embrace a strange woman or gaze upon her nakedness? Intuitively, we may feel certain that our duty toward the life of a fellow human being weighs more heavily than the obligations of sexual modesty and agree with the Talmud that he who hesitates in such a situation is indeed a *chasid shoteh,* a pious fool![143] However, the question remains as to how to formally justify such a decision within Jewish morality? Obviously, there might be other cases of conflicting duties where one's intuitions would be of little help, as in the case discussed in an earlier chapter which involved a conflict between one's obligation to oneself and one's love for one's fellow man.[144]

In order to understand the possibilities that might exist in Jewish morality for the resolution of such conflicts, we must ask whether the

Torah itself has made any distinctions between the various precepts, indicating that they vary in importance or that priorities are to be observed in carrying them out. As a matter of fact, we find that the rabbis sometimes said things which appear to imply the absolute equality of all the precepts. On the one hand, in discussing the *mitzvot* they often did make distinctions between more-important and less-important commandments according to various criteria.[145] Thus, we find that the precepts are categorized as "light" or "severe" on the basis of the severity of the penalty that their violation entails.[146] A prohibition punishable by *karet*, "cutting off," or death by the courts would be considered "severe." On other occasions, the precepts may be evaluated on the basis of the effort or the expense involved in fulfilling them. Earlier we cited a *Mishnah* which drew our attention to a group of precepts in regard to the great rewards they could bring:

> These are the thing whose fruits a man enjoys in this world while the capital is laid up for him in the world-to-come: honoring father and mother, practice of loving-kindness, and making peace between a man and his fellow, but the study of Torah is equal to them all.[147]

The point here seems to be that certain moral precepts have obvious immediate social benefits in addition to the spiritual rewards that await the doer in the future. However, the rabbis were not suggesting that the relative importance of the precepts be evaluated on the basis of the rewards they bring about. In regard to *mitzvot* and their rewards, the consensus among the rabbis was that (1) the observance of each and every precept will result in inestimable good, and (2) while there may be differences in the rewards for the *mitzvot*, we do not know precisely what they are.[148]

In terms of our positive obligations, therefore, the precepts are to be regarded as of equal importance. This is reflected in the Halakhah that "He who is occupied with a precept is exempt from performing another precept" and is not obliged to interrupt his present performance.[149]

In regard to the negative precepts, the Torah does disclose the penalties involved for transgression. One could certainly assume that a precept whose violation entails the death penalty is in some sense more important than one which entails flogging. Yet these gradations in penalties do not always yield a schedule of priorities. For example, we have already alluded to the principle that in Judaism, the preservation of life takes precedence over all the precepts except three: idolatry, incest, and murder. In respect to these, a person should prefer death to violation. Is there any correlation between the priority given these three prohibitions and their designated penalties? While it is true that all three carry the death penalty, the form of death varies, so that they are not all equal in severity. Furthermore, there are other precepts, like the Sabbath, whose violation also entails the death penalty, yet a Jew is not required to give his life for their observance. We must, therefore, conclude that "these three offenses were singled out not on account of the punishment they involve but because they rest on fundamental principles, the abolition of which undermines the entire existence of Judaism."[150] Indeed, when circumstances create the possibility of *kiddush ha-shem*—sanctification of the divine name—then every precept is given this highest priority. For then it is not the content of the precept that is significant but the fact that it is a command of God.[151]

In commenting on direct conflicts between our obligation to God and our duties to others, the Talmud teaches: "Wherever there is profanation of the name of God, we withhold honor to the teacher,"[152] and if parents advise children to violate the Torah, we are reminded: "You all, parents and children, are under obligation to honor Me."[153]

In another example of a conflict between Jewish values, invasion of economic rights versus increase of Torah knowledge, the latter is ranked higher. The Talmud rules that elementary teachers cannot complain that their source of livelihood is being impaired by an influx of teachers from another town, because of the principle that "Competition among the scribes increases wisdom."[154] If some other profession was involved, we would probably view this as a case of *hassagat gevul* and respond to the claim of the resident professionals. However, where dissemination of the Torah was involved, particularly among the young, Halakhah placed Torah higher than the monetary loss to individuals.[155]

While for pedagogical purposes, the rabbis often urged a greater stringency with rabbinic enactments than with biblical precepts, they never forgot the basic distinction between Torah and rabbinic legislation, which is reflected in the operational principle: "A doubtful case involving biblical law must be decided stringently; a doubtful case involving rabbinic law is decided leniently."[156]

In examining some of the positive precepts of the Torah and the conditions of their observance, it becomes clear that many of them could only be carried out at the expense of violating a negative precept. Thus the observance of the levirate marriage is possible only if a man marries his brother's wife, which is otherwise forbidden under the severe penalty of death. The stipulations requiring the bringing of sacrifices in the Temple on the Sabbath or on the Festivals are in direct conflict with the command to refrain from certain types of work on those days. The command to circumcise a male child on the eighth day may sometimes conflict with the Sabbath. Yet the rabbis ruled that when a specific time is given for an observance, the time must be observed even at the expense of the Sabbath.

From these instances, there emerges the general rule that "A positive precept overrules a negative precept," (1) where the positive precept is given a specific time, or (2) where the positive precept has no other possibility of being realized (as in the case of the levirate), or (3) where circumstances link the observance of the positive precept with violation of the negative precept. This latter category is exemplified by the precept to attach woolen fringes on all four-cornered garments. Since most garments were made of linen, fulfilling the precept would have involved transgressing the prohibition against sha'atnez, wearing garments made of linen and wool. This does not fit into the second category since it is possible to wear all-wool garments.[157] Additional applications of this principle are found in the Talmud, where the rabbis developed its limiting conditions by analysis of the instances found in the Torah.[158]

Another principle involving the relationship between precepts, which in a sense seems opposed to the previous one, is the concept rejecting "a mitzvah that comes about through a transgression." This is exemplified by the prohibitions against using a stolen lulav and against making a blessing after performing the mitzvah of challah from dough made of stolen wheat.[159] But why shouldn't we say that the positive precept of taking the lulav overrules the negative precept of stealing?

Consider the following passage: "And when ye reap the harvest of your land, thou shalt not wholly reap the corner of thy field, neither shalt thou gather the gleaning of thy harvest; thou shalt leave them for the poor and for the stranger; I am the Lord your God.[160] Rashi comments that this is merely a reiteration of the precept to leave the agricultural gifts of *leket, shikchah,* and *pe'ah* for the poor. Nachmanides, however, connects this passage with the earlier precept concerning the bringing of the *omer,* the offering of the first fruit of the harvest.[161] It is in connection with the performance of that important precept, that particular "harvest," that the Torah reminds you to leave the corner of your field and the gleaning of the *harvest* for the poor. In other words, the positive precept of the *omer* does not override the negative precept against taking those portions for oneself. While the positive precept of the *omer* does override the prohibition against doing work on the Sabbath, it does not override negative precepts that involve violating the rights of others. This would constitute a *mitzvah* that comes about through a transgression and is prohibited.[162]

As to the reason why a positive precept has the power to overrule a negative one, the suggestion has been made that the two kinds of precepts appeal primarily to different attitudes in man and involve different motivations. To go out and expend energy and substance in the bidding of one's master is generally prompted by love, which in turn evokes a response of compassion; i.e., the divine attribute of mercy, *rachamim.* However, to refrain from doing that which is forbidden by one's master is generally prompted by fear, to which God responds with his attribute of justice (*din*). But since love of God is greater than fear of God, the power of the positive precept is greater than the power of the negative, so that in cases of conflict, the positive overrules the negative.[163] This may also explain why the Torah prescribes penalties of all sorts for violation of the negative precepts while generally no penalties are ordered for nonfeasance or neglecting to perform the positive commands.

On the face of it, however, the priority given to the positive over the negative seems to be a formal one, while the priority given to human life over other rules, and to sanctification of the name over human life, is based upon a determination of the intrinsic superiority of the values involved.

In assigning different "weights" or significance to the various values in Jewish morality, the rabbis appear to favor considerations involving the dignity and respect due to man, *kavod ha-beriyot,* in one-self or in others, over other values. Thus, the rabbis found in Scripture a warrant excusing a scholar or elder from returning a lost animal to its owner if handling it was beneath his dignity. The criterion used is the following: If this was the scholar's own animal, he would pass it up because of his dignity; thus he may do the same with someone else's property.[164] Surprisingly, Maimonides adds that he who walks in the "ways of the right and the good" and acts *lifnim mi-shurat ha-din* should always return the lost item even if it is not in accordance with his dignity! This ruling would seem to evaluate benevolence as ultimately higher than *kavod ha-beriyot.* Actually the source for Maimonides' ruling is an incident recorded in the Talmud in which Rabbi Ishmael's going "beyond the line of the law" consisted in compensating the owner for his loss rather than doing what was beneath his dignity. A more consistent view would appear to be that if indeed the Torah discloses that human dignity is more important than returning lost property, it is not within the prerogative of the individual to forfeit that dignity even as *lifnim mi-shurat hadin.* In short, perhaps that is not the "right and the good" in that particular case.[165]

We have already discussed the moral evil of deception, which is forbidden even when the deception is purely psychological. The Talmud records a case where a host led his guest to believe wrongly that the very lavish and expensive service was all in his honor. This was, of course, immoral, but we are told that if it was done in the presence of others, so as a result of the pretense, the esteem and honor of the guest actually increase in the eyes of those present, this practice is permitted.[166] It is *genevat da'at* to encourage another person to have a false impression about my benevolence toward him. However, if his honor is involved, it is best not to disillusion him.

This leads to a general consideration of the role of the abstract values of truth and honesty in the actual practice of Jewish morality. Indeed, the Torah tells us, "Keep thee far from a false matter" and "Ye shall not . . . deal falsely nor lie one to another," and the rabbis tell us that "The seal of the Holy One, blessed be He, is truth."[167] Yet the rabbis taught that one may lie for the sake of domestic peace, even as God did, or in order to save someone from embarrassment.[168] We find in the Talmud the following esoteric teaching: "There are three excep-tions to the rule of truthfulness: tractate, bed, and hospitality."[169] If truth-telling were an absolute, we would all be at the mercy of every inquisitive person brazen enough to ask embarrassing questions. Where the lie serves some moral purpose, one may lie. If asked probing ques-tions about the state of your knowledge (tractate), you may feign ignorance for the sake of humility. If asked questions about your sex life (bed), you may lie for the sake of morality. If asked about the generosity of certain families (hospitality), you may lie in order to save the generous ones from being victimized.

An interesting conflict of duties is reported in the name of Rabbi Israel Salanter. Reuben had once spoken *lashon ha-ra* against his friend Simeon without Simeon ever finding out about it. Regretful and repen-tant, Reuben now wishes to attain expiation and forgiveness for his sin. But in order to achieve that, he must first ask Simeon for forgiveness. To do so, however, would be to reveal the entire matter to Simeon, who would undoubtedly experience great pain and aggravation. Yet without securing forgiveness from Simeon, Reuben cannot hope to achieve expiation for his transgression. What is he to do? Rabbi Salanter is said to have ruled that avoiding pain and aggravation to his friend stands higher than his own personal spiritual needs in these cir-cumstances.[170]

Although we have designated the Biblical rules, the *de-oraita,* as the superior legislation, and the rabbinic extensions as subsidiary, the Halakhah has enunciated a surprising set of priorities in regard to cer-tain situations where the rabbis can actually legislate against biblical law.[171]

The Talmud states: "The rabbinic courts have the power to suspend a law of the Torah in a passive way." That is to say, the rabbis have the authority to enact legislation by which the people would be restricted from observing some positive precept of the Torah. For example, the rabbis ruled that when Rosh Hashanah falls on the Sab-bath, the *shofar* (ram's horn) should not be sounded lest it inadvertently be carried in a public domain and thus violate the Sabbath.[172] Again, we are forbidden "to take the name of the Lord thy God in vain." Yet the rabbis in a certain period, in order to counteract the influence of atheism, decreed that one should greet his fellow man by invoking the name of God.[173] Earlier, in the days of Ezra, two biblical commands involving the giving of levitical tithes were suspended and the people were instructed to give them instead to the priests because the Levites had not responded adequately to the call for *aliyah*.[174]

After considerable debate, it was decided in the Talmud that the rabbinical court does not have the power to set aside biblical injunctions in an active manner; i.e., to call for actions forbidden by the Torah. However, in the very process of deciding this general principle, the Talmud outlines three broad exceptions that permit rabbinic legislation in these very circumstances. These, in turn, become in themselves important principles of the rabbinic judicial process.[175]

1. *Hefker bet din hefker*. The rabbinical courts have the power to deprive an owner of his property and fortune. This is a very wide-ranging principle and was utilized by the rabbis as the basis for many different types of legislation, including matters of ritual law.[176] According to one view in the Talmud, this was the legal basis for Hillel's *prosbul*. That enactment was clearly a case of a rabbinic court setting aside a biblical injunction in an active way, for Hillel was allowing the creditor to collect his debt and the debtor to pay it even after the Sabbatical year, which the Torah explicitly prohibited! By invoking the principle of *hefker bet din hefker* we are saying, in effect, that the creditor is simply collecting money that had already been transferred to his ownership by the rabbis.[177]

2. The rabbinical court may prescribe lashes or capital punishment, even in cases where the Torah does not call for such punishment, if the purpose is to preserve the Torah. It once happened that a man had sexual relations with his wife in a semipublic place. He was brought before the court and flogged. Although there is no express Torah prohibition against such conduct, and therefore, according to the Torah, the man did not deserve to be beaten, the court can act if, in its judgment, the times or the norms of public morality require it.[178]

> The court is authorized to flog one who may not be liable thereto by the Torah law and to execute one who may not be liable to capital punishment, which power is given not for the purpose of transgressing the Torah, but to build a fence around the Torah. Similarly, a judge may always expropriate money belonging to whomsoever, destroying it or giv-

ing it away, if, in his judgment, this would serve to prevent the breaking down of the fences of the Torah, strengthen its structure or to punish a mighty offender.

Significantly, the Rambam concludes:

> . . . but whatever expedient he [the judge] sees fit to resort to, all his deeds should be done for the sake of heaven. Let not human dignity be light in his eyes, for the respect due to man supersedes a negative rabbinic command. This applies with even greater force to the dignity of the children of Abraham, Isaac, and Jacob, who adhere to the true law. The judge must be careful not to do anything calculated to destroy their self-respect . . .[179]

3. A third principle appealed to was the concept of "temporary ruling," *hora'at sha'ah,* a sort of declaration of "national emergency" in which some policy is adopted in order to "bring back many to religion" or "to safeguard some principle." This type of action is exemplified by Elijah the prophet, who in his crucial contest with the false prophets brought sacrifices on Mount Carmel, contrary to the Torah, which prohibits all sacrifices outside the Temple precincts.[180]

In justification of these extraordinary priorities, the rabbis often cited Psalm 119:126, "it is time to do for the Lord; they have made void Thy Torah," which they interpreted as follows:

> "It is a time to do something for the Lord; *therefore* make void thy Torah"; i.e., there are times when to abrogate a single law of the Torah is, in effect, to do something for the Torah as a whole.

> Just as the physician amputates an arm or a leg in order to save the whole body, so also the *bet din* can and may, on a particular occasion, direct that some of the commandments be disregarded as a temporary measure so that all of them, as a body, may be preserved, as the early sages used to say, "He desecrated one Sabbath so that he might keep many Sabbaths."[181]

In offering guidance for the resolution of possible conflicts within the system, not only did the Halakhah anticipate conflicts between biblical negative precepts and positive precepts and between rabbinic and biblical legislation, but it also discussed the possibility of conflicts between the results obtained by applying different hermeneutical rules. For example, what is one to do if a *kal va-chomer* eventuates in a conclusion in conflict with the conclusion yielded by a *binyan av* on the same subject?[182] The rabbis also discussed the possibility of conflict between Jewish law and the secular law of the state in which Jews may reside.[183]

Concluding Remarks

It should be clear from the foregoing that what gives Jewish morality its integrated character is, first, the sense that the ultimate origin of all values is in God, whose essence is morality, and second, the logical connectives that relate principles to rules and rules to moral judgments.

The ideal of consistency is rendered attainable in Jewish morality by the presence of a hierarchy of values which offer guidance in cases of conflict. Except for that ultimate test when man must be prepared to give his life for *kiddush ha-shem,* human life and human dignity set aside ritual obligations, love of God stands higher than fear of God, mercy higher than justice, and peace higher than truth.

In terms of comprehensiveness, the material we have presented indicates that the basic reasoning processes employed by the original rabbis in interpreting the talmudic texts are still available to those of us today who would decide the moral issues that confront us by the perceptions of Jewish morality. This, it will be recalled, was the pointed claim of Moses: "It is not too hard for thee . . . it is not in heaven . . . but the word is very nigh unto thee, in thy mouth and in thy heart, that thou mayest do it."[184]

One of the most important claims of Jewish morality is that it is eminently practicable; that these values can be realized in real life. Judaism believes that the variegated richness and complexity of the real world is penetrable by human reason not only in the domain of pure knowledge but also by practical reason in the domain of morality. Stimulated by his intuitions and guided by the teachings of the Torah, the Jew should be able to work out what is right and good by himself.

It is ironic that some of the most attractive moral theories in the general field of ethics exhibit an almost fatal weakness precisely at the point where the individual, in the bewilderment of his concrete situation, is expected to make a moral judgment. Utilitarianism has never been able to provide a formula by which the utility of the various dimensions of pleasure could be transposed into a common factor for purposes of summing and evaluation. Even the very cogent intuitionist theory of W. D. Ross must acknowledge the uncertainty that often accompanies the individual moral judgment:

> Where a possible act is seen to have two characteristics, in virtue of one of which it is prima facie right and in virtue of the other, prima facie wrong, we are, I think, well aware that we are not certain whether we ought or ought not to do it. We come . . . after consideration to think one duty more pressing than the other, but we do not feel certain that it is so. In this respect the judgment as to the rightness of a particular act is just like the judgment as to the beauty of a particular natural object or work of art.[185]

We are not suggesting that Jewish morality offers a formula for decision procedures that can be mechanically applied to every concrete case and that will always yield a valid judgment or blissful certainty. In difficult cases of conflicting values or duties, the agony of uncertainty and the sense of moral risk will undoubtedly persist. In Judaism one has the further recourse of consulting with the rabbis and teachers, whose knowledge and experience can be helpful, and with whom one can share responsibility for the moral decision. However, the more than three thousand years during which the Jewish people have wrestled with moral issues, and recorded their struggles, have encouraged the development of a Jewish moral system that contains a pool of insightful moral teachings, a ranking of values, and a workable method of moral reasoning. In a sense, the history of Judaism, in its moral as well as its ritual aspects, has successfully carried out the original task given to it by the Torah: "'And these are the judgments that you shall *set* before them'—as a set table ready for human use and consumption."[186]

> The fire for lighting the lamps of the menorah had to come from the fires that burned continuously on the outer altar. The modest, sheltered, and

pure light of the menorah represents the intuitively grasped moral ideals of Judaism. The exposed fires of the outer altar, where the various votive and sin offerings were brought, symbolize the religious life that is intimately involved with the lives and circumstances of men, their struggles and failures, their temptations and aspirations. The periodic input from the outer altar to the menorah, the frequent contacts between the theoretic teachings and the pressures of human experience, gave us our Jewish morality, which illuminates the mind even as it warms the heart; even as it burns away the dross.

Notes

1. See R. M. Hare. *The Language of Morals* (New York: Oxford University Press, 1964), p. 122.

2. This material is from H. L. A. Hart, *The Concept of Law* (Claredon Law Series, Oxford University Press, 1961), chaps. 8 and 9.

3. This point is missed by S. Federbush, (המוסר והמשפט בישראל ירושלים תש"ח, מוסד הרב, קוק), who states on p. 27, המוסר כולל בתוכו גם את המשפט.

4. *Nicomachean Ethics,* 1094 a/19.

5. G. E. Moore. *Principia Ethica* (Oxford University Press, 1966), p. 188.

6. David Hume. *A Treatise of Human Nature,* bk. II, pt. II, sec. III.

7. H. B. Veatch. *Rational Man* (Bloomington: Indiana University Press, 1966), p. 70.

8. See the distinction made by Kenny, "Happiness," understood as a dominent end and as an inclusive end, in *Moral Concepts,* ed. J. Feinberg (Oxford University Press, 1970), p. 48.

9. *Nicomachean Ethics*, bk. I.

10. F. H. Bradley. *Ethical Studies* (Oxford University Press, 1962), pp. 95–97.

11. The traditional view of the Old Testament, and of the Jewish morality based upon it, is that we have here a deontological ethic. The following is typical: "The original core of Hebraic ethics is contained in a view of life that conceives of the good man as essentially the righteous man. This means living in accordance with the commandments laid down by a Supreme Being who is at once the Creator of all things and the Legislator for all mankind. His commandments are contained in the Holy Scriptures and enjoin a pattern of correct behavior for all true believers. The primary demand is study and fulfillment of the Law. William Paley, an eighteenth century divine put the matter succinctly in his *Principles of Moral and Political Philosophy* (1785): 'As the will of God is our rule; to inquire what is our duty, or what we are obliged to do, in any instance, is in effect, to inquire what is that will of God in that instance, which consequently becomes the whole business of morality.'" M. K. Munitz, *A Modern Introduction to Ethics* (Glencoe, Ill.: Free Press, 1958), p. 219.

12. I. Kant. *Fundamental Principles of the Metaphysics of Morals.*

13. C. D. Broad. *Five Types of Ethical Theory* (Totowa, N.J.: Littlefield, Adams 1959), pp. 127–128.

14. *A Treatise of Human Nature,* sec. I.

15. See Veatch, op. cit., pp. 48–49.

16. C. L. Stevenson. *Ethics and Language* (New Haven: Yale University Press, 1944), p. 116.

17. See H. Feigl, "Validation and Vindication: An Analysis of the Nature and Limits of Ethical Arguments," in *Readings in Ethical Theory,* ed. W. Sellars and J. Hospers (New York: Appelton-Century-Crofts, 1952), p. 674.

18. Abraham Edel, *Science and the Structure of Ethics: Foundations of the Unity of Science* (Chicago: University of Chicago Press, 1961), p. 13.

CHAPTER 2   The Place of Morality in Judaism

1. See the discussion by צבי הירש חיות in his (הוצאת דברי חכמים, ספר תורת הנביאים, also see מהר"ץ חיות בחידושיו, נדרים כ"ב ירושלים, תשי"ח(, כל ספרי מהר"ץ חיות פרק א'.

2. Genesis 19:56.

3. See below, p. 19.

4. Compare the Code of Hammurabi, where items of civil law are listed apart from ritual law. See „מהבין משפטי התורה לבין חוקי עמורבי?", מילר-כבוד פרסומי החברה לחקר המקרא בישראל, ספר זיידל, ספר י"א (ירושלים תשכ"ב) Of the accepted total of 613 commands in the Pentateuch, about 60 are moral rules.

5. See Federbush in his המוסר והמשפט, p. 26.

6. The rabbis often define *mishpatim* as laws whose rationale is clear and compelling, while *chukkim* appear obscure and irrational, provoking criticism from non-Jews. See Rashi on Leviticus 18:4–5 and Rambam in *Hilkhot Me'ilah* 8:8. See also M. Elon, *Jewish Law,* Part I (Heb.) (Jerusalem: The Magnes Press, Hebrew University, 1973), p. 146 and p. 148, n. 39.

7. E. Berkovits, "The Biblical Meaning of Justice," *Judaism* 18, no. 2. See also K. Kahana, *Jewish Civil Law* (London: Soncino, 1960), where he points to the use of the word *tasim* with *mishpatim,* which he suggests implies not "imposition" but "rational presentation," so that judges can intelligently apply these principles and rules to new cases.

8. Genesis 18:25 and 19:19.

9. Leviticus 18:4–5, 25:18, 26:46, Deuteronomy 26:16–18.

10. See I. Herzog, *Main Institutions of Jewish Law,* appendix, "Morality and Law." Also Rambam, *Hilchot Sanhedrin* 2:12.

11. Deuteronomy 23:21, 22:7, 24:13, 15:18, 15:10.

12. See his commentary on Deuteronomy 23:20. See also מוסר המקרא והתלמוד, ש.ז. פינס כ"ט-ט"ל (מוסד הרב קוק, ירושלים תש"ח) and fn. 29, where he interprets the talmudic passage in *Chullin* 110b, שמצוה שמתן שכרה בצדה אין בית דין שלמטה מוזהרין עליה, as reflecting this principle. Since these commandments for which reward is promised involve moral concerns beyond legal rights, human courts ought not to enforce them through compulsory means.

13. Exodus 21.

14. Commentators differ as to the number of actual *mitzvot* contained in the Decalogue.

15. Exodus 34:28; Deuteronomy 4:13, 10, 4. See also I Kings 8:9 and 8:21.

16. M. Buber, *Moses* (Oxford: East & West Library), p. 130. "It is both legislation and promulgation."

17. Talmud *Berakhot* 12a. It was discontinued out of fear that the Decalogue might tend to replace the other commandments.

18. Jerusalem Talmud, *Sanhedrin* 49b, *Sotah* 22b.

19. See Rashi on Exodus 24:12 that the Decalogue encompasses all of the 613 commandments. See E. E. Urbach, *The Sages* (Jerusalem: The Magnes Press, Hebrew University, 1975), pp. 360–364, who maintains that the rabbis, for the reasons we mentioned in note 17, refrained from any teachings which implied that the Decalogue in some sense embodied all of the 613 *mitzvot*. Philo, however, was quite explicit in favoring this doctrine. The source of the later Midrashim that mention this teaching and of Rashi's comment, according to Urbach, is to be traced to Sa'adiah Gaon. However, we do find a genre of *piyyut* (religious poetry) which appears shortly before the period of the Geonim, the *azharot,* recited on the Festival of Shavuot, which listed the 613 commandments and sometimes grouped them around the Ten Commandments. The idea was that each of the Ten Commandments entailed a number of different commandments whose grand total was 613. Since Shavuot is celebrated as the "season of the giving of the Torah," and since the Torah reading indicates that what was received by Israel on that day was the Ten Commandments, it was apparently considered important that the worshipper be made aware of the fact that the Decalogue actually incorporates all 613, so that acceptance of the former includes a commitment to the latter.

Enumerations of the 613 *mitzvot* around the Decalogue were made not only by Sa'adiah but also by the Ramban and by Rabbi Bachya ben Asher. (See the translation of *Kad ha-Kemach* in C. B. Chavel, *Encyclopedia of Torah Thought* (New York: Shilo, 1980), p. 628.

The concept that the Ten Commandments in some sense include all the *taryag mitzvot* is also found in the Midrash *Numbers Rabbah* 13:15.

20. See his Commentary on Leviticus (Hebrew trans., Shefer and Liberman), vol. 2, pp. קסו–קסז.

21. Exodus 3:12.

22. Exodus 10:25-26.

23. Jeremiah 7:22.

24. On this view, the placing of the Ark containing the two Tablets in the Holy of Holies of the Tabernacle and later of the Temple of Solomon appropriately stored the covenant in an area that could be regarded as "belonging" to both parties to the agreement. Referring to a treaty between the Egyptians and the Hittites concluded by Ramses II, considered by many to be the Pharaoh of the Exodus, John A. Wilson writes: ". . . the text [of the treaty] was newly engraved upon two silver tablets. One of these was carried back to Hatti and deposited 'at the feet of' the Hittite storm-god; the other copy was laid 'at the feet of' the god Re in Egypt." *The Culture of Ancient Egypt* (Chicago: University of Chicago Press, 1951), p. 248.

25. See Buber, *Moses,* and י. רוטשילד, in (ירושלים תשי״ח 1 מעינות "עשרת הדיברות„.

26. The fifth commandment, "Honor thy father and thy mother, "which is a moral rule, is followed by a promise of reward. This can be explained by applying the princi-

ple noted by the Ramban and referred to earlier. Since the "honor" called for goes beyond the strict requirements of justice and is a positive expression of love and reverence, special blessing will follow. See Y. Kaufmann, "The Biblical Age," in *Great Ages and Ideas of the Jewish People,* ed. L. W. Schwarz (New York: Random House, 1956), p. 23. "Thus the Bible itself implies that the universal moral rules of the Sinaitic covenant were already well known and in force among men whether in theory or practice long before Israel stood at Sinai."

27. Comp. Y. Kaufmann, *The Religion of Israel,* trans. M. Greenberg (Chicago: University of Chicago Press, 1960), p. 322.

28. Rabbi Akiva called "Love thy neighbor as thyself" a *kelal gadol ba-Torah,* "a great principle of the Torah." See ירושלמי נדרים ל:ד and ספרא, קדושים ז'.

29. See Rambam *Hilkhot Avel* 14:1, and *Sefer ha-Chinukh, mitzvah* 219. Compare the discussion in M. G. Singer, *Generalization in Ethics* (New York: Knopf, 1961), chap. 5, "Moral Rules and Principles."

30. See Berkovits, op. cit.

31. A. J. Heschel, *The Prophets* (New York: Harper & Row, 1955), pp. 200–201.

32. Deuteronomy 4:5–8.

33. Deuteronomy 16:18.

34. Exodus 34:13, Psalms 103:7; *Rosh Hashana* 17:2; *Pesikta Rabbati* 16.

35. See Cassuto on Exodus 34:5.

36. See ג"י, "זאב יעבץ & כרק י"ב, ניב המדרשיה של רחמים", "שלש עשרה מידות של רחמים", מאיר גרוזמן מדות יערכן"-מוצא דבר י"ז, תולדות ישראל חלק א'.

37. Rambam, "Eight Chapters," introduction to *Avoth* chap. 4.

38. *Nicomachean Ethics,* bks. I & II.

39. Genesis 6:9, Numbers 12:3.

40. Saadia Gaon, *The Book of Beliefs and Opinions,* trans. S. Rosenblatt (New Haven: Yale University Press, 1948), p. 129.

41. Moses Maimonides, *The Guide for the Perplexed,* trans. M. Friedlander (New York: Dutton, 1942), p. 76.

42. Exodus 33:13, 18.

43. Israel Efros, *Ancient Jewish Philosophy* (Detroit: Wayne State University Press, 1964), p. 83.

44. Kaufmann, "The Biblical Age," p. 24.

45. ש. ז. שפירא, תורת משה והנביאים, (מוסד הרב קוק p. 73 זאב יעבץ, תולדות ישראל, חלק ג' ירושלים תשכ"א)

46. Kaufmann, *The Religion of Israel,* p. 37.

47. Deuteronomy 10:12.

48. Kaufmann, *The Religion of Israel,* p. 385.

49. Leviticus 26, Deuteronomy 28.

50. Kaufmann, *The Religion of Israel,* p. 366.

51. It has been pointed out that often in the Book of Psalms, the personal involvement of the individual wilth moral inwardness often reaches a degree of intensity and penetration that surpasses the writings of the prophets themselves. Thus, while Isaiah (58:7) and Ezekiel (18:7) speak of satisfying the basic needs of the poor, the psalmist

(37:26) speaks of constant preoccupation with the needy so that one seeks them out rather than waiting to be asked for help. Similarly, Zechariah (8:16) bids us speak the truth to each other, while the psalmist (15) describes the individual whose heart is penetrated through and through with truth.

chap. 4. ש. ז. פינס, מוסר המקרא והתלמוד (מוסד הרב קוק, ירושלים תש"ח) See

52. Proverbs 2:6–10, 10:27–29.

53. See ד. ש. שפירא, „עשרת הדיברות במשלי שלמה", ארחים (ירושלים תשל"ז), pp. 172–179, who notes a certain sequence of the subject matter after Proverbs 1:10–11 and 2:12

54. I Kings 5:10

55. Kaufmann, The Religion of Israel, p. 326.

56. See R. B. Y. Scott, Introduction to The Book of Proverbs (Anchor Bible, New York: Doubleday, 1965), pp. xlii and xliv.

57. Proverbs 6:23, 10:17.

58. Proverbs 10:21–23, 3:33–35.

59. Proverbs 16:32, 6:30.

60. J. Guttmann, Philosophies of Judaism (New York: Holt, Reinhart & Winston, 1964), chap. 3.

61. Sefer haChinukh, mitzvot 546 and 547.

62. Exodus 20:12, Leviticus 19:3.

63. Sefer HaChinukh, mitzvot, 33, 48, and 212.

64. See חיים סבתו, „האגדה שבמשנה", כתלנו ח'.

65. This was supplemented by Avot de-Rabbi Nathan and tractate Derekh Eretz.

66. Avot 5:22, 5:23, 5:10.

67. Avot 4:4, 4:1.

68. Avodah Zarah 20.

69. M. Lazarus, The Ethics of Judaism (Philadelphia: Jewish Publication Society, 1901), pt. II, chaps. 4 and 7.

70. D. S. Shapiro, "The Meaning of Holiness in Judaism." Tradition 7, no.1 (Winter 1964–65): 48.

71. Ibid., p. 62.

72. Lazarus, op. cit., pp. 25, 176.

73. Leviticus 11:44–45, 20:8, 26. See Rashi on Leviticus 19:2.

74. Genesis 6:5.

75. M. Buber, Good and Evil (New York: Scribner's 1953), p. 91.

76. Aaron Barth, quoted by B. S. Jacobson, Meditations on the Torah (Tel Aviv: Sinai, 1956), p. 285.

77. Eliezer Berkovits, "A Jewish Sexual Ethic," in Crisis and Faith (New York: Sanhedrin Press, 1976), pp. 48–82.

78. A. J. Heschel, God in Search of Man (New York: Farrar, Straus & Cudahy, 1955).

79. Bava Kamma 30a.

80. Avot 2:1, 2:2, 3:14, 3:17.

81. Sifra on Leviticus 19:18.

82. M. Kadushin, Worship and Ethics (New York: Bloch 1963), p. 32.

83. See Maharsha on Shabbat 83 as to why Hillel used the negative form.

84. *Kiddushin* 41a.

85. *Sanhedrin* 45, *Ketubbot* 37.

86. Guttmann, op. cit., p. 36.

87. *Makkot* 23, 24.

88. See Albo, *Sefer ha-Ikkarim*, 3:10. See also I. Jacobson, חזון המקרא, חלק א', p. 405. Urbach op. cit., p. 344.

89. *Bava Metzia* 83a. *Mekhilta de'Rabbi Ishmael, Yitro.*

90. See the discussion in Urbach, op. cit., pp. 330–333.

91. *Kiddushin* 49–50.

92. Kadushin, op. cit., p. 55; *Yoma* 85b.

93. On Exodus 21:1.

94. *Sifre,* Deuteronomy 323; 138b.

95. *Kiddushin* 40a.

96. On Deuteronomy 12:28.

97. A biblical source for the distinction between duties toward God and duties toward man may be the passage in Deuteronomy 12:28 taken in conjunction with Proverbs 3:4. See, the Sifre on Deut. 12:28 and the discussion in *Sefer Hamitzvohs Hashem* by J. Steif Introduction to Part 2.

98. J. M. Guttmann, *Bechinat Kiyyum ha-Mitzvot* (Jerusalem: Makor, 1978), pp. 19–23.

99. Deuteronomy 24:15, *Bava Metzia* 111b.

100. Deuteronomy 24:17, *Bava Metzia* 115a.

101. Deuteronomy 25:4, *Bava Metzia* 90b.

102. Deuteronomy 24:6, *Bava Metzia* 115a.

103. Exodus 30:9, *Menachot* 3b.

104. Exodus 30:32, *Keritot* 6b.

105. Exodus 34:20, *Kiddushin* 29a.

106. Exodus 23:19, *Sanhedrin* 4b.

107. Numbers 35:25.

108. Maimonides, *Guide,* p. 331.

109. *Pe'ah* 1:1.

110. Rambam, *Hilkhot Berakhot* 11:2. See *Kesef Mishneh.*

111. *Torat Kohanim, Kedoshim.*

112. See the comments of Rabbi Jacob Emden in his הגהות מהר"יעבץ לשמונה פרקים א בר תנא, פרקי בראשית במחשבת See also the discussion in להרמבם (וולינא ש"ס) מסכת אבות ישראל (Israel, 1973), pp. 88–90.

113. (1) Jerusalem *Shekalim* 47c, (2) *Kiddushin* 40a, (3) *Avot* 3:13, (4) *Mekhilta* on Exodus 15:26, (5) *Shabbat* 31a, (6) *Shabbat* 31a, (7) *Shabbat* 119b, (8) *Sotah* 14a, (9) *Avodah Zarah* 17, (10) *Avot* 4:22.

114. The term *musar* is used in the Bible to mean "personal exhortation" but in later rabbinic literature was given the meaning of "moral teaching."

115. תנועת המוסר, ד. כץ (הוצאת בית הספר ת"א תש"ו) vol. 1 pp. 60–70.

116. Albo, *Sefer ha-Ikkarim* 3:2.

117. See (הוצאת גנזי ראשונים ירושלים תש"ו) י"ב, י"ב כ', p. מהר"ל, דרוש על התורה ועל המצות.

He explains that man is called Adam from *adamah,* "the earth," because just as the earth has the generative power to give forth clean and nourishing grains and fruits, so too is man capable of giving forth a moral personality that is divine-like quality.

118. See Seforno on Genesis 2:15, who suggests that the words לעבדה ולשמרה may refer to man's soul. Thus, man was placed in Eden to "cultivate and guard" his own spiritual capacity.

119. Urbach, op. cit., pp. 420–425.

120. See Leo Black, *God and Man in Judaism* (New York: Union of American Hebrew Congregations, 1958), pp. 36–37.

121. אליהו בן אמוזג, בשבילי מוסר (מוסד הרב קוק ירושלים תשכ"ו). p. 70.

122. Guttmann, *Philosophies of Judaism,* pp. 177–178.

123. C. Pearl, *The Medieval Jewish Mind,* (Hartmore House, 1972), p. 105. See the entire discussion in Chapter 7.

124. See Guttmann, *Philosophies of Judaism,* pp. 232–236.

125. Albo, *Ikkarim,* 3:28.

126. Isaiah 32:17.

127. *Tifereth Yisrael,* chap. 9.

128. I. Grunfeld, Introduction to *Horeb* (London: Soncino Press, vol. I, p. lxxxiii

129. M. Buber, *I and Thou* (New York: Scribner's, 1958), p. 75.

CHAPTER 3   The Grounds of Morality

1. See J. Guttmann, (הוצאת מאגנס, אוניברסיטה העברית, דת ומדע) p. 266. Also M. Lazarus, *The Ethics of Judaism* (Philadelphia: Jewish Publication Society, 1900), p. 112.

2. Micah 6:8.

3. *Sanhedrin* 56. Rambam, *Hilkhot Melakhim* 8:9. Some say six commands were given to Adam and a seventh to Noah.

4. שי"ז-שי"ח p. ספר משך חכמה, נצבים. See discussion in Urbach, *The Sages,* pp. 315–342. Also in ארחיים by ש. ד. שפירא pp. 33–36 (ירושלים תשל"ז מוסד הרב קוק, ירושלים).

5. *Deuteronomy Rabbah* 5:2, *Exodus Rabbah* 46:1.

6. *Leviticus Rabbah* 9:3.

7. *Genesis Rabbah* 76:3.

8. Aharon Lichtenstein acknowledges that "the existence of a natural morality is clearly assumed by tradition." However, after stating that "they may have felt that one could not ground specific binding and universal rules in nature," he makes no suggestion as to the form this natural morality may have taken.

See "Does Jewish Tradition Recognize an Ethic Independent of Halakha?" in *Modern Jewish Ethics,* ed. Marvin Fox (Columbus: Ohio State University Press, 1975), p. 62.

9. See (ירושלים תשי"ד), חלק א', p. 14 טעמי המצוות בספרות ישראל, יצחק היינמן.

10. Albo, *Sefer ha-Ikkarim* 3:7, p. 63.

11. *Sifra,* Leviticus 13:10. See Lazarus, op. cit., vol. I, p. 118

12. Urbach, op. cit., pp. 316–320.

13. *Eruvin* 100b.

14. Urbach, op. cit.

15. See below Chapter 9 regarding the use of *sevharah*.

16. J. Guttmann, *Philosophies of Judaism,* (New York: Holt, Rinehart, J. Winston, 1964), p. 64.

17. Albo, *Ikkarim* 1:7 and 8; bk. III, p. 64.

18. Quoted in "Three Jewish Philosophers," p. 103. (New York, Atheneum 1972).

19. See Fox, *Modern Jewish Ethics,* p. 174.

20. See S. B. Rabinkow, "יחיד וציבורר ביהדות„ in ירושלים, (מוסד הרב קוק, בין אדם לחבירו) (1975 Heinemann reports that the first Jewish thinker to speak of an "inner revelation" in which man can recognize in his perceptions of truth and justice an expression of God's revelation within man was I. Barnays, who in turn influenced S. R. Hirsch.

For a balanced survey of the literature on the question whether Judaism and particularly Maimonides advocated a "natural law" theory, see Norman Lamm and Aaron Kirschenbaum, "Freedom and Constraint in the Jewish Judicial Process," *Cardozo Law Review* 1, no. 1 (Spring 1979).

21. *Avot* 3:18. See the commentaries of Rambam and Abarbanel (*Nachlat Avot*) on this *Mishnah.* Abarbanel points out that the proof-text given in support of this statement is Genesis 9:6, which was said to Noah, and which, in its entirety, reads: "Whoso sheddeth man's blood, by man shall his blood be shed; for in the image of God made He man." Earlier passages referring to man's creation in the image of God were not used, says Abarbanel, because they were mere descriptions by the Torah. This passage was said to Noah and thereby "made known" to man that he is formed in the image of God. But this information is given to Noah as an explanation of the prohibition against murder. Thus we have here a connection between the awareness of being created in the image of God and the moral sense.

22. See O. G. Ramberan in *Religious Studies,* 14, no. 2, p. 214. See also הרב קוק, אגרות הראיה, אגרת מ"ד p. מה, "מפני שאנחנו יודעים שעצם שאיפת הצדק באיזו צורה שתהיה היא בעצמה ההשפעה האלהית היותר מאירה..."

23. Albo, *Ikkarim,* bk. II, p. 54.

24. Deuteronomy 30:14.

25. Exodus 34:6.

26. Y. Kaufmann, *The Religion of Israel,* trans. M. Greenberg (Chicago: University of Chicago Press, 1960), p. 327.

27. Leviticus 19:2.

28. Genesis 18:25. See Rabinkow, op. cit., p. 95.

29. Baeck, *God and Man in Judaism* (New York: Union of American Hebrew Congregations, 1958), p. 27.

30. Exodus 3:13–14.

31. See Rashi on Exodus 3:14.

32. See Lazarus, op. cit., pt. I, p. 123; Guttmann, "קאנט והיהדות„ in דת ומדע, p. 218; E. Fackenheim, *Encounters Between Judaism and Modern Philosophy,* (New York: Basic Books, 1973), pp. 31–79.

33. P. A. Hutchings, *Kant on Absolute Value* (Detroit: Wayne State University Press, 1972), p. 234.

34. Ibid., p. 241.

35. Ibid., p. 245.

36. Ibid., p. 250.

37. In his recent *Introduction to the Code of Maimonides* (New Haven: Yale Judaica Press, 1980), pp. 453–457), Isadore Twersky correctly points out that "Maimonides' insistence upon the imperatival aspect . . . rules out completely autonomy for law," and that for Maimonides the ultimate authority of the law including morality is God. However, some of the evidence he adduces for this conclusion seems misplaced.

It will be remembered (see above, p. 54) that Maimonides in his *Shemonah Perakim* discusses an apparent conflict between the philosophers' view and the view of our Jewish sages. The former claim that the innately good person with no inclination to evil is superior to the individual who has to overcome evil desires and only after a struggle performs the good. The rabbis seem to suggest the reverse. Maimonides' resolution of the problem was to suggest that the rabbis were referring only to ritual laws, while in regard to the rational commandments (*mishpatim*) the philosophers' view is correct.

Professor Twersky interprets this issue as being the Kantian one of heteronomy versus autonomy, with Maimonides apparently adopting a compromise position. However, he then asks us to consider the ruling of Maimonides to the effect that "where penitents stand, the completely righteous cannot stand," which implies, according to Professor Twersky, "that Maimonides in the *Mishneh Torah* comes down on the side of heteronomy," having made no distinction between *hukkim* and *mishpatim!*

According to our own reading of the texts, both citations are irrelevant to the issue of autonomy/heteronomy as applied to Maimonides. In the discussion in *Shemonah Perakim,* the only question is whether having ongoing inner impulses and desires toward evil, although they are controlled at the behavioral level, is in itself bad. But even after Maimonides' "compromise" solution, both individuals, the one doing *mishpatim* wholeheartedly and the other doing *chukkim* after a struggle, do so in obedience to the will of God. So that Maimonides never really abandoned his heteronomous position.

Moreover, Maimonides' ruling in regard to the penitent is irrelevant to the discussion in *Shemonah Perakim.* In the latter nobody actually sins. The issue is only whether a repressed inclination to do evil is, in itself, bad. On this motivational question, Maimonides suggested the distinction between *mishpatim* and *chukkim*. The penitent, however, is one who has actually sinned and who goes through a process of total personality transformation known as *teshuvah,* or repentence. On this, Maimonides rules that one who does so is religiously superior to the one who has never sinned. Again, this has nothing to do with the discussion in *Shemonah Perakim.* Of course, the penitent too does what he does in obedience to God.

True, Professor Twersky is correct; in the context of Maimonides' teaching, heteronomy survives intact. But then again, it was never threatened!

38. J. Rachels, "God and Human Attitudes," *Religious Studies* 7, pp. 325–337.

39. P. L. Quinn, *Religious Studies* 2, no. 3, p. 250.

40. Ibid., p. 274.

41. *Avot* 1:3. See Commentary of Abarbanel, נחלת אבות, on this *mishnah*.
42. See discussion in Urbach, op. cit., pp. 326–340, *Eruvin* 21b, *Berakhot* 20b.
43. *Midrash Tanchuma,* Ki tavo. See also Urbach, op. cit.
44. *Kiddushin* 31a.
45. This is suggested by Rashi on Leviticus 1:1.
46. *Midrash Tanchuma, Lekh Lekha, Parshah* 1.
47. Genesis 1:28.
48. Genesis 1:26.
49. Genesis 1:11–20.
50. Genesis 2:7 and 1:27. See interpretations of Rashi and Ramban.
51. See Kariv, מסוד חכמים, pp. 121–122.
52. *Sifrei,* Ha'azinu, sec. 306.
53. Genesis 2:19–20.
54. Deuteronomy 30:19.
55. Genesis 3:22.
56. Psalms 8:4–7.
57. *Sifra* on Leviticus 19:18.
58. *Sanhedrin* 37a.
59. Kariv, מסוד חכמים, p. 133. See commentary of Rashi on Ecclesiastes 3:11—"Also He hat set the world in their heart."
60. G. Vlastos, "Human Worth, Merit and Equality," in *Moral Concepts,* J. Feinberg (Oxford University Press, 1970), p. 148.
61. Hutchings, op. cit., p. 342.
62. See Alan Donagan, *The Theory of Morality* (Chicago: University of Chicago Press, 1977), pp. 57–66, who argues that the Golden Rule as formulated by Hillel or by Kant's first formula of the categorical imperative is a principle of impartiality but cannot serve as a substantive first principle of a moral system. However, he interprets the commandment "Thou shalt love thy neighbor as thyself" as ordaining behavior which shows respect to one's fellow human beings as rational creatures and thus as akin to Kant's second formulation, "Act always so that you respect every human being, yourself or another, as being a rational creature."
63. C. D. Broad, *Five Types of Ethical Theory,* (Totowa, N.J.: Littlefield, Adams, 1959), p. 128.
64. Hutchings, op. cit., p. 310.
65. See above, p. 15.
66. Deuteronomy 32:6, 15, 18.
67. Exodus 24:7, Deuteronomy 29:14. Urbach points out that the Midrash which reads a hint of "coersion" into the account of the giving of the Torah is the view of an individual; דעת יחיד.
68. Ze'ev Falk has pointed out ערכי משפט ויהדות [Jerusalem, 1980] pp. 66–67) that the original conception in the Torah of the judgment by which disputants were urged to seek a resolution of their disagreement was not necessarily to be delivered by an officially appointed judge within an established judicial system. Jacob says to Laban in answer to his accusations, "Set it here before my brethren and thy brethren, that they

may judge betwixt us two" (Gen. 31:37). Any impartial third party ought to be able to discern what is fair and just. A similar implication may be found in the following reference to the *congregation* as the dispenser of justice: "Then the congregation shall judge between the smiter and the avenger of blood according to these ordinances" (Num. 35:24). Similarly, the following passage suggests that justice is to be found simply in the act of the disputants agreeing to bring their case to judgment. "If there be a controversy between men *and they come to judgment* and they judge them by justifying the righteous and condemning the wicked," (Deut. 25:1). This seems to suggest that the necessary conditions for justice—which is what the judgment is supposed to bring about—are recognizable by an objective, intelligent mind and corresponds to our intuitive notion of fairness.

69. An observation made by Rabbi Hutner in פחד יצחק, volume on Shavuot.

70. Since man was driven out of Eden, it is no longer self-evident to him that existence is such a blessing.

71. *Mekhilta* on Exodus 5.

72. Bachya Ibn Pakuda, in his philosophical-ethical treatise, *Chovot ha-Levavot,* ("Duties of the Heart") grounds the human obligation to God on the basis of gratitude. "After having explained the manner of studying the good that the Almighty has bestowed upon man, we shall now mention that which man must perform, which is the service of God, insofar as reason obligates man to benefit the one who has benefited him." Intro. to Gate III.

73. *Avot* 4:29.

74. A. J. Heschel, *Who Is Man,* p. 97.

75. Ibid., p. 98.

76. Ibid., p. 108; Psalms 116:12.

77. *Niddah* 30b. See discussion in Urbach as to question of Platonic influence, op. cit., p. 245.

78. Ecclesiastes 6:7.

79. Ecclesiastes 5:9.

80. *Leviticus Rabbah* 4:2. See *Kariv,* מסד חכמים, pp. 125–126.

81. M. Buber, "Imitatio Dei," in *Israel and the World,* pp. 70–71.

82. Deuteronomy 13:15, 4, 24. *Sotah* 14a.

83. Deuteronomy 28:9, 11:22.

83a. Genesis 18:19.

84. *Sotah* 14a; Genesis 3:21, 18:1, 25:11; Deuteronomy 34:6.

85. *Sifrei,* Deuteronomy 49; 85a.

86. Exodus 15:2, *Mekhilta* 37a, *Shabbat* 133b.

87. Genesis 1:27.

88. *Pesikta Rabbati* 46b, *Genesis Rabbah* 49:29, *Yalkut Reuveni* on Genesis 1:27.

89. Alexander Pope, *Essay on Man,* Epistle II.

90. *Avot* 3:18.

91. Buber, "Imitatio Dei," p. 73.

92. W. D. Hudson, "Fact and Moral Value," *Religious Studies* 5, no. 2 (December 1969).

93. S. Toulmin, "The Logic of Moral Reasoning," in *Readings in the Problems of Ethics* ed. R. Ekman (New York: Schribner's, 1964), p. 356.

94. Fackenheim, *Encounters Between Judaism and Modern Philosophy,* p. 48.

95. Leviticus 5:21.

96. *Sifra* 372:4. See Rashi and see comment of D. T. Hoffmann: „משום שמעילה בבן אדם חברו נחשבת כמעילה ב"ה"

97. Albo, *Ikkarim* 3:35, 318.

98. H. Sidgwick, *The Methods of Ethics* (Chicago: University of Chicago Press, 1962), p. 204, fn. 3.

99. Quoted by L. Roth, *Judaism: A Portrait* (New York: Viking Press, 1961), p. 172.

CHAPTER 4   Morality and the Will of God

1. Genesis 22:2.

2. See נושא העקידה בתפילות in 'חקרי זמנים, חלק א by אלתר הילביץ (1976) מוסד הרב קוק ירושלים), p. ל"ו.

3. See E. Fackenheim, *Encounters Between Judaism and Modern Philosophy* (New York: Basic Books, 1973), for a thorough discussion of the problem.

4. *Midrash Tanchuma, Va-yera* 23 (Buber 46). *Yalkut Midrash Tehillim* 29:1.

5. Shalom Spiegel, *The Last Trial* (New York: Pantheon Books, 1967), p. 93.

6. *Avot* 1:3.

7. Deuteronomy 6:5.

8. See the discussion of this distinction, above p. 9.

9. Deuteronomy 22:7, 15:10; Leviticus 18:5.

10. Exodus 12:15.

11. See the discussion in Urbach, *The Sages,* p. 366. See Ramban on Deuteronomy 22: 6.

12. Deuteronomy 4:40, 5:30, 6:24.

13. This was interpreted by the rabbis as both early death and the loss of the here-after, *olam haba.*

14. Exodus 20:12, Deuteronomy 5:16.

15. Y. Kaufmann, *The Religion of Israel,* trans. M. Greenberg (Chicago: University of Chicago Press, 1960), p. 321.

16. Ibid., p. 328.

17. Deuteronomy 13:12.

18. Albo *Sefer ha-Ikkarim,* vol. IV, pt. II, p. 388.

19. See Urbach, op. cit., pp. 368–369, for a discussion of these examples.

20. Leviticus 23:42–43.

21. *Rosh Hashanah* 28a. See Urbach, op. cit., pp. 339 and 344.

22. *Avot* 4:16.

23. Rambam, *Hilkhot Teshuvah,* chap. 10.

24. *Sifrei* on Deuteronomy 11:22.

24a. *Nachlat Avot* on *Avot* 1:3. See also Malbim on Deuteronomy 6:18.

25. Psalms 112:1–2, *Avodah Zarah* 19a.

26. *Avot* 4:2.

27. *Nazir* 23b.

28. Jeremiah 9:22.

29. Psalms 1:1, Psalms 15.

30. *Avot* 6:8.

31. *Avot* 2:12.

32. *Berakhot* 57.

33. Quoted in ארץ חפץ by ישעיה שפירא p. ט‎"‎י‎.

34. Proverbs 30:9–10.

35. *Avot* 4:1.

36. Leviticus 6:11, *Ta'anit* 11a.

37. Talmud Yerushalmi, end of *Kiddushin*.

38. J. Guttmann, *Philosophies of Judaism* (New York: Holt, Rinehart & Winston, 1964), p. 15.

39. Kaufmann, *The Religion of Israel*, p. 331. Jonah 4:2, Genesis 15:16.

40. Jeremiah 12:1, Habakkuk 1:13.

According to Albo (*Ikkarim* 3:15), Asaph in Psalm 73 has already given all of the important answers to the problem of theodicy. If so, Albo asks, why did Jeremiah and Habakkuk, who came later, raise the old questions once again? To this he gives the following wise reply: "We might say that the matter was no longer a problem to the prophet, since Asaph had given the solution; but that they mentioned these two points because it gave them great pain when they saw with their own eyes wicked men prospering and righteous men suffering. For actual seeing of a thing causes more pain than mere knowing about it."

41. Kaufmann, op. cit., p. 338; Guttmann, op. cit., p. 15.

42. Deuteronomy 32:4.

43. See Rambam, *Hilkhot Teshuvah*, chap. 8, and his commentary on the Mishnah, *Sanhedrin, Chelek*.

44. *Kiddushin* 39b, *Pe'ah* 1:1, *Genesis Rabbah* 33:1.

45. The role of the resurrection of the dead in the scheme of Jewish eschatology is not very clear. Maimonides subordinated it to the concept of *olam ha-ba* viewed as an existence of the disembodied soul, which he saw as ultimate. In the Talmud we find the consideration that since the individual acts in life as an organic entity consisting of body and soul, he ought to be rewarded and punished as such. Abarbanel speaks of resurrection of the dead as the only truly convincing "mighty act" through which an omnipotent God can eventually bring about universal recognition of His truth by publicly vanquishing death. From another perspective, resurrection of the dead can be seen as the event which conflates the group *eschaton* with the individual *eschaton*. In the historical, empirical realm, God's plan is fulfilled with the Messianic redemption. For the many individuals who die before the advent of the Messiah, ultimate destiny is personal and metaphysical in terms of immortality and fellowship with God. Resurrection of the dead restores the righteous briefly to the historical realm to participate in the triumph of God in history at the "end of days."

It is perhaps in this vein that the blessing over the resurrection of the dead was included in that section of the *Amidah* called *gevurot*—"The mighty acts of God." For it is only in the fulfillment of the *eschaton*—the "end things"—in the *acharit ha-yamim,* "end of days," of both the nation and the individual that we have the clear vindication and manifestation of God's goodness and God's power—the ultimate solution to the dilemma of theodicy.

46. *Kiddushin* 39b.

47. Urbach, op. cit., p. 442.

48. *Yevamot* 121b.

49. *Berakhot* 5a, Proverbs 3:12.

50. *Avot* 4:19.

51. J. Hick, *Evil and the God of Love* (New York: Harper & Row, 1966), p. 369.

52. *Menachot* 29a.

53. *Avot* 3:19.

54. *Sifre* Deuteronomy 307.

55. See S. Spero, "Is the God of Maimonides Truly Unknowable?" *Judaism,* Winter 1973.

56. Hick, op. cit., pp. 360–361.

57. See *Genesis Rabbah* 9:2, 5–9; *Shabbat* 77b.

58. Urbach, op. cit., p. 92.

59. *Lamentations Rabbah* 1:45, Ber 3a.

60. See Maimonides, *Guide* 3:15 (Friedlander trans., p. 279).

61. Genesis 6:6. See *Genesis Rabbah* 27:4.

62. *Sanhedrin* 38b.

63. *Genesis Rabbah* 8:6, 8:5.

64. *Eruvin* 13b.

65. *Chullin* 60b. See Rashi on Genesis 1:16. See also Rashi on *Berakhot* 31b, where God admits bringing pain to man by having created the *yetzer ha-ra.*

66. See S. Spero, "Is Judaism an Optimistic Religion?" *Tradition,* Fall 1961.

67. Exodus 34:6,7.

68. Urbach, op. cit., p. 450.

69. *Genesis Rabbah* 12:15.

70. *Pesachim* 87b.

71. Urbach, op. cit., pp. 453–456.

72. *Rosh Hashanah* 17a.

CHAPTER 5   The Qualities of Jewish Morality

1. See Y. Kaufmann, "The Biblical Age," in *Great Ages and Ideas of the Jewish People,* ed. L. W. Schwarz (New York: Random House, 1956), p. 23.

2. Malachi 2:10. See H. M. Orlinsky, "Nationalism Universalism and Internationalism in Ancient Israel," in *Essays in Biblical Culture and Bible Translation* (New York: KTAV, 1974), 80–82. Orlinsky is correct in pointing out that the statement was uttered in a context wherein Malachi is referring not to all the peoples in the world but only to his own countrymen. However, the logic of the statement remains constant. That is to

say, since Judaism unequivocally does affirm in other texts that one God created all human beings, Malachi, as well as others who appreciate the logic, would have to acknowledge that the same moral inferences he drew for the people of Israel are to be drawn for all men. Perhaps the passage in Job 31:15 is less controversial: "Did not He that made me in the womb make him? And did not one fashion us in the womb?" See also Pines, op. cit., p. 55.

3. Genesis 6:13.

4. Deuteronomy 23:5.

5. Kaufmann, op. cit., p. 24.

The following was said by C. S. Lewis: "The third stage in religious development arises when the numinous power of which men feel awe is made the guardian of morality to which they feel obligation. . . . Perhaps only a single people, as a people, took the next step with perfect decision . . . for it was the Jews who fully and unambiguously identified the aweful Presence haunting the bleak mountain-tops and thunderclouds with the 'righteous Lord' who loveth righteousness" (*The Problem of Pain,* pp. 22–23).

6. See *Encyclopaedia Judaica,* vol. 6., col. 934, and Leo Baeck, *God and Man in Judaism* (New York: Union of American Hebrew Congregations, 1958), pp. 26–27.

7. A. J. Heschel, *The Prophets* (New York: Harper & Row, 1955), p. 3.

8. Amos 8:4–6.

9. Heschel, op. cit., p. 9.

10. Amos 8:7.

11. Habakkuk 2:6, 9, 11, 12.

12. Exodus 3:7.

13. By this we are to understand that God is involved in history—in the affairs of men—to a degree which is best described by saying that "He is affected" by the deeds of man. If Heschel's notion of "Divine Pathos" is taken too literally, it leads to theological problems. See E. Berkovits, "Dr. A. J. Heschel's Theology of Pathos," *Tradition* 6 (Spring—Summer 1964).

14. Exodus 22:26.

15. Heschel, op. cit., p. 16.

16. Genesis 18:2.

17. Genesis 18:7–8.

18. I. Efros, *Ancient Jewish Philosophy* (Detroit: Wayne State University Press, 1964), p. 85.

19. *Midrash Tehillim, Midrash Shocher Tov,* Psalm 110.

20. Here again is Efros (op. cit., pp. 148–149): "Biblical ethics is not staticism but activity . . . the chief thing is always the deed. Not to be but to do. . . . The Bible knows of a zealous God and a consuming fire and it demands moral zeal also from man, what we called the principle of involvement, the constant wakeful reaction to every crime committed somewhere in the world. . . . The restless mind of the Bible must look with astonishment at the marble faces of the Gods: Why are they so calm and why the happy smile on their faces? Would artists in ancient Israel even without the prohibition, have carved such faces? In the Hebrew divinity affliction and suffering would shine forth from its face."

21. H. L. A. Hart, *The Concept of Law,* p. 156.

22. M. G. Singer, *Generalization in Ethics* (New York: Knopf, 1961), chaps. 2 and 4.

23. Ibid., pp. 48–49.

24. *Avot* 3:18.

25. Leviticus 19:18.

26. Baeck, op. cit., p. 55.

27. Efros, op. cit., p. 92; see also Psalms 89:15, 97:2, Genesis 18:19, and Jeremiah 23:5.

28. Numbers 15:16.

29. Exodus 22:21.

30. Exodus 23:33 and Leviticus 19:15.

31. *Bava Metzia* 39b.

32. Leviticus 19:33–34.

33. Zephaniah 3:9. See also Isaiah 56:1–7 and 66:18–21.

34. E. Simon, "The Neighbor Whom We Shall Love," in *Modern Jewish Ethics,* ed. Marvin Fox (Columbus: Ohio State University Press, 1975), 29:55.

35. Compare Exodus 11:2, 2:13, 12:35, 3:21, with Deuteronomy 19:14.

36. Exodus 21:35.

37. Exodus 21:14.

38. Leviticus 19:16.

39. Leviticus 19:18.

40. *Bava Kamma* 37, 38; *Mekhilta* on Exodus 21:14.

41. Deuteronomy 23:8.

42. Deuteronomy 23:16–17, see Rashi.

43. Deuteronomy 24:14.

44. Rambam, *Hilkhot Gezelah* 1:1.

45. *Chullin* 94.

46. Leviticus 25:35. See Rashi.

47. See Rashi on Leviticus 26:1 and *Kiddushin* 20; also *Bava Metzia* 71.

48. *Avot* 1:12. The word *beriyot* denotes the entire human family and in some contexts includes the animal kingdom as well.

49. *Avot* 2:16.

50. *Avot* 4:1.

51. *Berakhot* 17a.

52. *Sifra, Acharei mot,* 13.

53. *Bava Kamma* 38a.

54. *Sanhedrin* 105a.

55. *Sha'arei ha-kedusha.*

56. See H. Fisch, "A Response to Ernst Simon," in *Modern Jewish Ethics,* ed. M. Fox; also E. Benamozegh, *Bi-Shevilei Musar* (Jerusalem: Mosad Harav Kook, 1966), pp. 118–120.

57. Deuteronomy 23:21, 15:3.

58. See Pines op. cit., p. 67, and Federbush, op. cit., p. 129. Compare *Bechorot* 13, for moral reasoning based on reciprocity.

59. Rambam, *Hilkhot Nizikei Mamon* 8:5.

60. *Shitah Mekubbetzet* on *Bava kamma* 38.

61. See discussion in J. Katz, *Exclusiveness and Tolerance* (Oxford, 1961), p. 116.

62. Genesis 9:5–6.

63. The Talmud (*Sanhedrin* 81b) relates how the rabbis had stringent requirements for witnesses and for warning (*hazharah*) in cases involving capital punishment which were designed to obviate the death penalty. They believed that since the judicial process, with its reliance on witnesses, did not yield certain knowledge, it was preferable to leave the matter to the justice of heaven when a person's life was at stake.

64. Leviticus 19:16.

65. *Hilkhot Rotze'ach* 4:2.

66. Ramban, *Mitzvah* 16 in *Sefer ha-Mitzvot* of Rambam.

67. See Albo, *Sefer ha-Ikkarim* (op. cit., 25 p. 237); also J. Steif, *Mitzvot ha-Shem*, p. 33.

68. Aaron Soloveitchik, "Jew and Jew, Jew and non-Jew," *Jewish Life*, May–June 1966, pp. 6–12.

69. Kaufmann, *The Religion of Israel*, p. 323 and footnote. See also *Sefer Ha-Chinnukh, Mitzvah* 83, where he says that from this *mitzvah* and from the reason given for the *mitzvah* (". . . for you were strangers . . ."), it follows that we ought to have compassion on every human being who finds himself in the anxious situation of being among strangers.

70. *Sifra Kedoshim* 4:12.

71. See Pines, op. cit., in his introduction; E. Simon, *Modern Jewish Ethics*, p. 37; and R. T. Herford, *Talmud and Apocrypha*, p. 44.

72. *Gittin* 61.

73. *Gittin* 59b.

74. *Yoreh De'ah*, 151:12.

75. Isaac Elchanan Spektor, *Nachal Yitzchak*, Declaration before his introduction to the book.

76. *Kiddushin* 31a.

77. Sanhedrin 106b.

78. *Avot* 3:12, 3:22.

79. *Avot* 1:17.

80. See *Kiddushin* 40b; Albo, *Ikkarim*, vol. III, p. 263.

81. Exodus 21:12 ff. We see that the Mishnah (*Keritot* 1) limited the need for a sin-offering for unintentional transgressions to thirty-six ritual violations between man and God, implying that for unintentional transgressions against one's fellow man there is no "sin" at all. Federbush, op. cit., p. 16.

82. *Pesachim* 50b.

83. *Kiddushin* 40a, except, of course, for the sin of idolatry.

84. See Albo, *Ikkarim*, vol. III, p. 255.

85. A. Kariv, *Shivas Amudei Ha-Tanakh*, p. 231.

86. Exodus 20:13, 20:14; see also Deuteronomy 5:18.

87. See *Sefer ha-Chinnukh, Mitzvah* 38. Even if one pays money for the object covet-

ed, if it was sold through any pressure against the will of the seller, one has violated the command "Thou shalt not covet." However, the *Chinnukh,* in *mitzvah* 416, following the Rambam (*Hilkhot Gezelah ve-Aveidah* 1:10–12), considers the *lo titaveh,* "Thou shalt not desire" in Deuteronomy 5:18 as prohibiting the desire alone even if it is not followed by any action designed to acquire the object.

88. *Avot* 4:28.

89. *Yoma* 29a, see Rashi.

90. Leviticus 25:36, *Ketubbot* 17a.

91. Although *kavvanah* is not required, the agent should be aware of performing an act of service to God. See *Orach Chayyim, Hilkhot Keriyat Shema.*

92. *Torat Kohanim, Kedoshim.*

93. *Avot* 2:4.

94. *Nazir* 23a. See *ha-Midrash ve-ha-Ma'aseh* on the portion of *Re'eh.*

95. See Rambam, Introduction to *Avot,* in his commentary on the Mishnah, chap. 6 of his *Eight Chapters.*

96. *Avot* 2:4.

97. See Rabbi Jonah Gerondi, *Sha'arei Teshuvah,* p. 28.

98. Deuteronomy 8:11, 9:4, 7:17, 20:1.

99. Deuteronomy 15:10.

100. Deuteronomy 15:7, Leviticus 19:18.

101. *Yoma* 23a.

102. Leviticus 19:17.

103. Deuteronomy 23:10, *Ketubbot* 46a.

104. Numbers 15:39.

105. Proverbs 6:16, 18.

106. Deuteronomy 15:9.

107. Deuteronomy 15:7.

108. Deuteronomy 22:1–3.

109. Leviticus 19:16.

110. Gerondi, *Sha'arei Teshuvah,* p. 68. Isaiah 58:7.

111. *Avot* 2:13.

112. *Avot* 2:15.

113. *Avot* 2:16.

114. *Avot* 4:4.

115. Psalms 51:12.

116. Psalms 24.

117. Proverbs 4:23.

118. *Avot* 2:13.

119. Deuteronomy 8:14.

120. Proverbs 16:5.

121. *Avodah Zarah* 20b; *Orchot Tzaddikim,* p. 13.

122. *Nedarim* 38a, *Berakhot* 43b, *Avot* 6:6.

123. Moses Chayyim Luzzatto, *Mesillat Yesharim,* p. 80.

124. Ibid., p. 44.

125. *Orchot Tzaddikim,* p. 23.

126. *Yoma* 86.

127. Rambam, *Hilkhot De'ot* 2:3.

128. *Avot* 4:12.

129. *Sotah* 5a.

130. I Samuel 15:17.

131. *Orchot Tzaddikim,* p. 14.

132. Ibid., pp. 8, 19.

133. See *Midrash Shemu'el* on *Avot* 2:1 by Rabbi S. Uceda. See also D. Katz, *Tenuat ha'Musar,* end of chap. 1, on the difference between the Chasidic and Musar movements.

134. Gerondi, *Sha'arei ha-Avodah.*

135. Commentary on Leviticus 19:18.

136. *Bava Metzia* 62.

137. *Avot* 4:1.

138. A. M. Amiel, "Ha-Tzedek ha-Sotziali ve-ha-Tzedek ha-Mishpati ve-ha-Musar Shelanu," in *Bain Adam le-Chavero* (Jerusalem: Mosad Harav Kook, 1975).

139. See comments of Ibn Ezra on Exodus 20:14.

140. *Avot* 5:13.

141. Proverbs 18:21.

142. Jeremiah 9:7.

143. *Arakhin* 15b.

144. I. M. Hakohen, *Shemirat-ha-Lashon* (New York: Shulsinger Bros., 1943). See first two chapters. See also *Targum Onkelos* on Genesis 2:7.

145. Jerusalem Talmud, *Pe'ah,* chap. 1.

146. See Rashi on Leviticus 13:46.

147. *Avot* 4:28.

148. *Pe'ah* 15d, *Arakhin* 15b.

149. Leviticus 19:11, 19:14, 19:16.

150. Exodus 23:7.

151. Deuteronomy 22:14.

152. Exodus 23:1.

153. Deuteronomy 23:10.

154. *Torat Kohanim* on Leviticus 19:17.

155. Leviticus 25:17, *Bava Metzia* 58b.

156. *Berakhot* 43, *Bava Metzia,* loc. cit.

157. Numbers 35:32, Isaiah 9.

158. I. M. Hakohen, *Sefer Chofetz Chayyim* (New York: Shulsinger Bros., 1943), p. 42.

159. *Avot* 1:15, 3:16, 12.

160. *Bava Batra* 9, *Taanit* 22a.

161. *Bava Batra* 165a.

162. *Megillah* 18a, *Pesachim* 99a, *Avot* 1:17.

163. *Bava Metzia* 49a.

164. S. Belkin, *In His Image,* p. 196.

165. *Kiddushin* 28b.

166. Rambam, *Hilkhot Mekhira* 22:17; *Yoreh De'ah* 256:6.

167. Numbers 30:3.

168. Psalms 145:9, Proverbs 12:10.

169. Genesis 9:9–17.

170. Psalms 147:9.

171. *Bava Metzia* 85a.

172. A. A. Harkavi, *Sefer Teshuvot ha-Geonim* (New York: Menorah, 1959), sec. 375, pp. 190–191.

173. *Bava Metzia* 32b, *Shabbat* 128b.

174. Activities such as the following, which are ordinarily forbidden on the Sabbath, are permitted for animals in order to relieve discomfort and pain: (1) using pillows and bedding to aid an animal that has fallen into a ditch; (2) certain materials ordinarily considered *muktseh* could be handled when being used as fodder for living creatures; (3) a non-Jew can be instructed to milk the cows on the Sabbath when not doing so would cause the animal pain; (4) an animal suffering from fresh wounds may be smeared with oils and salves. *Orach Chayyim,* Hilkhot Shabbat 324 and 332:2.

175. Exodus 23:5.

176. Deuteronomy 22:4.

177. *Rav Shulchan Arukh,* sec. 8.

178. Leviticus 22:27, Exodus 22:29.

179. *Deuteronomy Rabbah* 6:1; see also Maimonides, *Guide,* Friedlander trans., p. 360.

180. Leviticus 22:28. See *Chullin* 79a, *Yoreh De'ah* 15:2. This law applies to either the male or the female parent.

181. Maimonides, *Guide* 3:48.

182. Deuteronomy 22:6–7. See comments of Rashi on Exodus 19:4.

183. *Guide,* p. 372.
Any attempt to interpret the *mitzvah* of the "birds' nest" as an expression of God's mercy must deal with the difficult *mishnah* in *Berakhot* 33b: "If a man said in his prayers, 'To a bird's nest do Thy mercies extend,' they put him to silence." Maimonides sees the *mishnah* as following a general view that *mitzvot* ought not to be rationalized, a view which Maimonides himself rejects. Nachmanides distinguishes between having mercy on the animals for the sake of the animals per se, which he interprets the *mishnah* as rejecting, and having mercy on the animals in order to develop in human beings the quality of mercy, which he sees as the correct view. Others see the *mishnah* as irrelevant to the question of the actual reason for the commandment. Instead, it is viewed as an admonition about the proper expression to be used in prayer. In the public language of liturgy we must be cautious about making flat statements about God. In this case, the individual presumes to know the exact extent of God's mercies. It is for this reason that the *mishnah* advises that he be silenced.

184. Deuteronomyy 25:4.

185. Deuteronomy 22:10.

186. See *Exodus Rabbah* 31:7.

187. *Bava Metzia* 90b; Rambam, *Hilkhot Shekhirut* 13:3.

188. See Leviticus 19:19.

189. *Sefer Ha-Chinukh, mitzvah* 550.

190. See his comments on Deuteronomy 22:10. See also the interesting theory of the Ba'al ha-Turim (on Deuteronomy 22:10), who states that since the ox, as a kosher animal, ruminates constantly, while the ass, as a nonkosher animal, does not, it will appear to the ass that the ox is "eating" all day, and as a result it will become aggravated with envy.

191. Exodus 20:8–10, Deuteronomy 5:14.

192. Indeed, the early involvement of animals in the sacrificial ritual should be seen, at least from the perspective of man, not as a victimization of the beast but as a sort of compliment. In reality, it is man himself who should be on the altar. The acceptability before God of the animal as a surrogate for man reflects the high station that these living, sentient beings occupy on the ladder of life. This thought may also reverberate in the biblical narrative of Cain and Abel, wherein God accepts the animal sacrifice of Abel but not the offering of Cain, which consisted of agricultural produce.

193. Deuteronomy 11:15, *Gittin* 62a, *Berakhot* 40a.

194. Genesis 24:22–33.

195. *She'elot Ya'vetz* 1:17.

196. Exodus 21:28.

197. *Sanhedrin* 1:4, *Bava Kamma*, 24a; see also Ramban on Genesis 9:5.

198. Leviticus 20:15, Exodus 22:18.

199. *Sanhedrin, Mishnah* 7:4; also 54a.

200. *Avodah Zarah* 18b.

201. Josephus, *Antiquities* XV, 8:1.

202. *Nodah bi-Yehudah*, p. 48.

203. See J. Hurewitz, "The Care of Animals in Jewish Life and Lore," in *The Jewish Library,* ed. Leo Jung 1st Series (New York: Bloch, 1943), p. 113.

204. See *Guide* 3:48.

205. *Sanhedrin* 56a.

206. Rema, *Even ha-Ezer* 5:14. See also Responsa by J. M. Breisch, *Chelkat Ya'akov* 1:30, and article by A Haputin in *No'am* 4 (Jerusalem, 5721).

207. Isaiah 65:25.

208. Hosea 2:20.

209. Psalms 36:7.

210. Deuteronomy 24:10–11.

211. *Chagigah* 5a, *Kiddushin* 31a.

212. *Hilkhot De'ot* 6:10, *Bava Batra* 10b.

213. *Bava Batra* 2b, 6b.

214. Norman Lamm, "The Right of Privacy," in *Judaism and Human Rights* ed. Milton R. Konvitz (New York: Norton, 1972), p. 228.

215. Deuteronomy 25:11–12.

216. *Bava Kamma* 8:1 and 8:6.

217. The Mishnah (*Bava Kamma* 8:6) relates the following: "It once happened that a man unloosed a woman's hair in the street, and she came before Rabbi Akiva and he made the man liable for four hundred *zuz*. Said the culprit: 'Rabbi, extend for me the time.' And Rabbi Akiva extended for him the time of payment. The man watched for the woman standing before her courtyard and broke before her a cruse that held an *issur* worth of oil. She then unloosed her hair and scooped up the oil in her hand and laid her hand on her head. The man set up witnesses against her and came before Rabbi Akiva and said to him: 'Rabbi, should I give to such a one four hundred zuz?' Rabbi Akiva answered: 'Thou hast said nothing at all. For he who inflicts wounds upon himself, even though he is not permitted to do so, is not culpable, but if others wound him they are culpable.'"

219. *Avot* 2:15.

220. Deuteronomy 22:1.

221. *Bava Metzia* 30a–30b. See Rambam, *Hilkhot Gezelah ve-Avedah* 18:11. The rabbis in *Berakhot* 19–20 ruled that considerations of *Kavod ha-beriyot* cannot overrule a biblical negative command but oknly a rabbinical ordinance or a biblical positive command.

222. *Bava Kamma* 79b.

223. *Sifre Shoftim* 192.

224. Leviticus 6:18.

225. See C. W. Reines, *Torah u-Musar* (Jerusalem: Mosad Ha-Rav Kook, 5714), pp. 211–216. See also J. B. Soloveitchik "The Lonely Man of Faith," *Tradition,* Summer 1965, p. 13 note.

226. Genesis 49:6; Psalms 16:9, 30:13, 7:1, 13:10.

227. See his comments on Genesis 1:26.

227a. See "The Lonely Man of Faith," pp. 13–16.

228. *Kiddushin* 40b.

229. *Berakhot* 19b, *Shabbat* 81a, *Eruvin* 41b.

230. *Avot* 4:21.

231. Lamm, op. cit., p. 231.

232. Deuteronomy 21:22–23.

233. *Sanhedrin* 46b.

234. See *Megillah* 3b, *Berakhot* 2a. See also the discussion in E. Berkovits כוחה ההלכה (ותפקידה (מוסד הרב קוק ירושלים 1981), pages 105–108 as to whether the concept of *kavod ha-beriyot* can override a biblical law.

235. *Shabbat* 64b, *Yoma* 73a.

236. *Mo'ed Katan* 27b.

237. Psalms 147:19–20.

CHAPTER 6   Morality and Halakhah

1. See Menachem Elon, *Ha-Mishpat ha-Ivri* (Jerusalem: Magnes Press, 1975), 1:143, and C. Tchernowitz, *Toledot ha-Halakah* (New York, 1945), 1:23.

2. See the discussion in Elon, op. cit., p. 152.

3. See above, p. 43.

4. M. Silberg, op. cit., p. 83.

5. An example of this is the change that took place in the law regarding the extinguishing of a fire on the Sabbath (*Shulchan Arukh, Orach Chayyim* 334:26, Rema). While the Talmud and the *Shulchan Arukh* prohibited the extinguishing of fires on the Sabbath and permitted the rescue only of enough food and clothing for immediate use, the Rema remarks: "All of these aforementioned laws apply only in their day, but in our time, living among the non-Jews, the authorities have already ruled that fires may be extinguished on the Sabbath, because of the danger to lives which exists." An uncontrolled conflagration in the Jewish quarter or ghetto frequently resulted in looting and pillage and, if Jews resisted, rioting and death. The point is that an awareness of a generalized threat to the Jewish community was sufficient to set aside a well-established halakhic prohibition. See the discussion in Tzevi Hirsch Hayyot, Sefer Torat Nevi'im, *Darkhei ha-horaot* (Jerusalem, 1958), p. רכה.

6. *Bava Metzia* 30b.

7. Ibid. 52b and *Shabbat* 120a. See E. Berkovits, (ירושלים ותפקידה כוחה ההלכה 1981), pp. 102–105, where the author in his analysis of these different expressions used by the rabbis, claims that each expresison was applied to a somewhat different type of situation which called for a different level of moral response. In general, Berkovits follows the lead of Tosafot, to which we refer later.

8. Note the careful wording of the Ḥazon Ish, "Moral obligations are *sometimes* one corpus with the halakhic ruling" (chap. 3, of ועוד ובטחון אמונה עניני על איש חזון ספר, [תשי״ד ירושלים]).

9. See J. D. Bleich, "What Must a Jew Believe?," *Jewish Life,* 54, no. 1, for an attempt to place Jewish philosophy under the rubric of Halakhah.

10. See A. Lichtenstein, "Does Jewish Tradition Recognize an Ethic Independent of Halakha?" in *Modern Jewish Ethics,* ed. M. Fox (Columbus: Ohio State University Press, 1975), p. 68.

11. See above, p. 44.

12. Exodus 18:20; *Mekhilta, Yitro*; *Bava Kamma* 100.

13. *Sefer Mitzvot Katan.*

14. Deuteronomy 6:18; see Rashi.

15. Proverbs 2:20.

16. See Federbush, op. cit., p. 21.

17. A Donagan, *The Theory of Morality* (Chicago: University of chicago Press, 1977).

18. Introduction to *Derekh Chayyim,* by Rabbi Judah Loew of Prague. The talmudic teaching is in *Bava Kamma* 31.

19. See above Chapter 2.

20. *Avot* 3:1.

21. Rabbi Jacob Emden, in his opening comment in *Etz Avot.*

22. View of Obadiah Bertinoro in his commentary on the Mishnah.

23. Bachya Ibn Paquda, *Duties of the Heart,* pp. 213–217.

24. Genesis 1:28, Psalms 112:5.

25. Proverbs 23:20, 10:19, 24:4.

26. Proverbs 3:6.

27. Rambam, *Mishneh Torah, Hilkhot De'ot* 1:1.

28. Rambam, *Commentary on the Mishnah,* Introduction to *Avot,* chap. 4.

29. Tosafot, *Bava Metzia,* 24, *"Lifnim . . ."*

30. *Bava Metzia* 30b, *Bava Kamma* 100.

31. *Bava Metzia* 24b.

32. Ibid. 83a.

33. *Pe'ah* 1:1.

34. *Ketubbot* 50a.

35. Nachmanides on Leviticus 19:2 and Deuteronomy 6:18.

36. A. Lichtenstein's elegant translation is, "a scoundrel with Torah license."

37. See Rashi on Leviticus 19:1.

38. *Bava Metzia* 16a

39. *Choshen Mishpat* 175.

40. Silberg, op. cit., p. 103.

41. *Teshuvot Maimoniyot, Sefer Kinyan,* sec. 32 (quoted by Silberg).

42. *Hilkhot Shekhenim* 14:5.

43. Commentary of Rabbi Joseph Karo on *Mishneh Torah* of the Rambam. This comment is on *Hilkhot Shekhenim* 14:5.

44. See Elon, op. cit., 2:513.

45. See Federbush, op. cit., 18–19.

46. Ibid., pp. 20–21.

47. Maimonides, *Guide,* p. 392.

48. See the comprehensive discussion in Federbush, chaps. 6 and 7. I am indebted to him for these examples

49. *Ketubbot* 50, 69.

50. *Kiddushin* 32, *Yoreh Deah* 240.

51. *Bava Batra* 147, *Eruvin,* 49.

A. M. Amiel (*Bein Adam le-Chavero,* pp. 10–11) draws our attention to the discussion in *Bava Kamma* 20b, as to whether someone who "squats" on another's property which the owner is not using really has to pay rent! He also points to the Ran in *Nedarim* 85a as to whether others can freely help themselves to fruit belonging to someone who has taken a vow prohibiting himself from deriving any benefit from it. He infers that the rabbis did not seem to consider property or ownership rights as absolute in the sense that they could be used by themselves, in the absence of any other reason or purpose, simply to deprive others of the use of the said property. This attitude the rabbis associated with the evil Sodom.

52. For a listing of the sources, see Federbush, op. cit., pp. 84–85, and Elon, op. cit., 1:172–178.

53. Commentary of the *Bayit Chadash* (R. Joel Sirkes) on *Choshen Mishpat* 12:2.

54. Elon, op. cit., 1:173.

55. See the Me'iri on *Bava Kamma* 56a.

56. *Ketubbot* 77; see the comments of the Rosh.

57. Rema, *Even ha-Ezer* 154.

58. See Pines, op. cit., p. 66.

59. This is perhaps why the moral rules in the Decalogue are primarily negative.

60. Exodus 23:3, Psalms 62, *Chullin* 134.

61. *Ketubbot* 84.

62. *Avot* 5:13.

63. The Talmud and Rashi's comment on *Bava Metzia* 33a is most pertinent. The Gemara had asked the source of the teaching in the Mishnah that a man may save his own property before that of others. "Rav Judah said in the name of Rav, 'The Torah says, "Howbeit there shall be no needy among you" [Deut. 15:4]; yours, is before that of any man.' But Rav Judah also said in the name of Rav, 'He who fulfills this in himself [placing himself before all others] will in the end come to this condition [poverty].'" To which Rashi comments: "Although the Torah has not imposed it upon him, a person should enter 'within the measure of the law' and not insist what is mine comes first, unless an obvious loss is involved. For if he is constantly concerned about his own, he will throw off from himself the yoke of *gemilut chasadim* and *tzedakah*, and in the end he will become dependent upon others."

64. *Sanhedrin* 10.

65. *Avot* 1:2, 18.

66. Silberg, op. cit., pp. 89–91. I am deeply indebted to the late Justice Silberg for his insightful analysis of talmudic law in terms of "formalism" and "quantification" and for his many well-selected illustrations. However, drawing the implications of halakhic formalism for the question of *lifnim mi-shurat ha-din* is my own.

67. See the comment of Rashi on Exodus 21:1.

68. Deuteronomy 17:8–10.

69. Silberg, op. cit., p. 42.

70. *Ketubbot* 104a.

71. *Bava Batra* 23b.

72. *Bava Metzia* 24b.

73. Ibid. 51b, 52.

74. Ibid. 24b.

75. Shevu'ot 10:9.

76. *Shabbat* 120a.

77. *Bava Kamma* 55b, 56a; *mishnah* 6:4.

Jewish law distinguishes between *garme,* an act which, although indirect, will inevitably and necessarily lead to harm or damage for which the agent is held liable, and *gerama,* an act which in itself may or may not inflict damage, where the agent is not held liable by the human court.

78. The concept of causation in law and philosophy continues to defy precise formulation. See the readings in chap.6 of H. Morris, ed., *Freedom and Responsibility,* (Stanford, Calif: Stanford University Press, 1961).

79. See E. Berkovits, "The Concrete Situation and Halakhah," in *Crisis and Faith* (New York: (Sanhedrin Press, 1976), p. 84.

80. Deuteronomy 19:15.

81. *Gittin* 2b.

82. See discussion in Elon, op. cit., pp. 428–434.

83. *Yevamot* 88a, Tosafot *Nazir* 43b. The term *agunah* means "tied"; i.e. "tied forever to the man who disappeared."

84. In recent generations, rabbinic authorities such as Rabbi Isaac Elchanan Spektor of Kovno and the rabbinate of Israel have been successful with many problems of this kind working within the framework of Halakhah. See in Eliezer Berkovits, ההלכה כוחה ותפקידה, pp. 132–155, for a comprehensive discussion of the introduction between morality and Halakhah in the Jewish laws of marriage and divorce.

85. Deuteronomy 15:1–2.

86. Mishnah *Shevi'it* 10:3–4.

87. See discussion in Elon, pp. 418–420.

88. *Kiddushin* 28b.

89. *Sh'ma*, 10/192 (April 18, 1980).

90. *Kiddushin* 71a; see Berkovits, "The Concrete Situation and Halakhah," p. 89.

91. Proverbs 3:17.

92. *Gittin* 59b, *Nedarim* 62a.

93. M. Elon "Moral Principles as Halakhic Norms" *De'ot* 20 (5722): 62.

94. Leviticus 23:40.

95. *Sukkah* 32.

96. Deuteronomy 25:5.

97. *Yevamot* 87b.

98. See another case in *Yevamot* 13a.

99. See *Chokhmat Shelomoh* on *Yevamot* 87b.

100. *Bayit Chadash, Tur, Choshen Mishpat* 275.

101. *Gittin* 59a, *Avodah Zarah* 26a, *Bava Metzia* 32a, 10a, *Ketubbot* 58b.

102. E. Berkovits, ההלכה כוחה ותפקידה, 88.

103. Rambam, *Hilkhot Shabbat* 2:3.

CHAPTER 7   The Self and the Other

1. Leviticus 19:18.

2. *Shabbat* 31a, see also *Targum Jonathan ben Uzziel* on Leviticus 19:18.

3. See comments of Nachmanides and Malbim, on Leviticus 19:18.
The verb "to love" is usually used in the Hebrew in the accusative case (as in Deut. 6:5) with the article et, which denotes a more direct object, but in this case the object stands in the dative case (*le* . . .), which generally signifies a more indirect relationship. Thus, this passage should perhaps be translated as, "Be loving to thy fellow man" with the emphasis on deeds or works of love rather than emotions. Toward God one is directed to develop a more personal and intense love. See Rambam, *Hilkhot Teshuvah* 10:3.

4. Rambam, *Hilkhot De'ot* 6:3.

5. Rambam, *Hilkhot Aveil* 14:1.

6. *Sifra* on Leviticus 19:18.

7. *Bava Metzia* 62a.

8. *Ha-Ketav ve-ha-Kabbalah* (R. Jacob Meckleinburg) on Leviticus 19:18.

9. See Maharsha (R. Samuel Edels) on *Shabbat* 31a.

10. Attributed to N. H. Wesseley

11. See commentary of D. T. Hoffmann on Leviticus 19:18.

12. R. M. MacIver, "The Deep Beauty of the Golden Rule," in *Moral Principles of Action,* ed. R. N. Anshen (New York: Harper & Row, 1952).

13. M. G. Singer, *Generalization in Ethics* (New York: Knopf, 1961), p. 13; see also H. Sidgwick, *The Methods of Ethics* (Chicago: University of Chicago Press, 1962), chap. 5.

14. See K. Baier, *The Moral Point of View* (Ithaca, N.Y.: Cornell University Press, 1958).

15. See A. T. Cadoux, "The Implications of the Golden Rule," *International Journal of Ethics* 22 (1912), and J. D. Hertzler, "On Golden Rules," ibid. 44 (1934).

16. Matthew 7:12.

17. An echo of this bias is found in the following observation by John Stuart Mill: "In justice to the great Hebrew lawgiver, it should always be remembered that the precept of love thy neighbor as thyself already existed in the Pentateuch; and very surprising it is to find it there." (*Three Essays on Religion,* p. 98)

18. *Avot* 1:12.

19. C. W. Reines, "The Self and the Other in Rabbinic Ethics," in *Contemporary Jewish Ethics,* ed. M. M. Kellner (New York: Sanhedrin Press, 1978), p. 164.

20. Federbush, op. cit., pp. 41–42.

21. Psalms 34:15.

22. *Ahad Ha'am: Essays, Letters, Memoirs,* trans. and ed. Leon Simon (East-West Library, 1946), p. 136.

23. *Genesis Rabbah* 24.

24. Sidgwick, op. cit., pp. 379–380.

25. Ahad Ha'am, op. cit., pp. 132–133.

26. See Singer, op. cit., pp. 184–185.

27. Matthew 5:43.

28. Leviticus 19:17–18.

29. See Commentary of Abarbanel

30. *Berakhot* 10a.

31. Psalms 139:21–22.

32. *Shabbat* 115a. *Sefer ha-Chinnukh, mitzvah* 238; *Orchat Tzaddikim,* p. 44; Rambam, *Commentary on the Mishnah, Sanhedrin, Chelek.*

33. Exodus 23:5; *Pesachim* 113b; Rambam, *Hilkhot Rotze'ah* 13:14.

34. *Meshech Chokhmah* on Deuteronomy 22:4.

35. *Arakhin* 15.

36. *Avodah Zarah* 26b; Rambam, *Hilkhot Mamrim* 3:2.

37. Chazon Ish, *Yoreh De'ah* 13:16.

38. *Avot* 1:12, 2:16, 6:1, 6:6. See commentary *Lechem Shamayim* on *Avot* 1:12; see also Psalms 97:10. Buber notes: "Hate is by nature blind. Only a part of a being can be hated. He who sees a whole being and is compelled to reject it is no longer in the kingdom of hate, but is in that of human restriction of the power to say Thou." *I and Thou,* p. 16.

39. *Bava Metzia* 32b.

40. Proverbs 24:17–18.

41. See the discussion in E. Benamozegh, *Bi-Shevilei Musar* (Jerusalem: Mosad ha-Rav Kook, 1966), pp. 110–117, 130–133, 134–140.

42. Luke 10:25–37.

43. Deuteronomy 23:8.

44. *Sanhedrin* 72a.

45. Deuteronomy 23:15.

46. See Rabbi Shaul Yisraeli, *Amud ha-Yemini* (Tel Aviv, 5726), sec. I, chap. 16; Rabbi J. Gershuni, "The Redemption of Captives in the Light of Halakhah," *Hadarom* 33 (Nisan 5731).

47. A Response to M. Pail, "The Dynamics of Power: Morality in Armed Conflict After the Six Day War." See also the article by Z. Yaron in the same section in *Modern Jewish Ethics*, 227.

48. Genesis 9:5, Deuteronomy 4:9, Shevuot 36a, *Ta'anit* 22b, Rambam, *Hilkhot Rotze'ah* 11:4, *Yoreh Deah* 116.

49. Leviticus 19:16, *Sanhedrin* 73a.

50. See the very comprehensive discussion by Rabbi B. Wein, "Aspects of the Prohibition of Standing Idly by the Blood of Thy Neighbor," *Hadarom* 33 (Nisan 5731).

51. See the sources cited in the article by Rabbi Wein.

52. *Bava Metzia* 62a; *Sifra, Be-har* 5:3.

53. See Pines, op. cit., p. 70.

54. *Chazon Ish,* section on *Choshen Mishpat* and *Nezikin, Bava Metzia, Likutim,* item 20.

55. Rabbi Y. Weinberg, *Seridei Esh,* pt. I, p. 313.

56. Ahad Ha'am, op. cit., p. 132.

57. *Ketubbot* 50a.

58. *Pesachim* 25b, *Sanhedrin* 74a.

59. S. Belkin, *In His Image,* p. 183.

60. See discussion in Wein op. cit.

61. A. Donagan, *The Theory of Morality,* (Chicago: University of Chicago Press, 1977), p. 183.

62. *Bava Metzia* 71a; Rambam, *Hilkhot Matnot Aniyim* 7:13.

63. *Nedarim* 80b.

64. *Bava Metzia 33a.*

65. *See N. Samuelson in Sh'ma* 7/125.

66. Your father has given you existence in this world, but your teacher, who teaches you the Torah, brings you into the world-to-come, the world of eternal spirit. Of course, if your father has also taught you Torah, then he has priority.

67. Deuteronomy 15:16, *Bava Metzia* 62a; see the comments of Maharam Schiff.

68. L. Jacobs, "Greater Love Hath No Man," in Kellner, *Comtemporary Jewish Ethics,* p. 181.

69. S. Schwarzchild, *Shm'a* 7/134, 7/124.

70. John 15:13.

71. See Jacobs, op. cit., p. 181.

72. *Choshen Mishpat* 42b.

73. See J. J. Petuchowski, "The Limits of Self Sacrifice," and remark by N. L. Rabinovitch in Modern Jewish Ethics, p. 95.

74. Rabbi Kook, *Mishpat Kohen,* no. 143.

75. Jacobs, op. cit., p. 182.

76. See A. Kariv, *Mi-Sod Chakhamim,* p. 313, who suggests that in a real-life situation Rabbi Akiva himself would probably have acted in accordance with the ruling of Ben Petura. See his reference to S. Y. Agnon.

77. Leon Roth, *Judaism: A Portrait* (New York: Viking, 1961), p. 68.

78. Deuteronomy 6:5, see Rashi.

79. Leviticus 18:5, *Yoma* 85b.

80. See *Meshekh Chokhmah* on Exodus 31:14, who explains why desecration of the Sabbath is punishable by death even though the Sabbath was given to serve man and one may violate the Sabbath to save a life!

81. *Sanhedrin* 74a.

82. Leviticus 19:2.

83. Leviticus 22:32.

84. Exodus 38:21, 25:16; Deuteronomy 31:26.

85. Isaiah 43:10.

86. Leviticus 5:1, *Leviticus Rabbah* 6:5.

87. Rambam, *Hilkhot Yesodei ha-Torah* 5:11.

88. Ibid. 5:1–4.

89. *Lekhem Mishneh;* see the discussion by Y. Nachshoni in *Hagos be-Parshiyot ha-Torah,* vol. *Va-yikra,* pp. 614–615.

90. *Hilkhot Yesodei ha-Torah* 5:4; see *Kesef Mishneh.*

91. *Avodah Zarah* 27b, *Yoreh De'ah* 157:1; see Belkin, op. cit., p. 209.

92. "Whatsoever the Holy One, blessed be He, created in His world, He created but for His glory, as it is said: "Everything that is called by My name, it is for My glory, I have created it. I have formed it, yea, I have made it" [Isa. 43:7]." *Avot* 6:11.

93. Rabbi Kook, *Mishpat Kohen,* 142, 144.

94. Judges 5:18. There is the case of the martyrs of Lud (*Pesachim* 50a), where two brothers accepted the blame for a crime in order to save an entire community and were killed. Although the rabbis approved of this act of martyrdom to save an entire community, it is not clear evidence of the principle of self-sacrifice for *Kelal Yisrael,* because it seems from the story that had they not done so, they would have died anyway, with the rest of the community.

95. Rambam, *Hilkhot Melakhim* 5:1.

96. S. Gorin, *Machanayim,* no. 21.

97. See the sources in Rabbi S. Y. Zevin, *Le'or ha-Halakhah* (Tel Aviv 1964), "Ha-Milchamah," chap. 7, pp. 16–17.

98. Rav Kook, *Mishpat Kohen,* loc. cit.

99. S. Belkin, op. cit., p. 120.

100. Deuteronomy 13:11–12, 17:13, 21:21.

101. Nachmanides on Deuteronomy 21:21.

102. *Kuzari,* 3:19.

103. *Sanhedrin* 44. See the comments of *Meshekh Chokhmah* on Numbers 25:11. See Tosafot, *Yevamot* 103, which indicates that Esther submitted to the king in order to save the Jewish people.

104. M. L. Shachor, *Avnei Shoham*

105. See *Berachot* 10a. Isaiah told Hezekiah he was being punished because he had not married, to which Hezekiah responded: "It was because I foresaw through the Divine Spirit that bad children will come forth from me." Isaiah said: "What have you to do with the secret of the Almighty? Whatever *you* are commanded to do, you ought to fulfill, and whatever pleases the Holy One, praised be He, let *Him* do."

CHAPTER 8   Freedom and Responsibility

1. See B. A. O. Williams, "Freedom and the Will," in *Freedom and the Will,* ed. D. F. Pears (New York: Macmillan, 1966), pp. 2–3.

2. There are several commentators who, like Sforno, see the concept of man created in "the image of God" as referring primarily to man's unique gift of freedom of the will. See the *Meshekh Chokhmah* on Genesis 1:26 that man's freedom involves a self-limitation on the part of God. The plentitude of Divinity must "withdraw" to make room for the world; so too must the will of God "restrain" itself to make room for human choices and decisions. The word *tzelem,* usually rendered "image" or "form," may be related to *tzel,* meaning "shadow." A shadow is an area empty of the light, blocked out by the body. Man (*tzelem*) exists in the "shadow" of God; i.e., he operates in a "free zone" in which God voluntarily refrains from exercising His complete sovereignty.

3. Y. Kaufmann, *The Religion of Israel,* trans. M. Greenberg (Chicago: University of Chicago Press, 1960), p. 329.

4. Ibid., p. 76.

5. Genesis 3:12–13.

6. Genesis 4:5.

7. Genesis 4:6.

8. Genesis 4:8.

9. *Genesis Rabbah* 22:28.

10. Deuteronomy 30:19.

11. Lamentations 3:38.

12. Deuteronomy 5:26.

13. Numbers 35:30.

14. Numbers 35:1–34, Deuteronomy 19:4–7.

15. See Ramban and Sforno.

16. Mishnah *Bava Kamma* 8:4.

17. *Eruvin* 65a.

18. Rambam, *Chovel u-Mazik* 1:5, 11.

19. *Eruvin* 64a.

20. *Gittin* 23a.

21. See the discussion in G. Libson, "Criminal Liability of the *Shikur* in Jewish Law," *Din Israel* 3 (Tel Aviv University, 1972): 71–89.

22. Deuteronomy 22:25–26.

23. *Makkot* 10b.

24. *Bava Kamma* 26.

25. Belkin, op. cit., pp. 211–213.

26. *Chovel u-Mazik* 5:9.

27. See Belkin, *In His Image,* and Rambam, ibid. 6:3–4.

28. *Berakhot* 33b.

29. *Niddah* 16b.

30. *Sanhedrin* 38a.

31. *Antiquities* 18:13.

32. Genesis 42:28.

33. Proverbs 19:3, *Ta'anit* 9a.

34. Williams, op. cit., p. 5.

35. While man experiences a sense of freedom in important matters, where he agonizes over the question and weighs the pros and cons, he is also very conscious of his control in very trivial matters, where there are really no reasons or pressures either way; where it makes no difference. Here the decision is quite arbitrary, so that I do it *this* way simply because *I choose* to do it this way.

36. Martin Luther, *The Bondage of the Will,* in *Martin Luther: Selections* (New York: Doubleday Anchor Books, 1961).

37. It has been suggested that when Cain replied to God's question as to the whereabouts of his brother Abel, with the brazen, "Am *I* my brother's keeper?" he meant to imply: "After all, God—aren't *you* really the keeper of all the brothers who are your children? If you are the Creator and possess the power and the goodness; then surely it is your responsibility to protect the innocent from the likes of me!"

38. See, for example, Albo, *Ikkarim* 4:5.

39. Psalms 115:16.

40. Genesis 50:20.

41. See Maimonides, *Guide,* 3:17; see also note 99 on Chap. 2:4 of Guttmann, *Philosophies of Judaism.*

42. *Makkot* 10b

43. *Shabbat* 104a, *Yoma* 39a.

44. Rambam, *De'ot,* 5:4; see his letter to the community of Marseilles.

45. Deuteronomy 2:30, Joshua 11:20.

46. Rambam, *Hilkhot Teshuvah* 6:3.

47. See Abarbanel.

48. *Avot* 3:19.

49. *Hilkhot Teshuvah* 5:5; see comment of Ra'avad.

50. *Guide,* p. 295.

51. See *Or Same'ach,* pt. I, on *Hilkhot Teshuvah* 4:4, also *Tosafot Yom Tov* on *Avot* 3:19, discussion by N. L. Rabinovitch in *Peirush Yad Peshutah,* comment of Nachmanides on Exodus 3:13.

Imagine a person in 1980 getting into an H. G. Wells time machine which projects him into 1990, where he witnesses A killing B and then returns to tell us about it. Can the murderer after his crime in 1990 claim he was "compelled" to do it because of this foreknowledge?

52. R. L. Purtill, "Foreknowledge and Fatalism," *Religious Studies,* 10, no. 3 (Septemper 1974): p. 323.

53. D. P. Lackey, "A New Disproof of the Compatibility of Foreknowledge and Free Choice," *Religious Studies,* 10, no. 3 (September 1974).

54. S. T. Davis, "Divine Omniscience and Human Freedom," *Religious Studies* 15, no. 3 (September 1979).

55. J. Sachs in a recent article ("Philosophy and the Language of Religion," *Proceedings of the Association of Orthodox Jewish Scientists* 3:4 [1976]) attempts to use the problem of free will as the example of how Wittgenstein's observations about different "language games" can "disolve" some classic problems in philosphy of religion (see my review article in *Tradition* 9, no. 4, "Does the Science-Religion Conflict Rest on a Mistake?"). He concludes, "This then is the reconciliation of divine omniscience and providence with human freedom. Freedom is a reality from our point of view, especially bound as we are in time: it is not a reality from a vantage point outside of time (God's) and neither of these aspects is false." But this is no better than Kant's formula that the self as noumena is free while the empirical self as phenomenon is subject to causality. Besides what Sachs forgets is that in Judaism, it is precisely God who tells us that also from *His* point of view (reward-punishment, accountability) human freedom is a reality.

56. Hosea 14:2-3.

57. Deuteronomy 4:30-31.

58. Deuteronomy 30:11-14.

59. *Deuteronomy Rabbah* 11, 12; Ezekiel 33:11; *Kiddushin* 40b.

60. Isaiah 55:7.

61. See Baeck, op. cit., p. 48.

62. Malachi 3:7.

63. *Hilkhot Teshuvah* 2:2.

64. *Al ha-Teshuvah,* ed., P. Peli (Jewish Agency, 5735), pp. 191-259.

65. Compare I Samuel 25: ". . . in the morning when the wine had left him."

66. *Hilkhot Teshuvah* 7:7.

67. See M. H. Spero, "Perspective on the Yetzer ha-Ra," in *Judaism and Psychology: Halakhic Perspectives* (New York: Yeshivah University Press, 1980), pp. 64-82.

68. *Sukkah* 52a.

69. *Yoma* 29 on Psalms 22.

70. See Tosafot in *Berakhot* 46a.

71. See the discussion in I. Hutner, *Pachad Yitzchak,* vol. on Yom Kippur, *ma'amar* 13.

72. John Stuart Mill.

73. J. Hospers, "Free Will and Psychoanalysis," in *The Problem of Free Will,* ed. W. F. Enteman (New York: Scribner's, 1967). See also Spero, op. cit., chap. 3.

74. F. H. Bradley, *Ethical Studies* (London: Oxford University Press, 1927), p. 3.

75. C. A. Campbell, "Is 'Free Will' a Pseudo-Problem?" in *A Modern Introduction to Philosophy,* ed. P. Edwards and A. Pap, Glencoe, Ill.: 1960), p. 368.

76. W. T. Stace, "The Problem of Free Will," in *Philosophy and Contemporary Issues,* ed. J. R. Burr and M. Goldinger (New York: Macmillan), p. 27.

77. M. Schlick, *Problems of Ethics* (New York: Dover, 1962), p. 153.

78. Campbell, op. cit.

79. M. Mandelbaum, "Determinism and Moral Responsibility," *Ethics,* 1960.

80. H. L. A. Hart, "Legal Responsibility and Excuses," in *Determinism and Freedom in the Age of Modern Science,* ed. S. Hook (New York University Press, 1958).

81. P. H. Nowell-Smith, *Ethics* (Penguin, 1954).

82. J. L. Austin, "Ifs and Cans—A Plea for Excuses," in *Freedom and Responsibility,* ed. H. Morris (Stanford University Press, 1961).

83. Nowell-Smith, op. cit., p. 275.

84. D. Browning, "The Feeling of Freedom," in *The Problem of Free Will,* ed. W. F. Enteman (New York: Scribner's 1967), p. 237.

85. J. Howie, "Is Effort of Will a Basis for Moral Freedom?" *Religious Studies* 8, no. 4 (December 1972).

86. P. D. Gosselin, "C. A. Campbell's Effort of Will Argument," *Religious Studies* 13, no. 4

87. F. Ferré, "Self-Determinism," in *Philosophy and Contemporary Issues,* ed. J. R. Burr and M. Goldfinger (New York: Macmillan), p. 38.

88. S. Freud, *General Introduction to Psychoanalysis* (Garden City, N. Y., 1938), p. 95.

89. I. Pavlov, *Lectures on Conditioned Reflexes* (New York: International Publishers, 1941), 2:144.

90. R. Blatchford, "The Delusion of Free Will," in *Philosophy and Contemporary Issues,* ed. Burr and Goldinger, p. 16.

91. A. Castell, *The Self in Philosophy* (New York: Macmillan, 1965), pp. 68–69.

92. W. D. Ross, *Foundations of Ethics* (Oxford: Clarendon Press, 1939), p. 327.

93. See J. Grunblatt, "Freedom of the Will—A Traditional View," *Tradition* 10, no. 4.

94. Deuteronomy 21:18–21.

95. Campbell, op. cit.

96. W. I. Matson, "On the Irrelevance of Free-Will," *Mind,* 1956.

97. Gosselin, op. cit., p. 430.

98. See the comment of the Rema on *Shulchan Arukh, Orach Chayyim* 6:1.

99. Genesis 39:7–12.

100. W. James, "Will," in *Freedom and Responsibility,* ed. H. Morris (Stanford University Press, 1961), p. 82.

101. Compare the following from *The Dilemma of Determinism* by William James: What is meant by saying that my choice of which way to walk home after the lecture is ambiguous and matter of chance as far as the present moment is concerned? It means that both Divinity Avenue and Oxford Street are called; but that only one, and that one *either* one, shall be chosen. Now, I ask you

seriously to suppose that this ambiguity of my choice is real; and then to make the impossible hypothesis that the choice is made twice over, and each time falls on a different street. In other words, imagine that I first walk through Divinity Avenue, and then imagine that the powers governing the universe annihilate ten minutes of time with all that it contained, and set me back at the door of this hall just I was before the choice was made. Imagine then that, everything else being the same, I now make a different choice and traverse Oxford Street. You, as passive spectators, look on and see the two alternative universes—one of them with me walking through Oxford Street. The other with the same me walking through Divinity Street. Now, if you are determinists you believe one of these universes to have been from eternity impossible: you believe it to have been impossible because of the intrinsic rationality or accidentality somewhere involved in it. But looking outwardly at these universes, can you say which is the impossible and accidental one, and which the rational and necessary one? I doubt if the most ironclad determinist among you could have the slightest glimmer of light on this point. In other words, either universe *after the fact* and once there would, to our means of observation and understanding, appear just as rational as the other. There would be absolutely no criterion by which we might judge one necessary and the other matter of chance. Suppose now we relieve the gods of their hypothetical task and assume my choice, once made, to be made forever. I go through Divinity Avenue for good and all. If, as good determinists punctually do affirm, that in the nature of things I couldn't have gone through Oxford Street—had I done so, it would have been chance, irrationality, insanity, a horrid gap in nature—I simply call your attention to this, that your affirmation is what the Germans call a Machtspruch, a mere conception fulminated as a dogma and based on no insight into details. Before my choice, either street seemed as natural to you as to me. Had I happened to take Oxford Street, Divinity Avenue would have figured in your philosophy as the gap in nature; and you would have so proclaimed it with the best deterministic conscience in the world.

102. C. S. Lewis, *Miracles,* p. 61. Also see the *Sefat Emet* on *Va-yeira,* where he relates *nes* (miracle) to *nisayon* (moral test) in that both involve a transcending of nature.

103. Numbers 28:19, *Yalkut Shimoni* 782 on Numbers 29:2.

104. For this thought I am indebted to Israel Efros, *Ancient Jewish Philosophy* (Detroit: Wayne State University Press, 1964), pp. 120 and 132.

105. C. A. Campbell, "In Defense of Free-Will," in *A Modern Introduction to Ethics,* ed. M. K. Munitz (Glencoe, Ill.: Free Press, 1958), p. 386.

106. Thus we follow with interest the debate between the defenders of the "steady state" theory and the "big bang" theory as to the origin of the universe. To be sure, the truth of Judaism does not depend on the outcome of this debate. That is to say, the vindication of one or the other theory would not prove or disprove the theistic position. However, the "big bang" theory, which states that the universe as we know it today had, in some sense, a beginning in time in a cataclysmic explosion, with matter

expanding from this initial explosion and being transformed, by laws known to us today, to form our present-day stars and galaxies, is certainly more consistent with the Torah doctrine of creation. Phenomena discovered during the past two decades have been interpreted as evidence in support of the "big bang" theory, so that scientists refer to it today as the "standard model" of the early universe. The scientists, of course, cannot go beyond that primeval explosion. They cannot tell us what or who caused the explosion. They cannot tell us who or what put the matter or energy into the universe or whether the universe was created out of nothing or out of some preexisting material. Scientific inquiry would seem to end at this "big bang" because the force of the exploding fire-ball must have destroyed any traces of what might have been before. The point of mystery before which science must pause is for the religionist the exact location where he expects to find mystery, for behind it is God. Dr. Arno Penzias, one of the Nobel Prize laureates who discovered the traces of the original radiation emanating from the "big bang," said in an interview: "My argument is that the best data we have are exactly what I would have predicted had I had nothing to go on but the five Books of Moses, the Psalms, the Bible as a whole." And as Robert Jastrow concludes: "For the scientist who has lived by his faith in the power of reason, the story ends like a bad dream. He has scaled the mountains of ignorance; he is about to conquer the highest peak; as he pulls himself over the final rock, he is greeted by a band of theologians who have been sitting there for centuries" (*New York Times*, March 12, 1978; *New York Times Magazine*, June 25, 1978). S. Weinberg, *The First Three Minutes*, (New York: Basic Books, 1977); Z. Zahavy, *Whence and Wherefore* (New York: Barnes, 1978).

107. See S. Spero, "Israel in Eschatological Perspective," in *The Religious Dimensions of Israel* (Synagogue Council of America, 1968).

108. See the references in I. G. Barbour, *Issues in Science and Religion* (Englewood Cliffs, N.J.: Prentice-Hall, 1966), pp. 348–351.

109. H. J. Campbell, "Pleasure-Seeking Brains," *Smithsonian*, October 1971.

110. *Beyond Freedom and Dignity.*

111. *New York Review of Books*, December 30, 1971.

112. Noam Chomsky, *Reflections on Language* (New York: Pantheon, 1975), pp. 12, 40.

113. Genesis 2:7.

114. "Man is unique in his world as God is unique in His" (*Genesis Rabbah* 21:5). See also *Meshekh Chokhmah* on Leviticus 19:18.

115. I have deliberately not included in our discussion of freedom of will the developments that have taken place in physics in connection with the uncertainty principle enunciated by W. Heisenberg in 1927. While some have argued that this discovery destroys the position of determinism at least on the micro-physical level and is therefore supportive of the concept of free will, others have interpreted the data differently. They argue that the uncertainty principle represents a temporary epistemological difficulty which may someday be overcome. In any case, the difficulty we have today in predicting the behavior of an electron has no clear metaphysical implications for the free will–determinism issue. Because of the inconclusive nature of the discussion, I have not

referred to it in the text. For balanced discussions of the issue, see Enteman, "Micro-Physics and Free-Will," and Barbour, op. cit., pp. 273–317.

116. *Avot* 3:1.

CHAPTER 9   Systemic Aspects of Jewish Morality

1. A. K. Bierman and J. A. Gould, *Philosophy for a New Generation,* 2 ed. (New York: Macmillan, 1973), p. 80.

2. See above, Chapter 2.

3. See above Chapter 3.

4. C. Tchernowitz, *Toledot ha-Halakhah* (New York: 1945), 1:151–152; see also N. Bronznick, "The Significance of Rational Interpretation of *Mitzvot* in Rabbinic Thought," *Or Hamizrach* (Fall 1980): p. 134.

5. M. Elon, *Ha-mishpat ha-Ivri* (Jerusalem: Magnes Press, Hebrew University, 1973), 1:223–228.

6. Albo, *Ikkarim* 3:23 p. 203.

7. J. S. Mill, *Utilitarianism,* Everyman's Library ed. (New York: Dutton, 1910), p. 23.

8. M. G. Singer, *Generalization in Ethics* (New York: Knopf, 1961), p. 103.

9. See above Chapter 2.

10. Tchernowitz, op. cit. p. 151.

11. Tzevi Hirsch Chajes, *Mevo ha-Talmud,* chap. 4. See also E. Berkovits, op. cit., pp. 24–33.

12. *Ketubbot* 22, *Bava Kamma* 46b.

13. See Rashi on Exodus 38:22, where it is stated that Bezalel, taking a position in accord with *minhag ha-olam,* correctly judged what God had actually instructed Moses.

14. C. Wellman, *Morals and Ethics* (Glenview, Ill.: Scott, Foresman, 1975), p. 301.

15. *Bava Kamma* 46b. See Elon, op. cit., 2:805–808.

16. *Pesachim* 25b.

17. *Ketubbot* 22a. A revealing indication of the high regard in which the rabbis held the concept of *sevarah* is the law that one owes greater respect to the rabbi from whom one learned *chokhmah,* which Rashi defines as "*sevarah* and the reasoning of the Mishnah" (*Bava Metzia* 33a).

18. Actually there are two types of *sevarah* used in the Talmud; one is the self-evident type, while the other simply means "a reasoned argument" and may be rejected by one of the disputants. See L. Jacobs, *Studies in Talmudic Logic and Methodology* (London: Vallentine, Mitchel, 1961), p. 37.

19. *Mishneh Torah, Hilkhot Avel* 14:1; see also *Sefer ha-Chinnukh* on Leviticus 19:18.

20. Fred Rosner, *Modern Medicine and Jewish Law* (New York: Yeshiva University Press, 1972), pp. 28–29.

21. Deuteronomy 4:9, 4:15.

22. *Rotze'ah* 11:4.

23. *Yoreh De'ah* 116:5.

24. Tchernowitz, op. cit., pp. 102–104.

25. *Bava Kamma* 28b.

26. Abraham Edel, *Science and the Structure of Ethics* (Chicago: University of Chicago Press, 1961), p. 75.

27. R. G. Olson, *Meaning and Argument* (New York: Harcourt Brace, 1969), pp. 297–299.

28. *Bava Metzia* 28a

29. Deuteronomy 22:2; see Tchernowitz, op. cit., 1:162–163.

30. *Bava Metzia* 32b.

31. *Gittin* 59b.

32. M. Mielziner, *Introduction to the Talmud,* 4th ed. (New York: Bloch, 1968), p. 119.

33. Elon, op. cit., 2:244–446.

34. Ibid., p. 261.

35. Deuteronomy 24:12–13.

36. Deuteronomy 24:17.

37. *Bava Metzia* 115a.

38. Based on Exodus 21:22–23 and Leviticus 24:17.

39. Mishnah *Ohalot* 7:6, *Arakhin* 1:4.

40. *Yevamot* 69b.

41. See the sources and discussion in Rosner, op. cit., chaps. 4 and 5, and in J. D. Bleich, "Abortion in Halakhic Literature," in *Jewish Bioethics,* ed. F. Rosner and J. D. Bleich (New York: Sanhedrin Press, 1971), p. 134.

42. This method of "categorization," a term used by Rabbi Bleich is similar to the type of reasoning utilized by lawyers and judges in courts of law where it sometimes happens that there is agreement as to the facts but a question as to whether certain behavior constitutes "reasonable care," whether or not a ledger is a "document," and whether a certain institution was or was not a "public authority." John Wisdom points out that this sort of argument is not a chain of demonstrative reasoning but rather "a presenting and representing of those features of the case which *severally cooperate* in favor of the conclusion . . . in favor of calling the situation by the name by which he wishes to call it. The reasons are like the legs of a chair not the links of a chain. . . . And because the premises are severally inconclusive the process of deciding the issue becomes a matter of weighing the cumulative effect of one group of severally inconclusive items against the cumulative effect of another group of severally inconclusive items and thus lends itself to description in terms of conflicting 'probabilities' . . . the solution of the question at issue is a decision. A ruling by the judge . . . and though the decision manifests itself in the application of a name it is no more *merely* the application of a name than is the pinning of a medal *merely* the pinning on of a bit of metal."

43. See the responsa of Rabbi Isaac ben Sheshet Perfet, no. 239, and Rabbi Asher ben Yehiel (17:1) in *Jewish Law and Jewish Life: Selected Rabbinical Responsa,* ed. J. Bazak (New York: Union of American Hebrew Cong., 1979), pp. 209, 213, 219.

44. Leviticus 19:16, *Sanhedrin* 73a.

45. *Bava Kamma* 117a.

46. Tradition asserts that these thirteen *middot* were themselves given to Moses at Sinai. (*Sanhedrin* 99a)

47. See the controversy Between Maimonides and Nachmanides on the status of laws derived from the thirteen *middot*; *Sefer ha-Mitzvot, shoresh sheni.*

48. Beginning of *Sifra, Torat Kohanim*; we use here the translation of J. J. Hertz in *The Authorized Daily Prayer Book,* p. 43.

49. Elon, op. cit., 2:271.

50. Exodus 22:9.

51. Elon. op. cit., 2:280.

52. Deuteronomy 22:1–3.

53. Mishnah *Bava Metzia* 2:5.

54. Sanhedrin 86a.

55. Exodus 21:16, Deuteronomy 24:7, Leviticus 19:11.

56. Elon, op. cit., p. 284.

57. Leviticus 19:13.

58. Deuteronomy 24:14–15.

59. *Bava Metzia* 110b.

60. Exodus 23:4–5.

61. Elon, op. cit., pp. 286–287.

62. Deuteronomy 22:25–27.

63. *Sifra* 243.

64. Deuteronomy 24:6.

65. Mishnah, *Bava Metzia* 9:13.

66. Elon, op. cit., p. 289.

67. *Sanhedrin* 74a.

68. See Rashi on Exodus 6:12, *Genesis Rabbah* 92:7.

The *kal va-chomer* pattern of reasoning occurs altogether in the Bible about twenty times, ten of which may be found in the wisdom literatures, six in Proverbs, and four in Job. Generally the argument follows a structure in which the major premise is based either on an event known to have occurred or on some well-known maxim which is assumed to be self-evident.

M. Paran ("The A Fortiori Pattern in the Book of Proverbs," *Beth Mikra* 73 [Jerusalem: World Jewish Bible Society, p. 221] shows how all of the uses of *kal va-chomer* in Proverbs have as their premise a maxim which occurs elsewhere in our wisdom literature and that the word or phrase which connects the premise to the conclusion is always the same: *af* or *af ki.* The following are two instances of the use of *kal va-chomer* in Proverbs for a moral teaching: "Overbearing speech becometh not a churl; much less do lying lips, a prince" (Prov. 21:27); "The sacrifice of the wicked is an abomination; how much more when he bringeth it with the proceeds of wickedness" (Prov. 17:17).

69. Genesis 44:8.

70. *Chullin* 142.

71. Jacobs, op. cit., p. 3.

72. Ibid., pp. 4–5.

73. See the entry by Jacobs in the *Encyclopaedia Judaica,* s.v. "Hermeneutical Rules."

74. Mielziner, op. cit., p. 130.

75. Ibid., p. 251.

76. Ibid., p. 130.

77. How would we transpose the *kal va-chomer* used by the brothers of Joseph referred to earlier? Here only one step appears necessary, because unlike the previous *kal va-chomer,* which involved two sets of elements, effort and expense/divine reward and SFM/WM, this one deals with only two elements.

(1) There are two moral traits, X (refusing to keep strange valuables found in one's possession) and Y (not stealing valuables from another's possession), which are related in such a way that if A has X then A has Y.

(2) The brothers of Joseph have X.

(conclusion) The brothers of Joseph have Y.

Our final example will be of a complex *kal va-chomer* used in the Talmud to derive an important law regarding the responsibilities of *shomrim* (bailees) who undertake to take care of things belonging to others. The rabbis distinguished between different types of bailees—the borrower, the gratuitous bailee, the bailee-for-hire—and their different degrees of responsibility. The Torah states that the borrower must pay if the object breaks or the animal dies. However, asks the Talmud, what is the law if the object is stolen or lost? This, replies the Talmud, can be derived by means of a *kal va-chomer* from the law of the bailee-for-hire. If a keeper for a fee, who does not pay in case of breakage or death, does, in fact, pay in case of theft or loss, then a borrower, who does pay in case of breakage or death, must certainly pay for theft or loss.

In this instance, the factor that makes A "more severe" than B is not assumed or considered self-evident but is supplied.

I.

(1) Liability X (for death and damages) is related to liability Y (for theft and loss) in such a way that if a certain type of bailee, A, is considered more responsible than bailee B in regard to liability X, then A is also more responsible than B in regard to liability Y.

(2) The borrower is more responsible than the bailee-for-hire in regard to X.

(conclusion) The borrower is more responsible than the bailee-for-hire in regard to liability Y.

II.

(1) The borrower is more responsible than the bailee-for-hire in regard to theft and loss.

(2) The bailee-for-hire must pay in case of theft and loss.

(conclusion) The borrower must (certainly) pay in case of theft and loss.

78. See Mielziner, op. cit., pp. 137–139.

79. Elon, op. cit., p. 295.
80. *Niddah* 19b, *Sukkah* 11b.
81. Exodus 21:26–27.
82. *Mekhilta* 9:96.
83. *Kiddushin* 25a.
84. Jacobs, op. cit., p. 12.
85. Exodus 21, 22.
86. Mishnah *Bava Kamma* 1:1.
87. Elon, op. cit., p. 302; see also *Talmudic Encyclopedia* (Heb.), s.v. *hekaish* (vol. 10), *gezeirah shavah* (vol. 5), and *binyan av* (vol. 4). See. also Rashi on *Sanhedrin* 73.
88. Deuteronomy 19:14.
89. Deuteronomy 27:17.
90. Hosea 5:10, Proverbs 22:28.
91. Mishnah *Bava Metzia* 4:12, *Bava Batra* 21b.
92. *Kiddushin* 49a.
93. Responsa Maharshal, no. 89.
94. See entry on *hassagat gevul* in *Encyclopaedia Judaica*, written by M. Elon.
95. Exodus 20:3.
96. Leviticus 19:13.
97. Leviticus 19:11.
98. Leviticus 25:14.
99. *Mekhilta, Mishpatim* 13.
100. *Chullin* 94.
101. See the sources in E. Shohatman, "Consumer Protection in the Halakhah," *Dine Israel* 3, p. 227. See also Rabbi Jonah Gerondi, *Sha'arei Teshuvah* 3:184, and Ritva, novellae on *Chullin* 94.
102. Elon, op. cit., pp. 344–347.
103. Responsum 85.
104. Responsum 78.
105. Responsum 7.
106. Edel, op. cit., pp. 56–59.
107. Deuteronomy 17:9.
108. Ibid. 17:11.
109. Ibid. 32:7.
110. Maimonides, *Commentary on the Mishnah, Introduction to Seder Zeraim,* trans. F. Rosner (New York: Feldheim, 1975), pp. 78–79.
111. Leviticus 18:6–20, *Yevamot* 21a.
112. Deuteronomy 6:17–18.
113. *Bava Metzia* 108a; see above Chapter 6.
114. *Bava Batra* 5a, *Choshen Mishpat* 175:26.
115. *Bava Kamma* 80b; Rambam, *Nizkei Mamon* 5:3; see also Joshua 24:25 and commentary of Nachmanides on Exodus 15:25.
116. *Bava Kamma* 82a.
117. See Rashi on *Shabbat* 14b.

118. Deuteronomy 15:9–11.
119. Mishnah *Shevu'ot* 10:3, *Gittin* 34b, 37a.
120. Horowitz, *The Spirit of Jewish Law,* p. 496.
121. Deuteronomy 19:16, *Gittin* 2b.
122. Mishnah *Yevamot* 16:7.
123. Leviticus 5:23, *Gittin* 55a.
124. Mishnah *Bava Kamma* 2:6, Tosefta *Gittin* 4–5.
125. See Elon, op. cit., p. 633.
126. Responsa Rashbah 3:411; Elon op. cit., 570.
127. Edel, op. cit., pp. 68–69.
128. See Tchernowitz, op. cit., p. 159.
129. *Gittin* 28.
130. *Eruvin* 31b.
131. *Bava Batra* 5.
132. *Ketubbot* 10.
133. Ibid. 75b.
134. *Bava Batra* 146b.
135. *Yevamot* 116a.
136. *Pesachim* 9a.
137. Tchernowitz, op. cit., 158.
138. Henry Sidgwick, *The Methods of Ethics,* p. 303. Compare Rabbi Jonah Gerondi, *Sha'arei Teshuvah, Sha'ar* 3, p. 183.
139. Deuteronomy 23:24, Numbers 30:3.
140. *Sefer ha-Mitzvot le-Rambam,* positive command 94; see comments of Ramban. See also *Sefer ha-Chinnukh, mitzvot* 407 and 575.
141. Sidgwick, op. cit., p. 279.
142. Deuteronomy 28:9, 10:12, Genesis 18:19; *Sefer ha-Chinnukh, mitzvah* 611.
143. *Sotah* 21.
144. See Chapter 7.
145. See Urbach, op. cit. (Heb.), p. 308.
While throughout rabbinic literature we find a number of rabbinic expressions in which some particular commandment, such as charity or honoring parents or *tzitzit,* is extolled for some particular characteristic that it possesses, and is proclaimed as "equal to all the precepts put together," these are to be considered as essentially pedagogic in nature, responding to special social and economic conditions and were designed to endear certain precepts to the people (Urbach, p. 305).
146. *Shevu'ot* 12b.
147. Mishnah *Pe'ah* 1:1.
148. *Avot* 2:1.
149. *Sukkah* 25a.
150. Urbach, op. cit., p. 308.
151. *Shabbat* 34a.
152. *Berakhot* 19.
153. *Bava Metzia* 32.

154. *Bava Batra* 21b.

155. See discussion in *Sefer Chazon Ish* (Jerusalem, 5714), chap. 3, p. 21.

156. Mishnah *Tohorot* 4:1.

"Despite all the distinctions that we find in their relative assessment of the precepts and the emphasis given to one or another commandment, the sages never attained to a comprehensive and final classification of the precepts either according to their inner character or on the basis of the source of their revelation and the ways of their promulgation" (Urbach, 316).

157. See Y. M. Guttmann, *Bechinat ha-Mitzvot* (Jerusalem: Makor, 1978), p. 38.

158. Thus, if a *kohen* sees a lost object in a cemetery he is not obliged to return it and thus make himself "unclean," because while the return of the lost object is a positive command, his obligation to remain *tahor* is based both on a positive command and on a negative command, which a positive command cannot overrule. See Rambam, *Hilkhot Gezelah ve-Avedah* 11:18, and *Maggid Mishnah*.

159. *Sukkah* 30a, *Sanhedrin* 6b.

160. Leviticus 23:22.

161. See Nachmanides on Leviticus 23:22, Mishnah *Menachot* 10:3–4.

162. Guttmann, op. cit., p. 39.

163. Nachmanides on Exodus 20:8.

164. *Bava Metzia* 29b, 30b.

165. Rambam, *Gezelah ve-Avedah* 11:17; see also *Kesef Mishnah*; see also *Yoreh De'ah* 244:14, *Piskai Teshuvah* 4.

166. *Chullin* 94a.

167. Exodus 23:7, Leviticus 19:11, *Yevamot* 65a.

168. *Bava Metzia* 23b.

169. *Sanhedrin* 11b.

170. Mentioned by Rabbi Hutner, *Pachad Yitzchak,* Vol. on Yom ha-Kippurim, p. 60.

171. Elon, op. cit., 2:414–438; Tchernowitz, op. cit., p. 119.

172. *Yevamot* 90a.

In the light of what we said earlier in connection with the biblical precepts—that the force of a positive command is stronger than a negative one—the question may be raised as to why a biblical positive command does not overrule a rabbinical negative enactment. (See Radvaz on Rambam, *Hilkhot Nedarim* 3:9.) But perhaps where both precepts are from the Torah, it can be argued that if, for example, the Torah commands to perform a circumcision on the eighth day, knowing full well that it can sometimes fall on the Sabbath, then it is, in effect, saying that the obligation to circumcise overrules the Sabbath. The rabbinic prohibition, however, is enacted on a different level and so is unaffected by the positive imperative of the Bible. Thus, the very subsidiary nature of the rabbinic precept turns out to be the source of its stringency! (See Tchernowitz, p. 119, n. 4.)

173. *Berakhot* 54a, *Makkot* 23b.

174. *Yevamot* 86b, *Sotah* 47b.

175. *Yevamot* 89b–90a.
176. Mishnah *Shekalim* 1:2.
177. *Gittin* 36a.
178. *Yevamot* 90b, *Sanhedrin* 46a.
179. Rambam, *Sanhedrin* 24:4–6, 24:10.
180. *Yevamot* 90b.
181. Rambam, *Mamrim* 2:4.
182. See entries in *Talmudic Encyclopedia* listed above in note 87.
183. See *Encyclopaedia Judaica,* s.v. "Conflict of Laws."
184. Deuteronomy 30:11–14.
185. W. D. Ross, *The Right and the Good* (Oxford: Clarendon Press), p. 30.
186. See Rashi on Exodus 21:1.

Index

379